MAIMONIDES

MAIMONIDES Life and Thought

MOSHE HALBERTAL

Translated from the Hebrew by Joel Linsider

Princeton University Press

Princeton and Oxford

First published in Israel under the title *ha-Rambam* © Zalman Shazar Center (Jerusalem), 2009
English translation copyright © 2014 by Princeton University Press
Requests for permission to reproduce material from this work
should be sent to Permissions, Princeton University Press
Published by Princeton University Press, 41 William Street,
Princeton, New Jersey 08540
In the United Kingdom: Princeton University Press, 6 Oxford Street, Woodstock,
Oxfordshire OX20 1TW

With thanks to the Center of Jewish Studies at Harvard University for permission to include
"What Is the Mishneh Torah," previously published in *Maimonides After 800 Years*. Cambridge:
Center for Jewish Studies, 2007.

press.princeton.edu

Library of Congress Cataloging-in-Publication Data

Halbertal, Moshe.
[ha-Rambam. English]
Maimonides : life and thought / Moshe Halbertal ; translated from the Hebrew by Joel Linsider.
        pages cm

Includes bibliographical references and index.
ISBN-13: 978-0-691-15851-8 (cloth : alk. paper)
ISBN-10: 0-691-15851-7 (cloth : alk. paper)   1. Maimonides, Moses, 1135–1204.   I. Linsider,
Joel A.   II. Title.
B759.M34H3513 2014
296.1'81—dc23
[B]
                2013008398

British Library Cataloging-in-Publication Data is available

This book has been composed in Garamond Pro

Printed on acid-free paper. ∞

Printed in the United States of America

10 9 8 7 6 5 4 3 2 1

For Rivkah and Akiva

CONTENTS

Chapter Seven: The *Guide of the Perplexed* and Its Critique of Religious Language

Chapter Eight: The *Guide of the Perplexed*: Will or Wisdom?

Conclusion

MAIMONIDES

INTRODUCTION

Moshe ben Maimon (known in Hebrew by the acronym "Rambam" and in English as Maimonides) attempted to bring about two far-reaching and profound transformations in the Jewish world. The first pertained to the *halakhah* (Jewish law, broadly construed) which he sought to change, in a fundamental way, from a fragmented and complex system to one that was transparent and unambiguous. In his great code *Mishneh Torah*, he consolidated the array of halakhic rules and norms and set them in an orderly, unified, and accessible structure. This brilliant work represented a mighty effort to extract the *halakhah* from the thicket of Talmudic discussions, marked by frequent disagreement and tangled debate. Maimonides set out to create a systematic structure, arranged by subject, from the randomly presented Talmudic material, in which a given issue might be dealt with in various places and diverse contexts. In his *Mishneh Torah*, Maimonides created an unambiguous, comprehensive, and exhaustive halakhic text; he did so by omitting the halakhic give and take, the disagreements, and the minority opinions that appear in earlier halakhic writings. This transformation of Jewish law was unprecedented in the world of *halakhah*, as Maimonides himself declared:

> I have been preceded by *Geonim* and great scholars who compiled treatises and issued rulings, in Hebrew and in Arabic, on matters that are known. But not since our holy Rabbi [R. Judah the Prince, the editor of the *Mishnah*] and his holy associates has anyone resolved halakhic matters regarding the entire Talmud and all the laws of the Torah. (*Iggerot*, pp. 439–440)

In truth, even the *Mishnah* as edited by R. Judah the Prince at the beginning of the third century is not really a precedent for *Mishneh Torah*, for it retains unresolved disputes and minority opinions. A code such as *Mishneh Torah*—comprehensive, exhaustive, accessible, and unambiguous—had never been written before Maimonides' time and has not been written since.

The second transformation that Maimonides sought to accomplish was a substantive shift in Jewish religious consciousness. That far-reaching and penetrating transformation, in turn, had three main components.

First, there was the struggle against anthropomorphism, against seeing God as a personality possessed of a body and emotions. Maimonides gave new meaning to the biblical struggle against idolatry. As he saw it, that struggle goes beyond merely shattering the idols found in pagan sanctuaries; it extends to a confrontation with the internalized image of God envisioned by the person worshipping Him. A worshipper who envisions God as a merciful grandfather seated on a throne is worse than one who worships statues. A person worshipping a statue may see the statue as nothing more than a symbolic representation of the exalted God, but a worshipper of God who imagines Him as a human body internalizes the statue and the image into his own consciousness. Maimonides thus turned the biblical iconoclastic fervor toward the shattering of the mental image. Because the tradition itself, both biblical and midrashic, describes God in terms of a human body and attributes to it such emotions as anger, jealousy, love, and mercy, Maimonides is compelled to offer a systematic reinterpretation of Jewish religious language and of religious language in general.

The *second*, no less radical, element of the transformation in religious consciousness was the placement of the natural and causal order at the center of the divine revelation and presence. God's wisdom, as revealed in nature, was to be seen as the highest expression of His revelation—a position very much at odds with the conventional view that God's presence in the world was expressed primarily through the extraordinary and the miraculous. This fundamental change in religious sensibility away from miracle and toward causality, or, as Maimonides formulated it, from *will* to *wisdom*, required Maimonides to reinterpret some of Judaism's basic concepts, such as providence, creation, prophecy, and revelation, all of them seemingly based on a revelation of divine will and a fracturing of the normal causal order.

Third, the change in religious consciousness entailed ending the distinction between what was within the tradition and what was outside of it. In all his writings, halakhic as well as philosophical, Maimonides saw philosophy and science as the medium for attaining the heights of religious experience—love and awe of God. In his scientific and philosophical worldview, Maimonides belonged to the school of Aristotle and his Muslim interpreters, al-Farabi, Ibn Bajja, and Ibn Rushd (Averroes). Maimonides accepted the insights offered by these scientific and philosophical streams as substantively true; accordingly, where they conflicted with Jewish tradition, he saw a need to reinterpret the tradition to reconcile it with these truths. But philosophy, in Maimonides' world, was more than a critical method of use in drawing conclusions about the world, conclusions to which traditional views had to be conformed. Beyond that, it was considered to be a spiritual discipline and way of life, a stance taken within the world, a system dealing first and foremost with how a person's life should be lived. Through philosophy and science, whose sources of information would appear at first blush to be outside the Jewish tradition, a person can reach the pinnacle of religious life and realize his perfection as a human being. Philosophy does more than criticize; it serves a redemptive purpose as well.

Any one of these three elements of the Maimonidean religious transformation could shake the entire Jewish tradition; occurring all at once, they could be devastating. Accordingly, instilling the new religious sensibility into the heart of Judaism required a new and comprehensive interpretation of the tradition. Moreover, in an effort to ground the basic insights of the religious transformation as binding and authoritative Jewish perspectives, Maimonides integrated them into his code, *Mishneh Torah*. He thereby rendered his spiritual and religious positions binding status, and he turned his halakhic treatise into a model of integration between philosophy and *halakhah*. To be sure, historically speaking, he did not succeed in bringing about the change in religious consciousness that he hoped for. Nevertheless, once Judaism had passed through the refining blaze of Maimonidean interpretation, it acquired a different and distinctive voice that offered a genuine alternative to the then conventional understanding. This distinctive Maimonidean voice shook the rafters in its day and posed a lasting challenge to all later Jewish thought.

Medieval Jewry had its share of great thinkers and halakhists, but Maimonides was the only one who attempted to bring about, simultaneously, two such profound and far-reaching transformations, one in the domain of *halakhah* and the other in that of philosophy. For that reason, none of them had such a complex set of relationships, comprising both esteem and polemic, with his contemporaries. The oft-stated comparison between Moses son of Maimon and Moses our Teacher (that is, the biblical Moses)—a comparison involving his self-perception and the way in which he was perceived by his contemporaries and by succeeding generations—is no exaggeration and contains more than a kernel of truth. In his life and oeuvre, Maimonides belonged to the rare and unique species of religious reformers—even, one may say, of religious founders.

Maimonides' efforts to bring about these transformations lacked the institutional backing that might have provided him social and political support. He was not a "prince," as was R. Judah the Prince, the third-century editor of the *Mishnah*, and he did not lead either of the Babylonian yeshivas that saw themselves as heirs to the great court of Jerusalem of old. Born in Cordoba, Andalusia, in 1138, Maimonides at a young age became a refugee and an émigré following the rise of the Almohads, a radical Muslim movement that shattered the Judeo-Arabic culture of Andalusia. After years of wandering and persecution in North Africa, he reached Egypt in 1166. Following inner communal political struggles, he attained a position of leadership in the Egyptian Jewish community, serving as its head, and his stature continued to grow until his death in 1204. In no way, however, did his position provide an institutional framework that could legitimate the transformations he attempted to bring about. Moreover, Maimonides claimed no divine revelation that might have afforded his words a quasi-prophetic standing. He did not attribute his writings to pseudepigraphal ancient authorities, as did the authors of the *Zohar*, who ascribed their works to R. Simeon ben Yoḥai; and he did not presume to be the custodian of some received and authoritative secret tradition, transmitted to him through the generations, as did R. Moses Naḥmanides a generation later (though he claimed that through his power of reasoning he had managed to revive such an old, lost tradition). In his effort to bring about vast changes, Maimonides, the refugee from Andalusia, relied on his own great ability, his prodigious halakhic and philosophical learning, his linguistic and literary Midas touch, and his profound inner certainty and sense of mission.

∼

In this book, I will present the range and depth of the changes Maimonides sought to bring about, the nature of his oeuvre, and his self-perception and its relationship to his biography. The first chapter, "Moses the Man," is devoted to Maimonides' self-image and how it developed in response to the events of his life. From there, the book takes up Maimonides' teachings, treating them in the order in which his books were completed. Chapters 2 and 3 consider the *Commentary on the Mishnah* and the *Book of*

Commandments written in the third decade of his life, between the ages of twenty-three and thirty. These chapters consider whether these youthful works represent the efforts of a novice writer who has not yet found his unique and brilliant voice or are better seen as prefiguring the great works yet to be written, manifesting early stages of the lines along which their author would later develop.

Chapters 4, 5, and 6 deal with *Mishneh Torah*, which Maimonides wrote in Egypt over a ten-year period while he was in his thirties, from 1168 to 1177. Chapter 4 considers the goal of *Mishneh Torah* and two different readings of the work: its character as a treatise and its status as an authoritative source in the eyes of its author. The fifth chapter analyzes the philosophical elements included in this great halakhic treatise, while the sixth is focused on Maimonides' concept of *halakhah* and how it informs the organization of *Mishneh Torah* and its halakhic rulings.

Chapters 7 and 8 take up the *Guide of the Perplexed*, a work that Maimonides began to write at the age of forty-eight and completed at the age of fifty-three, between 1186 and 1191. Maimonides himself affirmed that he had concealed the *Guide*'s deeper meanings from the reader; hence, it is not surprising that the greatest work of Jewish thought through the ages is also the most enigmatic. The discussion here will offer the reader four possible readings of the book, differing substantively with regard to the key questions that preoccupy Maimonides. These chapters are meant not to determine the true meaning of the *Guide*, but only to present four possible understandings that close readings through the ages have identified. The concluding chapter will describe the common kernel shared by all the readings of the *Guide*, reflecting the religious transformation Maimonides tried to engender.

No one in the history of Jewish thought and philosophy has received more detailed attention than Maimonides. Intensive exegesis of his writings began while he was still alive, and generations of scholars and critics have gone through those writings with the most fine-toothed of combs. The greatest halakhists have repeatedly examined the sharply worded formulations in *Mishneh Torah* as a basis for halakhic rulings, and the treatise eventually gave rise to a mountain of interpretive literature—a literature that treated *Mishneh Torah* as an endless resource for understanding Talmudic passages and *halakhah* overall. Modern scholarship in the field of Jewish thought has carried on the tradition of the medieval interpretation of the *Guide*: it has attempted to determine the enigmatic meaning of the treatise, it has examined the Arab and Greek influences on Maimonides' thinking, and it has sought to parse the complex relationships between *halakhah* and philosophy in Maimonides' teaching and personality. Throughout the book I will avoid supplementing my arguments with detailed footnotes, which might interrupt the flow of the presentation and its clarity. It goes without saying, however, that the positions I take in this book are based on those of interpreters, scholars, and teachers who have come before me, from whose learning and wisdom I have greatly benefited. To fill the gap in acknowledgments, at least in part, I have included at the end of the book a bibliography of the works related to each chapter, identifying those that I have relied upon and whose positions I consider, directly or indirectly. The bibliography begins with a listing of abbreviated citations to the various editions and translations of Maimonides' writings used.

That said, there are several individuals whose help I would like to acknowledge here. I am deeply grateful to teachers, colleagues, and friends, who offered me their wisdom and support. Menachem Fish, Dov Halbertal, Menachem Lorberbaum, and Toby Freilich read the whole manuscript and provided me with helpful insights. I have learned a great deal from discussing different aspects of the work with my teachers, David Hartman and Haym Soloveitchik, and my friend, Daniel Wolff. I wish to thank as well the anonymous readers of Princeton University Press for their most helpful suggestions, my editor at the Press, Fred Appel, for his advice and encouragement, copyeditor Karen Verde for her patient reading and valuable comments, and to Eli Fischer who translated the second chapter of the book from Hebrew to English.

I am grateful to the New York University Filomen D'Agostino Foundation for the grants that supported the writing of the book.

CHAPTER ONE

Moses the Man

"Moses of his Generation"

In his introduction to the first chapters of Part III of the *Guide*, Maimonides took the rare step of disclosing his self-image and the role he set for himself in the complex times in which he lived and worked. While writing this section of the *Guide* around the year 1180, he was forty-two years old and at the height of his power. Those chapters are devoted to interpreting "the Account of the Chariot" (*maʿaseh merkavah*, the term applied to the prophet Ezekiel's vision of the divine chariot), the holy of holies of Jewish mystical teachings. According to a ruling in the *Mishnah*, "the Account of the Chariot" may only be elaborated orally and only to one person, and that person must be capable of apprehending the matter on the basis of his own understanding. To write a commentary on Ezekiel's vision, even one limited to chapter headings only, thus constitutes a breach of the accepted boundaries of esotericism. Maimonides' introduction to the chapters is meant to justify the literary transgression of committing the Torah's mysteries to writing, and much can be gleaned from it about the writer's self-image.

Maimonides understood himself to have been born into a period of devastation and loss in which the inner meaning of the Account of the Chariot disappeared from the world. He attributes that loss in part to the earlier generations having been so cautious about disseminating and transmitting it that it failed to endure. But even though the information was entirely lost, Maimonides claimed that he was able to apprehend the meaning of the Account the of the Chariot by the sheer force of his own intellect: "in that which has occurred to me with regard to these matters, I followed conjecture and supposition; no divine revelation has come to me to teach me that the intention in the matter in question was such and such, nor did I receive what I believe in these matters from a teacher" (*Guide*, p. 416).

The historical desolation in which he lived, and his status as the only person holding the key to the deep significance of the tradition, were the factors that led him to commit his interpretation of the Account of the Chariot to writing, in the form of chapter headings, even though doing so was forbidden and information of that sort was to be transmitted only orally and in private. He justified this literary transgression in the following terms: " . . . if I had omitted setting down something of that which has appeared to me as clear, so that that knowledge would perish when I perish, as is inevitable, I should have considered that conduct as extremely cowardly with regard to you and everyone who is perplexed" (*Guide*, pp. 415–416).

Maimonides thus believed that his life offered a unique opportunity to reveal the inner meaning of Judaism, a possibility that would disappear from the world upon his death. Were he to feel bound by the traditional prohibition on committing the material to writing, the deep meaning of Israel's Torah, which he had apprehended through the power of his intellect, would have been denied to future generations. Moreover, understanding the hidden meaning of the Torah could, he believed, resolve the great crisis afflicting the perplexed of his time. Accordingly, revealing the mysteries of the Torah in the *Guide* was the best hope for saving the perplexed from the confusion in which they found themselves in the wake of the encounter between the Torah and wisdom.

How did Maimonides understand the perplexity generated by the encounter between Torah and philosophy? And how did he think his proposed interpretation of the Jewish tradition would be able to resolve that perplexity? These questions are among the important foci of the book, and we shall deal with them extensively. In this chapter, I want to examine a different question: what was Maimonides' perspective on himself and his times, and how did the events of his life contribute to the shaping of that self-image? In that context, the introduction to Part III of the *Guide* makes evident the great audacity underlying Maimonides' philosophical work, an audacity flowing from his sense of historical crisis that imposed on him personally a mighty historical responsibility, and from his self-perception as the last and sole opportunity to reveal and preserve the inner meaning of Torah. Boldness of this sort has no parallel in the history of Jewish philosophy, either prior to Maimonides or after.

This historical consciousness and sense of self drove Maimonides' halakhic activity as well as his philosophical work. In the introduction to his legal magnum opus, *Mishneh Torah*, he paints a starkly sorrowful picture of the state of *halakhah* in his time. According to Maimonides, the deterioration in halakhic knowledge and in the ability of scholars to produce any sort of unity and clarity in the halakhic corpus began immediately after the completion of the Talmud in the sixth century, some six hundred years before the writing of *Mishneh Torah*:

> After the Court of Rav Ashi, who compiled the Gemara which was finally completed in the days of his son, an extraordinarily great dispersion of Israel throughout the world took place. The people emigrated to remote parts and distant isles. The prevalence of wars and the march of armies made travel insecure. The study of the Torah declined. The Jewish people did not flock to the colleges in their thousands and tens of thousands as heretofore; but in each city and country, individuals who felt the divine call gathered together and occupied themselves with the Torah; studied all the works of the sages; and from these learned the methods of legal interpretation. (Introduction to *Mishneh Torah*, pp. 37–38)

Maimonides refers here to the decline of the Babylonian center's power as new Jewish communities were established in the wake of the spread of Islam to North Africa and all the way to Spain. This geopolitical change, which followed the completion of the Talmud, led to the dismantling of the relatively solid structure of *halakhah*, and this process of disintegration continued with even greater force in Maimonides' own time:

> In our days, severe vicissitudes prevail, and all feel the pressure of hard times. The wisdom of our wise men has disappeared; the understanding of our prudent men is hidden. Hence, the commentaries of the *Geonim*, and their compilations of laws and responses, which they took care to make clear, have in our times become hard to understand so that only a few individuals properly comprehend them. Needless to add that such is the case in regard to the Talmud itself—the Babylonian as well as the Palestinian, the *Sifra*, the *Sifre*, and the *Tosefta*, all of which works required, for their comprehension, a broad mind, a wise soul, and considerable study. (Introduction to *Mishneh Torah*, p. 39)

Maimonides regarded the achievements of the *Geonim*, the rabbinic authorities during the centuries following the completion of the Talmud, as more limited and local than those of the Talmudic period. In his time, their writings, too, became obscure and difficult to explain, and even the words of the Talmud came to be beyond the understanding of most of the public.

Late in his life—in 1199, some twenty-two years after having written the introduction to *Mishneh Torah*—Maimonides, in his letter to the sages of Lunel, again described this sad state of affairs, this time in greater detail. The letter was addressed to a circle of scholars living in Provence, led by R. Jonathan Hakohen, who regarded Maimonides as an authoritative and dominant figure; in his exchange with them, Maimonides adopted a posture of first among equals. His words therefore warrant careful attention:

> As for yourselves, my esteemed friends, be confident and strong of heart! For, alas, I am constrained to inform you that in our day the people of your community and only a few of the neighboring communities stand alone in raising the banner of Moses and engaging in the study of the Talmud and in the pursuit of wisdom. Your people are preeminent in cherishing knowledge and wisdom. But in other communities in the East, the study of the Torah has ceased and especially is this true in most of the large cities where a process of spiritual decay has set in. In all of Palestine there are only three or four Jewish places that have survived, and even they are spiritually impoverished. In Syria, as well, there is only the community of Aleppo where some people are still engaged in the study of Torah, although they are not prepared to sacrifice themselves for it. In the Babylonian Diaspora there are only two or three grapes [men of learning]; in Yemen and the rest of Arabia they know little of the Talmud save for having some superficial acquaintance with Aggadic expositions. (*Letters of Maimonides*, pp. 164–165)

This bleak account of the demise of the halakhic world encompasses the entire Jewish world known to Maimonides, from Babylonia and Yemen to the Maghrib and Aleppo. Within the context of this historical picture, Maimonides regarded himself as one who was capable of bolstering the halakhic structure with his great work, *Mishneh Torah*. That treatise was meant to provide a clear, comprehensive, unambiguous, concise, and approachable picture of the entire halakhic system at the very moment this tradition stood on the brink of collapse. And so, in the introduction to the treatise, following a description of the crisis faced by *halakhah* in his time, he writes:

> On these grounds, I, Moses the son of Maimon *the Sefaradi*, bestirred myself, and, relying on the help of God, blessed be He, intently studied all

these works, with the view of putting together the results obtained from them in regard to what is forbidden or permitted, clean or unclean, and the other rules of the Torah—all in plain language and terse style, so that the entire Oral Law might become systematically known to all. (Introduction to *Mishneh Torah*, p. 39)

The treatise, then, was to encompass all areas of *halakhah*; impart the *halakhah* without any give-and-take or dissenting opinions; transform its intricacies into something accessible to all, great and small; and present, once and for all, the world of *halakhah*. But this sort of treatise was a literary act unprecedented in the history of the *halakhah*. Maimonides recognized that he was risking literary transgression, and—as in the case of the *Guide*—his justification for what he was doing was deeply rooted in his self-image and his comprehension of the historical circumstances.

Through *Mishneh Torah*, Maimonides sought to bring about a far-reaching and profound change in the history of *halakhah*. The nature of the change is conveyed a few lines later in the passage from the introduction just cited, in the most ambitious statement ever uttered by a Jewish scholar about himself and his treatise: "Hence, I have entitled this work *Mishneh Torah* (Repetition of the Law), for the reason that a person who first reads the Written Law and then this compilation, will know from it the whole of the Oral Law, without having occasion to consult any other book between them" (Introduction to *Mishneh Torah*, p. 39). The precise meaning of this statement, which at least appears to claim that all of halakhic literature has been encapsulated in the treatise, will be considered more broadly in the chapter on the nature of *Mishneh Torah*. Even at this point, however, we can appreciate the great hope raised by the statement as well as the penetrating criticism leveled against it.

The grim picture painted by Maimonides notwithstanding, the eleventh and twelfth centuries were a time of efflorescence in the history of the *halakhah*. Rashi's (1040–1105) wonderful commentary on the Talmud, composed in the eleventh century, made that text approachable. The Tosafists, especially R. Jacob ben Meir (Rabbeinu Tam, Rashi's grandson) (1100–1171) and R. Isaac ben Samuel (Ri the Elder, Rashi's great-grandson), developed a rich and sophisticated conceptual system that enabled them to shed startling new light on the Talmudic sources. In addition to the new analytical tools developed during the twelfth century, the Tosafists approached the Talmud from a synoptic perspective, in which every Talmudic passage was examined in light of the other passages in the Talmudic literature that dealt with the same issue, directly or indirectly. Seen in this comparative light, a passing mention of a subject or an indirect allusion to it can mandate a change in the interpretation of the primary passage in which the subject is discussed—in other words, can alter that passage's meaning. The conceptual breakthroughs and synoptic perspective, forged in the study halls of the great twelfth-century Talmudists, made the accomplishments of the *Geonim* who preceded them seem unsophisticated and raw. Maimonides himself was unaware of these developments in France and Germany, far from the Jewish world known to him, and his works contain not one quotation from or reference to even so central a work as Rashi's commentary on the Talmud. Maimonides' familiarity with the Jews living under Christian rule extended no further than Provence, and, as we have seen, he treated the Jews of Provence as the surviving remnant of the halakhic world.

And so, halakhists of stature were active in Maimonides' time. Rabbeinu Tam and R. Abraham ben David (Ra'abad, a Provencal scholar, 1125–1198), described as men who were able "to find 150 grounds for declaring an impure insect pure," formulated far-reaching halakhic innovations on the basis of the new methods they had developed. Nahmanides (R. Moses ben Nahman, 1194–1270), born about a decade before Maimonides' death, wrote Talmudic novellae in which he refined and burnished these accomplishments. But none of these giants of Talmud had Maimonides' sense of self, and none took on a foundational project like the one Maimonides did. His sense of history and his self-image make him not simply a great figure but rather a monumental one.

Letters from one scholar to another during the Middle Ages would typically contain poetic and highly rhetorical exaggerated words of praise for the addressee. That style was foreign to Maimonides and he avoided it, as might be expected of one whose magnificent Hebrew in *Mishneh Torah* and in his letters is clear and precise, refined as fine, white flour. A review of letters written to or about Maimonides shows, even after discounting the excesses typical of the genre, that scholars and philosophers saw him, even during his lifetime, as an overpowering figure.

Maimonides' admirers, among them men of high stature in their own right, saw him as he saw himself—as a sort of redemptive figure. His life was understood as a one-time revelation—the appearance of a man who, through his halakhic and philosophical work, contributed to the healing of a deep wound. R. Aaron ben Meshullam, a scion of the rabbinic elite of Provence, wrote in the midst of one of the earlier polemical storms that concerned Maimonides' theology in 1202, the following comments about Maimonides in a letter to his adversary, R. Meir Abulafia of Toledo:

Indeed, his God sent him [that is, Maimonides] to restore His people, for He saw that the sages' capacity had fallen short and the lot of the children of Israel was becoming more and more dismal. And so he raised his arm and extended his mighty rod over the sea of the Talmud so that the children of Israel might enter the sea on dry land; and from the sea of foolishness he drew[1] his people, instilling His Torah in their hearts, written and etched. And as it is written before me, I will not be silent, for since the days of Ravina and R. Ashi none has arisen in Israel like Moses, of wondrous counsel and great understanding.

The term "Moses of his generation," appearing in many references to Maimonides, is no empty rhetorical flourish. It echoes here in every sentence of the letter, which analogizes Maimonides' halakhic effort to the salvation brought about through the agency of the earlier Moses when the Red Sea was split.

In his commentary on Ecclesiastes, Samuel Ibn Tibbon, the great translator of the *Guide* into Hebrew, wrote in similar terms about Maimonides' philosophical work:

Since the sages of the Talmud, almost no one has been inspired to compose a book or write something about these sciences ["the Account of Creation" and "the Account of the Chariot"]; it was enough for them to write about laws, about what is prohibited and what permitted. [This continued] until God, seeing the poverty of His people's thought and their great ignorance regarding all matters of wisdom, sent them a redeemer, a wise and understanding man, a wise artisan with an understanding of mysteries. Since the time of R. Ashi and his cohort, we have not known one like him among our people with respect to all matters of wisdom. [He is] a true sage, a divine philosopher, our master and our teacher, Moses, the servant of God, the son of the great sage R. Maimon, may his memory be for a blessing.

[1] "He drew" translates the Hebrew *mashah*, alluding to Moses (Moshe) and the Bible's explanation of Moses' name; see Exod. 2:10. In general, the passage is poetic and rhetorical, and it is sometimes difficult to tell whether the pronoun should be he/his, referring to Moses, or He/His, referring to God.

The goal of Maimonides' major works was not only to deepen and extend the study of the authoritative traditions of Judaism; they were intended to bring about a profound change in the lives of the Jewish people. *Mishneh Torah* was written to bring about an overall change to the structure of *halakhah* and to alter the fundamental belief system of Jews by integrating a theological-philosophical element into a halakhic work. The *Guide* grew out of the need to reveal and reinterpret the inner meaning of Judaism as a one-time opportunity to resolve the crisis that was slowly crippling the elite of the Jewish communities in Arab lands.

The repeated comparison between Maimonides and Moses, heard in his own generation and since, is not simply a turn of phrase growing out of the coincidence that they share a name. The name was shared as well by other Jewish luminaries across the generations, such as Moses ben Naḥman, Moses De Leon, and Moses Cordovero, but the comparison was made, for good reason, only in the case of Moses ben Maimon. The monumental character of his life's work invites the association, and Maimonides himself internalized it. At the start of a response to R. Jonathan ha-Kohen, Maimonides describes his reaction to the letter he had sent him, repeatedly comparing himself to Moses:

> Said Moses [that is, Maimonides, but the passage has numerous references to the biblical Moses], "Let me turn aside and see this great sight." And when he heard the mighty voice of the questions, brought by a fierce wind, Moses said, "it is the voice of those who cry for being overcome" . . . and replied with a few words, but the hands of Moses were heavy. But when he saw there was none other, he went in his usual way and sat in the crevice of the rock, and Moses said to the Lord: "You said You have known me by name and you have pleased Me, but now, in later times, my children have defeated me. (*Iggerot*, pp. 500–501)

Andalusia: 1138–1159 (?)

Maimonides' self-image and historical consciousness are deeply rooted in his biography. His sense of ruination and loss took shape in the wake of the events that led to the destruction of the Jewish communities of Andalusia in the southern part of Spain, his familial and cultural homeland. Moses ben Maimon was born in Cordoba, Andalusia, most likely in 1138. While still a youth, he became a refugee and migrant. His family was forced to flee from Spain to Morocco following the rise of the Almohads, a radical Islamic movement rooted in the Berber tribes of North Africa; its name ("the unifiers") reflects its intense emphasis on God's unity. This movement, which proclaimed its unwillingness to compromise, gained control of North Africa and Andalusia. In its religious zealotry, it unraveled the marvelous cultural tapestry that had led to the flourishing of Spanish Jewry during the tenth and eleventh centuries and the first half of the twelfth.

The great Hebrew poetry of the Middle Ages was created in Andalusia by such dazzling and accomplished poets as Samuel Hanagid (993–1056), Solomon Ibn Gabirol (1021–1058), Moses Ibn Ezra (1055–1138), Judah Halevi (1075–1141), and Abraham Ibn Ezra (1089–1164). Andalusia was where the leading Jewish thinkers developed their ideas; noteworthy writers and their works include Bahya Ibn Paquda of the first half of the twelfth century, author of *Hovot ha-Levavot* deeply immersed in the Sufi tradition; Solomon Ibn Gabirol, the Neo-Platonist author of *Fons Vitae* (*Meqor Hayyim*); Abraham Ibn Ezra, whose scientific and astronomical works, philosophical treatise (*Yesod Mora*), and commentary on the Bible decisively influenced the course of Jewish thought and exegesis; and Judah Halevi, author not only of marvelous poetry but also of the theological-philosophical dialogue the *Kuzari*, which exerted immense influence on the future of Jewish thought. This literature, written mostly in Arabic though in Hebrew script ("Judeo-Arabic"), was the product of a fruitful encounter between the Jewish world and the great poetic, scientific, and philosophical achievements of Islamic culture.

Andalusia was home as well to a halakhic tradition and a school of Talmudic interpretation that overshadowed the Babylonian center. The scholar who stood at the center of that tradition was R. Isaac Alfasi (1013–1103), who emigrated late in life from Morocco to Spain and became head of the yeshiva in Lucena (Arabic, al-Yussana), in Andalusia. His treatise, *Hilkhot ha-Rif* (Rif is an acronym for R. Isaac Alfasi), became a central component of the curriculum for Torah study and had considerable influence on the history of *halakhah*. His great student, R. Joseph Halevi Ibn Migash (1077–1141), succeeded him as head of the yeshiva, and was the teacher of R. Maimon, Maimonides' father. The latter served as *dayyan* (judge of the Jewish court) in Cordoba and attended the yeshiva in Lucena.

This great but delicate cultural world unraveled in all directions in the mid-twelfth century with the Almohad rise to power. Maimonides' family wandered south, to Morocco and the Maghrib, while other families headed

north, to Christian Spain and to Provence. Among the prominent Andalusian families who settled in Provence were the Kim<u>h</u>i family of Bible
scholars and the Ibn Tibbon family of translators and philosophers. Members of the Ibn Tibbon family produced Hebrew translations of Andalusian
Jewish literature and of substantial portions of the Muslim philosophical
tradition, thereby integrating the Judeo-Arabic world of Andalusia into the
culture of the Hebrew-speaking Jews of Christendom. Judah Ibn Tibbon
translated the writings of Solomon Ibn Gabirol, Ba<u>h</u>ya Ibn Paquda, and
Judah Halevi, and his son Samuel Ibn Tibbon later played an important
role in Maimonides' life, translating the *Guide* into Hebrew and serving as
a prominent representative of the Maimonidean culture that developed in
Provence.

Moses ben Maimon lived at the pinnacle of the Jewish world of Andalusia. His family, whom he refers to as "among the exiles from Jerusalem
who are in Spain," had deep roots in Al-Andalus. At the end of his *Commentary on the Mishnah*, Maimonides set forth a seven-generation geneal-
ogy; it included five generations of *dayyanim* going back to the *dayyan*
Ovadiah, after whom the family was known as Ben Ovadyah or, in Arabic,
Ibn Abdallah.[2] Long after emigrating from Andalusia, having lived in
Egypt for more than thirty years, Maimonides still referred to himself as
"the Spaniard (*ha-sefaradi*)" or "the Andalusian." His cultural homeland
was Andalusian through and through, and it was there that his worldview
took shape. He spent all his productive years outside his homeland, but it
was in Andalusia that he gained his Talmudic and philosophical training.

Maimonides received his Talmudic education in the home of his father,
R. Maimon, in Cordoba. In the *Commentary on the Mishnah*, in *Mishneh
Torah*, and in his responsa, one can find evidence of the halakhic traditions
he learned from his father. In *Mishneh Torah*, for example, he writes that
he disagrees with his father's position on one issue regarding the kashrut of
an animal that has been slaughtered. But his father's role in his education
was more a matter of transmitting the Andalusian halakhic tradition than
of exercising personal influence.

Wherever Maimonides uses the term "my teachers" in his *Mishneh Torah*
and other writings, he is referring to R. Isaac Alfasi (the Rif) and to his father's teacher, R. Joseph Halevi Ibn Migash. Maimonides did not study directly with these teachers; the Rif died years before Maimonides was born

---

[2] Hebrew Ovadyah and Arabic Abdallah both mean "servant of God."

and R. Joseph Ibn Migash died in 1141, when Maimonides was still a child. That he adopted as his teachers men who were no longer alive supports the belief that even at a young age he overshadowed his immediate circle. He knew of these sages' teachings from their writings or through traditions that he heard from his father or others who were learned in the Spanish tradition. Maimonides had R. Joseph Ibn Migash's novellae on tractates *Bava batra* and *Shevu'ot* and his responsa, which were still extant; in addition, he had the summaries of Ibn Migash's lessons that he received from his father. In one of his responsa, Maimonides notes that he consulted those booklets to clarify a point that was unclear to him: "This lottery [used by the priests to allocate tasks in the Temple] posed great problems to all who came before, and I have heard no interpretation of it that comports with the statements in the Talmud. But I found in a booklet of my teacher and father, of blessed memory, something about this by R. Joseph Halevi, may the memory of the righteous be for a blessing" (*Teshuvot*, sec. 126, pp. 223–224).

Maimonides' commitment to R. Isaac Alfasi's halakhic tradition is evident in his statement, in the introduction to the *Commentary on the Mishnah*, that he disagreed with Alfasi no more than ten times. In a letter that he wrote following the completion of *Mishneh Torah*, he raised that number to about thirty.[3] (In fact, a careful study of Maimonides' rulings will show that number to be substantially greater.) But while disagreements with the Rif certainly existed, they required more substantial justification than did disagreements with other earlier halakhists. Maimonides declared that he had written, in his youth, a compilation explaining his criticisms of the Rif. Later on, he advised his student Joseph to study *Mishneh Torah* and, where he found disagreements with the Rif, to examine carefully the Talmudic passage that gave rise to the dispute. Like others who maintained the Andalusian halakhic tradition, Maimonides saw *Hilkhot ha-Rif* as an independent foundational treatise to be used in the training of scholars, a sort of primary substitute for the Talmud. By his own account, he taught *Hilkhot ha-Rif* in his yeshiva several times as an independent treatise.

Maimonides' esteem for R. Joseph Ibn Migash, the Rif's successor, is evident in an unusually forceful comment: "And I gathered what I was able to obtain of my father's interpretations, may the memory of the righteous be for a blessing, and also those uttered by R. Joseph Halevi [Ibn Migash], of blessed memory. For that man's Talmudic reasoning is astonishing—

---

[3] Maimonides' Responsa 251.

God knows—to anyone who considers his comments and the depth of his probing, to the point that I would say of him that no one who preceded him was a king like him in this way" (Introduction to the *Commentary on the Mishnah*). Maimonides was one who showed no favor in judgment, and his standard for assessing intellectual accomplishments was severe and critical. His intellectual and halakhic independence requires no proof, for at several points in his responsa and in *Mishneh Torah*, he mentioned the positions of his teachers, the Rif and R. Joseph Migash, only to disagree with them. These words of praise, accordingly, evidence a tremendous degree of esteem.

We do not know the exact year in which Maimonides' family was forced to emigrate from Andalusia. The family seems to have left Cordoba upon its conquest by the Almohads in 1148 but remained in Andalusia, apparently in Seville, for another few years before leaving for the Maghrib. In any event, Maimonides eventually left Andalusia as a well-versed scholar. The *Commentary on the Mishnah*, which he began to write at the age of twenty-three and completed seven years later, in 1168, shows that he had acquired his breathtaking mastery of the Talmudic literature while still a young man. He wrote the *Commentary* during his years of wandering, after he left Andalusia, finishing it two years after his arrival in Egypt. Moreover, Maimonides recounts that even before writing the *Commentary*, he wrote a commentary on difficult Talmudic passages in the orders of *Mo'ed*, *Nashim*, and *Neziqin* as well as tractate *Hulin* in the order of *Qodashim*. His extensive knowledge of the Talmud Yerushalmi, or Jerusalem Talmud—the Talmud produced in the Land of Israel—allowed him to write, while still in his youth, *Hilkhot ha-Yerushalmi*, a treatise analogous to the Rif's work on the Babylonian Talmud. Maimonides mentions another book that he wrote, containing critical comments on rulings by the Rif that he considered to be in error. He did not consider these works to be polished enough, and so he withheld them from publication; manuscripts of some of them remained in Maimonides' family for generations. So extensive a halakhic oeuvre indicates that the foundation for Maimonides' halakhic greatness was laid while he still lived in Andalusia.

An interesting piece of evidence for the total mastery of the Talmudic literature that Maimonides acquired during his youth appears in a comment about him by Joseph Ben Aknin, written even before Maimonides had published his *Commentary on the Mishnah*. Joseph ben Aknin was living in Morocco when Maimonides' family reached Fez. In his commentary on Song of Songs, he cited Maimonides' arrival in the city as an expression of the Maghribi Jews' faithfulness to the Torah even in a time of persecution: "And the proof for what I am saying is the appearance in Fez of the great sage, our Rabbi Moses, son of his honor, R. Maimon, whose stature in wisdom is unparalleled" (Ibn Aknin, *Perush le-Shir ha-Shirim*, p. 398).

Maimonides' deep attachment to the Andalusian halakhic tradition stayed with him throughout his life. Thirty years after his departure from Andalusia, that attachment came into play in a halakhic and personal dispute with his bitter adversary, Samuel ben Eli, which took place between 1189 and 1191. Samuel ben Eli was head of the yeshiva in Baghdad, the successor to the Babylonian *Geonim*, at a time when the geonic establishment, which had dominated the Jewish world from the eighth century to the eleventh, was in an extended decline. As often happens, the heirs to the geonic center continued to demand the status accorded their predecessors and struggled against the changes in their situation. The blossoming of Andalusia, which produced great scholars in their own right, symbolized in many ways the demise of the Babylonian center.

Maimonides did not accept the halakhic authority of the *Geonim*. In the introduction to *Mishneh Torah*, as we shall see, he determined that the rulings of the *Geonim* had local authority only and bound neither Jewish communities overall nor succeeding generations. In *Mishneh Torah*, he rejected some of the geonic enactments, accepting only those that he believed to have been accepted by all Israel. It is fair to assume that Maimonides from the start was not admired by the heirs of the *Geonim*, and his rise as a halakhic authority throughout the Arabic-speaking Jewish world threatened what little was left of their standing. Not surprisingly, therefore, *Mishneh Torah* received hostile criticism in Baghdad on the part of the *ga'on* Samuel ben Eli, and he did all he could to undermine *Mishneh Torah*'s authority and Maimonides' standing. As we shall see later in this chapter, the documents that were preserved from this bitter struggle are of great importance to the understanding of Maimonides' inner sense of self and his reaction to hostile reception. They attest, among other things, to his great attachment to Andalusian tradition until the end of his life.

The principal halakhic issue raised in the polemic against Maimonides' rulings pertained to his claim that it was permitted to sail on the Sabbath in the great rivers of Babylonia (the Euphrates and the Tigris) and of Egypt (the Nile). Samuel ben Eli believed such sailing to be forbidden, on the grounds that the passenger would go beyond "the Sabbath boundary."[4] The dispute centered on whether the prohibition against going beyond the Sabbath boundary applies to rivers and seas and on whether the prohibition is a matter of biblical law or only of rabbinic decree. Beyond his halakhic arguments, the head of the Babylonian yeshiva enlisted the Babylonian geonic tradition that forbade sailing in these rivers on the Sabbath. Maimonides responded to that argument with his own account of established practice:

> It is well known that the Seville River [near Cordoba] runs for about eighty *mil* until it comes to the salt sea. Ships sail upon it and are laden with oil, and they sail down the river to the salt sea and regularly go to Alexandria. And Jews sail on them, sages and students before all the *Geonim* who are there. And I recall that among them were R. Hanokh and R. Moses his son, R. Isaac ben Gi'at, R. Isaac ben Barukh, R. Isaac, author of the *Halakhot*, and R. Joseph Halevi his student, of blessed memory; and never did I hear from any of them of any prohibition, nor from anyone in Egypt. (*Iggerot*, p. 390)

Maimonides adds that even though there were *Geonim* who forbade it, "there are other *Geonim* among us who have resolved the practical halakhic issue by permitting it." He thus did not want to treat earlier practice as a consideration in determining the halakhic question. But since R. Samuel ben Eli had cited the geonic tradition, Maimonides countered with the Andalusian tradition, from R. Ḥanokh to R. Joseph Ibn Migash. Though its provenance was not Babylonian, he considered that tradition to be highly superior, as he points out with some biting irony: "But if these *Geonim* of ours are not worthy of being heeded because they are not from Babylonia and what matters is location—it is possible (*Iggerot*, pp. 390–391).

Maimonides' Andalusian legacy exercised philosophical as well as halakhic influence. The Andalusian Jews absorbed the many achievements and methods of Arabic science and thought, and the inner tensions among the competing worldviews in the Arabic world manifested themselves in the various streams of Judeo-Arabic thought in Andalusia. Solomon Ibn Gabirol and Baḥya Ibn Paquda belonged to the Neo-Platonic and Sufi Arab tradition; Abraham Ibn Ezra internalized, in his interpretation of the Jew-

---

[4] In general, *halakhah* prohibits one from going more than 2,000 cubits beyond one's city's limits on the Sabbath.

ish tradition, the science and Arabic astrological thought of al-Biruni, the Brethren of Purity, and others; and the thought of Judah Halevi had a deep connection to that of al-Ghazali and various streams within the Shi'ite world. In stark contrast to his practice in halakhic inquiry, Maimonides made little reference to his predecessors in medieval Jewish thought, nor did he debate them. His writings make little express reference to Sa'adyah Ga'on, Ibn Gabirol, Ibn Ezra, or Judah Halevi, even though he systematically refers to and many times attacks the Arabic schools of thought to which these thinkers belonged. In the *Guide*, he attacks the Muslim theological stream known as the Kalam, which exerted great influence on Sa'adyah, as religious apologetics having nothing to do with genuine philosophy; he rejects the astrology that appears in Ibn Ezra as useless and empty; and he does not consider al-Ghazali to be a philosopher of stature worth engaging. In Maimonides' view, the principal flaw in the Jewish thought that preceded him is its overreliance on erroneous and misguided sources of influence.

As for the sources on which Maimonides himself drew, we learn about them in a letter he wrote to Samuel Ibn Tibbon, in which he defines the philosophical canon that one should study and take guidance from:

> Generally, I would advise you to study only the works of logic composed by the scholar Abu Naṣr al-Farabi, for everything he has written, especially *The Principle of Existing Things*, is like fine flour. . . . Similarly, Ibn Bajja (Abu Bakr Ibn al-Ṣa'igh) was a great philosopher. All his writings are lucid to one who understands, and correct to those that find knowledge.
>
> The works of Aristotle are the basis for all these philosophical books and, as I indicated before, they can be understood only with the help of the commentaries of Alexander, Themistius and Averroes. . . . For Aristotle reached the highest level of knowledge to which man can ascend, with the exception of one who experiences the emanation of the Divine Spirit, who can attain the degree of prophecy, above which there is no higher stage. (*Letters of Maimonides*, p. 136)

His adulation for Aristotle, as a man who had attained all that could be attained through reason and without revelation, and his profound praise for al-Farabi, who died in 950, for Ibn Bajja who died in 1138, and for Aristotle's interpreters, place Maimonides within the stream of thought referred to in the Arab world as Falsafa. This stream drew its inspiration from Aristotle and, transmitted through such intermediaries as al-Farabi, Ibn Bajja, and their students, became central to the lives of educated Muslims.

This tradition also included Ibn Rushd (Averroes) of Cordoba, Maimonides' contemporary and home-town native, whose writings reached Maimonides at a later point in his life and of whom he speaks highly: "I have now obtained everything written by Ibn Rushd about Aristotle's works except for the *Commentary on the Parva Naturalia*, and I see that his expounding is well done, but I have not yet had time to examine all his books" (*Iggerot*, p. 312). Like Maimonides, who integrated *halakhah* and philosophy, Ibn Rushd also enjoyed legal and religious authority in Cordoba, serving there as chief *qadi* as well as being a philosopher of stature. Their philosophical proximity suggests that Ibn Rushd was part of the same philosophical stream in which Maimonides was educated in his youth. As we shall see, Maimonides' association with that school of thought had a critical effect on his philosophical interpretation of the Torah.

We do not know the identity of Maimonides' science and philosophy teachers in Andalusia. In the *Guide* (II: 9), he mentions the son of Ibn Aflah (an astronomer from Seville) as well as a student of Ibn Bajja as men with whom he associated and studied. It is clear that his training in these areas began at an early age, and his affiliation with the school of Aristotle and his interpreters, of al-Farabi and the Falasifa, was set in his youth.

Maimonides was only sixteen or seventeen years old when he wrote his first book, *Milot ha-Higayon* (*Treatise on Logic*). The book, written in Arabic in Hebrew letters and first translated into Hebrew by Moses Ibn Tibbon, is a clear and concise introduction to logic as taught in Maimonides' time. It demonstrates its author's mastery of Aristotelian logic as developed by al-Farabi. The *Commentary on the Mishnah*—written, as noted, when Maimonides was between the ages of twenty-three and thirty—likewise incorporates substantial philosophical elements. For example, the introduction to the commentary on tractate *Avot* (known as *Shemonah peraqim* ["Eight Chapters"]) encompasses a view of man drawn from that philosophical school. It is no wonder, then, that in that same introduction, Maimonides advised his readers to "hear the truth from whoever utters it." Truth is truth and one must accept it without regard to its source; in this instance, the truth appears in the writings of Aristotle and al-Farabi. Maimonides' integration of *halakhah* and philosophy in the *Commentary on the Mishnah*, and his mastery of both areas at an early age, demonstrate that these facets of his personality and his world had already been set in place at the beginning of his career.

If Maimonides' halakhic and philosophical influences have their source in his native Andalusia, it follows that he left Andalusia as a mature and fully formed person. The destruction of Andalusia was a traumatic event of personal and cultural loss in his life, and it set the perception of crisis within which he worked. From the day he left Andalusia, Maimonides' life can be seen in some sense as an effort to preserve and reconstruct his homeland in his writings and to save the Jewish world from the halakhic and spiritual ruin he had experienced.

Maimonides' sense of loss and fracture, and his perceived role as a refugee preserving a world that was lost, are evident in a letter he wrote in 1172 to a Yemenite sage who had conveyed his admiration for Maimonides. In that letter, he described himself in the following terms:

> I am one of the humblest scholars of Spain whose prestige is low in exile. I am always dedicated to my duties, but have not attained the learning of my forebears, for evil days and hard times have overtaken us and we have not lived in tranquility; we have labored without finding rest. How can the Law become lucid to a fugitive from city to city, from country to country? Have everywhere pursued the reapers and gathered ears of grain, both the solid and the full, as well as the shriveled and the thin. Only recently have I found a home. ("Epistle to Yemen," p. 95)

The Maghrib and Persecution: 1159–1166

In his conclusion to the *Commentary on the Mishnah*, which also offers a sort of apology for the errors it may contain, Maimonides describes the frenzied conditions under which the work was written:

> We have completed this treatise as we intended it, and I beseech Him, may He be exalted, and plead before Him that he save me from error. But anyone who finds reason to raise a question or believes he has an interpretation of any of the halakhot that is better than mine should so note and judge me favorably, for what I have taken upon myself to do here is no small matter easily discharged by one possessed of righteousness and a good sense of discernment. That is especially so because my heart is often burdened by the troubles of the time and what God has decreed for us with regard to exile and wandering the world from one end to the other; and perhaps we have

already received the associated reward, for exile atones for sin. He, may He be exalted, knows I wrote my interpretation of some halakhot while I was journeying on the road, and I listed some of them while I was aboard ship on the Mediterranean Sea. (*Commentary on the Mishnah*, conclusion to *Seder Taharot*)

Maimonides' family emigrated to the Maghrib, coming first to Fez, Morocco. The wanderings in the Maghrib continued throughout the third decade of his life and those years were accompanied by harsh religious persecutions. We cannot know why the family emigrated into the belly of the beast of the Almohad domain, in the Maghrib interior, instead of heading northward toward Christian Spain or Provence. It may be that conditions were easier near the Almohad center of power than at the margins. It is also possible that commercial or family ties account for the move.

The intensity of the tribulations endured by the Maghribi Jews is evident in a terrifying letter sent from Fustat in 1148. The letter was written by Solomon ben Judah Hakohen of Sijilmasa, a refugee from the Maghrib, to his father, whose commercial activities had brought him to Mirbat, a port city at the southern tip of the Arabian Peninsula on the India Ocean:

You will want to know news of the Maghrib, which will cause the ears of all who hear it to burn . . . After that, he [Abd al-Mu'min] conquered Tlemcen and killed all those within it except for those who transgressed [that is, converted to Islam] . . . After he entered the city [of Sijilmasa], he gathered all the Jews and offered them the option of transgressing [converting to Islam], and after seven months of enticing them, during all of which time they fasted and prayed, one of his officers came and demanded that they transgress. They declined, and one hundred fifty Jews were slaughtered for the unity of God's Name . . . and the remainder transgressed. The first of the transgressors was Joseph ben 'Imran, the *dayyan* of Sijilmasa. For this I mourn and cry . . . And the communities of the Maghrib were all destroyed on account of their sins; not one remained . . . bearing a Jewish name. Those who were killed were killed, and those who transgressed, transgressed. (Hirschberg, "On the Decrees of the Almohads")

The Almohad conquests led by Abd al-Mu'min destroyed the Jewish communities of the Maghrib. Some Jews died while resisting the forced conversion; some accepted Islam under compulsion, continuing to live as Jews in secret (among them the rabbi of the Sijilmasa community, Joseph ben 'Imran, as well as Joseph ben Aknin, previously mentioned); and some fled beyond the reach of the Almohad regime. The Almohad dynasty sought to create a Muslim expanse with no Jews or Christians, rejecting the traditional Muslim view that the "people of the book"—Jews and Christians—were *dhimmis*—entitled to protection. According to Muslim historians of the time, Jews who took on the trappings of Islam were not afforded equal status to Muslims. The Almohads confiscated estates, denied commercial rights, kidnapped Jewish children to raise them as Muslims, and required Jews to wear special clothing that marked them as alien and degraded.

The Muslim historian Ibn al-Qifti maintained that Maimonides and his family suffered a similar fate in the Maghrib and that Maimonides was required to pretend to have become Muslim; only after moving to Egypt was he again able to be openly Jewish. As Ibn al-Qifti tells it, a Muslim scholar named Abu al-Arab Ibn Ma'isha, who had come from Spain and was an adversary of Maimonides, told the Egyptian vizier, the *qadi* al-Fadil, that Maimonides had converted to Islam in his youth. That accusation had extremely serious implications, for according to Islamic law it is a capital crime for one who has converted to Islam to later leave it. But the vizier had extended his protection to Maimonides, who was serving as his personal physician, and argued that conversion to Islam under compulsion is not effective conversion pursuant to Islamic law.

Ibn al-Qifti's account raised a considerable ruckus among Maimonidean scholars. The conversion to Islam of one of the leading post-Talmudic halakhists, even if under compulsion, was a sensational piece of information. But Ibn al-Qifti's unique report is uncorroborated by any other independent source known to us and is open to question. If the report were accurate, it could not readily have been denied, for Maimonides was already a prominent and renowned figure in the Maghrib. If the conversion to Islam of a relatively marginal figure such as the rabbi of Sijilmasa became known throughout the region, any such act on the part of Maimonides and his family certainly would have become known, even if Maimonidean loyalists had tried to conceal it.

Moreover, refugees from the persecutions wandered throughout North Africa, and many of them reached Egypt. Had Maimonides in fact converted under compulsion, many people would have made use of that fact against him. Maimonides had more than a few enemies in Egypt and Babylonia, and they would have been delighted to use such information to undermine his halakhic and spiritual authority once and for all. To be sure, Maimonides himself took the view, as we shall see, that a Jew under compulsion to become Muslim may do so rather than suffer death. It is therefore conceivable that Maimonides, if faced with that decision, might have chosen under compulsion to declare his belief in Islam, thereby saving his life, and flee to a place where he could again live openly as a Jew. But since al-Qifti, as noted, remains the only source for this story, one may well be skeptical of his account.

The status of Jews who had converted under compulsion but remained Jews in secret turned into a matter of intense controversy, and Maimonides became involved in it while still in the Maghrib. At issue was whether a Jew might elect to remain alive by affecting Muslim appearance until the furor passed. Complicating the question is the fact that if he were to die rather than accept Islam, his surviving young children would be raised as Muslims. One responsum of unknown authorship that was widely disseminated in the Maghrib claimed decisively that Islam was idolatry and that one must give up his life rather than declare belief in it. That declaration, termed *shahada* in Arabic, required the Jew to attest that there was no god other than Allah and that Muhammad was His prophet. That sage equated this to the acceptance of idolatry, subject to the Talmudic rule of "be killed rather than transgress"; and a court may impose capital punishment on one who chooses to transgress to save his life. Moreover, the ruling held that any commandments of the Torah fulfilled in secret by one who has converted lack any value, and since he has removed himself from the community of Israel, his prayer is repugnant: "One who utters that confession is a gentile, though he fulfills the entire law publicly and privately . . . If one of the forced converts enters one of their houses of worship [that is, a mosque], even if he does not say a word, and then goes home and offers his prayers, this prayer is charged against him as an added sin and transgression" (*Epistle on Martyrdom*, p. 16). This responsum firmly spurned all those in the Maghrib who had converted under compulsion, ousting them from the community of Israel. It denied them any prospect of a continued link to Judaism, even a partial one, and severed absolutely their ties to Israel. Even before he became known as a prominent and ultimate authority, Maimonides responded to this ruling in his *Epistle on Martyrdom* (*Iggeret ha-shemad*).

The *Epistle on Martyrdom* offers an important statement of Maimonides' self-understanding as a legal scholar and of his concept of *halakhah*. From his viewpoint, the issue at hand was more than a purely legal one; it was also—indeed, primarily—the fate of a community at risk of being cut off from the Jewish world due to the heavy burden cast upon it. This ruling risked their effectively being pushed to change from being Muslims by compulsion (and superficially only) to Muslims by will:

> Therefore I was afraid that the response that turns people away from God would fall into the hands of an ignorant individual, and he would conclude that he will receive no reward for praying, so he will not pray. This, he will assume, is true of the other commandments; if he performs them, he will get no reward for performing any of them. (*Epistle on Martydrom*, p. 22)

His alarm over that sage's condemnation of people submitting to forced conversion led Maimonides to begin his own response with an effort to undermine the sage's standing in the eyes of those raising the question. He portrayed the sage as an empty vessel, as one not even worthy of a reply: "The man of whom the inquiry was made offered a weak and senseless reply, of foul content and form. He made statements in it distinctly harmful" (*Epistle on Martydrom*, p. 15). He concluded by mocking that sage and applying to him the verse in Ecclesiastes (10:13): "His talk begins as silliness and ends as disastrous madness" (ibid., p. 17).

As his next step, Maimonides attempts to ease the compelled converts' sense of rejection by transforming the author of the responsum from accuser to accused. His offense is grounded in the fact that his words of admonition are actually a slanderous utterance against a group beloved of God. Greater men than he have been punished for the sin of slandering Israel—among them, Moses, Elijah, and Isaiah:

> If this is the sort of punishment meted out to the pillars of the universe— Moses, Elijah, Isaiah, and the ministering angels—because they briefly criticized the Jewish congregation, can one have an idea of the fate of the least among the worthless who let his tongue loose against Jewish communities of sages and their disciples, priests, and Levites, and called them sinners, evildoers, gentiles, disqualified to testify, heretics who deny the Lord God of Israel? These are verbal quotations from his response; can you picture his punishment? . . . This man did not realize that they are not rebels by choice. God will not abandon nor forsake them, *for He did not scorn, He did not spurn the plea of the lowly* [Ps. 22:25]. (ibid., p. 19)

Maimonides goes on to reinforce the compelled converts' sense of belonging by citing a range of authoritative sources to demonstrate that Jewish sages, including such sages of the *Mishnah* as R. Eliezer and R. Meir, put on the appearance of having transgressed their faith during times of persecution but continued in secret to carry out the Torah and commandments. The compelled converts of the Maghrib therefore should not be regarded as people who have set themselves outside the Jewish community. On the contrary; their difficult straits, and their resolution to continue observing the commandments in secret, place them squarely within the tradition of great Talmudists.

Replying to the claim that the compelled converts enjoy no reward for the commandments they observe, Maimonides cites midrashic statements arguing that the virtuous acts of even great sinners such as Ahab, Nebuchadnezzar, and Esau are not considered to be repugnant and receive abundant reward. If such is the case with respect to willful sinners, how much more with respect to people who were compelled and had no desire to sin? Maimonides understood that he had to prepare the ground in this way in the opening paragraphs of the letter, before providing the detailed legal support for his position, for halakhic explanations alone would not suffice to liberate these communities from the heavy onus of accusation and rejection.

The detailed halakhic case comprises two central arguments. The first argument, which informs the entire letter, holds that one who has failed to fulfill his obligation to die rather than convert is not on that account considered to be a sinner or an apostate. One who transgresses under threat of death, even where he is obligated to suffer death rather than transgress, is considered to have acted under compulsion and therefore to be exempt from court-imposed capital punishment. That claim was accepted by a few of the medieval rabbinic authorities, and, years later, Maimonides ruled thus in his *Mishneh Torah*. It made no sense to consider those who had converted under compulsion to be sinners expelled from the community of Israel, as urged by the sage Maimonides was reacting to, for doing so failed to distinguish between willful behavior and acting under compulsion.

Maimonides' second argument is more far-reaching. He maintains that the Jews of the Maghrib were not obligated even in the first instance to die rather than convert, because all that was being required of them was a mere declaration: "There has never yet been a persecution as remarkable as this one, where the only coercion is to say something. When our rabbis ruled that a person is to surrender himself to death and not transgress, it does not seem likely that they had in mind speech that did not involve action" (*Epistle on Martydrom*, pp. 30–31). This distinction has to be examined carefully. A speech act can constitute an idolatrous worship, as the *Mishnah* in Sanhedrin rules that one forbidden form of idolatrous ritual is to state regarding an idol—"you are my god"; such a statement is forbidden because through it, the speaker accepts the foreign god as his divinity. But Maimonides believes that to be the case only when the words are uttered voluntarily, whereas a declaration made under compulsion is an empty act, lacking all meaning. Moreover, the gentiles compelling the act know that the words are mere lip service: "They know very well that we do not mean what we say, and that what we say is only to escape the ruler's punishment and to satisfy him with this simple confession" (ibid., p. 30). Speech thus differs from action. An idolatrous ritual action remains an action even if performed under compulsion and is forbidden, whatever the cost. Speech, in contrast, requires intention and assent. If done under compulsion, it is nothing more than a sequence of noises. Consistent with his distinction between speech and action, Maimonides formulates his halakhic conclusion as follows:

> Anyone who suffered martyrdom in order not to acknowledge the apostleship of 'that man' [Muhammad], the only thing that can be said of him is that he has done what is good and proper, and that God holds great reward in store for him. His position is very high, for he has given his life for the sanctity of God, be He exalted and blessed. But if anyone comes to ask me whether to surrender his life or acknowledge, I tell him to confess and not choose death. (ibid.)

But the distinction between speech and action seems forced in this context. It could be argued that a public declaration, like any other deed, has an active quality. Moreover, according to Maimonides' own ruling, consistent with the *halakhah* in the Talmud, in a time of persecution one is obligated to give up his life rather than succumb to even the slightest demand of the oppressor, even changing the manner in which one ties one's shoelaces. Can one say that a declaration of faith is not equivalent to at least the smallest of sins? To be sure, declaring the first part of the *shahada*—"There is no god but Allah"—poses no difficulty, especially for Maimonides, who believes Islam to be a monotheistic religion in all respects. But the second

part, in which the speaker attests publicly that Muhammad is Allah's messenger—is more problematic. A declaration of this sort undermines the
principle of the Torah's eternity, and it signifies an uprooting of the Jewish
religion. In a time of persecution, it would be difficult to argue that a public declaration in this spirit is less significant than a compelled minor alteration in an item of clothing, which one would be required to suffer death
for rather than submit to. Maimonides' further finding—that one who
dies rather than declare his faith in Islam has fulfilled a commandment and
is greatly rewarded—also shows that it is more than pure halakhic logic
that dictates his ruling.

This attitude toward one who suffers death is clearly opposed to the
position that appears in *The Epistle on Martyrdom* and is reiterated in *Mishneh Torah*. There, he rules in practice that a person who submits to death
where he is not obligated to do so has committed a capital offense. In
contrast to the Ashkenazi halakhists, Maimonides believed that when it
came to dying in sanctification of God's name, there are no voluntary acts
of piety. As he puts it in *The Epistle on Martyrdom*: "And our sages ruled [in
certain cases] 'Let him transgress and [not] surrender his life.' [Yet] this
man [sees himself] of higher status than the sages, and more punctilious
about the Law. By word of mouth and the use of his tongue, he surrenders
himself to death and claims to have sanctified God's name. But by his actions he is a sinner and rebellious, and he makes himself guilty against his
life" (ibid., p. 30). How can he rule, on the one hand, that there is no obligation to give up one's life in the Maghribi persecutions and, on the other,
that one who acted stringently and did so receives a great reward? Evidently, as Haym Soloveichick pointed out, Maimonides himself recognized
that the lenient ruling he propounded in *The Epistle on Martyrdom* was not
firmly enough grounded to make one who does not accord with it into a
sinner.

Even if the distinction between speech and action is possible, it cannot by
itself adequately support the lenient ruling Maimonides issued. The ruling
rests on Maimonides' broad position toward the value of human life vis-à-vis
the obligation to sanctify God's name and on his attitude toward the complex
situation of the community that posed the question. In unambiguously forbidding a person to give up his life when he is not obligated to do so, Maimonides shows that he regards the preservation of life as a central halakhic
value. In *Mishneh Torah*, he formulated the duty to preserve life even at the
cost of Sabbath desecration not as a limitation on what the *halakhah* de-

mands of one but as a value in its own right, one that is characteristic of the Torah's overall goals: "For Scripture says 'Which if a man do, he shall live by them' (Lev. 18:5), that is to say he shall not die by them. Hence you learn that the ordinances of the Law were meant to bring upon the world not vengeance but mercy, loving-kindness, and peace" ("Laws Concerning the Sabbath"). Given this broad understanding of the Torah's purpose and the value of life, it is easy to comprehend the use of the distinction between speech and action, however strained, as a means for narrowing the scope of the martyrological obligation. Moreover, the halakhic determination is driven not only by broad systemic values but also by the nature of the specific situation to which it pertains. Maimonides found himself confronting a dilemma. On the one hand, he wanted to lend support to the compelled converts, and he therefore ruled permissively, on the basis of the distinction between speech and action. On the other hand, he could not disparage the Maghribi Jews who had given their lives rather than declare their allegiance to Islam. These sanctifiers of God's name were presumably admired even by those who had decided to convert outwardly.

As is clear from his treatment of forced conversions in the Maghrib, Maimonides took the view that a responsum of this sort should not be limited exclusively to formal considerations. A ruling is a complex product, and the decision maker's interpretation of authoritative halakhic sources must be integrated with larger value considerations and responsiveness to the particular circumstances in which the questioner finds himself. The circumstantial constraints that a scholar must consider in the course of arriving at a decision continued to have a bearing on Maimonides' activities as halakhist throughout his career.

In a responsum from a later period, when he was already living in Egypt, he considered the case of a man who had acquired a beautiful Christian maidservant who was living in the same courtyard as he. The maid converted to Judaism, and the question posed was whether the man was permitted to reside with her or whether the court was obligated to compel him to remove her from his house. Maimonides was well aware that the *halakhah* forbade a master's marriage to his freed maidservant, given the suspicions that he had engaged in relations with her before she was freed. Nevertheless, he replied as follows:

> We have ruled several times in this sort of situation that he may emancipate her and marry her. And we did so to facilitate repentance. We said it is bet-

ter that he eat [forbidden] gravy rather than the fat itself, relying on the sages' determination that "It is a time to act for the Lord; they have violated Your Torah" (Psalms 119, 126). So we help him to marry her with delicacy and blessing, setting for him a time by which he must either marry her or remove her, as Ezra did. (*Teshuvot*, sec. 211)

Maimonides recognized that an uncompromising insistence here on compliance with the letter of the *halakhah* would only aggravate the master's offense and complicate his situation, for he would continue to live with the former maid in sin. There can be a gap between the *halakhah*'s abstract demands and their practical application. Maimonides looked to the principles of the *halakhah* itself to justify departures, in specific cases, from the law's abstract principles. According to Talmudic sources, a scholar must sometimes deviate from the *halakhah* because exigent circumstances call for violating the Torah's commands for the sake of heaven: "It is a time to act for the Lord; they have violated Your Torah."[5]

The Epistle on Martyrdom, then, had a purpose broader than that of simply replying to a halakhic question. In its wider role, as David Hartman noted, it was an effort to revive flagging spirits and restore a people's self-esteem. The sensitivity to those needs pervades the letter, from beginning to end. That is why it encompasses so much more than a series of references to the specific sources needed to resolve the question. The responsum takes account of the intolerable threat posed by the earlier rabbi's treatment of the issue and of the possibility that the community would be crushed under the burden of sin cast upon it. The sensitivity to the community's distress and the need to raise its spirits appear not only in the responsum's rhetorical envelope but at the heart of the halakhic distinction Maimonides drew. This multifaceted grappling with the issue led Maimonides to a position that is not entirely in line with his own position in principle or with the written halakhic sources.

At the conclusion of the letter, Maimonides pressed the members of the communities under Almohad pressure to leave their homes and emigrate to areas where they could live full Jewish lives, openly observing the Torah and its commandments. The compelled converts had sinned not by their superficial proclamation of the Muslim credo but by continuing to live in the same place following the proclamation that had saved their lives. Their

[5] The midrashic reinterpretation of the verse, meant to justify action in exigent circumstances to prevent a greater evil, reads it as "It is a time to act for the LORD; violate the Torah."

messianic hope for some external force that would improve their condition was mere self-deception; they were obligated, instead, to uproot themselves from their residences and move somewhere else. One version of *The Epistle on Martyrdom* contains the following passage: "What I counsel myself, and what I should like to suggest to all my friends and everyone else that consults me, is to leave those places and go to where he can practice religion and fulfill the Law without compulsion or fear. . . . He must leave everything he has, travel day and night until he finds a spot where he can practice his religion. The world is sufficiently large and extensive" (*Epistle on Martyrdom*, pp. 31–32). Among other things, Maimonides suggests that the compelled convert who saves his life by uttering the *shahada* emigrate to the Land of Israel: "In my opinion, one can escape from them by uttering that word, namely, acknowledging that man [that is, Muhammad] and then going to the Land of Israel to dwell there, and not remaining on any account in the place of persecution" (*Iggerot*, p. 57).

Maimonides' use of the first person suggests the responsum is directed not only at the fate of the compelled converts but also at that of Maimonides himself and his family. And so, in or around 1166, Maimonides took flight from the persecutions in the Maghrib and moved to the Land of Israel. We learn of his stay there through an important letter, written twenty years later in 1185 to R. Japhet, the *dayyan* of Acre, who hosted members of Maimonides' family. In the letter, Maimonides longingly recalls his visit to Jerusalem: "For I, and he [that is, David, Maimonides' brother], and my honored father, and you, the four of us, walked through the House of the Lord with great feeling . . . and we walked through the deserts and the forests seeking God; I will not forget it" (*Iggerot*, p. 230). Evidently because they could not earn a living in the Land of Israel, however, Maimonides and his family emigrated to Egypt.

Fustat: 1166–1177

Maimonides' years of wandering, during which he endured harsh religious persecution, came to an end when he and his family arrived in Egypt, then ruled by the Fatimid dynasty and free of Almohad influence. They came to Egypt in 1166, going first, it appears, to Alexandria and then moving to Fustat, near Cairo, where he remained until his death in 1204. Maimonides' father, R. Maimon, died soon after the family's arrival in Egypt, and we know nothing of Maimonides' mother, not even her name. In addition to Maimonides himself, the family included his younger brother David, whom he loved deeply and to whose education he was devoted, and at least three sisters. In an important letter to Maimonides, found in the Cairo Genizah by Solomon Dov Goitein, his sister Miriam, who had remained in Spain or the Maghrib, sorrowfully requests her brother's help. She writes that her son has gone missing and has not been heard from for three months, and she is concerned about his fate. She hopes that her renowned and influential brother can use his connections to help find her son and tell him to write home as soon as possible. The letter conveys greetings to Maimonides' sisters—the plural informs us that he had at least three sisters overall—and to David.

Not long after arriving in Egypt, Maimonides married; he was then in his early thirties, a relatively advanced age for marriage. In delaying his marriage beyond the norm, he acted consistently with his position, set forth in *Mishneh Torah*, that one was permitted to defer marriage in order to study Torah. Moreover, Maimonides ruled in accord with a minority view in the Talmud that one who craved only Torah was exempt from the commandment to procreate.[6]

Maimonides' views about delaying marriage may also flow from his negative attitude toward sexuality conveyed throughout his writings. At several points in the *Guide*, he approvingly cites Aristotle's attitude to the effect that "the sense of touch is a disgrace for us."[7] Sexuality is a necessity that should be confined to preservation of the species and not otherwise engaged in. He takes this view with respect not only to physical sexuality but also to everything related to the possibility of intimate relationships with women. Even before marrying, he wrote harshly, consistent with the spirit of his times, of contact with women. In his commentary on *Avot* 1:5, he considers the *Mishnah* that states, "Do not engage much in conversation with a woman. That is so of his own wife, and a fortiori of his fellow's wife. Hence the sages said: One who engages much in conversation with a woman causes harm to himself, and abandons words of Torah, and his destiny is Gehenna." Maimonides comments: "And it is known that most conversation with women relates to sexual intercourse, and he therefore says that to converse much with them is forbidden, for he causes harm to himself, that is, he develops a flaw in his character, namely, excessive lust."

[6] Laws of Marriage, 15, 2–3.
[7] See for example *Guide* II, 36.

Maimonides inherited from Talmudic *halakhah* various discriminatory rules toward women such as disqualifying them from serving as witnesses or from attaining public office. The problematic attitude toward women was aggravated in Maimonides' writings because of the impact of the Aristotelian picture and contemporary Islamic practice on his thought and rulings. He repeatedly attributed to women an inferior intellectual standing, and lack of stable and strong character.[8] This was in line with the Aristotelian stance that he took in his allegorical readings of Scripture, identifying the female with inferior matter, and the male with superior form. Yet, such a position was not based in his thinking, on a rigid ontology which is immutable, but rather on social standing and education that were subject to change. Given his non-ontological stance, Maimonides thought that women were, in fact, capable of achieving the highest form of prophetic perfection. Such an accomplishment he ascribed to Miriam, Moses's sister, who achieved a "death by kiss," the most exalted form of the prophetic mystical state:

> Because of this the *Sages* have indicated with reference to the deaths of *Moses, Aaron* and *Miriam that the three of them died by a kiss* . . . . And they say of *Miriam* in the same way: *She also died by a kiss.* But with regard to her it is not said by *the mouth of the Lord*; because she was a woman and the use of the figurative expression was not suitable with regard to her. (*Guide,* 3, 51)

In addition to the misogynistic Aristotelian attitude that Maimonides internalized, the impact of Islamic patriarchal tendencies is present in rulings in *Mishneh Torah* in which he deviated from his Talmudic sources toward a more restrictive and harsher attitude toward women; deviations that were recognized by other medieval halakhists who debated these rulings. One such ruling not explicitly mentioned in the Talmud and practiced in the Islamic custom of his time restricts women's movement in the public sphere:

> For every woman is entitled to go to her father's house to visit him, or to a house of mourning or a wedding feast as an act of kindness to her friends and relatives, in order that they in turn might visit her on similar occasions, for she is not in a prison where she cannot come and go. On the other hand,

---

[8] Laws of Repentance, 10, 1; Laws of Idolatry 11, 17; *Guide of the Perplexed*, 3, 37.

it is unseemly for a woman to be constantly going out abroad and into the streets, and the husband should prevent his wife from doing this and should not let her go out, except once or twice a month, as the need may arise. Rather, the seemly thing for a woman is to sit in the corner of her house, for so it is written, All glorious is the king's daughter within the palace. (Ps. 45, 15) (Law of Marriage 13, 10)

In line with this restriction, Maimonides supported in a responsum of his the claim of a husband who wished to prevent his wife from teaching Torah to children and insisted she should stay at home though she was in a grave economic state.[9] In another controversial ruling in *Mishneh Torah,* the influence of patriarchal Islamic habits that he shared becomes clearer and harsher: "A wife who refuses to perform any kind of work that she is obligated to do, may be compelled to perform it, even by scourging her with a rod" (Laws of Marriage 21, 10). Scholars argued whether this ruling grants the husband a right to force his wife with lashes, or, since the verb "compel" in Hebrew is in the plural, such a right is granted only to a court. In any event, this extreme measure, which has no basis in the Talmud, was criticized by the great Provençal scholar, R. Abraham Ben David, who points to its strangeness: "I have never heard of afflicting women with rods."[10]

We should not conclude from Maimonides' attitude toward sexuality that he was a man lacking in passion. As we shall see, he believed that love of God and truth is the greatest religious and philosophical attainment a man can experience in his life. He describes that love in blatantly erotic terms, and its climax is the lover's "death by a kiss." Eros was a central element in Maimonides' life, but it was directed only to God and truth—the sole worthy object, he believed, of this sort of desire. Love of God is described in his writings in terms of a powerful, debilitating desire:

What is the love of God that is befitting? It is to love the Eternal with a great and exceeding love, so strong that one's soul shall be knit up with the love of God, and one should be continually enraptured by it, like a love-sick individual, whose mind is at no time free from his passion for a particular woman, the thought of her filling his heart at all times, when sitting down or rising up, when he is eating or drinking. Even intenser should be the love of God in the hearts of those who love him. (Laws Concerning Repentance, 10:3)

[9] Responsa 34 and 45.
[10] See the strong language of R. Moshe Isserlis, in *Shulchan Arukh*, Even ha-Ezer, 154, 3.

In *Mishneh Torah*, toward the end of "Laws Concerning Forbidden Inter-course," Maimonides treats sexuality as an impulse difficult to resist: "There is no prohibition in the whole of Scripture which the generality of the people experience greater difficulty in observing than the interdict of forbidden unions and illicit intercourse" ("Laws Concerning Forbidden Intercourse," 22:18). The struggle with sexuality requires discipline and warnings, which he goes on to enumerate: "In like manner, man should keep away from levity, drunkenness, and lewd discourse, since these are great contributory factors and degrees leading to forbidden unions. Nor should a man live without a wife, since married estate is conducive to great purity" (ibid., 22:21). Following the Talmud, Maimonides thus recommends conduct that he himself did not adopt: early marriage that helps one channel his sexuality and prevail over it.

Maimonides' own way of dealing with sexuality is expressed, evidently, in the following passage: "But above all this, as the Sages have declared, a man should direct his mind and thoughts to the words of Torah and en-large his understanding with wisdom, for unchaste thoughts prevail only in a heart devoid of wisdom, and of wisdom it is said, *a hind of love and a doe of grace, let her breasts satisfy thee at all time, with her love be thou ravished always* (Prov. 5:19)" (ibid.). As a foil to sexual Eros one must set the desire for wisdom, described here in powerfully erotic terms. The love of wisdom fills one's entire consciousness, and its interaction with sexual Eros consti-tutes a zero-sum game.

Maimonides was forty-eight years of age in 1186, when his son Abraham was born. He appears to have had a daughter who died while still very young. In a letter to his beloved student Joseph written while Abraham was still a boy, the proud father spoke warmly of his son, whom he saw as a source of great consolation in a life of harsh travail:

> Concerning my personal welfare, I find comfort only in two things: In an ability to indulge in speculative investigation and, secondly, in blessed en-dowments vouchsafed unto my son, Abraham. Like his namesake, the pa-triarch, may he be sustained and granted long life. For he is most humble and unpretentious, excelling in unusual fine qualities of character and im-bued with an exemplary good nature and a subtle mind scintillating with innovate ideas. I am sure he will be held in high esteem by all people and I beseech the Almighty to watch over him and recompense him for his good deeds. (*Letters of Maimonides*, pp. 83–84)

His warm feelings for his son are evident as well in a particularly valuable letter—found in the Genizah and published by Paul B. Fenton—describing a meeting with Maimonides at his home in Fustat. The writer had been requested to bring Maimonides a personal letter, and he assumed that the important and busy addressee of the letter would simply accept it and that his assignment would thereby be completed. To the excited messenger's surprise, Maimonides invited him from the entry way, past the guard, to his own chamber, where he opened the letter in the messenger's presence and even took counsel with him about something related to the letter. The messenger was accompanied by a friend named al-Fakhr, who was so awe-struck by the important figure that he waited outside. The messenger's young son al-Galal, however, accompanied his father into Maimonides' chamber, since his father did not want him to miss the opportunity to see the great man; as a typical child, he was unimpressed by Maimonides' majesty and personality. Refreshment was brought into the room, and the messenger recounts that Maimonides ate some of the lemon cake that was served. Also in the room was Maimonides' son Abraham, then a lad.

Maimonides evidently sought to expose Abraham to the ways of the world and to leadership. He therefore took pains to ensure that his son was present when he dealt with the questions of the hour; as we have seen, he expected great things of his son. In circumstances such as these, children find each other, and while the adults were dealing with the affairs of the world, Abraham was cheerfully teaching al-Galal one of the forms of address used for his father. Maimonides listened happily to the chatter between the boys, and the messenger, who made sure to describe the meeting in detail, tells that Maimonides played with al-Galal. Maimonides appointed Abraham to no office during his lifetime, but the story makes clear that he tried to expose him to community business.

Maimonides' great hope was realized, and, after his death, his son was appointed leader of the Jews in Egypt and became an important thinker and halakhist in his own right. Notwithstanding his consistent defense of his father's teachings, R. Abraham imported elements of Sufi Muslim mysticism into his interpretation of Judaism, a worldview quite distant in many ways from Maimonides' basic ideas. At one point of disagreement with his father's halakhic stance, R. Abraham makes an interesting observation about his father's method:

Had my father and teacher heard this, he would have acknowledged it [that is, Abraham's position on a matter on which they disagreed]; as he himself said, "acknowledge the truth." And we always saw him, may his memory be for a blessing, agreeing with the least of his students when something was true, despite his wealth of learning, which did not stand at odds with the greatness of his piety. (*ha-Maspiq le-Ovdei ha-Shem*, p. 70)

In the patriarchal societies of the Middle Ages, women's names go un-mentioned in family genealogies, and they and their biographies drop out of the collective memory, which focuses on male heroes. Maimonides' wife, therefore, like his mother, is largely unknown to us, and even her name is unreported. We do know, however, that her family was esteemed and in-fluential in the Egyptian Jewish community and in the court of the Muslim ruler. Her father's Hebrew name was Mishael Halevi ben Isaiah.

One Genizah fragment contains the genealogical roll of Maimonides' father-in-law; it describes a particularly noble lineage comprising fourteen generations of a prominent family in the Land of Israel and in Egypt on his mother's side, and six generations of sages, physicians, and government officials on his father's side. At several points in this family tree, we find a significant title that says much about the family's spiritual direction: "Rab-beinu Isaiah, leader of the order, leader of the pious ones (*ḥasidim*) and of the men of accomplishment, and his beloved [son] Daniel, glory of the pious ones, and his beloved [son] Isaiah, the precious possession of the pious ones and his brother Daniel, the pious and his beloved [son] Isaiah the pious." Repetition of the designation "pious" is rare in genealogical lists, and it indicates a distinctive tradition within the family. It may be that this tradition of pietism within his mother's family influenced Abraham, and he eventually became the spokesman and leader of a stream of Judaism with pietistic tendencies in the spirit of Sufi Muslim mysticism.

One of Maimonides' sisters was married to Uzziel, known as Abu al-Maʿali, a senior officer in the Sultan's court and secretary to the mother of al-Afdal, the son of Saladin. We learn of that marriage through the writings of the Arab historiographer Ibn al-Qifti, who provides the following data about Maimonides: "And he [Maimonides] in Egypt married the sister of a Jewish official; he [Uzziel] was known as Abu al-Maʿali . . . Abu al-Maʿali married the sister of Moses [Maimonides] and begat children from her, among them the wise physician Abu al-Riḍa." In one of his letters, Maimonides refers to his nephew Abu al-Riḍa as a member of his household. Marriages, of course, have political and economic significance; for an immigrant—even a vastly learned one—a marital connection with a distinguished local family can provide an important platform for participation in the life of the community.

Maimonides enjoyed a meteoric rise within the Egyptian Jewish community. Even before writing *Mishneh Torah*, he had become, as author of the *Commentary on the Mishnah*, an irresistible force. Egypt had not produced any sages whose stature could match that of the imposing immigrant from the ruins of Andalusia. Soon after arriving in Egypt, he became a sort of High Court of Appeal, and local judges voluntarily submitted to his authority. As he wrote to Pinḥas the judge long after immigrating: "To sum it up, I have been in the land of Egypt about thirty years, and all or most of the judges of Alexandria come before me" (*Iggerot*, p. 463).

Also contributing to Maimonides' integration into the leadership of Egyptian Jewry—whose influence extended as well to the Jews of the Land of Israel and of Syria—was his continuous and active involvement in public affairs. His lifelong and multifaceted participation in the day-to-day life of the community, extending far beyond his halakhic rulings and responsa, shows that his life was far removed from a philosophical ideal of seclusion and from confinement to the four cubits of the *halakhah*.

He first became involved in public life as a figure to be reckoned with in 1169, only three years after coming to Egypt; the matter was one that did not bear directly on any complex halakhic questions. It involved letters sent around that time to Jews throughout Egypt, on which Maimonides was a signatory, urgently pleading for contributions to a fund for the ransoming of prisoners. It appears the prisoners had been taken in Bilbays—a city on the caravan route between Egypt and the Land of Israel—by Crusaders who had penetrated into the Egyptian border areas. The Crusaders retreated to the Land of Israel, taking their prisoners with them, and demanded ransom for their release. The demand came to 33 1/3 dinars per prisoner, an amount that required broad participation by the Jewish community throughout Egypt. In one of the fund-raising letters, Maimonides declared that he had put his money where his mouth was:

> So do as we have done, all the judges, elders and sages. All of us go forth, by
> night by and day, rousing people in synagogues and markets [and at?] door-

ways until we achieve something for this great cause. Since we have contributed what we were able to, [we ask that] you do for them in accord with your honor, generosity and love to purchase the right [of freedom]. (*Iggerot*, p. 65)

In the best fund-raising manner, the request provides an example of intercommunal responsibility and recognizes, from the outset, the generosity of the community being turned to so that the request will bear fruit. Maimonides did not rest content here with listing his name as a signatory; in addition, he actively participated as a fund-raiser. The Cairo Genizah contains a document, written in 1170 in Maimonides' hand, confirming receipt from an emissary named Hiba ben R. Eliezer of nine dinars collected in the city of al-Maḥalla and transferred to Maimonides as campaign treasurer. Later, as shown by the Genizah documents, Maimonides would be involved in all the details of administering the property, known as *heqdesh*, whose earnings were directed to charitable causes. For example, a letter in Maimonides' hand provides detailed instructions for dealing with an orchard that had been dedicated to charity.

Maimonides' involvement extended to the highest political reaches of the Jewish community in Egypt, and in 1171, only some five years after arriving in Egypt, he was named to the office of *ra'is al-yahud*, the head of Egyptian Jewry. As a rule, one could be named to the office only with the approval both of the leadership of the Jewish community and of the Muslim government. In appointment letters, the occupant of the office is given responsibility for all matters pertaining to Jews within the area governed by the Muslim authorities. He is considered the highest judicial authority and is charged with enforcement of religious law and with oversight of public order and the proper behavior of the members of the community. The *ra'is al-yahud* administered the *heqdesh* and the community's charitable funds, and he could issue and revoke excommunication orders. He was responsible for the appointment of various religious functionaries, including kosher slaughterers, cantors, judges, and synagogue leaders, and for defining the scope of their authority, overseeing their activities, and removing them from office if they failed, in his judgment, to perform satisfactorily. The influence of the *ra'is* was derived in part from the influence he wielded within Muslim government circles. The members of the Jewish community saw him as their representative before the government and sought his intervention when they were mistreated by the government or its officials. In short, he was regarded as responsible to the government for the conduct of the minority he headed and as their emissary to the government.

Maimonides' responsa show that upon his arrival in Egypt, he was considered to be the highest halakhic authority, and all segments of the community turned to him with a wide range of questions. In addition, as noted, he functioned as a sort of high court of appeal and sometimes, following an appeal by a litigant, demanded that a judge change his decision. His unquestioned halakhic standing was almost self-evident, given the recognition by all who were in contact with him of his powerful control of all the halakhic sources. In addition to his halakhic rulings, he was involved in the enactment of community rules whose violation could be punished by banning. One of the more daring enactments issued by Maimonides in agreement with his fellow scholars was eliminating the worshipers' silent recitation of the *amidah* prayer while counting solely on the cantor's loud recitation of the *amidah* prayer which ordinarily is performed after the silent individual prayer.[11] This enactment was motivated by the fact that during the loud recitation of the cantor after the silent prayer by each individual member of the synagogue, the community that had already silently recited the *amidah* behaved in a disrespectful manner, causing desecration of God's name in the eyes of the Muslim environment.

At the same time, the office of the *ra'is al-yahud*, head of the Jews, was clearly a political and institutional one. Successfully discharging the responsibilities of the office required skills and connections extending far beyond mastery of the halakhic literature. It is no surprise, therefore, that the office had been held by the local Jewish aristocracy, whose members were wealthy merchants with access to government circles. Its occupants had come mainly from families close to the leadership of the yeshiva of the Land of Israel, which had taken up residence in Egypt during the 1130s. Maimonides' appointment as *ra'is al-yahud* only a few years after his arrival in Egypt entailed, by the nature of things, a persistent political struggle with the powerful and established families who had dominated the office and had close ties to the Muslim government. A reference to the harsh struggle in the wake of his appointment—a struggle that included threats on his life—appears in Maimonides' comments to Japhet the judge, in which he described his early years in Egypt in these terms: "Many and severe misfortunes befell me in Egypt. Illness and material loss overwhelmed me. Informers plotted against my life" (*Letters of Maimonides*, p. 72). The

[11] Maimonides' Responsa, 256; 258.

great immigrant from Andalusia challenged the families of the Jewish nobility who had exercised highhanded authority in the Land of Israel, Egypt,
and Babylonia. In his *Commentary on the Mishnah* (*Bekhorot* 4:4), Maimonides speaks disparagingly of the titled figures associated with these
families, recounting his direct impression of them:

> In the Land of Israel and in Babylonia, they call some men "*rosh yeshivah*"
> [head of the academy] and others "*av bet din*" [chief judge], and they distin-
> guish between "*rosh yeshivat ge'on ya'aqov*" and "*rosh yeshivah shel golah*" . . .
> but these are nothing more than a pile of meaningless titles . . . And I have
> seen men in the Land of Israel called "*ḥaverim*" ["members," a title indicat-
> ing membership in the Palestinian yeshivah] and others called "*rosh yeshi-
> vah*," and they are not equal in learning to one who has been in the study
> hall only one day.

Maimonides' central adversary in the clash over Jewish leadership was a
scion of one of these families: Sar Shalom Halevi. As Menaḥem Ben-Sasson
and Mordecai Akiva Friedman have shown, this individual, like many of
his contemporaries, was known by several names: Abu Zikri, Yaḥya, Sar
Shalom. His opponents in Maimonides' camp referred to him as "Zuta"—
the small one.

We know of the first flare-up of the struggle between Maimonides and
Sar Shalom thanks to a question posed to Maimonides by the community
of al-Maḥalla. Sar Shalom Abu Zikri, who was then the *ra'is al-yahud*, had
ordered the judge in al-Maḥalla, Peraḥiah ben Joseph, to collect a tax from
anyone asking him for a halakhic ruling. A certain portion of the tax would
go to the *ra'is al-yahud*'s account, to fund the payment he was required to
make to the Muslim ruler in order to keep his office. Charging this sort of
fee for a halakhic ruling was the practice in Babylonia but not in the Land
of Israel or in Egypt, and the judge declined to impose it. The community
feared that Sar Shalom would remove the judge and replace him with one
of his sycophants, and it therefore vowed to remain loyal to Peraḥiah ben
Joseph and not accept the authority of any other judge. Anyone who refused to take the oath and submitted to the *ra'is al-yahud* would be subjected to a ban. The community well recognized that this constituted a
substantial challenge to the authority of the *ra'is al-yahud* and that doing
so required the backing of a great halakhist. It therefore looked to Maimonides to confirm that the oath and the ban were binding.[12]

[12] Maimonides' Responsa 270; and see as well Maimonides' Responsa volume 4, pp. 8–9.

In his *Commentary on the Mishnah*, Maimonides forcefully attacked the practice of imposing a tax or raising funds to support those who study Torah or provide instruction. In interpreting the Mishnaic teaching "make of them neither a crown of which to boast nor a pickaxe with which to dig," he offers the following sharp observations:

> I had thought to say nothing about this provision, because it is clear but also because I know that what I have to say about it will displease most, if not all, great Torah scholars. But I will have my say and not pay attention to [them]. Know that it says "make not of the Torah a pickaxe with which to dig"; that is, do not consider it a means for earning a living. This means that one who obtains this-worldly benefit from the honor of the Torah has cut off his soul from the life of the world to come. . . . For when we consider the practice of the sages of blessed memory, we find that none of them raised funds from people or sought contributions for the exalted and distinguished yeshivas or for the Exilarch or for judges or teachers or any appointees or other people. (*Avot* 4:7)

The geonic *yeshivas* conducted fund-raising campaigns for the support of halakhic scholars, but Maimonides rejected the practice as one that turned Torah into a means for worldly gain. Scholars should support themselves, he believed, and one who desecrates the Torah by making it into a mere instrumentality forfeits his place in the world to come. Maimonides himself never accepted any public or charitable funds as payment for studying Torah or providing halakhic guidance. He recognized that he was attacking the practice of the geonic elite, both past and present. And so, consistent with his overall position and without mentioning it in the responsum, he affirmed the force of the oath taken by the al-Maḥalla community and thereby effectively went on the attack against the *ra'is al-yahud* Abu Zikri Sar Shalom and against his ability to impose his authority.

Another responsum, sent to Alexandria in 1169 or 1170, similarly attests to the way in which Maimonides used his halakhic authority in his ongoing struggle with the *ra'is al-yahud* Sar Shalom. One clear indicator of the *ra'is al-yahud*'s status was the widespread practice within the Jewish communities of beginning legal documents with an invocation of the *ra'is al-yahud*'s authority, using the formula "by the authority of Rabbi [name]." The Jews of Alexandria asked Maimonides about their vowing to ban the use of that formula in their documents, forbidding as well any mention of the name of the Exilarch or the head of the yeshiva. This enactment partook of open rebellion against the authority of the *ra'is al-yahud*. The questioners wrote that the *ra'is al-yahud* did not remain silent, and his loyalists tried to annul the vow: "many sages, including the prince, the Exilarch, may the memory of the righteous be for a blessing, taught that this vow was invalid from the outset and has no force." It is hardly surprising that the halakhists who were close to the *ra'is al-yahud* took the view that the vow was null and void.

The writers turned to Maimonides in the hope that he would lend his halakhic weight to their move against the sages and the Exilarch and would enable them to fulfill their vow. Maimonides did not disappoint them, ruling that the vow was binding on those who were present at the time of its enactment and took it upon themselves. Moreover, he said, if the vow had been instituted by a majority of the community, even the minority who had not taken it upon themselves would nevertheless be subjected to its stipulations. That obligation was not tied to the force of the vow itself, for they had not taken it on, but to the factionalization of the community that would result from their not submitting to it—something to which the *halakhah* was opposed. His raising the specter of communal division as a reason for imposing the terms of the vow even on the minority is of particular interest. Presumably, it was the same concern about fragmentation of the community that also underlay the *ra'is al-yahud*'s halakhists' annulment of the vow, on the grounds that it struck at legitimate authority and gave rise to disagreement. The halakhic force that Maimonides assigned to these vows entailed the linkage of a halakhic position to a political struggle, and his doing so no doubt substantially weakened the power of the *ra'is al-yahud* and his loyalists. *Halakhah* even in the hands of its most exalted figures cannot be separated completely from power struggles.

Because the role of the *ra'is al-yahud* was dependent on his being appointed by authority of the Muslim ruler, Maimonides' rebellion against the representative of a powerful and established family may have been made possible, in part, by the Ayyubids' overthrow of the Fatimid dynasty in 1171, around the time of Maimonides' ascent to the post of *ra'is al-yahud*. The previous Jewish leadership had been based on close ties to the Fatimids, and the latter's fall undermined the former's standing. It is possible as well that the relatively large influx of immigrants from the Maghrib likewise contributed to the ability of an immigrant like Maimonides to

attain a position of high influence, as did his marriage into a local aristo-
cratic family.

Still, Maimonides did not attain full and final control over the internal
affairs of the Jewish community in Egypt. He had served as *ra'is al-yahud*
for only two years when another reversal took place and Abu Zikri Sar
Shalom, known as Zuta, was again appointed to the office. These appoint-
ments entailed intrigue, bribery, and struggle, and throughout Abu Zikri's
term as *ra'is al-yahud*, Maimonides not only refused to recognize his authority, but with the force of his halakhic standing, even supported challenges by various communities to his leadership. In his letter to Pinḥas the
judge, who had evidently been intimidated by the *ra'is al-yahud*, Maimonides described the latter as a corrupt and insubstantial figure:

> You have asked about Abu Zikri, who seized power in a contemptible and
> morally impoverished manner. He fears the least person in the community
> and has no one to help him. Do not be concerned about him and do not be
> frightened by the words of passersby. He wasted the ninety dinars that he
> gave, receiving no appointment document from the king, but only the fol-
> lowing authorization: If the Jews want you, they will want you. He then
> came and said to the elders, "If you expel me, I will go." He wept before
> them all night until they allowed him [to remain]. This is a true account.
> (*Iggerot*, p. 450)

Maimonides called on Pinḥas to oppose the rule of Abu Zikri and his
adherents. Abu Zikri had in fact bribed the king, but in exchange he received only a conditional and half-hearted appointment, dependent on
the acquiescence of the community. He is portrayed as a coward and a
scoundrel, and the elders who were required to confirm the appointment
for it to be effective responded only after the fact to Abu Zikri's pitiful
entreaties.

Still, this rather harsh portrayal of Abu Zikri may not present the complete picture. He appears to have had a substantial power base within the
community, as is evident in the comments of R. Abraham, Maimonides'
son. In his book, R. Abraham tells of his father's efforts to bring liturgical
unity to the Egyptian Jewish community through universal adoption of the
Babylonian version of the liturgy. Fustat, like many other places, had two
synagogues—one for the Babylonian Jews and one for the Land-of-Israel
Jews. A distinguishing feature of the Land of Israel liturgy was its triennial

Torah-reading cycle, in contrast to the Babylonian practice of reading the entire Torah annually. Maimonides sought to eliminate differences of this sort, and R. Abraham claimed that the "prince of princes"—evidently, Abu Zikri—had thwarted his father's efforts. Abu Zikri was a member of the geonic family in the Land of Israel, and it comes as no surprise that he would defend the Land-of-Israel liturgical practices within the Egyptian community.

His rival's relatively powerful position seems to have been responsible for Maimonides holding office as *ra'is al-yahud* for only two years, 1171–1172, and he regained the office only toward the end of his life, from 1196 to 1204. His return to office and his ousting of Sar Shalom Abu Zikri is alluded to in "The Scroll of Zuta the Wicked," a polemical tract written by Abraham ben Hillel, a supporter of Maimonides, in 1197: "until the mighty One on high gazed down and dispatched the envoy to the faithful, the sign of the ages and the wonder of the time, Moses the rabbi. He restored religion to its former [glory], properly reestablished it, and removed the idol from the sanctuary."[13]

Yemen and Islam: 1172

While only in his mid-thirties, Maimonides was already looked to as Rabbi of all Israel throughout the Muslim lands. This is clearly evidenced by the leader of the Yemenite Jews, R. Jacob ben Netanel, looking to him for help in the wake of the harsh circumstances that had befallen Yemenite Jews at the time. In 1150, an Islamic awakening had begun in Yemen, led by Ali Ibn Mahdi. His son, Abd al-Nabi Ibn Ali Ibn Mahdi, succeeded his father as leader of the movement and conquered almost all of Yemen. The movement pressed for religious reform within Islam, but it also impaired the standing of the Jews as a tolerated minority and brought pressures to bear on the Jewish community. Maimonides' Letter, written in 1172 and referred to as the *Epistle to Yemen (Iggeret Teiman)*, reflects the harsh conditions and religious persecution to which the Jews of Yemen were subjected, their resulting perplexity and bewilderment, and Maimonides' efforts to deal with this difficult reality.

The first and most difficult source of bewilderment was tied to Islam's complicated challenge to the Jewish tradition. The challenge was unprece-

[13] The Hebrew is written in verse, which the translation does not attempt to reproduce.

dented, precisely because of the two faiths' great degree of similarity with regard to monotheism and rejection of idolatry. That closeness undercut the Jew's historical and traditional image of himself as standing apart from his surroundings, an image that allowed him to preserve his identity even under difficult conditions of exile and persecution. In this historical and traditional picture, Jews saw the religion of the dominant majority as idolatrous, at odds not only with Judaism but with divinity itself. The downtrodden Jewish minority in the midst of a pagan world saw itself as endowed with spirit in a world of falsehood and error. The Jews preserve the true faith under difficult and trying conditions, and all of humanity will ultimately recognize the error of its ways and come to accept the one exalted God. That image generated a sense of election and uniqueness under conditions of suffering and explained the difficulties of exile as a trial of the chosen people that would end in salvation and recognition.

That historical perception—the Jews standing, as in the Bible, against the great idolatrous religions of Egypt, Assyria, and Babylonia or, as in the rabbinic literature, against Greek and Roman paganism—began to unravel in the new circumstances in which Jews confronted a triumphant Islam. The Jews of Yemen could not treat Islam as a world of lies, based on a struggle against God Himself. Moreover, the Jews of the Islamic lands and their spiritual leaders absorbed the poetic, scientific, and theological achievements of the impressive Muslim culture. The result was a mortal blow to what had been a source of consolation for all the suffering and destruction—the vision of the dominant and prospering religion as a religion of falsehood and the persecuted minority's sense of being uniquely chosen. The great historical battle against idolatry—a battle that was to be waged until the day when God will be one and His name will be one and in which Israel stood courageously against the nations of the world—seemed all at once to have become moot. Moreover, Islam was especially unrelenting in its rejection of idolatry, and seemed to have replaced Israel as the historical carrier of that banner.

Within the Yemenite Jewish community, the feeling of affinity to Islam was especially profound. A pinnacle of Jewish-Muslim integration can be found in *Gan ha-Sekhalim*, a book by Netanel ben Fayyumi, the leader of the Yemenite community and the father of Jacob, Maimonides' questioner. In *Gan ha-Sekhalim*, Netanel treats the Qur'an as a divine revelation to Muhammad, and he tries to prove from the text of the Qur'an that its purpose was not to replace the Torah: "Therefore let every people practice what it has received, following its prophets, priests, and leaders; and none is left without Torah, for it is all from one God to Whom they all return, and all pray to Him and look to Him" (*Gan ha-Sekhalim*, p. 114). Beyond any doubt, Netanel ben Fayyumi took an extraordinary stance within the history of religious tolerance and of Judaism's attitude toward competing religions. But it is precisely that sort of position that can make it harder for a community to maintain its distinct identity in a time of stress.

This challenge left the Jewish minority in the Muslim lands in a posture quite different from that of the Jewish Diaspora within Christendom. The latter were able to maintain the basic outlook inherited from the biblical and rabbinic texts, for the Ashkenazi Jews saw Christianity as a clearly idolatrous faith and the Christian empire as the heir to Rome. Moreover, Sefardi and Ashkenazi Jews differed greatly in the degree to which they internalized the ambient culture. Jewish sages in Ashkenaz did not write so much as one line in Latin, the language of high culture in their part of the world, and, in contrast to their brethren in the Muslim world, they could easily maintain a sense of spiritual and cultural superiority to their surroundings under conditions of political stress.

The doubts associated with a weakened image of time and place and with a sense that Jewish suffering and distinctiveness had lost their meaning appear in the *Epistle to Yemen* in the particular context of the traditional historical drama—the coming of the Messiah. From Maimonides' response to him, one can infer that Jacob ben Netanel wondered whether Islam itself might not be fulfilling the Jewish messianic hope. And if it is, the only thing that remained was to join up with Islam.

That view was supported by propaganda produced by a Jew who had converted to Islam and maintained that the Torah itself foretold the appearance of Muhammad and the rise of Islam as fulfillment of the biblical historical destiny. Maimonides' treatment of the convert's supposed proofs, including his item-by-item refutation, make it plain that they resonated deeply among his readers.

Another front in the battle was opened because of astrological forecasts—regarded as genuine science—according to which the stars showed that Israel would not be redeemed. Maimonides worked to show that there was nothing to these arguments, incidentally attacking astrology overall as charlatanism having nothing in common with a sound view of the world.

Yet another factor that weakened the Yemenite Jews' belief in the redemption was an end-reckoning in a book by R. Saʿadyah Gaʾon, according to which the still-unrealized redemption ought to have taken place quite some time ago. Should not the passing of that predicted date prove that hope was lost? Maimonides responded that an end-reckoning was nothing more than a scholar's estimate, meant to calm a community in difficult straits. And yet, in his effort to ease the painful loss of faith and hope, he refers in the *Epistle* to an end-reckoning tradition he had from his own father—notwithstanding his comment in *Mishneh Torah* that end-reckoning was to be rejected as something that did not contribute to fear of God and might even detract from it. That tradition calculates that the End will begin to eventuate in 1220 and that the renewal of prophecy—an advance sign of the Messiah's coming—will take place in that year. (Later, after Maimonides' death, his son Abraham had to deal with the disappointment of Yemenite Jews when that end-reckoning also proved incorrect.)

In such a time of growing despair, with believers casting doubt on the possibility of redemption, it is hardly surprising that someone would arise and claim to be the Messiah, heralding the approaching End. Although his name remains unknown, this man attracted many followers, who saw him as a wondrous messianic figure. The false hopes he aroused were likely to intensify the despair when their failure would become evident and lead to acts of apostasy and in any case to generate dangerous friction with the Muslim government, which did not look favorably on Jewish messianic movements. Maimonides sensed correctly that the torment of despair had led even R. Jacob ben Netanel to pin his hopes on that false messiah, and he therefore devoted considerable rhetorical talent to revealing the false-hood of his messianism and rejecting this individual as mentally unstable.

But these questions and Maimonides' various ways of dealing with them were not the central feature of the *Epistle*. At the heart of the work is Mai-monides' effort to provide the Jews living under Muslim rule with a credi-ble historical picture that would preserve the historical sense of time that was now threatened with collapse. Maimonides well understood that the distress evident in the *Epistle* was severe enough to undermine that histor-ical consciousness. Impairing the texture of time under conditions of tor-ment could shake the most basic layers of Jewish identity.

The greatness of the *Epistle to Yemen* lies not in its brilliant halakhic ex-planations or profound philosophical arguments. Its power comes through in Maimonides' ability to tell the Jewish story anew, in a historical con-struct that allows Jews, despite the sharp change in their circumstances, to bear suffering and recognize their destiny, seeing themselves and their lives as carrying on the traditional chain of history. Maimonides anchored this construct in biblical exegesis, attempting thereby to show that the Jewish experience under monotheistic and victorious Islam does not shatter the traditional picture of time; on the contrary, it is foreseen in Scripture.

The historical construct forged by Maimonides sets the torment of the Yemenite Jews at the apex of a series of struggles and trials that the Jewish people have endured since the beginning of their history. To do so, he provides a bird's-eye view of the historical clashes between Israel and the nations, comprising, as he sees it, three stages.

In the first stage, the nations used force of arms in their effort to compel the Jews to abandon their faith: "Ever since the time of revelation every despot or rebel ruler, be he violent or ignoble, has made it his first aim and his final purpose to destroy our Law and vitiate our religion by means of the sword, by violence, or by brute force. Such were Amalek, Sisera, Sennacherib, Nebuchadnezzar, Titus, Hadrian, and others like them" (*Epistle to Yemen*, p. 97).

In the second stage of their struggle against Israel, the nations of the world brought to bear not only physical force but also arguments and contradictions meant to undermine the Jewish faith: "The second class consists of the most intelligent and educated among the nations, like the Syrians, Persians, and Greeks. They also endeavor to demolish our Law and to abrogate it by means of arguments they invent and controversies that they institute" (ibid., p. 98).

The third and most dangerous stage involves the nations' efforts to undermine the religion of Israel by imitating it: "After that a new class arose . . . [that] resolved to lay claim to prophecy and to found a new Law, contrary to our divine religion, and to contend that it also came from God, like the true claim. Thus doubts will be generated and confusion will be created, since one is opposed to the other and both supposedly emanated from one god, and it will lead to the destruction of both religions" (ibid., p. 98). That is the sort of battle waged against Judaism by Christianity and Islam. Muhammad claimed to have received a new divine revelation, and Jesus of Nazareth saw himself as the emissary of God, fulfilling the goals of the Torah through an interpretation that results in negation of the Torah and its commandments.

The continuity of this historical picture—which affords meaning to the Jews' terrible suffering—can be demonstrated, according to Maimonides,

by reference to the Book of Daniel. Daniel foretold the rise of Christianity
when he spoke of a subversive impulse appearing at Judaism's very heart,
presenting itself as a reinterpretation of it: "*The children of the impudent
among your people shall make bold to claim prophecy, but they shall fall* [Dan.
11:14]" (*Epistle to Yemen*, p. 98). The rise of Islam likewise was foreseen:
"This was predicted by the divinely inspired prophet Daniel, according to
whom, in some future time, it would happen. Sometime later a person will
appear with a religion similar to the true one, with a book and oral com-
munications, who will arrogantly pretend that God has vouchsafed him a
revelation, and that he held converse with Him, and other extravagant
claims" (ibid., p. 100).

Of the four beasts seen by Daniel in his vision, symbolic of the ancient
empires that displaced one another, the fourth and last represents Islam.
This creature, with a long and powerful horn, triumphs over its enemies,
and its eyes resemble a human's. The similarity between the fourth beast
and the human represents the similarity between the religion of Islam and
the true religion. And just as Daniel foresaw its rise, he also foresaw its
demise:

> [A]nd behold, the horn had two eyes similar to they eyes of a human, and a
> mouth speaking big things. This obviously alludes to the person who will
> found a new religion similar to the divine religion and make claim to a
> revelation and to prophecy. He will produce much talk and will endeavor to
> alter this Torah and abolish it. . . . But God informed [Daniel] that He
> would destroy this person, notwithstanding his greatness and his long en-
> durance, together with the remaining adherents of his predecessors. For the
> three parties that warred against us will ultimately perish: the one that
> sought to overpower us with the sword, the second that claimed it had ar-
> guments against us, and the third that claims to have a religion similar to
> ours. (ibid., pp. 100–101)

In Maimonides' sketch of the historical panorama, then, the ascent of
Islam is not a breach; it is, rather, the pinnacle. The resemblance between
Judaism and Islam does not blur Judaism's status; on the contrary, the resemblance is the decisive stage in the nations' battle with Judaism. That
stage, which incorporates as well the earlier stages of physical persecution
and intellectual disputation, represents the most difficult trial of all. Its
purpose is also to separate the wheat from the chaff within the Jewish nation, leaving only the remnant worthy of being part of it.

Maimonides saw Islam as a monotheistic religion in all respects. In his letter to Ovadyah the proselyte—who evidently had been a Muslim before converting to Judaism—he writes that "These Ishmaelites are in no way idolaters. It has already been excised from their mouths and hearts, and they properly regard God as a unity, a unity with no exception" (*Iggerot*, p. 238). Consistent with this perspective, Maimonides ruled, in *Mishneh Torah*, that the prohibitions relating to various sorts of dealings between Jews and gentiles do not apply to relations between Jews and Muslims. Wine produced by Muslims, for example, may not be drunk lest doing so promote overly intimate relations, but deriving benefit from such wine— by selling it, for example—is not forbidden, for Muslims do not pour libations in honor of idols.[14]

In contrast to Islam, Christianity is an idolatrous religion, and the prohibitions pertaining to relations between Jews and idolaters apply to Christians.[15] According to Maimonides, the Christian doctrine of the Trinity detracts from the concept of divine unity, as does the belief that Jesus is the embodiment of God in human flesh. But despite this failing of Christian belief with respect to monotheism, Christianity, in Maimonides' view, enjoys one advantage over Islam, in that it recognizes the authoritativeness of the Scriptures. While Muslims regard the Hebrew Bible as a forgery, Christians, though regarding the New Testament as its complement, still consider it to be God's initial revelation. Consistent with that approach, Maimonides rules, uniquely, that Torah may be taught to a Christian, since he considers it to be sacred, but may not be taught to a Muslim, who may misuse it aggressively.[16] And so, the resemblances between Judaism and Islam and between Judaism and Christianity are a complex matter: Islam resembles Judaism in its uncompromising monotheism, and Christianity resembles Judaism in its acceptance of the Hebrew Bible. The former resemblance, as Maimonides sees it, poses a novel threat to Judaism, more dangerous than those that came before. At the same time, the similarity represents a significant historical advance, for it paves the way for the messianic age in which all the nations of the world will accept both monotheism and the authoritativeness of Moses' Torah.

That Judaism and Islam share a strong monotheistic belief shifts the conflict between them to the question of revelation. The claim of a second

---

[14] *Mishneh Torah*, Law of Prohibited Foods, 11, 7.
[15] *Mishneh Torah*, Law of Idolatry, 9, 4.
[16] Responsa 149.

revelation sows a new sort of perplexity, for it transforms all claims of revelation into something relative. Accordingly, in the *Epistle to Yemen*, Maimonides grounds the uniqueness of the Jewish religion in the enduring quality of the revelation in the Torah, thereby rejecting Islam's claim of a later, competing revelation. Judaism's credibility is derived from the great difference between its view that the foundational revelation was granted to Moses, and the Muslim view that the foundational revelation was given to Muhammad. The giving of the Torah was a public affair, taking place before all of Israel; all were present to see the visions and hear the sounds. Moses' credibility is not grounded in the miracles he worked, for miracle stories abound in all traditions and all religions. It follows, rather, from the participation of the entire nation in the giving of the Torah: "This event is analogous to the situation of two witnesses who observed a certain act simultaneously. Each of them saw what his fellow saw, and each of them is sure of the truth of his fellow's statement as well as of his own, and does not require proof or demonstration . . . Similarly, we of the Jewish faith are convinced of the truth of the prophecy of Moses, not simply because of his wonders, but because we, like him, witnessed the theophany on Mount Sinai" (*Epistle to Yemen*, pp. 112–113). It is not the monotheistic faith that is to be contrasted with Islam; it is the force of the revelation at Sinai. The giving of the Torah must therefore be set at the center of Judaism's view of history:

> Now, all my fellow countrymen in the Diaspora, it behooves you to hearten one another, the elders to guide the youth, and the leaders to direct the masses. Gain the assent of your community to the Truth that is immutable and unchangeable, and to the following postulates of the true faith that shall never fail. God is one in a unique sense of the term. And Moses, His prophet and spokesman, is the greatest and most perfect of all the seers. To him was vouchsafed the knowledge of God, what has never been vouchsafed to any prophet before him, nor will it be in the future. The entire Torah from beginning to end was spoken by God to Moses, of whom it is said: *With him I speak mouth to mouth* [Num. 12:8]. It will never be abrogated or superseded, neither supplemented nor abridged. Never shall it be supplanted by another divine law containing positive or negative duties. Keep the revelation at Mount Sinai in mind in accordance with the divine precept to perpetuate the memory and not to forget this occasion. He enjoined us to teach it to our children so that they grow up knowing it. . . .

It is imperative, my fellow Jews, that you make this great spectacle of the revelation appeal to the imagination of your children. Proclaim at public gatherings its nobility and its momentousness. For it is the pivot of our religion and the proof that demonstrates its veracity. Evaluate this phenomenon in its true importance, as God pointed out its importance in the verse: You have but to inquire about bygone ages that came before you, ever since God created man on earth, from one end of heaven to the other: has anything as grand as this ever happened or has its like ever been known? Has any people heard the voice of a god speaking out of a fire? [Deut. 4:32–33]. (*Epistle to Yemen*, pp. 103–104)

The *Epistle to Yemen* is neither a halakhic responsum nor a resolution to a philosophical conundrum. Its purpose was to raise the consciousness of the contemporary public and reinforce the continuity of the historical narrative at a time when, Maimonides believed, it was at risk of coming apart as it confronted new realities. The *Epistle* therefore has the quality of a large-scale historical epos, written anew by Maimonides and anchored in Scripture. The historical banner unfurled in the *Epistle* assigns a new interpretation to suffering, and the sense of uniqueness that made it easier to tolerate suffering is preserved by placing it in a different focus. A community's image of its time is the faith in which its members are raised. It is only natural, therefore, that they do not learn that faith so much as they are assimilated into a consciousness—through stories to which they are exposed from infancy, through prayers, and through the cycle of the calendar. The fabric of time is so fundamental that when things are going well, it is not something that is up for discussion. But a profound historical dislocation can make the no-longer self-evident framework seem problematic and force the members of the community to reexamine their identity.

Maimonides was well aware that the *Epistle*'s addressees were not limited to scholars or to people who were educated yet perplexed. The contemporary crisis that the Epistle was meant to deal with affected the most basic layers of the community—young men and women and the simple Jew who bore the burden of suffering that his ancestors had been able to endure loyally because of their sense of uniqueness and of hope. And so, at the conclusion of the letter, Maimonides emphatically (and uncharacteristically) urges Jacob ben Netanel to publicize the *Epistle* as much as possible:

I beg you to send a copy of this missive to every community in the cities and hamlets, in order to strengthen the people in their faith and to put them on their feet. Read it at public gatherings and in private, and you will thus become a public benefactor. Take adequate precautions lest its contents be divulged by an evil person and mishap overtake us. (God spare us therefrom). When I began writing this letter I had some misgivings about it, but they were overruled by my conviction that the public welfare takes precedence over one's personal safety. (ibid., p. 131)

In 1172, when the *Epistle to Yemen* was written—evidently during Maimonides' first term as *ra'is al-yahud* in Egypt—Maimonides was already a well-known figure. His words therefore resounded not only in the closed Jewish world, but also within Muslim governing circles. Given that the *Epistle*'s central concern was bolstering Judaism's distinctiveness in the face of the historic challenge posed by Islam, its public nature partook of a political challenge, and Maimonides assumed some considerable risk in writing it. Publishing this grand epistle could incur a heavy price, and although Maimonides was anxious about it, he was prepared to pay it in order to strengthen the Jewish community.

In the Sultan's Palace: 1178–1204

Despite the shadow cast by Andalusia's destruction and the ensuing years of wandering and suffering in the Maghrib, Maimonides' first decade in Egypt was a time of great growth and prosperity. In Fustat, his fame soared within the segment of the Jewish world that was under Muslim rule. He dispatched responsa to communities in Egypt, the Land of Israel, Syria, Yemen, Babylonia, and the Maghrib. In the ensuing years, mediated by scholars who had immigrated from Provence to Egypt and by Andalusian translators in Provence, his reputation crossed the Pyrenees and penetrated the Ashkenazi Jewish world. The first ten years of Maimonides' stay in Egypt, from 1168 to 1177, also saw his greatest literary output; it was during those years that he wrote *Mishneh Torah*.

A treatise like *Mishneh Torah* cannot be written on the run. As a gloriously organized structure whose parts complement one another as it strives to encapsulate the entire Talmudic tradition down to Maimonides' time, its writing required the time that would allow for systematic and highly concentrated work. Looking back in 1199, Maimonides described his decade of labor on *Mishneh Torah* in a letter to R. Jonathan Hakohen of Lunel and his circle: "I am sure you realize how I labored day and night for almost ten years to compose [*Mishneh Torah*]. Men of your scholarly attainments appreciate the significance of this work. I have gathered materials that were dispersed and separated between the hills and the mountains, and I called them forth 'one from a city and two from a family' (Jer. 3, 14)" (*Iggerot*, pp. 542–543).

Mishneh Torah is not only a huge treatise; it is also a beautiful and elegant one. Its aesthetic component lies in its giving no hint of the great effort invested in it. To the casual reader, the treatise is simple and clear, like a dancer executing complex movements without showing any sweat. Great scholars like Maimonides' correspondents in Lunel, who knew their way around the thicket of Talmudic discussions, recognized the great accomplishment in each and every chapter. Generations of scholars strived to reconstruct, after the fact, the interpretive decisions that led Maimonides to his conclusions and to uncover the new insights into fundamental halakhic concepts that he wove into his book. Serious scholars knew that to write even one chapter of the thousand making up *Mishneh Torah*, Maimonides would have had to acquire complete and concurrent mastery of all the scattered halakhic literature—a mastery that only he could distill into so clear and organized a work.

At times, as Maimonides attested years after writing *Mishneh Torah*, he himself had difficulty reconstructing the processes and sources that led him to a ruling that seemed so simple. In a poignant passage in a letter to Pinḥas the *dayyan*, following an account of the effort he invested in the treatise and the need at times to draw the sources for a single chapter from ten or more places in the Babylonian Talmud and the Talmud Yerushalmi, he writes as follows:

> I will tell you of what just happened to me in this regard. A pious *dayyan* came to me, bearing a booklet from this treatise [that is, *Mishneh Torah*] that contained the "Laws Concerning Murder" from the *Book of Torts*. He showed me one *halakhah* and said "Read it." I read it and said to him "What is uncertain here?" He said, "Where were these words said?" I said, "In their place, either in the chapter *Elu Hen ha-Golin* or in [tractate] *Sanhedrin*, in the laws pertaining to murder." He said to me, "I have already reviewed all of that without finding it." I said to him, "Perhaps it is in the *Yerushalmi*?" He said to me, "I sought but could not find it, not in the *Yerushalmi* and not

in the *Tosefta*." I wondered for a while and said to him: "I recall that these words were set forth at some point in [tractate] *Gittin*. I took out *Gittin* and searched, but did not find it. I was shocked and alarmed, and I said, "Where were these words said?" But now, before I could remember their source, he left; and I then remembered. I sent a messenger and had him return and I showed him the words explicitly stated in the *Gemara* of *Yevamot* . . . He was amazed and went his way. (*Iggerot*, pp. 444–445)

One must keep in mind that this was not simply the forgetfulness that afflicts everyone, even Maimonides. His letter to Pinḥas the *dayyan* was written at a time when he was busy and burdened to the point of exhaustion. He no longer enjoyed the leisure and perseverance that made it possible to keep things in his mind as sharp and as fresh as they were when he was writing the treatise. *Mishneh Torah* was composed during a ten-year period when he was free to work on it day and night. He was able to do so thanks to his younger brother David, who assumed the burden of supporting the family. As Maimonides says in his letter to Japhet the *dayyan*: "He went abroad to trade that I might remain at home and continue my studies" (*Letters of Maimonides*, p. 73).

Maimonides' situation was radically changed by the tragedy that befell his brother. On a commercial journey to India in 1177, David went down in the Indian Ocean along with the family's assets; he left a wife and young daughter who became Maimonides' responsibility. The crisis that ensued in Maimonides' life is described in that same letter to Japheth: "But the heaviest blow, which caused me more grief than anything I had ever experienced to this day, was the death of the most saintly man I knew, who was drowned while journeying in the Indian Ocean. With him went down a considerable fortune belonging to us as well as to others. His little daughter and his widow were left with me" (ibid., p. 72). Maimonides was familiar with the ways of commerce and involved in his brother's commercial ventures, but he was concerned about commercial journeys to India. In a farewell letter to his brother before one such journey, he wrote: "God, may He be exalted, is the One who knows the sorrow and desolation I feel at the departure of my brother from birth and loving friend. May God protect me from misfortune to him and unite me with him in Egypt" (*Iggerot*, p. 76).

A valuable document found by Goitein in the Cairo Genizah is a heartfelt letter from David to his brother, written in 1171, six years before David's death. It was sent from Aidhab, an East African port city from which trading ships sailed to India and China. David, who was then making his first commercial trip to East Africa, sailed up the Nile to Luxor, a journey of about fifty days. From Luxor, caravans set out for Aidhab, an exhausting trek of more than four hundred kilometers across the desert. A Jewish merchant who joined up with David persuaded him to leave the organized caravan and cross the desert on his own. Because of his inexperience, David agreed to this hasty adventure, and finally reached Aidhab after a difficult and dangerous journey. David and his partner reached Aidhab ahead of the caravan, and when the caravan arrived, they learned that it had been attacked by brigands and some of its people had been killed. Maimonides was acquainted with some of the travelers, and David was concerned that when word of the murders reached Fustat, his brother would worry about his fate. He therefore hastened to write to him. Because the port city turned out not to have the proper goods, David had decided to sail to India. In his letter, he apologizes to his brother for doing so despite his brother's instructions to the contrary, and he concludes with an effort to calm his fears about the journey. A later journey, as we know, saw the realization of the older brother's fears, with David drowning in the Indian Ocean.

Later in his letter to Japhet the *dayyan*, Maimonides describes the painful, suicidal mental state to which he deteriorated in the wake of his brother's death: "For almost a year after receiving the sad news I lay on my couch stricken with fever, despair, and on the brink of destruction" (*Letters of Maimonides*, p. 74). This depression, which silenced Maimonides for about a year, appears even worse in light of the discussion of mourning in *Mishneh Torah*: "One should not indulge in excessive grief over one's dead, for it is said: *Weep not for the dead, neither bemoan him* (Jer. 22:10), that is to say, (weep not for him) too much, for that is the way of the world, and he who frets over the way of the world is a fool" (Laws of Mourning 13:11). That stoic recommendation to accept death as part of the world's normal course collapsed in the face of his enormous personal loss. Even years after the tragedy, the breach in Maimonides' life was not repaired:

> Close to eight years have now elapsed and I still mourn for him for there can be no consolation. What can possibly comfort me? He grew up on my knees, he was my brother, my pupil. He went abroad to trade that I might remain at home and continue my studies. He was well versed in Talmud and Bible and an accomplished grammarian. My greatest joy was to see

him. Now every joy has been dimmed. He has departed to his eternal life and left me confounded in a strange land. Whenever I come across his handwriting on one of his books my heart turns within me and my grief reawakens. (*Letters of Maimonides*, p. 73)

Many mourners experience guilt following the death of someone beloved, and it appears that Maimonides' sorrow over the loss of his brother was accompanied by a heavy sense of guilt. He, the older brother, had been unable to protect the younger brother who had been like a son to him; indeed, the younger brother could be seen to have sacrificed his life for the elder: "He went abroad to trade that I might remain at home and continue my studies" (lit., "remain securely at home"). It is no surprise that Maimonides refused to be comforted and that every encounter with his brother's memory reopened the wounds.

For many immigrants, close family members can serve as a replacement for the sense of security that had been provided by the familiar homeland, providing both emotional and economic support. The loss of his brother undermined Maimonides' feelings of emotional and economic security, effectively becoming a second exile: "[it] left me confounded in a strange land." From that point on, Maimonides bore the scars of two major losses: the forced exile from Andalusia with the ensuing wanderings in the Maghrib, and the death of his brother. The former entailed the loss of a communal and cultural homeland, while the latter amounted to the collapse of the security framework afforded by a refugee immigrant's family.

But the effects of the tragedy extended beyond the existential sense of estrangement and alienation that it generated. Its harsh economic consequences wrought a significant change in Maimonides' day-to-day life. From that year forward, Maimonides' time was not his own, and his accounts of his days speak repeatedly of his burdens and resultant fatigue. He declined to receive a salary for his rabbinic office and turned to medicine for a living. He advised his student Joseph, then in Baghdad, to do the same, after cautioning him not to be supported by the Exilarch or to accept a salary for providing halakhic guidance: "It would be better for you to earn a single drachma as a weaver, tailor or carpenter than to be dependent on the license of the Exilarch. If you dispute with any of them, you will lose your earning. And if you accept from them favors you will be humiliated.

My advice to you is to pay full attention to your trade and the practice of medicine and at the same time continue to study the Torah faithfully" (*Letters of Maimonides*, p. 83).

Maimonides received his medical training in Spain and the Maghrib before coming to Egypt. In his book on asthma, he told of his contacts with physicians in Morocco. He wrote as follows of a particular illness: "I too have not seen it in the West nor did any of my teachers under whom I studied mention that they had seen it. However, here in Egypt, in the course of approximately ten years, I have seen more than twenty people who suffered from this illness" (Maimonides' Medical Writings, *Medical Aphorisms*, p. 140).

We see, then, that Maimonides practiced medicine while still in the Maghrib, studying with his unnamed teachers. Medical training at an early age was a typical pedagogic practice within the educated class of Spanish Jews during the Middle Ages. Knowledge of medicine was a portable resource that could accompany a man and be in demand wherever a member of a minority group might find himself. Maimonides' life as a refugee demonstrates the wisdom of being given this sort of training. Moreover, the ruling classes often preferred to put themselves in the hands of Jewish doctors and to select them as court physicians because they lacked any real power base within the general population and therefore could be trusted.

Medical expertise thus afforded the Jewish elite a degree of influence, however limited. A clear example is provided by Ḥasdai Ibn Shaprut, who gained influence in the Andalusian court of Abd al-Raḥman III during the tenth century. When Maimonides arrived in Egypt, Netanel ben Moses (known in Arabic as Hibat Allah Ibn Jami' al-Isra'ili) was leader of the Jewish community and also serving as court physician, in which capacity he wrote some important medical texts. Given the economic and political opportunities opened by the medical profession and the tradition of educated Jews, it is hardly surprising that Maimonides' son Abraham also received medical training, as did his brother-in-law Abu al-Ma'ali, his nephew, and his student, Joseph ben Judah.

For Maimonides, however, the practice of medicine was more than a political or economic opportunity; it also had broad religious meaning. While receiving his medical training, he wrote as follows in his *Commentary on the Mishnah*: "The practice of medicine brings much by way of virtue, knowledge of God, and attainment of true perfection, and [medical] study and inquiry are among the greatest of works" (*Eight Chapters*, chapter 5). A sound body is essential for attaining perfection, which is knowledge of God, and medicine therefore is a way of serving God.

Moreover, Maimonides' concept of medicine—consistent with that of Galen (second century CE) and of the Arab physicians influenced by Galen—saw a close connection between sound living and good health. Since most diseases resulted, he believed, from poor nutrition, they originated in uncritical consumption of food, driven solely by pleasure. Man differs from other animals in that he can select his food not only for its taste but also for the higher purpose of promoting bodily well-being:

> For if a man comes to eat pleasurable food, pleasing to the palate and fragrant, thereby harming himself, perhaps bringing about a dangerous illness or sudden death—he is no different from a beast. This is not the action of a man in his humanity. . . . Rather, it will be human action if he partakes only of what is useful, sometimes setting aside what is tastier and eating what is unpleasant. (*Eight Chapters*, chapter 5)

For Maimonides, medicine was first and foremost the promotion of health through preventive practices, that is, proper consumption and a sensible way of life. There is thus a close tie between virtue and physical health—a link that imparts a spiritual and religious dimension to the practice of medicine.

This concept of medicine led Maimonides to include *halakhot* of a medical character in *Mishneh Torah*, *halakhot* meant to offer counsel on a proper way of life. The preventive value of that counsel is emphasized in the promise that Maimonides incorporated into the chapter on medicine that appears in the midst of the halakhic work: "Whoever lives in accordance with the directions I have set forth, has my assurance that he will never be sick till he grows old and dies; he will not be in need of a physician, and will enjoy normal health as long as he lives" (Laws Relating to Moral Dispositions 4:20).

Underlying the connection between uncontrolled desire and illness is the argument that the distinction between body and soul is an artificial one from a medical perspective. The physician should treat the patient, not merely the illness, and should provide him not only with medical prescriptions but with training in how to direct his desires and personal attributes. This psychophysical attitude toward medicine forges the tie between Maimonides the halakhist and philosopher and Maimonides the physician. Ibn

Sana' al-Mulk, a Muslim poet and *qadi* (Arabic, judge) and contemporary admirer of Maimonides, described his medical stance as follows: "Galen healed the body alone; Ibn Imran (=Maimonides) [heals] the body and the spirit as well. In his knowledge, he stands at the head of the physicians of our age, and in his wisdom he also cures the illness of foolishness."

Maimonides began to practice medicine in 1178. After a few years, he recounts in a letter written in 1191, he reached the height of his medical career by being appointed physician to al-Faḍil, vizier to Saladin. Al-Faḍil, who lived from 1135 to 1200, was the second most important figure in the Ayyubid government of Egypt. He served Saladin in many governmental roles, from raising revenues to organizing the military. When Saladin was leading a military campaign in Syria, the vizier, along with Saladin's brother, were entrusted with the entire government of Egypt. Saladin is reputed to have said that he owed his conquests not to the sword but to al-Fāḍil's pen. In addition to playing a central political role, the vizier was a literary man and a patron of scholars, assembling a highly important collection of manuscripts in his library.

One member of this circle was the Arabic poet Ibn Sana' al-Mulk who, as already noted, knew Maimonides as an interlocutor and a physician. A glance at the atmosphere that prevailed in the discourse between Jewish and Muslim scholars in al-Faḍil's circle can be derived in the poet's direct report, as published by Franz Rosenthal. In the poet's home, known as a center of good conversation, a discussion of theological questions took place between Abu al-Qasim al-Halabi, identified as a Syrian-born Shiite thinker who had come to Egypt from Aleppo, and Maimonides. Unfortunately, we lack a full summary of that discussion, which took place around 1186, but the report conveys the unique atmosphere that dominated al-Faḍil's circle. We learn as well that Ibn Sana' al-Mulk, a member of the Sunni nobility, hosted an important Shiite immigrant from Syria and the great Jewish immigrant from Andalusia for a discussion of important issues of faith.

The vizier's physician had daily access to the ruler's ear and thereby gained trust, protection, and political influence. But medical success came at a high price. Maimonides described the rise to prominence and its price in a letter to his beloved student, Joseph ben Judah:

> I tell you that I have become known as a physician among the mighty, such as the chief judge, the emirs, and the house of al-Faḍil and the other princes

of the land, those who lack nothing. But as for the masses, I am beyond
their reach, and they have no way to approach me. And this causes me to
spend the entire day in Cairo, tending to the sick, and when I get back to
Fustat, all I can do for the rest of the day and into the night is to examine
the medical texts that I need to consult. . . . As a result, I do not have a
moment to study Torah except on the Sabbath, and as for other sciences, I
do not have a moment to study any of them, and this harms me greatly.
(*Iggerot*, p. 313)

After his brother's death, then, Maimonides had to move from a way of
life that allowed him to devote day and night to the writing of *Mishneh
Torah* to one in which the only time he could devote to Torah study was on
the Sabbath. Evidence of this transition appears in letters from this period,
in which he repeatedly apologizes for the tardiness and brevity of his responsa. When one of his admirers in Egypt wanted to learn Torah from
him, he suggested that he come only on the Sabbath, for he was burdened
and exhausted: "Without doubt he has (=you have) already seen and heard
some of the state I am in, a state of *betwixt morning and evening they are
shattered* [Job 4:20]. And when night comes . . . I am ill, filled with sighs,
unable because of my tiredness to sit up, able only to lie supinely" (*Iggerot*,
p. 563). When the sages of Lunel asked him to translate the *Guide* into
Hebrew, he replied sadly: "Alas, my honored friends, I do not even have the
leisure to write a small chapter and it is only out of respect for your congregation that I have painfully exerted myself to write this epistle with my
own hand" (*Letters of Maimonides*, p. 164). In another letter to those same
sages, he connects the loss of leisure to the gilded cage of his medical career:
"Compounding my physical condition, I am burdened with a multitude
of patients, who exhaust me and give me no respite day and night. Alas,
one has to pay a price for a reputation that has spread to even neighboring
countries" (ibid., p. 161). In this stressful condition, even important statements and letters were squeezed out of the overburdened Maimonides
under pressure; such was the case of the *Letter on Astrology* that he sent to
the scholars of Montpellier in the year 1185 or 1186: "Do not censure me,
my masters, for the brevity of these remarks, for the writing makes it clear
that I wrote it to fill a present need. For I was very busy with many Gentile
affairs. The Deity knows that if Rabbi Pinhas had not sent a messenger who
'urged me till I was ashamed' (Kings 2, 17) and did not leave my presence

until I had written it, I would not be replying now since I have no leisure. On this account, judge in my favor" (*Letter on Astrology*, p. 473).

During these years of overwork, Maimonides wrote the greatest work in the history of Jewish philosophy, *The Guide of the Perplexed*. It is possible that the limitations under which it was written had an effect on its literary style. In the introductory letter to the *Guide*, Maimonides identified the work's intended audience: his student Joseph ben Judah and others like him.

Joseph ben Judah was born in the city of Sebta (Ceuta), Morocco and immigrated to Alexandria. From there, he sent Maimonides a rhymed letter describing his great desire to acquire wisdom. Maimonides could not discern Joseph's character from the poem itself, but he could see his intense desire for learning and accepted him as his student in Fustat. Joseph studied astronomy and mathematics with Maimonides, later moving on to logic—the disciplines that, at the time, were prerequisite to metaphysics. At these preparatory stages to metaphysics, Maimonides found that his student's yearning for wisdom was joined to genuine talent.

From that point on, Maimonides began to introduce Joseph to the hidden meanings of Scripture and the metaphysical tradition he knew: the Aristotelian Arab *falsafa*. This gradual and careful initiation was interrupted by Joseph's necessary departure for Aleppo. That parting of the ways moved Maimonides to write the *Guide*, which he sent to Joseph piece by piece:

> When God decreed our separation and you betook yourself elsewhere, these meetings aroused in me a resolution that had slackened. Your absence moved me to compose this Treatise, which I have composed for you and for those like you, however few they are. I have set it down in dispersed chapters. All of them that are written down will reach you where you are, one after the other. Be in good health. (*Guide*, Epistle Dedicatory)

But the composition of the *Guide* as a series of epistles sent to an individual student chapter by chapter was motivated by more than historical circumstances and the exigencies of writing. This unique method of writing suits the treatise's esoteric character as a work directed to a perplexed individual rather than the masses. Maimonides' preface to the book describes how it came to be written, presents it as a continuation of a process of personal and cautious instruction, and defines it as a collection of letters sent to Joseph and those like him—all for the purpose of addressing the book solely to the proper class of readers. Similarly, the piecemeal dispatch of the book to Joseph represents a gradual entry into metaphysics and suggests that the book's structure—a series of chapters rather than a clear and orderly presentation of a case—was meant to conceal its meaning. A reader who finds himself perusing a letter not addressed to him must look into whether he is among the perplexed individuals who are the treatise's legitimate addressees. Writing the book as a series of epistles, then, was an effort to preserve the personal and gradual initiation of Joseph ben Judah into the world of mysteries while at the same time addressing not only him but also others similarly situated.

The *Guide*, then, is a book that is, in effect, a letter. It therefore must be seen as a unique genre, representing a balance between quiet, oral instruction and broad dissemination to all who are interested. Consistent with that understanding of the work, Maimonides had reservations about its dissemination to the public at large and imposed limitations on its copying. We see this in the admonition he sent to Joseph along with a group of chapters he forwarded to him:

> I am here sending you six booklets of the Guide which I have taken from the others, and they complete the first part. I am uncertain if I have already sent you the introduction included with them or not, and I am therefore sending it to you now. They have been copied only by the pious *dayyan* and Abu al-Maḥasin, so treat them carefully and do not lose them, so I am not harmed by the gentiles or by the many wicked Israelites. (*Iggerot*, pp. 310–311)

Careless copying and distribution of the *Guide*, which attacks the prevailing doctrines of the Muslim Kalam and what God-fearing Jews take to be principles of Jewish belief, could have jeopardized Maimonides.

This unique literary genre, and the cautious way in which the book was written and disseminated, show impressively how Maimonides saw the book and its intended audience. But those precautions failed to provide the degree of protection that Maimonides had hoped for. Once the ideas were committed to writing following Joseph's departure, and despite the limits on allowed copying, the book was no longer within Maimonides' control, and it began to fall into the possession of those who did not share the distress of Jewish intellectuals in the Muslim world. They saw the *Guide* as a serious threat to the integrity of the Jewish tradition.

And so, in 1232, three decades after Maimonides' death, his fears came to pass: a violent controversy over his legacy broke out in Provence. In this *Kulturkampf,* Maimonides' opponents imposed a ban on anyone reading the *Guide*, and copies of the book were burned. The seeds of trouble had already been sown during Maimonides' lifetime, given that the *Guide* had been circulated beyond the circles of Jewish intellectuals in Muslim lands. It reached Maimonides' supporters in Provence, where it was translated into Hebrew and fell into the hands of his adversaries.

In contrast to his express direction that the *Guide* not be widely copied and disseminated, Maimonides hoped that *Mishneh Torah* would become available to all Jews, and he took pains to have it copied and disseminated. The original, authorized version of the work, in Maimonides' own hand, was kept in his home. From that *editio princeps*, corrected on occasion by Maimonides himself, additional copies were made. Those manuscripts were certified as authoritative by Maimonides' signed statement that he had examined and approved the copy. These copies were sent to various communities, and, during Maimonides' lifetime, the treatise reached all parts of the Jewish Diaspora, all the way to India. Maimonides was following carefully and attentively the fate of *Mishneh Torah* and could provide a detailed account of its dissemination, in times when manuscripts and letters moved in slow motion. Such was his account to the scholars in Montpellier given around 1185, eight years after the completion of *Mishneh Torah*: "It seems to me that it (*Mishneh Torah*) will come to you before this reply, since it is already widespread on the island of Sicily, as well as in the West and the East and in the South" (*Letter on Astrology*, p. 464). The presence of the manuscript of *Mishneh Torah* in Sicily assured Maimonides that it would reach Provence before the letter that he sent from Cairo.

Mishneh Torah's arrival in Provence raised a substantial stir, and the work was enthusiastically received in the circle of scholars associated with the study hall of R. Jonathan Hakohen of Lunel. These scholars, who had corresponded with Maimonides about matters related to *Mishneh Torah*, and the Andalusian families who had immigrated to Provence and were tied to Maimonides' native culture, were his primary supporters among the Jews living under Christian rule.

But there were those in Provence who saw things differently. While his supporters regarded Maimonides as highly authoritative, other Provencal rabbis and scholars had acute reservations about *Mishneh Torah*, about its pretense of authoritativeness, and about its religious perspectives. At their head was R. Abraham ben David (Ra'abad), an immensely learned halakhist who was equipped to go head-to-head with *Mishneh Torah* in all its breadth and depth and who critically annotated it during Maimonides' lifetime. These scholars and their successors stood at the center of the controversy that developed around *Mishneh Torah*'s *Book of Knowledge* (the first and most philosophical of the treatise's fourteen major units), and around the *Guide*.

Maimonides did not initiate the sending of the *Guide* to Provence. He responded, rather, to the request of R. Jonathan Hakohen, who got word of the treatise after he and his colleagues had already obtained copies of *Mishneh Torah*: "[we ask you] to satisfy us as well with the book *Moreh Nevukhim [the Guide]*, of whose reputation we have heard and which is known in the land of Egypt." And further: "We come before you to place us by your right hand regarding your other books as well, for our people live and our dead will rise, as we are bound up in admiration for them. If they are here, all is here" (*Iggerot*, p. 492).

Around 1197, Maimonides, whose time was no longer his own, sent the first two parts of the *Guide* to Lunel, in the original Arabic. The sages of Lunel did not know Arabic, and they gave the text to Samuel Ibn Tibbon to be translated. Samuel's high standing as the scion of a renowned Andalusian family of translators is mentioned in the thank-you letter that R. Jonathan Hakohen sent to Maimonides after receiving the two parts of the *Guide*. The letter, in its writer's hand, is preserved in the Genizah and includes the following passage:

> You have increased our wisdom and wellbeing, for you have sent us the book *Moreh Nevukhim* . . . but it would have been for us as a stone in a mortar, a rose among the thorns, a book given to an illiterate, had our Creator not caused there to be among us a sage, learned in all wisdom, taught by his father the literature and language of Arabia, the son of the glorious sage and exalted physician, the rabbi R. Judah Ibn Tibbon, the Spaniard. (*Iggerot*, p. 493)

Samuel Ibn Tibbon translated the first two parts of the *Guide* upon their receipt and posed to Maimonides some questions that had arisen in the course of the translation. Maimonides had heard good things about Judah Ibn Tibbon, Samuel's father, from Andalusians who had come to Egypt, and he understood from Samuel's questions that the son, like his father, was an excellent translator as well as a philosopher in his own right, who had managed to plumb the depths of the treatise. The strong impression the translator selected in Lunel made on him is evident from Maimonides' letter responding to his questions:

> When your Arabic and Hebrew letters reached me, they gave me an insight into your wide range of interest and beauty of style. When I noted further your doubts concerning some of the passages in my major exposition, *The Guide of the Perplexed* and the errors of the scribe you perceived therein, I repeated the words of the ancient poet: "if only they knew his ancestry, they would say the merit of the father is passed on to the son."
>
> Blessed be He who has granted a recompense to your learned father, and granted him such a son. . . . The questions you raised are all valid, and the omissions you noted of one or several words in many places are correct. . . . You are surely well equipped and qualified to engage in the work of translation, for the Almighty has endowed you with an understanding heart to comprehend similes and parables, the epigrams of the wise and their riddles. I recognized from your correspondence that you have the capacity to delve into the depth of a subject and reveal its hidden meaning. (*Letters of Maimonides*, pp. 131–132)

This letter was sent on 30 September 1199; immediately after, Maimonides sent the third part of the *Guide* to Lunel. Samuel Ibn Tibbon translated that as well, completing the entire project on 7 Tevet (30 November) in 1204, only a few days before Maimonides' death. The book, intended as a personal letter to select addressees, became open to all, including readers who knew no Arabic and were far removed from the questions that had troubled those for whom the book was written. It was not long before the book had become simultaneously the most important and highly esteemed work of medieval Jewish philosophy and a work that aroused controversy and harsh criticism to the point that its readers were banned and copies of the book were destroyed.

Samuel Ibn Tibbon was not content merely to send questions to Maimonides. It is evident from Maimonides' letter responding to the questions that Samuel wanted to meet Maimonides face to face and was prepared to travel from Provence to Fustat to do so. Such a meeting was presumably important to him not only to resolve translation issues but also—indeed, primarily—to discuss the meaning and secrets of the *Guide*. Maimonides replied that so long a journey would not be useful, for he lacked the time to engage in such conversations. At most, Samuel would be able to pay him a brief, and unnecessary, courtesy call.

It may be, as some have suggested, that Maimonides declined Ibn Tibbon's request out of concern about having to confirm for him the way in which he understood the *Guide*'s mysteries. Samuel, as we shall see, was the first to interpret the *Guide* as a treatise whose hidden meaning challenges the beliefs conventionally seen as basic to the Jewish tradition. The questions Ibn Tibbon posed had allowed Maimonides to discern the direction his interpretation was taking, and Maimonides preferred to leave the matter obscure. Any agreement with Ibn Tibbon's interpretation, even if conveyed orally and privately, would have immediately been publicized, and there are good reasons to believe that Maimonides had qualms about allowing that to happen. It is fair to assume that in the absence of these concerns, Maimonides would have found time to meet with the translator and discuss his questions despite the time constraints under which he worked. But Maimonides preferred to cite those time pressures as the reason for declining the meeting, and, in doing so, he gives us a rich picture of the last, austere years of his life:

> I reside at Misr (Fustat) and the Sultan resides at al-Qahira (Cairo); these two places are two Sabbath days' journey [about one mile and a half] distant from each other. My duties to the Sultan are very heavy. I am obliged to visit him every day, early in the morning; and when he or any of his children, or any of the inmates of his harem are indisposed, I dare not quit Cairo, but must stay during the greater part of the day in the palace. It also frequently happens that one or two of the royal officers fall sick, and I must attend to their healing. As a rule, I go to Cairo very early in the day, and even if nothing unusual happens, I do not return to Fustat until the afternoon. Then I am almost dying with hunger. I find the ante-chambers filled with people, both Jews and Gentiles, nobles and common people, judges and bailiffs, friends and foes—a mixed multitude, who await the time of my return.
>
> I dismount from my animal, wash my hands, go forth to my patients, and entreat them to bear with me while I partake of some slight refreshments, the only meal I take in the twenty-four hours. Then I attend to my patients. Patients go in and out until nightfall, and sometimes even, I solemnly assure you, until two hours or more into the night. I converse with and prescribe for them while lying down from sheer fatigue, and when

night falls I am so exhausted that I can scarcely speak. (*Letters of Maimonides*, p. 134)

The court physician at the seat of power must be prepared to respond to every ache, pain, or worry of the ruler and his entourage. In the atmosphere of suspicion and plotting that prevails in the palace, a physician accused of medical negligence—accidental or intended—would be at great risk indeed. The preparedness and availability the job required by, and the resultant adverse effects on Maimonides' life, are clearly evident in this passage.

The practice of medicine also put an end to Maimonides' powers of creativity. After completing the *Guide* in 1191, his literary efforts were directed solely to medicine, and in the last thirteen years of his life, he wrote only medical works. Ten such works can be attributed to Maimonides with certainty or near-certainty; one more is the subject of debate among experts on Maimonides' medical writings. Four of his medical works deal with medical training: *Extracts from Galen*; *Commentary on the Aphorisms of Hippocrates*; *Glossary of Drug Names*; *Medical Aphorisms of Moses*. These writings show the strong influence of Hippocrates and Galen and of the Arab medicine that followed them. This medical tradition was dominated by the "theory of fluids and humors." The most ambitious of these works was *Medical Aphorisms of Moses*, in which he set himself the goal of organizing medical knowledge in a series of well-ordered chapters, thereby allowing readers to find what they needed in Galen's vast corpus. As in his other writings, Maimonides did not shy away from criticizing Galen where he thought he had erred, even though he regarded Galen as the greatest of physicians. Writing the book took considerable time; Maimonides seems to have begun it no later than 1188 and continued working on it until the day he died.

Five other medical works were written in response to requests by high-ranking and influential Muslims for help in dealing with medical problems. The *Treatise on Asthma* was a reply to a member of the Muslim nobility whom Maimonides does not name. The man, about forty years of age and living in Alexandria, asked Maimonides to try to help him with his problem. The *Treatise on Hemorrhoids* was likewise written in response to a Muslim nobleman afflicted with that illness.

Maimonides wrote two treatises in response to requests by Prince al-Afdal, the eldest son of Saladin. At the time, the prince was living outside of Egypt, and Maimonides had treated him in the past for constipation, bad digestion, and depression. One of the treatises he now sent him was entitled *Regimen of Health*. Maimonides believed that illness was caused, for the most part, by poor nutrition, which leads to flaws in the initial digestive process in the stomach and, later, to flaws in the digestion that takes place, according to Galen, in the liver and other organs. Most of the book therefore is devoted to general guidance on proper nutrition. For example, it recommends avoiding fats, raw fruits, and white flour and counsels against eating before going to sleep. It is preferable to eat at set times and only when hungry, and not to eat to the point of feeling fully satiated. It is proper to exercise before eating and to be cautious about excessive activity right after eating. Wine aids digestion if drunk in moderate amounts during the meal.

The second work sent to Prince al-Afdal was *On the Causes of Symptoms*. The prince was pressuring Maimonides to journey to him to treat him, and Maimonides, true to the tradition of flattering the ruler, said nothing would delight him more than to come to care from the prince. Sadly, however, old age and the difficulty of travel precluded his doing so. Instead of undertaking the journey, Maimonides sent the prince a medical treatise. It is evident from the treatise that Maimonides had been asked, among other things, to assess the medical advice provided by the physicians in the prince's entourage. Maimonides' decisions regarding disagreements among the physicians reveal an important aspect of his medical thinking. As he saw it, medical intervention could often be harmful if it was based solely on guesswork and speculation. In such cases, it was preferable to allow nature to take its course. That was true in the prince's case, for Maimonides recognized that his problems were routine and that hasty intervention would cause serious side effects. In addition to the prince's routine problems, he suffered from hemorrhoids and heart irregularities, and Maimonides recommended a heart elixir devised by the school of Ibn Sina. He recommended to the prince—who seems to have been a serious hypochondriac—that he undertake a fixed daily regimen, including meetings with pleasant friends, reading, music, and rest, all of which would ease his depression.

Another treatise written for a Muslim nobleman is titled *Treatise on Cohabitation*. The nobleman, who is not named, asked for Maimonides' help because he was concerned about a diminution in his sexual potency. Maimonides believed that excess sexual activity was improper, especially if it was for the sake of pleasure, and that it could be harmful to health. And so, for example, when Prince al-Afdal reported to Maimonides on a reduction in his sexual activity, Maimonides encouraged him to continue on that course. But the unnamed nobleman who asked Maimonides about his impotence made clear that he was not at all interested in a response along those lines. In his possession were several young women he was required to satisfy, and he urgently sought help in improving his sexual prowess. The essay written in reply provides a wide range of advice on enhancing potency: foods that will increase the production of semen and foods that should be avoided; certain elixirs that enhance sexual ability; ointments, baths, and massages to the pertinent body parts; partners to be sought out and partners to be avoided; and needed mental preparation. It is fair to assume that the treatise was written from the perspective of a physician who understands that nothing he can do will change his patient's basic habits. Under those circumstances, the best that can be done is to enable him to live his life without frustration and bitterness.

At the request of his greatest patron in the Sultan's court, the vizier al-Faḍil, Maimonides wrote a book entitled *Treatise on Poisons and Their Antidotes*. Intended for a broad audience, the book details, among other things, ways of preventing and treating snakebites. It was written during Ramadan, as an act of charity performed by the ruler for his subjects.

From his letter to Samuel Ibn Tibbon, we see that Maimonides' standing as a physician went far beyond the palace and the upper-class Muslims he served. In a letter written eight years earlier to Joseph ben Judah, Maimonides reports for the first time on his becoming court physician. He describes his work as a physician and writes that he deals only with the upper, ruling class: "But as for the masses, I am beyond their reach, and they have no way to approach me." According to that letter, when he returns each day to Fustat after working at the palace, he devotes his time to medical studies to improve his job performance. During that same period, when he was still able to decline requests for medical services to the masses, he had the time to write the *Guide of the Perplexed*.

By 1199, when he sent his letter to Samuel Ibn Tibbon, the dam had burst and Maimonides had lost whatever control he had over his time. When he returned from caring for the court entourage, he found a large crowd awaiting his return and eagerly seeking medical advice. Dealing with these patients' needs went on into the night, and the exhausted Maimonides treated sick people while he himself was recumbent on his couch.

At the end of 1204, on 20 Tevet, Maimonides died. According to al-Qifti's account, he was buried in Tiberias: "He had asked of his heirs in advance that he be taken, when his spirit left him, to the Sea of Galilee and be buried there, in a place having the graves of Jews and their great Torah scholars, and that was done for him" (*Iggerot*, p. 578, notes).

The Man Moses

Maimonides' life is better documented than that of any other figure in the medieval Jewish world. Letters, responsa, and Genizah fragments afford us a rare glimpse into his life and inner world. Over time, the responsa of great halakhists undergo an editing process that strips them of their personal and narrative dimensions. Because responsa typically serve as halakhic precedents, they acquire a generalized, impersonal quality. Proper names are replaced by "Reuben" and "Simon" or "Ploni" and "Almoni" (that is, John Doe and Richard Roe), and the bright, specific colors of the incident inquired about become darkened over time as the responsum is transmitted. Maimonides' responsa and letters did not undergo that sort of editing, and they retain their original freshness. They reflect a living, complex give and take and suggest a wealth of psychological and institutional inferences. Maimonides' status as a unique personality afforded his writings protection again meddling by editors and copyists, and the same may be said of the documents preserved in the Genizah. Precisely because the Genizah is not an official archive, it preserved accounts of the world as it actually was, without the need for any intermediary to maintain it in the collective memory of ensuing generations.

And yet, despite this wealth of data, there is a wide gap between the conventional impression of Maimonides and his personality as revealed in letters and Genizah fragments. The gap results from the widespread image of Maimonides as an intellectualist and a rationalist. The adjective "intellectualist" is of only limited use in characterizing his oeuvre, and it contributes nothing to understanding his personality. The term suggests a man in control of his emotions and lacking passion; a man who is cold, elitist, and humorless; a man who invites esteem but not love. But the written sources reveal an entirely different personality. The severe, year-long depression following the death of his brother and the mourning that followed for at least eight years are hardly characteristic of a cold, stoic man. Maimonides' personality had a sensitive, delicate, and vulnerable streak—components that are hard to assess because of his primary image as a man too nearly perfect to be approached.

Certainly, Maimonides' own way of expressing himself contributed to his image as a distant giant, sometimes arrogant or even harsh. And, certainly, he was not tolerant of what he considered to be error, especially when it involved religious and scientific concepts he wanted to uproot. On the great questions of the nature of the Jewish tradition, his basic stance vis-à-vis his surroundings was one of conflict and struggle. A central goal of his work was to bring about a profound change in the beliefs of his contemporaries and those who would come after.

At the heart of his religious polemic was his effort to extirpate the idea that God possessed a body and an emotional life, a widespread belief that Maimonides considered to be worse than idolatry. In his *Essay on Resurrection*, he speaks as follows of several Jewish sages who maintain a belief in God's corporeality on the basis of a literal reading of Talmudic *aggadah*: "These exceedingly deficient folk . . . who, although they consider themselves sages in Israel, are in fact the most ignorant, and more seriously astray than beasts, their minds filled with the senseless prattle of old women" (*Essay on Resurrection*, p. 212).

A similar tone is evident in his comments on astrological literature and those who believe in it; he regarded astrology as having developed out of idolatry: "Thus you ought to know that fools have composed thousands of books of nothingness and emptiness. Any number of men, great in years but not in wisdom, wasted all their days in studying these books and imagined that these follies are science" (*Letter on Astrology*, p. 465). That literature, it should be recalled, included the writings of Jewish sages, among them Abraham Bar H̲iyya and Abraham Ibn Ezra. A sharp strain of rejection appears wherever Maimonides discusses something that he regards as a superstition that impairs Judaism's purity. In the *Guide*, for example, he comments on those who ascribe magical powers to divine names: " . . . do not let occur to your mind the vain imaginings of the writers of charms or what names you may hear from them or may find in their stupid books" (*Guide* I:61; Pines trans., p. 149. In *Mishneh Torah*, he speaks in similar tones against those who write sacred names on mezuzahs because they consider it an object with special powers, capable of protecting the house and those who dwell in it:

But those who write the names of angels, holy names, verses, or special shapes on the mezuzah are included in the category of those who have no share in the world to come, since these fools not only cancel the commandment but make of a great commandment, the unification of the Holy One, blessed be he, His love, and His worship, a charm for their own benefit since they, in their stupidity, think that this is a matter which benefits them concerning worldly vanities. ("Laws Concerning Tefillin, the Mezuzah and the Scroll of the Law" 5:4)

Maimonides was not much easier on those who disagreed with him on halakhic issues. His tone in halakhic discussions was less sharp than it was in polemics over beliefs, but it was still harsh, even when he was engaged in a dispute with the greatest of the *Geonim*. In the course of one dispute with the author of *Halakhot Gedolot* (R. Simeon Kayyara) and others, he said the following: "For them, the language of the Talmud is combined with a confused tongue and foreign language" (*Book of Commandments*, p. 11). In the introduction to the *Commentary on the Mishnah*, taking issue with the view of the *Geonim* regarding the origin of halakhic disputes, he describes their position as follows: "this type of contention God knows, an extremely depraved and ugly statement. These are words of someone without understanding, and who is not meticulous about fundamentals and who blemishes the people through whom the commandments were received. All this approach is void. That which brought one to believe in this depraved conviction was a paucity of contemplation into the works of the Sages that are found in the Talmud."

Maimonides observed that his taste for polemic subsided over time and that maturity tempered his youthful inclination to biting and aggressive forms of expression that could reduce his opponents to tears. In a letter to his beloved student Joseph ben Judah, in which Maimonides insisted that his student not allow himself to be drawn into the fray, he wrote of himself as follows:

When I was your age or even older, I was even more forceful than you in argument and, as you heard, I would take on with my word and my pen those great and wise men who sought to disagree with me. And you no doubt have heard of what transpired between me and R. Judah Hakohen of blessed memory, son of Mar Pirḥon, regarding two issues related to holding an animal to be non-kosher, and between me and the judge of Sijilmasa regarding a bill of divorce, and between me and Abu Joseph ben Mar Joseph, may his rest be in Eden, regarding a woman who had been taken captive, and many other similar cases. I there delighted my admirers and brought my adversaries to tears with my words and my pen—with my words to those who were in my presence, and with my pen to those who were distant. (*Iggerot*, pp. 421–422)

The force of Maimonides' reaction to his adversaries evidently resulted from the gap between his own talents and the grandeur of his native community and the lesser status of the people he encountered over the course of his life as a refugee in the Maghrib and an immigrant in Egypt, and as one who challenged what remained of the *geonic* tradition in the Land of Israel and in Baghdad. As a halakhist and philosopher, Maimonides lived in splendid isolation, having in his vicinity no worthy interlocutors of the stature of those in the lost world of Andalusia. Things might have been quite different had Maimonides' family emigrated northward, toward Provence, for when he happily discovered, late in life, the great sages of Lunel, he acted toward them as first among equals.

A sharp, almost violent tone was nothing unusual in twelfth-century halakhic polemic. Halakhists of stature, such as Rabbeinu Tam and Ra'abad, who towered over their surroundings, were known in their day as figures not to be trifled with. Maimonides himself, for example, was sometimes the target of piercing criticism by Ra'abad, who took issue with his rulings in *Mishneh Torah*. These figures, Maimonides among them, reacted to what they saw as errors in the field of *halakhah* as a gifted conductor would react to a dreadful rendition of a work of music. The slightest off-key note struck them as terrible dissonance that could not be disregarded.

Still, Maimonides' polemical approach to his halakhic and cultural environment went beyond the feelings of a genius toward what seemed to him to be almost harebrained amateurism. He found himself in fundamental conflict with his surroundings because he was engaged, as he saw it, in establishing a different religious consciousness. Rabbeinu Tam and Ra'abad did not live with that sense of mission. Even though they were drawn in to more than a few local confrontations over halakhic issues, they remained fundamentally at one with their communities. In contrast, Maimonides' monumentally transformative role placed him at odds with the world he inhabited. The certainty and self-assurance that marked his words, along with his dismissive arrogance toward his surroundings, made him one of a small and distinctive group of religious reformers and founders.

The sense of alienation and arrogance that Maimonides' writings sometimes convey is reinforced by, among other things, the attitude he developed toward the masses—an attitude that assumed a central place in his worldview and his spiritual attitude toward his surroundings. Most of the ignorant masses, as he saw it, were driven by vain illusions of hope and terror. Given that man is characterized as human by his ability to distinguish truth from falsity, it follows that most men do not live fully human lives. Full realization of human life is something quite rare, limited to isolated virtuosi. That sense marks all of Maimonides' writings, and his pen could produce some hair-raising formulations of that perspective on the world. Such a sentiment of alienation and isolation is expressed in Maimonides' description of the relationship of the prophet who achieved perfection toward his human environment:

> He should rather regard all people according to their various states with respect to which they are indubitably either like domestic animals or like beasts of prey. If the perfect man, who lives in solitude thinks of them at all, he does so only with the view of saving himself from the harm that may be caused by those among them who are harmful if he happens to associate with them, or to obtaining an advantage that may be obtained from them if he is forced to it by some of his needs. (*Guide*, p. 2, 36, Pines, p. 372)

The perspective resulted in ongoing tension with his surroundings, and Maimonides therefore was torn between the halakhist's sense of responsibility toward his community and a feeling of discomfort, sometimes approaching disgust, at the obligatory interaction with the stupidity and boorishness of human society. It is possible that this sense was sharpened by exile from his grand and sophisticated native community to an environment that struck him as poor and pretentious, an exile that produced harsh and unavoidable loneliness. As we shall see in the chapters on the *Guide*, this fundamental inner tension regarding his surroundings became quite significant in his consideration of human perfection and the philosopher's place in the world.

His indictment of the masses underlay another important complexity in Maimonides' basic stance between revolution and conservatism. He had his own way and did not hesitate to challenge existing traditions and worldviews, whether halakhic or philosophical. His worldview took shape through intensive contact with the Greek science and philosophy that had penetrated Arab culture, and he did not regard them as menaces that had to be avoided or approached cautiously. In our terms, he was "open." He therefore served as an inspiration to modern Jewish thought, which likewise rejected isolationism as a spiritual path and sought to locate a space in which intellectual discussion could be carried on with philosophical streams outside the tradition.

And yet, in his overall social outlook, Maimonides was a conservative, one of the most authoritarian halakhists within the Jewish tradition. His authoritarian strain is conveyed by his attitude in such areas as the struggle against heresy. The unpredictable and volatile masses are always vulnerable to being misled, and the maintenance of the social order depends on a firm and rigorous legal system. And so, despite the ongoing effort to elevate the entire community to higher and more truthful levels of understanding and awareness, he cautioned against revealing metaphysical truths to the community, lest they undermine obedience to the law. We therefore must distinguish clearly between Maimonides' philosophical openness and his authoritarian political views. He embodied a fascinating blend of intellectual independence and social conservatism.

Maimonides' letters and responsa show that there is more to his personality than is suggested by his harsh polemical tone, in which he adopts the posture of a superior mind utterly confident in his opinions. In the *Epistle on Martyrdom*, as we have seen, he applied his halakhic and literary talents to rehabilitating the crushed spirits of the Maghribi Jews. Alongside its uncompromising polemical streak, the *Epistle* conveys a great empathy that brings about a reinterpretation of authoritative halakhic sources. Sensitivity to suffering and generosity of spirit are evident as well in the second great epistle discussed above, the *Epistle to Yemen*. In that letter, which offers a magnificent application of the art of consolation, Maimonides establishes the historical construct that explains the suffering of the Yemenite community as the climax of the drama of Jewish history.

The delicate and merciful streak appears not only in Maimonides' enlistment in the resolution of communal problems but also in letters and responsa in which he dealt with individuals and the difficulties they faced. It is worthwhile to look at a few of these cherished moments in Maimonides' life, which would have fallen into oblivion but for the letters and responsa preserved in the Genizah. These texts are no match for Maimonides' monumental literary achievements in the *Commentary on the Mishnah*,

Mishneh Torah, or the *Guide*, but for that very reason, they shed additional light on the man's complex personality.

One of these minor yet illuminating artifacts appears in the correspondence between Maimonides and Joseph Ibn Jabir. Ibn Jabir is unusual among the people with whom Maimonides engaged; he was neither a student of Maimonides nor a rabbinic figure who sought his advice or disagreed with him. He was a simple admirer, the sort who hovers around great men without really understanding much of what they teach or write. Knowing no Hebrew, he was unable to read *Mishneh Torah*, but he tried his hand at the *Commentary on the Mishnah*, which was written in Arabic.

While in Baghdad, Ibn Jabir was exposed to the critique of *Mishneh Torah* by Samuel Ben Eli, the *ga'on* of the Baghdad yeshiva, and he turned to Maimonides for help in refuting it. Ibn Jabir's questions have not survived, but Maimonides' reply suggests that Ibn Jabir had apologized for his ignorance and his consequent need to burden Maimonides with his questions. Maimonides began his response on a charmingly reassuring note:

> First of all, I must tell you, may the Lord preserve and increase your welfare, that you are not justified to call yourself ignorant. You are my beloved pupil, and so are all those who are inclined to pursue zealously the study of Torah and attempt to understand even one biblical verse or a single *halakhah*. It makes also no difference whether one pursues his studies in the holy language or in Arabic or Aramaic, as long as one understands the issues involved. . . . I would suggest that you do not disparage yourself or abandon the prospect of achieving perfection. (*Letters of Maimonides*, p. 87)

After responding expansively to Joseph's questions one by one, Maimonides turned to a particularly sensitive problem. He heard that Joseph had stood up for his honor in Baghdad and confronted his rival on his behalf. For all the affection and support Maimonides lavished on Ibn Jabir, he certainly had no interest in having him serve as his ambassador in Baghdad; but how could he tell Joseph to refrain from fighting his battles without insulting him and seeming to reject his loyalty? Maimonides resolved the matter with delicacy and humor:

> I have learned—although I do not know whether it is true or not—that there is someone who speaks evil against me and tries to gain honor by

maligning me and misrepresenting my teaching. I also heard that you pro-
tested against this and reprimanded the slanderer. Do not act in this way!
I forgive anyone who opposes me because of ignorance, especially if he
derives from his opposition some personal advantage without harming
me. For are we not compelled to refrain from adopting the traits of Sodom
in cases where one derives a benefit and the other sustains no loss? (ibid.,
p. 94)

Maimonides' critics derive benefit from their attacks on him, which make
them seem wise to those around them. But since Maimonides gives their
attacks no regard and is utterly unaffected by them, the situation invokes
the Talmudic dictum that if A benefits from some action that in no way
disadvantages B, it would be wrong—"the trait of Sodom"—for B to de-
prive A of the benefit. If Joseph continues to do battle on behalf of Maimonides' honor when the heads of the Baghdad yeshiva derive benefit
from belittling it, he is acting in the manner of the people of Sodom.
Given that Maimonides himself wrote quite harshly in other contexts of
his rivals in Baghdad, the humorous elegance of his response here is even
more striking.

Maimonides' correspondence with Ovadyah the proselyte displays a delicate and sensitive treatment of a personal matter that also has broader
implications. Ovadyah turned to Maimonides after having been offended
by his rabbi, who is unnamed in the epistle. The incident between Ovadyah
and his rabbi centered on two questions. The first was whether Ovadyah
could recite the conventional prayer formulas that refer to ancestry, such as
"our God and God of our fathers, the God of Abraham, the God of Isaac,
and the God of Jacob." Given that Abraham, Isaac, and Jacob were not the
biological fathers of the proselyte, his rabbi ruled that Ovadyah was forbidden to recite those passages. The second question related to the Jewish view
of Islam—was it monotheistic or was it idolatrous?

The first question had already been dealt with in the *Mishnah* and Talmud,[17] and Maimonides ruled in accord with the view that permitted a
convert to refer to the patriarchs as his fathers. The ruling was grounded in
Maimonides' understanding of the significance of Israel's election, a matter
we will consider extensively below. What is of interest for present purposes
is less the way in which Maimonides treated the question as a broad halakhic and ideological problem than the manner in which he handled

---

[17] See *Mishna Bikurim* 1,4; *Talmud Yerusalmi Bikurim* 1, 4 64a.

Ovadyah's distress at being made to feel like a second-class member of the Jewish community. In an effort to confront Ovadyah's feelings of inferiority, Maimonides wrote to him as follows: "Do not see your descent as inferior. If we trace our descent to Abraham, Isaac, and Jacob, you trace your descent to the One who spoke and the world was created. As Isaiah says explicitly, 'One shall say: 'I am the Lord's; and another shall call himself by the name of Jacob' (Isa. 44:5)" (*Iggerot*, p. 235).

The personal dimension of the exchange is accentuated in Maimonides' response to Ovadyah's second question, related to his dispute with his rabbi over the status of Islam. Ovadyah evidently had previously been a Muslim, and he argued that Islam rejected idolatry; his rabbi argued to the contrary. In their discussion, the rabbi called Ovadyah a fool, and Ovadyah, feeling hurt, asked Maimonides to clarify the matter. As already noted, Maimonides took the view that Islam was a monotheistic religion in all respects, rejecting idolatry, and he explained the matter at length in his response to Ovadyah. At the end of the response, he turned directly to Ovadyah and, in an effort to alleviate his feelings of shame, challenged the authoritativeness of the rabbi who had insulted him:

> As for your rabbi having responded to you inappropriately, saddening you and calling you a fool—that was a great transgression on his part, and he sinned a great sin. But it seems to me likely that he did so through inadvertence, and that he should seek your forgiveness (though you are his student) and then fast, cry out, and pray, and perhaps God will grant him atonement. But was he drunk and unaware that the Torah warns thirty-six times about [the need to be kind to] proselytes? . . . And before wondering whether the Ishmaelites [that is, Muslims] are idolaters or not, he should have concerned himself with the anger that he felt, to the point of improperly humiliating a righteous convert; and our sages of blessed memory have already said "One who angers should be in your eyes as an idolater." (ibid., pp. 239–240)

One thing that Maimonides sought to do here was to reverse the authority vector between Ovadyah and his rabbi. It was the rabbi who was obligated to seek Ovadyah's forgiveness for having insulted a proselyte, and if the rabbi meant to demean Ovadyah as the descendant of idolaters, he would do better to look inward, for he might find that he himself is afflicted by idolatry.

In the following paragraph, Maimonides writes more directly to the offended convert:

> That he called you a fool is indeed strange: You, a man who leaves his father, his homeland, his nation, and their outstretched hand, achieving understanding with his own heart and cleaving to this nation—considered today "a nation despised," "the servant of rulers"—and knowing that its religion is a religion of truth and righteousness; coming to know Israel's ways and knowing that all religions are stolen from its religion . . . recognizing all, knowing and pursuing God; traversing the holy path and coming under the wings of God's presence; following Moses our Teacher and Teacher of all the prophets, and desiring his commandments. A man whose heart raised him to be close to God, to be illuminated by the light of life, and to ascend to the heights of the angels and rejoice with the joy of the righteous; and who cast the concerns of this world from his heart, turning away from emptiness and falsehood. Can such a person be called a fool? Heaven forbid; not "fool" did God name you but "wise man"[18]—understanding and bright, thinking logically, a student of Abraham our father, who left his parents and his homeland and turned toward God. (ibid., pp. 240–241)

People such as converts, who are situated at society's margins and lack pedigree and standing, tend to internalize the inferior status that society imposes on them. Maimonides recognized that he was dealing here not only with a sense of shame, but also—indeed, primarily—with a real risk of internalizing a damaging self-image. This heartfelt passage was intended to transform the convert's perception of himself from that of fool in the eyes of his rabbi to that of wise in the eyes of God.

As noted, Maimonides firmly believed that Islam was a monotheistic religion, and he reiterated the point in his response. The human feeling becomes evident at the point where he moves from theoretical analysis to personal address. That portion of the response shows that Maimonides took account not only of the question but also of the questioner. He well understood the shame and hurt endured by the proselyte and responded to them. A careful reading of Maimonides' writings affords us insights into his underlying and complex attitude toward the world around him. His personality manifests both the zealous—one might even say violent—tone of

---

[18] The Hebrew here has a play on words: "fool" is *kesil*; "wise man" is *maskil*.

the religious reformer and the vulnerability and thoughtfulness of an émi-gré acquainted with grief.

Talented people often suffer a degree of estrangement from their sur-roundings, and their social skills are sometimes as weak as their intellectual skills are powerful. Maimonides was not such a person. His letters demon-strate his ability to read the people around him, on both the personal and the institutional level.

An interesting example of that ability is provided by his conflict with Samuel Ben Eli and Samuel's son-in-law Zechariah ben Berakhel of Bagh-dad. As noted several times, Samuel Ben Eli, the *ga'on* of Baghdad, bitingly criticized some passages in *Mishneh Torah* and even accused Maimonides of denying belief in the resurrection of the dead. The struggle took place between 1189 and 1191, and some unique material related to it has survived. That material is of two voices. On the one hand, there is the correspon-dence between the two figures related to the issues themselves; Maimonides there sounds cold and distant as he criticizes Samuel's comments in ironic terms. A rather different voice can be heard, however, in Maimonides' letter to his student, Joseph ben Judah, updating him on the controversy. Had we only the former letters, we would have sensed a certain restrained hos-tility. But in his letters to his student Joseph, who had by then become a sort of pen pal, Maimonides revealed the personal attitudes concealed be-hind the official restraint and, even more, his penetrating interpretation of what underlay the halakhic discussion. Evidently, Maimonides saw the situation as one involving a power struggle having little if anything to do with substantive halakhic debate. As far as I can tell, this sort of dual cor-respondence was unprecedented in the history of *halakhah* and has re-mained unparalleled: on the one hand, a substantive correspondence be-tween halakhists; on the other, a more personal and open correspondence in which the great halakhist interprets the meaning of the dispute in which he is engaged, manifests a penetrating understanding of the power plays in which he has been caught up, and portrays what he takes to be the spiritual and institutional decline of his adversaries.

Maimonides well understood that the very composition of *Mishneh Torah*, and its ensuing acceptance as an authoritative halakhic source, tended to undermine the standing of the *ga'on*, which was based on his personal authority and institutional decision-making. A comprehensive and easy-to-use halakhic treatise could displace his institutional and per-sonal authority alike. Maimonides understood as much and interpreted his halakhic and theological disputes with Samuel Ben Eli in that light. In that spirit, he wrote as follows to Joseph:

> I know that as I gained fame there [in Baghdad], he [Samuel Ben Eli] and all who follow him and all who wish to aggrandize him in people's eyes would feel a need to diminish my treatise [*Mishneh Torah*] and appear so perfect as to have no need to consult it. On the contrary, they say that any one of them could have written a better treatise than mine and done so more quickly. (*Iggerot*, pp. 303–304)

Later in the letter, Maimonides offers one of the sharpest indictments of the corrosive effect of institutional hegemony on religious authority: "[Regarding] most men of religion who are possessed of authority—when something has a bearing on their authority, their piety leaves them" (*Iggerot*, p. 308).

Maimonides attributed the decline in the institution of the gaonate to the hereditary transmission of the yeshiva's leadership. He regarded his rival's personal and intellectual decay as the result of the combined effect of destructive institutional power and a perverse sense of spiritual superiority that lacked any real basis. He described Samuel Ben Eli as one "who grew up from childhood being told that he was unique in his generation and is now bolstered by old age, prominence, pedigree, and the absence of knowledgeable people in that land. He feels a need to instill in people the pathetic idea that everyone should look forward to hearing what comes from the yeshiva" (*Iggerot*, p. 303). There is a profound—albeit not uncommon—irony in that Maimonides, an independent émigré and prominent sage who saw hereditary leadership as something destructive, himself became the founder of a dynasty, whose descendants served as leaders of the Jewish community in Egypt for some two hundred years after his death.

In his letter to Joseph, Maimonides described what he believed to be the motives and abilities of his rival:

> I knew and it was evident to me when I wrote [*Mishneh Torah*] that it without doubt would fall into the hands of malevolent and jealous men who would disparage its merits, seeing it as unnecessary or flawed; and into the hands of foolish and naïve men who would not understand what it was about and think it of little use; and into the hands of silly and confused novices who would question it because of their lack of knowledge or limited ability to replicate my reasoning; and into the hands of those who

consider themselves to be God-fearing yet are stupid and will be critical of what is included in the code concerning fundamentals of faith. (*Iggerot*, p. 301)

Beyond the piercing comments here about his rival in Baghdad, it is hard not to see in this passage the plea of a sensitive writer, trying to defend himself by arguing that he had from the outset foreseen the criticism brought against his work. That criticism, he maintains, does not uncover any flaws in his work; rather, it demonstrates only the illegitimate motives and limited talents of his rivals. The critics are zealous and foolish incompetents, self-righteously pious in their own eyes.

Maimonides recognized that *Mishneh Torah*'s philosophical component could incur opposition, and we will consider that component in ensuing chapters. Still, his attitude toward the false piety that would serve as the basis for future criticism of *Mishneh Torah* was well founded. In addition to his halakhic criticisms of *Mishneh Torah*, Samuel Ben Eli argued stridently that the treatise made plain that Maimonides did not believe in resurrection of the dead. Maimonides was forced to defend himself against that charge in his *Essay on Resurrection*.

The personal letters to Joseph thus allow us to read the subtext of the struggle between the two halakhists. In a rare disclosure, the great halakhist reveals to his beloved student the dark and belligerent aspect lurking behind the official, putatively halakhic debate. In analyzing these harsh facts of life, Maimonides shows his sharp institutional and political insight, a quality that allowed him to act, over the course of his life, not only as a halakhic authority and philosopher but also as a man well equipped to navigate personal and institutional power struggles.

Maimonides' subtle understanding of the human environment is evident as well in more personal moments. One such comes to our attention through the correspondence between Maimonides and Japhet, the *dayyan* in Acre. Japhet's letter to Maimonides has not survived, but its tone and some of its content can be reconstructed through Maimonides' response. Japhet sought Maimonides' help in obtaining some authorization that evidently was important to him. He first came into contact with Maimonides when he met Maimonides' family in the Land of Israel, and his letter was written in 1186, some twenty years after they had gone their separate ways. During that long interval, Maimonides had neither seen nor heard from him.

Japhet began by chastising Maimonides for not having written since his departure for Egypt, and then went on to request his help. Maimonides well understood the context of the letter, sensing that Japhet was embarrassed to finally be writing to his acquaintance, after all these years, only when he needed assistance. He sought to overcome that embarrassment by criticizing Maimonides for seemingly turning his back on him. Maimonides portrays these sentiments elegantly:

> Your gracious epistle reached me but its content amazed me. You complain about my silence and my failure to ask about your welfare since I left the Land of Israel. Apparently, this is a case of one who comes to admonish others but deserves admonition himself. Indeed, you acted treacherously toward others but no one acted that way towards you. Since we separated, my father died. We received letters of consolation from distant lands of Idumea and the West but not a word from you.
>
> Many and severe misfortunes befell me in Egypt. Illness and material losses overwhelmed me. Informers plotted against my life. (*Letters of Maimonides*, p. 72)

Shifting blame is not an effective way to deal with abandonment. Japhet had certainly heard of the troubles Maimonides had encountered, and Maimonides had received condolences on the death of his father from throughout the world, including places more remote than the Land of Israel. Japhet, however, saw no need to be in touch with Maimonides during those difficult times, and wrote only now, when he needed assistance. Maimonides interpreted Japhet's words with the observation that "Apparently, this is a case of one who comes to admonish others but deserves admonition himself." None of this, however, freed Maimonides of the duty to help his former acquaintance, who had hosted his family in the Holy Land. At the end of the Epistle, he returns to that theme: "I would certainly be justified not to answer your letter that just arrived. But my love for you, which I have kept steadfast in my heart, cannot be severed and I shall never forget when we walked together through the deserts and the forests seeking God. I shall, therefore, bear no grudges against you as love obliterates all iniquity" (ibid., p. 73).

Thanks to his personal and political skills, the émigré from Andalusia had reached the pinnacle of the Egyptian Jewish community. He struggled with distinguished and long-established families for the position of *ra'is al-yahud* and, serving as a physician, survived the intrigues in the Sultan's court. His involvement with his surroundings is a central element not only in his ascent to institutional greatness but also—indeed, primarily—in his intellectual oeuvre. That oeuvre, as already noted, was meant to bring about a profound change in Jewish life.

The drive to exercise communal leadership and to produce a transformative oeuvre raises another aspect of Maimonides' personality, one that recurs in Maimonides' comments about himself. It pertains to the inner struggle occasioned by the tension between influence and personal integrity. The effort to attain a position of far-reaching political and intellectual influence can make a person unduly concerned about how he is regarded by those around him. That sort of dependence would not have arisen had Maimonides confined himself to the four cubits of *halakhah* and philosophy, or even if he had weighed in only occasionally on the issues of the day. Maimonides sought to escape that grip and achieve inner independence, but he never gave up his desire to wield influence. Clear evidence of his thinking on this can be found in his letters to his student Joseph, which contain acute and melancholy reflections on the risk of lost independence as the price of influence and status:

> My honored son knows that the high governmental offices some Jews hold today are not something I consider a mark of success . . . rather, they are the ultimate burden, a source of travail and exhaustion. The perfect man who achieves true success is one who concentrates on religious success, doing what he is obligated to do and distancing himself from the opinions of all people and from misguided ways and offensive traits. For one who holds office suffers much sorrow and worry, lest the gentiles mock and shame him or he fall into disfavor with the government and they torment him and break his bones. And if he pays attention to people and tries to please them, he will transgress the Law of God, may He be exalted, by exercising flattery and showing favoritism. (*Iggerot*, pp. 262–263)

Maimonides thus saw high office as a burden one was obliged to assume. Still, another observer, a Muslim who admired Maimonides' medical and philosophical eminence, attributed to him genuine political ambition: "He [Maimonides] felt a great love of leadership and of service to the rulers of the world" (Ibn Abi Uṣaybiʿa, p. 117). In any case, the tone of Maimonides' letter to Joseph shows that Maimonides recognized the need to please people in order to protect the fragile measure of power that one had managed to attain.

The dedication of his book on poisons provides a brief glimpse of the dependence and need to flatter that were part of Maimonides' political life. The book was dedicated to his patron, the vizier al-Faḍil, whose grandeur is described in greatly exaggerated terms in the introduction. Maimonides mentions, among other things, the vizier's military triumphs over the Crusaders, crediting him with expelling them from the holy cities and bringing about the triumph of monotheism. Maimonides' yearning for the perfected person, one unconcerned about public opinion, conveys his effort to maintain his inner integrity in the circumstances in which he worked.

This inner tension is evident not only in Maimonides' view of his moral standing but also in his attitude regarding the reception of *Mishneh Torah*. The public's acceptance of his ambitious and far-reaching treatise was significant to his success, and, as we shall see, it established his authoritativeness. Maimonides took pains to disseminate the treatise and was pleased by reports he received about the work's reception. But his aspiration to see the work disseminated was accompanied by a not insubstantial effort to be inwardly free of any concern about criticism of the book and to brace himself in advance for any disappointment. This psychological effort resonates in Maimonides' remarks to Joseph in reaction to the latter's account of the attacks on *Mishneh Torah* in Baghdad:

> Know that I did not write this treatise in order to become glorified in Israel or to acquire a name for myself . . . Rather, I wrote it—as God Himself knows—first for myself, to make it easier to find what I might need; and, in my old age, for the sake of God, may He be exalted; for, as God lives, I have been zealous on behalf of the Lord God of Israel, seeing a nation lacking a true and comprehensive book of its laws and lacking true and clear opinions; so I did what I did for the sake of God alone. (*Iggerot*, pp. 300–301)

In his struggle for inner freedom and independence from his surroundings, Maimonides used two strategies. One was his withdrawal into himself, into the "I," a posture conveyed by his claim that he wrote the treatise first and foremost for himself. The other was his effort to move beyond his surroundings and to stand before God, for whose sake the treatise had been written.

These two strategies—one personal, the other exalted; one involving withdrawal from his surroundings and the other ascent above them—were meant to forge the independence described by Maimonides later in the letter:

And if it turns out that people question my fear of God or what I have done, so be it. And all of this, my son, as God lives, does not distress me, even if I witness it as it is done before my very eyes. Rather, my speech will be calm, and I will be silent or respond on topic. For their neglect of truth is much greater than this. And I will not defend myself, for my self respect and my attributes call for me to be silent to fools, not to do verbal combat with them. (*Iggerot*, p. 304)

But there is another theme that recurs in Maimonides' stance vis-à-vis his environment. The temptation to engage in argument, in which a man might lose his dignity and independence, is replaced by the harsh criticism of his antagonists that Maimonides allows himself to express only to himself and to those close to him. That sharp judgment allows Maimonides to expel them from his sphere of interest, as can be seen in his harsh remarks, conveyed to Joseph, regarding Zechariah ben Berakhel, Samuel Ben Eli's son-in-law: "But this master Zechariah—he is a very naive man, teaching himself and exerting himself in those areas of discussion and commentary, and thinking of himself as one unique in his generation who has already attained greatness . . . how shall I pay any attention to a truly poor old man foolish in all matters, who is to me like a newborn babe; but one should give him the benefit of the doubt because of his folly (*Iggerot*, pp. 304–305).

Maimonides' disclosure of his inner state to his student Joseph allows us to reach a deeper understanding of his thinking during one of the most difficult confrontations of his life. They reveal what was going on beyond the official correspondence between the halakhists engaged, at least putatively, in a battle over Torah. At the center of Maimonides' inner drama lies the tension between his drive to gain influence and his desire to preserve his freedom and independence. His exhausting daily schedule at the end of his life was the high price Maimonides paid for the status he attained, but he valiantly strove to prevent that price from penetrating his innermost being.

Maimonides' rise as a force for change, as a figure having the qualities of the founder of a religion, took place in the context of two great losses. One was the destruction of Andalusia, his glorious homeland, and his ensuing flight to the Maghrib, with its religious persecution, and thence to Egypt, a relatively poorer area. All of these factors instilled in Maimonides' consciousness the impression of a halakhic and philosophical crisis. That impression, along with Maimonides' rare intellectual talents, his Andalusian origin, his personal and political abilities, and his powerful sense of mission, turned him into one perceived by himself and by those around him as the "Moses of his generation."

The second loss, the death of his brother, struck on a more intimate level. The tragedy left Maimonides broken-hearted for an extended time and deprived him of the economic and psychological support that a close family had provided the émigré in a strange land. The loss impelled him, as a practical matter, to the heights of medical and institutional success in the Sultan's court—something that also consumed what remained of his time and left him weakened. The letters that have survived reveal that behind the distant, extremely confident figure was a man suffering great pain, a sensitive and delicate personality struggling with, among other things, the difficulty of maintaining an even keel, the loss of freedom, and the dependence on others that comes with power and influence.

The *Commentary on the Mishnah*, the *Book of Commandments*, and the Philosophy of *halakhah*

In the Laboratory of the *Commentary on the Mishnah*

One of the most valuable manuscripts in the National Library of Israel in Jerusalem is of Maimonides' commentary on two orders of the *Mishnah*, *Mo'ed* and *Nashim*, written in Maimonides' own hand. This manuscript remained in the possession of Maimonides' descendants in Egypt, and when David (II) b. Joshua Maimonides (1335–1415), leader of the Jewish community in Egypt, moved from Cairo to Aleppo, he brought the authentic manuscript with him, to symbolize the continuity and authority of the Maimonides family.

The circumstances under which the manuscript survived are astounding. Edward Pococke, who taught Arabic at Oxford, purchased two volumes of the manuscript—containing the commentaries on the Mishnaic orders of *Zera'im*, *Neziqin*, and *Kodashim*—for Oxford's Bodleian Library. He published sections of the manuscript along with a Latin translation in 1655. The second part of the manuscript was acquired by the National Library of Israel from the family of David Solomon Sassoon, who had purchased it in 1908 from the brothers Jacob, Moses, and Barukh Toledano in Damascus.

Every remaining medieval manuscript carries a real risk of deviation from the original due to copyist errors or emendations. The original manuscript of the *Commentary on the Mishnah*, however, is free of such concerns. In addition to the complete reliability of the manuscript (if only we had the original manuscript of *Mishneh Torah*, from which other copies were made!), close scrutiny of it reveals how Maimonides composed the commentary. Maimonides began writing the commentary at the age of twenty-three and completed the first version of it in 1168 in Fustat, when he was thirty. Most of the commentary was written under harsh conditions while wandering through the Maghrib, as Maimonides attests in his epilogue. However, work on the commentary did not end there; we see from the manuscript that the *Commentary on the Mishnah* was an open book that Maimonides continued to revise many years after completing the first version.

In numerous instances, Maimonides revised the original version by deleting passages and adding superscript or marginal comments. Among the factors leading to these changes was his review of various subjects while writing *Mishneh Torah*, in the years after writing the *Commentary on the Mishnah*. By studying these topics afresh, he reached new conclusions and therefore revised the original text of the commentary to reflect his new views. As he wrote in a letter about one such change: "At that time [while I was writing *Mishneh Torah*], I was meticulously scrutinizing every law of my major work [i.e., *Mishneh Torah*], and the meaning of this Mishnah became clear" (*Iggerot*, p. 212). Indeed, Maimonides continued to revise his *Commentary on the Mishnah* throughout his life, even after writing *Mishneh Torah*. The introduction to his commentary on the tenth chapter of Tractate *Sanhedrin* contains a revision that was made after he wrote the *Guide of the Perplexed*, certainly after 1191. This *modus operandi* led to the proliferation of manuscripts and printed versions of the commentary, as the different printed editions reflect various stages of revision that Maimonides made to his initial text.

Tracking the differences between versions of the *Commentary on the Mishnah* or between the *Commentary* and *Mishneh Torah* can teach us about the direction of Maimonides' development as a halakhist. On several occasions, Maimonides addresses one of the principles that underlies these revisions—his increasing liberation from geonic positions: "these reservations that [the *Geonim* of Baghdad *yeshivot*] express about the *Commentary on the Mishnah* is solely because I revised it in places; God knows that in most of them I was misled by following the *Geonim*, like R. Nissim's *Megillat Setarim* and R. Hafetz's *Sefer ha-Mitzvot*" (*Iggerot*, p. 305). Critics of Maimonides in Baghdad attempted to undermine the stature of *Mishneh Torah* by pointing out where Maimonides recanted from positions he took in the *Commentary on the Mishnah*. If Maimonides indeed recanted, who could guarantee the credibility of the views he espouses in *Mishneh Torah* and that he would not discover mistakes there, too? Maimonides' response to these criticisms included a barb aimed at his critics. The mistakes in the

Commentary on the Mishnah stemmed from over-reliance on the *Geonim*, from whom the heads of the Baghdadi *yeshivot* drew their authority. Maimonides, however, put greater stock in his later, independent viewpoints. In one such responsum about a discrepancy his correspondents found between the version of the *Commentary on the Mishnah* they had and the law as recorded in *Mishneh Torah*, he wrote as follows:

> What I wrote in the work [*Mishneh Torah*] is doubtlessly correct, and so I wrote in the *Commentary on the Mishnah* [in a revision of the first version]. What you have is the first edition, which I published before close scrutiny, following, in this passage, what R. Hafetz wrote in *Sefer ha-Mitzvot*. The mistake is his, and I followed it without verifying. But when I examined and scrutinized these passages, it became clear that what I wrote in the work is correct, and I revised the commentary. Similarly, in that first version of the commentary are some ten matters on which I followed one of the *Geonim* and was later made aware of their mistake. (*Iggerot*, pp. 647–649)

The correspondents had a copy of the first version of the *Commentary on the Mishnah*, and Maimonides responded that he revised his own copy based on his conclusions in *Mishneh Torah*.

In this responsum, Maimonides referred to ten places where he changed his stance once liberating himself from the tendency to automatically accept geonic traditions. However, the number of revisions is far greater, indicating the evolution of his views in additional realms. Saul Lieberman, in his introduction to Maimonides' *Hilkhot ha-Yerushalmi*, lists dozens of such revisions, and Aaron Adler, who has studied these changes and described their characteristic features, has counted more than seven hundred such revisions of positions taken in the first version of the *Commentary on the Mishnah*. These changes show a steadily increasing independence not only vis-à-vis geonic attitudes, but in other areas as well.

Thus, for example, it is possible to identify the development of considerations for deciding halakhic disputes between the sages of the *Mishnah*, the *Tannaim*. In the first phase of writing the *Commentary on the Mishnah*, Maimonides tended to accept the decision-making principles enshrined in the Babylonian Talmud: in a controversy between a single sage and multiple sages, the law accords with the majority; the law follows R. Joshua against R. Eliezer; the law follows an anonymously attributed *Mishnah*; and so forth. Maimonides' revisions over time demonstrate that he liberated himself from the automatic application of these principles or from following the legal precedents common among halakhists who predated him.

This deviation from conventional precedent is connected, *inter alia,* with the stature of the Talmud Yerushalmi, which grew over time in Maimonides' eyes. Medieval halakhists relied on the Talmud Yerushalmi only to clarify views that appear in the Babylonian Talmud or as supplemental information on areas of the law around which no Babylonian Talmudic tractate was developed. Maimonides greatly enhanced the status of the Talmud Yerushalmi in halakhic decision-making. Thus, where there was no explicit ruling on the Babylonian Talmud on a given subject, Maimonides eventually began ruling in accordance with the decisions of the Talmud Yerushalmi, against the decision-making principles of the Babylonian Talmud.

One such example can be found in the commentary on Tractate *Bikkurim,* which addresses the question discussed in the last section of the previous chapter regarding Ovadyah the convert. The *Mishnah* (1:4) states that a convert must make an offering of his first fruits (*bikkurim*) but may not recite the accompanying formula: "The following bring [*bikkurim*] but do not recite [the formula]: a proselyte brings but does not recite, for he cannot say 'which the Lord swore to our fathers to give us.'" Since the recitation over the *bikkurim* includes a verse that refers to the Land of Israel that "the Lord swore to our fathers to give us" (Deut. 26:3), a proselyte cannot recite this segment; his forefathers were not Israelites.

In the first version of the *Commentary on the Mishnah,* Maimonides rules in accordance with the *Mishnah,* writing: "this is clear." Later, however, he revised the commentary, adding the following lines:

> But the halakhic ruling is that a proselyte himself brings and recites; this is based on what God said to Abraham, "for I have made you a multitude of nations" (Gen. 17:5), about which [the Sages] said: "in the past you were a father to Aram; now you are a father to the whole world." Therefore, any proselyte may recite "which the Lord swore to our fathers", for Abraham was a father to the whole world since he taught them faith and religion.
> (*Commentary on the Mishnah, Bikkurim* 1, 4)

Maimonides thus retracted and ruled that a proselyte may recite the *bikkurim* formula, against the halakhic principles which state that the law accords with the *Mishnah.* This change is based on the Talmud Yerushalmi, which cites an opinion that contradicts the *Mishnah* and maintains that a proselyte must bring *bikkurim* and recite the accompanying formula. It indeed rules in accordance with this view: "It was taught in the name of R. Judah: a proselyte himself brings and recites. Why? 'For I have made you a multitude of nations'—in the past you were a father to Aram; from now on you are a father to all nations" (*Bikkurim* 1:4, 64a). Later in the same discussion, the Talmud rules in accordance with R. Judah: "R. Joshua b. Levi said: The law accords with R. Judah." Maimonides thus based himself on the explicit ruling of the Talmud Yerushalmi and even quoted it in his commentary: "this is based on what God said to Abraham, 'for I have made you a multitude of nations.'" The growing stature of the Talmud Yerushalmi in the eyes of Maimonides caused him to deviate, in this instance, from the decision-making principles which state that the law accords with an anonymous *Mishnah*.

This example, one of many, shows how this priceless manuscript of the *Commentary on the Mishnah*, with the revisions Maimonides inserted over the years, presents an opportunity to actually enter into Maimonides' laboratory. Close study of this manuscript reveals the steadily increasing independence that Maimonides demonstrated in his rulings, whether vis-à-vis geonic traditions or with regard to previously accepted methods of reaching halakhic decisions.

The Purpose of the *Commentary on the Mishnah*

At first glance, the *Commentary on the Mishnah*—Maimonides' youthful composition—appears to be lacking the monumental and innovative character of his later work. In contrast to the *Commentary*, which, as its name indicates, is a running commentary on the *Mishnah*, *Mishneh Torah* was designed to change the face of *halakhah*, and the objective of the *Guide of the Perplexed* was to disclose the inner meaning of Judaism and offer a new interpretation of Jewish tradition, thereby rescuing the enlightened Jewish class from its perplexity.

The difference between the ostensibly trifling character of the *Commentary on the Mishnah* and the monumental character of *Mishneh Torah* and the *Guide of the Perplexed* is discernible from the dissemination of the works and the degree to which they occupied subsequent generations. There is no comparing the extent to which *Mishneh Torah* was studied by generations of scholars to the limited study and discussion of the *Mishnah* commentary. That the commentary was written in Arabic no doubt influenced the scope of its dissemination, but its lack of importance cannot be blamed solely on differences of language. After all, the *Guide* was written in Arabic as well, but its translation into Hebrew allowed it to influence Jewish thought for centuries. Yet, we should not confuse a work's popularity and impact with its originality and the energy invested in its composition. Indeed, the *Commentary on the Mishnah* is truly innovative; it prepares the ground for both Maimonides' monumental halakhic work and the synthesis of *halakhah* and philosophy that defined the course of his later life.

The first innovation, with far-reaching consequences for the understanding of *halakhah*, is the very transformation of the *Mishnah* into a text to be studied on its own. From close scrutiny of medieval *Mishnah* manuscripts and other indirect evidence, it emerges that *Mishnah* was not studied as an independent work in Babylonia; its study was always secondary to the study of the Babylonian Talmud, except in the case of the Mishnahic orders *Zeraʿim* and *Taharot*, on which there is no Babylonian Talmud. Things were different in the Land of Israel; there, as Jacob Sussman has shown, the *Mishnah* was studied on its own. The manuscripts in which the *Mishnah* appears as a separate work, not part of the Babylonian Talmud, all originated in the Land of Israel. In the Land of Israel and its sphere of influence—Byzantium and Southern Italy—students continued to study the *Mishnah* as a separate work, and it is from there that these manuscripts of the *Mishnah* have reached us.

The Babylonian tendency of neglecting the *Mishnah* continued in the communities of both Ashkenaz and Sepharad, due to Babylonian influence. This remains true until this day; *Mishnah* is not studied as a separate work in contemporary *yeshivot*, but is merely studied as a supplement to the Babylonian Talmud. Thus, a comprehensive commentary on the *Mishnah* as a free-standing work was an original idea; prior to Maimonides, no such attempt was made either by any of the Babylonian *Geonim* nor by leading halakhists in Spain, Provence, Germany, or France. The only known commentary on the entire *Mishnah* that preceded Maimonides' was written in the eleventh century by R. Nathan, the head of the Yeshiva in the Land of Israel. Yet even this commentary is primarily lexicographic and does not achieve the same quality and scope as Maimonides' commentary. The *Commentary on the Mishnah* was indeed a novel and unprecedented work, through which Maimonides attempted to change the conventional modes of study.

What led Maimonides to try to affect such a change? Maimonides thought that without a penetrating knowledge of the *Mishnah*, one lacked the essentials necessary to understand *halakhah* in its entirety. In his commentary on Tractate *Mikva'ot* (4:4), he addresses an error made by a halakhist, blaming it on the latter's lack of knowledge of the *Mishnah*: "what caused all of this torment is insufficient mastery of the *Mishnah* and study of its contents. How true are [the Rabbis'] words about a Torah scholar whose Talmud has been dulled like iron and whose Mishnah is not fluent in his mouth."

Maimonides, however, went even further. In his introduction to the *Mishnah*, he listed four goals that he set for his commentary; it emerges from them that this work was designed to prepare the ground for writing *Mishneh Torah*. The first goal is to know the interpretation of the *Mishnah* according to the conclusions of the Talmudic discussion: "For if you ask the greatest of the *Geonim* to expound the law from the *Mishnah*—he would not be able to say anything unless he remembers what the Talmud says about that law . . . and none are capable of remembering the entire Talmud" (*Introduction to the Mishnah*). The second goal is to decide from among the various opinions whenever the *Mishnah* records a controversy and indicate which opinion is followed. The third goal is to serve as a "primer for the novice scholar; from this he will understand how to scrutinize the words and their meanings and will be as one who has encompassed the entire Talmud. This will assist him greatly throughout the Talmud" (ibid.). The fourth goal is to assist those who have already studied and mastered Talmud to remember and review.

The *Commentary on the Mishnah* thus serves two overarching objectives, which will characterize Maimonides' later approach to *halakhah*. The first objective is to compose a work that will make it possible to organize and refine the principles and fundamentals of the halakhic material from within the convoluted discussions of the Talmud. By explaining the *Mishnah* according to the Talmud's understanding, Maimonides concisely summarized the long and occasionally hard-to-follow Talmudic discussions. The *Mishnah* is organized and succinct and can therefore be used to impose order, organization, and brevity on the chaos of the Talmud. Maimonides thought that his commentary would give beginners the comprehensive rudiments of the entire corpus of Jewish law and help more accomplished scholars to summarize and remember what they had learned.

The organizing and summarizing principle that underlies the work sheds light on why Maimonides occasionally interrupted his running commentary on the *Mishnah* to introduce overviews of the principles of various areas of *halakhah*. His introduction to Tractate *Taharot* is a masterpiece that makes order out of an extremely thorny area of *halakhah*. Additional examples include his overview of the laws of *muktzeh* and *nolad*—categories of objects that cannot be moved on the Sabbath—at the beginning of Tractate *Beitza*; principles of levirate marriage and divorce at the beginning of Tractate *Yevamot*; principles of forbidden sexual relations in Tractate *Sanhedrin* (7:4); principles of flogging administered by rabbinical courts in the commentary on Tractate *Makkot*; and others.

The second objective of the *Commentary on the Mishnah* is to issue halakhic rulings on each *Mishnah* according to the decisions of the Babylonian Talmud. The halakhic rulings in his commentary illustrate Maimonides' basic position, which underlies his composition of *Mishneh Torah*—that the purpose of studying *Mishnah* and Talmud is to decide the *halakhah*.

These two foci—organization and halakhic decision—lie at the heart of *Mishneh Torah* as a comprehensive halakhic work. By turning the *Mishnah*, via his commentary, into a work studied on its own, Maimonides served the basic purpose of his conception of *halakhah*, which reached its ultimate fruition in his magnum opus.

As we will see later on, Maimonides viewed the *Mishnah* as the precedent for his *Mishneh Torah*. He identified with the figure of R. Judah ha-Nasi, the *Mishnah*'s redactor, who in his time formulated the basis of *halakhah*, and from then on it continued to grow and develop. By writing a *Mishnah* commentary that incorporated insights of the Babylonian Talmud, but without the exhausting discourse that led to those insights, he laid the necessary foundations and paved the way for *Mishneh Torah*.

Controversy, Truth, and Interpretation

In the *Commentary on the Mishnah*, which, as noted, serves as the foundation for his entire halakhic oeuvre, Maimonides incorporated a principled and systematic philosophy of *halakhah*. This philosophical doctrine deals with the basic concepts of the Jewish legal system: the conception of halakhic authority, modes of understanding halakhic interpretation, the status of halakhic controversy and the question of whether one of the disputants is necessarily in error, the relationship between innovation and tradition in *halakhah*, and the role of prophecy within *halakhah*'s authority structure. These questions hold the key to understanding the halakhic system since they do not take a position on the particular content of one law or another, but address the halakhic corpus in its entirety.

Maimonides' occupation with the basic components of halakhic thought stemmed from both his general interest in philosophy and his affiliation with broader Islamic culture, in which philosophy of law was a highly developed field. Yet it seems that we must go even further. His treatment of *halakhah*'s theoretical basis in the *Commentary on the Mishnah* was intended as an advance preparation for his monumental attempt, in *Mishneh Torah*, to impose an ordered, exhaustive, and systematic structure on Talmudic discourse. Such an attempt forced Maimonides to develop a framework into which he could assimilate, refine, and formulate Talmudic discourse in a principled way.

Formulating a coherent and comprehensive philosophy of *halakhah* was a major component of Maimonides' methodology, in contrast to the leading twelfth-century halakhists of France and Provence. These halakhists, Maimonides' contemporaries, paved the way for the emergence of a literature of novellae and saw the purpose of Talmud study as being the broadening of the Talmudic discourse itself. The Tosafists, the commentaries of Ra'abad, and the novellae of Naḥmanides and his school represent an ever-increasing expansion of Talmud commentary, just as the Talmud itself, until its completion, was an ever-expanding work. Those who expand Talmudic discourse itself generally are not preoccupied with the theoretical basis of *halakhah*, which can be characterized by contemplating it from the outside. Maimonides was thus the first halakhist to formulate a systematic philosophy of *halakhah*.

As in other areas, Maimonides formulated a philosophy of *halakhah* independently and in opposition to the mainstream geonic tradition. It is worthwhile to first articulate the prevailing approach among the *Geonim* to the fundamental questions of halakhic philosophy. In the introduction to Abraham Ibn Daud's twelfth-century *Book of Tradition*, the author summarizes the approach of most *Geonim* in simple terms:

> This *Book of Tradition* I have written to inform the students that all the words of our rabbis, the sages of the Mishnah and Talmud, were all re-

ceived—great and righteous sage from great and righteous sage; *yeshiva* head and his cohort from *yeshiva* head and his cohort—from the Men of the Great Assembly, who received it from the prophets, of blessed memory. The sages of the Talmud and *a fortiori* the sages of the *Mishnah* never spoke their own thoughts, even on small matters, with the exception of regulations instituted by consensus in order to build a fence around the Torah. If a person imbued with a spirit of heresy whispered to you that he doubts the words of the sages because they argue in many places, blunt his teeth and inform him that he is a rebel according to the rabbinical court; our sages never debated the central aspects of a commandment, only its details. They had heard of the central aspects from their mentors but did not ask about the details because they did not adequately apprentice. As such, they did not argue about whether one lights a candle on the Sabbath eve; they debated what one may light and what one may not light. Similarly, whether or not we are obligated to recite the *Shema* morning and evening—what did they argue about? When must it be recited in the evening and when in the morning. So too with all their statements. (*Book of Tradition*, Introduction)

According to this approach, which we will term the "restorative approach," the revelation at Sinai contained all necessary halakhic knowledge. The sages did not invent anything on their own, and the authority of the Oral Torah is anchored in a tradition that transmitted the specific content of the revelation to subsequent generations. According to this conception, the purpose of the *Book of Tradition*, or any other work on the history of *halakhah*, is to trace the unbroken and reliable chain of transmitters, who ensure continuity from the *halakhah* as it was given at Sinai through the *halakhah* of the *Mishnah* and Talmud all the way until the time that the work was written.

This approach, which formed, *inter alia*, in reaction to polemics with the Karaites, who questioned the authority of the Oral Torah, had to deal with the phenomenon of controversy. If the entire corpus of *halakhah* was given, cut and dried, at Sinai, why do the sages debate what they should know by virtue of the tradition? The answer given is that controversy arose as a result of disruption in the transmission of halakhic information. For example, the answer to the question of when the *Shema* is to be recited in the evening was given at Sinai, but due to the negligence of students who did not sufficiently apprentice under their masters, the answer was forgotten and lost. As a result of this disruption and loss, the sages had to restore the lost knowledge using their intellects. This is why they argue about the sense of the expression "when you lie down," which is supposed to be the Written Torah's indication of the proper time for the evening *Shema*.

The approach of Ibn Daud and most of the *Geonim* bases the authority of the *halakhah* in its entirety on the revelation at Sinai but undercuts the credibility of the tradition in order to explain the proliferation of controversy. For that reason, Abraham Ibn Daud attempts to marginalize halakhic controversies in order to protect the tradition from being completely undermined: the sages did not disagree about the obligation to recite the *Shema* at night, only about the timeframe in which it could be done. Similarly, they never disagreed about the duty to light candles to usher in the Sabbath, only about the types of fuel that may be used, "what one may light and what one may not light." The nucleus of the tradition was, however, maintained, even if controversy attests to flaws in the chain of transmission. In this conception, the corrupted transmission process that leads to controversy only affects the margins of halakhic knowledge.

The *restorative* approach systematically presents positions on all of the components needed for a theoretical basis for *halakhah*—revelation, interpretation, truth, and authority. According to this approach, interpretation should not be viewed as a creative act of adding new knowledge to the basic *halakhah*, for ideally there is no room for human invention in a *halakhah* that is completely rooted in the revelation at Sinai. The need for interpretation is merely ex post facto, once the traditions were lost, and its sole purpose is to reconstruct and retrieve information that was given at Sinai but lost. The concept of halakhic truth derives, in this system, from its understanding of revelation and interpretation. According to the restorative approach, it is obvious that one party to a controversy is mistaken, and mistakes are evaluated on the degree to which they correspond to what was spoken at Sinai. It is possible that we will never know which of the disputants erred, since controversy originates in forgotten traditions, but it is clear that, in principle, there is one correct answer to the halakhic debate, and that answer was given at Sinai.

This conception of truth can be termed "truth as correspondence," based on the philosophical approach that defines truth in terms of correspondence to reality, the correspondence theory of truth. In this philosophical conception, any claim about the world is evaluated as true or false based on its correspondence to the facts as they are. In the restorative approach, a halakhic truth claim is evaluated on the degree to which it matches the content that God communicated at Sinai. Moreover, the approach of the *Geonim* bases authority on the temporal dimension of *halakhah*. Since halakhic knowledge is subject to forgetting and to corrupted transmission, the authority of a halakhist increases the earlier he appears in the chain of transmission. Historical proximity to the source of the tradition gives him greater credibility and mastery of the halakhic material before it was forgotten; for this reason, earlier sages are granted a preferred status to their successors.

In his introduction to the *Commentary on the Mishnah,* Maimonides challenged each element of this approach and alternatively proposed a completely different model, which can be termed the *"cumulative* approach." In his introduction to the *Commentary on the Mishnah,* he divided the halakhic corpus into three basic components:

(A) The first component includes all *halakhot* given to Moses at Sinai and transmitted by tradition. Regarding this component, Maimonides states, in opposition to the *Geonim,* that anything transmitted by tradition from Sinai was never subject to controversy: "The first category (consists of) explanations which were received from Moses, which are alluded to in Scripture, and may be derived by deductive reasoning. Here no difference of opinion exists; rather if someone states: 'Thusly I have received it', one should not question it further" (*Introduction to the Mishnah*).

(B) The second component of the halakhic corpus includes all of the commandments that the sages innovated relying on their interpretation of the written Torah. In this area of *halakhah* there is indeed controversy, for there is no given tradition: "Laws which are derived through methods of deductive reasoning, and concerning which dispute occurs . . ." (ibid.).

Controversies infiltrate *halakhah* in matters about which there is no tradition, when sages attempt to reason out answers to questions that arose during their studies:

> Matters about which he never heard anything from the prophet, from the branches—they would derive the law on these matters by inference . . . among those laws that they derived—there were matters about which there was no controversy, rather there was consensus; and others—there was controversy between two rationales, one following one inference and the other preferring

another inference. For it is the nature of this sort of rhetorical principles that while using them as guiding an inference such a thing might occur (ibid.).

(C) The third component of *halakhah* includes rabbinic decrees and amendments that are not passed on by tradition and are not derived through interpretation of the Written Torah.

Maimonides thus maintained, in opposition to the *Geonim*, that the revelation at Sinai did not include the entire contents of *halakhah*. Many halakhic matters originated in human exegetical creativity, and controversy develops whenever the human factor is introduced into the creation of *halakhah*. Controversy is not the result of a corrupt transmission process because the nucleus given to Moses at Sinai was preserved completely and without change. Controversy appears when sages attempt to create new laws by means of interpretation. Maimonides sharply attacked the geonic explanation for the emergence of controversy:

> However (there are) those who think that the laws which are disputed were also received from Moses, and who (further) believe that the controversy arose by way of errors in the transmitting them, or because of forgetfulness, and that one of the sages received the correct tradition whereas the other was mistaken in what he received, or forgot, or did not receive from his teacher all that which he was supposed to receive . . . this type of contention God knows, is an extremely depraved and ugly statement. These are words of someone without understanding, and is not meticulous about fundamentals and who blemishes the people through whom the commandments were received. All this approach is void. That which brought one to believe in this depraved conviction was a paucity of contemplation into the works of the Sages that are found in the Talmud. (Introduction to the *Mishnah*)

The geonic position is so sharply attacked because viewing controversy as the result of a corrupt transmission process undermines the validity of the tradition. According to Maimonides, on one hand, the tradition was pristinely preserved; according to him, there was no controversy about anything received from Sinai. On the other hand, he maintained that the vast majority of halakhic particulars originated as human interpretation and was not anchored in revelation. It was not dictated at Sinai when to recite the evening or morning *Shema*, for had this detail been given at Sinai, there would not be any controversy about it. The only revealed instructions pertaining to the time of the recitation of the *Shema* were the words in the verse "when you lie down and when you arise." Controversy arose when the sages attempted to determine a specific time from these expressions.

The debate between Maimonides and the *Geonim* about the phenomenon of controversy represents a basic tension between two possibilities of explaining it—a tension stemming from the complex relationship between revelation on one hand and tradition and controversy on the other. Choosing one of these options is a theologically and normatively problematic compromise. On one hand, the attempt—like that of the *Geonim*—to anchor the authenticity and authority of *halakhah*, in all its detail, in revelation undermines the credibility of tradition. On the other hand, claiming that the tradition has been preserved and not corrupted, as Maimonides maintained, precludes anchoring the entirety of *halakhah* in revelation. This model views *halakhah* as a human creation, at least whenever it is subject to controversy. The theological price of Maimonides' insistence on the intactness of the tradition was sharply formulated by the seventeenth-century Rabbi Yair Bacharach in his work *Havot Ya'ir*:

> Thus [Maimonides] built a fortified wall around the Oral Law by writing
> that it is impossible that it be forgotten . . . though any gain was outweighed
> by the loss incurred by writing that any other controversy among the sages,
> which represent the vast majority of the Oral Law and virtually the entire
> Mishnah, are not from Sinai at all. (*Havot Ya'ir*, no. 192)

R. Yair Bacharach pointed out that Maimonides defended the tradition by insisting that there was no controversy about anything received by tradition. However, he believed that the cost of this defense outweighed the benefits since it requires that one maintain that any controversial matter was not stated at Sinai. It seems, however, that this defense of the credibility of tradition is predicated on a principle that lies deeper within Maimonides' religious conception. According to him, the fact that the human component fulfills an important role in the creation of *halakhah* does not detract from its religious value. The faculty of reason has the power to create religiously significant norms as long as those norms derive from the consistent interpretation of the word of God Himself.

In opposition to the restorative approach, Maimonides presents a completely different conception of the fundamental concepts of *halakhah*. This debate is rooted in attitudes toward the scope and meaning of the revelation. The *Geonim* believed that halakhic knowledge began with a complete and total revelation that eroded over time due to corruptions in the transmission process. Maimonides maintained that halakhic knowledge did not atrophy over time, but steadily accumulated. The revelation, according to him, provided only a limited and fixed halakhic core, transmitted in its unadulterated form from generation to generation, to which were incrementally added, by means of interpretation, new normative content.

These two conceptions view the human contribution to the creation of *halakhah* in diametrically opposite manners. Interpretation, according to Maimonides, is not the retrieval of laws given at Sinai, but a creative framework through which new norms are derived from the legal material given through revelation.

Maimonides' approach also constitutes a turning point in the concept of the "truth" of each halakhic position. Maimonides thought that in cases of controversy, one party was mistaken, and controversy is the result of a diminution of capacity for legal reasoning or lack of consensus regarding hermeneutical principles. Like the *Geonim*, he bases himself on the Talmudic statement that controversy arose due to the proliferation of students of Hillel and Shammai who did not sufficiently apprentice—a statement that views controversy as a historical failure. But in contrast to the *Geonim*, the error of one disputant is not contingent upon the degree to which his opinion corresponds to what was stated at Sinai, since nothing about this matter was ever stated explicitly at Sinai.

Halakhic truth and error are determined, according to Maimonides, by the degree of consistency of the new norm with the norms given earlier, at Sinai. Maimonides replaced the earlier theory of truth with a different one, "the coherence theory," which parallels, though not completely, the philosophical theory known as the "coherence theory of truth." According to this theory, truth claims are evaluated based on whether they flow consistently and compatibly from previously derived truth claims. Since interpretation is the deduction of new norms from older norms, it is evaluated, like any other deduction, on the degree of the conclusion's coherence with the conclusions from which it derives.

Maimonides' position has ramifications for conceptions of halakhic authority as well. Since, according to Maimonides, halakhic material has been transmitted perfectly, temporal precedence offers no advantage to those who lived earlier. At any given phase of halakhic history the same revelatory information is available; the advantage of one sage over another is not by virtue of having lived first.

Thus, between these two conceptions—that of the *Geonim* and that of Maimonides—there are indeed substantive differences in their basic views on the history of *halakhah* and the role of revelation. These conceptions create real discrepancies in their understandings of some basic concepts of the philosophy of *halakhah*—revelation, interpretation, controversy, truth, and authority.

The *Book of Commandments* and the Structure of *halakhah*

This portrait of Maimonides' philosophy of *halakhah* is complemented by attitudes that emerge from his *Book of Commandments*. But before describing these attitudes, it is worthwhile to discuss Maimonides' goals for this work.

Maimonides wrote the *Book of Commandments* before *Mishneh Torah*, while writing the *Commentary on the Mishnah*, by all indications toward the end, as Maimonides wrote the first version of the commentary: "as will be explained to you in my work enumerating the commandments" (*Hullin* 1:5).

This work appears to raise basic questions about the character of Maimonides' literary activity while he was in his twenties. Unlike the *Commentary on the Mishnah*, which, as noted, is a novel and original work, books of commandments were a common genre within the geonic literature that preceded Maimonides. Geonic books of commandments sought to enumerate the 613 commandments and summarize their main features. Maimonides' enumeration was preceded by R. Shimon Qayyara's *Halakhot Gedolot*, the books of commandments composed by R. Saʿadia Gaon and R. Samuel b. Hofni Gaon, and the work of the Andalusian Rabbi Hefetz b. Matzliah. Maimonides very sharply criticized his predecessors who enumerated the commandments, be they rabbis or poets: to him, inconsistency and haphazardness were primary features of this genre. By his reckoning, the commandment enumerators uncritically followed the list espoused in *Halakhot Gedolot*: "as though thoughts were frozen by the words of that man" (*Book of Commandments*, Introduction).

However, the failures of earlier attempts do not really explain why Maimonides himself undertook his own counting of the commandments. Maimonides composed monumental works like the *Commentary on the Mishnah* and *Mishneh Torah*; intellectual challenges for their own sake do not characterize his oeuvre. Precisely tailoring his count of the commandments to the Talmudic tradition that establishes 613 as their number seems—at least prima facie—like the solution to a complex riddle; writing an entire work to solve a riddle, even if it superseded all earlier such works, is not the sort of literary task that suited Maimonides' self-image as a halakhist. So why did he expend literary and polemical efforts on such a project?

The answer is that this work plays a unique role in the organization of *Mishneh Torah*. In his introduction to the *Book of Commandments*, Maimonides explained the role of his enumeration of the commandments in his *Mishneh Torah* project:

> When I directed my thoughts toward this end, I contemplated how this work should be divided and arranged . . . it then became obvious to me that the best division would be to do it by groups of laws in lieu of the tractates of the Mishnah . . . and to that end I realized that I needed to first enumerate all of the commandments—positive and negative—in the introduction to the work, so that the divided book would still incorporate all of them, and no commandment would remain without a discussion of all its laws . . . this is all to make sure that there is nothing I do not talk about; if I include everything in the enumeration of the commandments, I will be secure [and protected] from this. (*Book of Commandments*, Introduction)

Thus, Maimonides first planned to organize *Mishneh Torah* based on the order of the *Mishnah*, but rejected that option. The *Mishnah* itself does not encompass all areas of *halakhah*. He therefore decided to enumerate all of the commandments and to structure his book around the commandments. And indeed, the commandments serve as subheadings to the different sections of *Mishneh Torah*. By itemizing the commandments and their legal details throughout the various books that comprise *Mishneh Torah*, he was assured of covering the entirety of *halakhah*. Maimonides therefore enumerated the positive and negative commandments in separate lists, and then combined this list as subheadings to the various books of *Mishneh Torah*.

This unique context for enumerating the commandments generates, for Maimonides, a different definition of commandment, a definition that is fundamentally different from the concept as espoused by his commandment-enumerating predecessors. Since the commandments are subheadings for the books of *Mishneh Torah*, and these books are themselves arranged in such a way that "no commandment would remain without a discussion of all its laws," each commandment is thus the category around which all of the associated halakhic details are organized. Enumerating all commandments in the book headings of *Mishneh Torah* and then listing all of the laws that branch out from each commandment would yield a complete account of all laws on all topics. For that reason, Maimonides did not consider every "thou shalt" and "thou shalt not" in the Torah to be a commandment. To his mind, a commandment is an organizing category of a group of laws, not merely an explicit ordinance.

In order to create a coherent framework for enumerating the commandments, one that would replace what he deemed to be the haphazard and arbitrary enumeration of the *Geonim* of the previous era, Maimonides prefaced his *Book of Commandments* with fourteen rules that conceptualized what a commandment is and defined what should and should not be counted as a commandment. Maimonides devoted most of these principles to making a distinction between a commandment that is an organizing principle and a commandment that applies under specific conditions.

A clear example of understanding a commandment as an organizing principle appears in the ninth of these fourteen rules. The Torah requires one to leave the gleanings of one's vineyards and unharvested olives for the poor. This duty appears in the Torah as two separate prohibitions: "do not glean your vineyard" (Lev. 19:10) and "when you beat your olive tree, do not go over the branches again" (Deut. 24:20). However, according to Maimonides they should not be counted as two separate prohibitions even though they are commanded separately, since they are particular instances of the same principle—there is an obligation to leave produce in the field for the poor. Not every explicit ordinance in the Torah should be enumerated as a separate commandment. A commandment is an organizing principle: "for these are not two negative commandments, but a single prohibition about a single matter, namely, that one should not take in what one has forgotten of his grain or fruits while gathering them" (*Book of Commandments*, ninth principle).

Another group of principles is devoted to formulating distinctions between true instructions and commandment-like linguistic structures that appear in the Torah, and which commandment-enumerators erroneously identified as commandments. The eighth rule provides an instructive example of the distinction between commandment verses and pseudo-commandment verses. This rule states: "negation should not be enumerated as a proscription." This is an important formulation of the problem of normative language as a whole. The Hebrew word "*lo*" does not only serve as a proscription of a particular action; it is a broader term of negation that can be imperative as well as descriptive. Thus, "**no** prophet has arisen in Israel like Moses" ("*lo qam navi od be-Yisra'el ke-Mosheh*"; Deut. 34:10) introduces no prohibition, but merely describes, and the word "*lo*" that introduces the phrase is a negation, not a proscription. In Arabic, there is separate terminology for negation and proscription—"*la*" and "*lam*"— and it is therefore easy to distinguish. In Hebrew, by contrast, only the words "*hishamer*" ("beware") and "*al*" ("do not") are exclusively proscriptive. "*Lo*," however, can be negative or proscriptive.

Maimonides claimed that his commandment-enumerating predecessors did not clearly distinguish these two senses of the word: "This matter escaped him and reached the point that he enumerated 'she shall not go free in the manner of slaves,' not realizing that this is a negation, not a proscription" (*Book of Commandments*, eighth principle). According to Maimonides, this verse is not proscriptive; it merely negates the application of a particular law to a Hebrew maidservant just as "but to the young woman you shall not do anything" (Deut. 22:26) states that a young woman who is raped is not punished; the "shall not" is not an indicator of any prohibition or proscription. The possibility of distinguishing cases where "*lo*" is used as a negation and cases where "*lo*" is used as a proscription is completely dependent on context, according to Maimonides, because there is no linguistic component that unequivocally differentiates between them: "There is no tool that makes it possible to distinguish negation from proscription aside from context; it cannot be done based on words since the Hebrew word for negation and proscription is the same— the word '*lo*'" (ibid.).

Another important principle derived from the conception of a commandment as an organizing principle relates to the Torah's all-inclusive directives. According to Maimonides, not every statement in the Torah's legal discourse adds new content. Occasionally, verses that are considered bona fide commands are not included in his enumeration since they do not add anything to existing proscriptions, merely reviewing and reinforcing them. Thus, he claims in the ninth rule: "the positive and negative commandments themselves are not counted, only the things to which the proscriptions and commandments pertain." And in the fourth rule: "It is not proper to enumerate commands that include all of the commandments." Here Maimonides establishes that there are general directives that do not contain any specific normative content, but are designed to reinforce and inspire meticulous observance of other instructions.

Thus, the *Book of Commandments* is a preparatory stage of *Mishneh Torah*. It can even be said that it was the first part of it that was committed to writing. As a preparation for *Mishneh Torah*, the work generated a new understanding of the concept "commandment/mitzva," from which Maimonides derived a different enumeration of the commandments from all those that preceded him. Maimonides attempted to build the foundations of *halakhah* through the *Book of Commandments*. His enumeration of the commandments presents the organizing categories from which *halakhah* spreads out. Maimonides decided to write the *Book of Commandments* as a detailed defense of the unexplained list of the commandments that forms the backbone of his *Mishneh Torah*; after all, there was a long tradition of enumerating the commandments, which he deviated from. The *Book of Commandments* is the only extant commentary on *Mishneh Torah* that was initiated by Maimonides himself, and it only deals with a limited portion of *Mishneh Torah*—the enumeration of commandments that appears in the introduction to each book. Maimonides attests to the centrality of his enumeration of the commandments in the organization of *Mishneh Torah*:

> When I thought about it, knowing how widespread this enumeration is among the people, I knew that if I record the correct, properly enumerated count simply and without providing evidence, the first reader would imagine that it is a mistake, and it would be evident to him that it is a mistake since it is the opposite of what so-and-so wrote. (*Book of Commandments*, Introduction)

On the Place of Revelation

In order to be considered an enumerable commandment, aside from the condition that the commandment must be an organizing command, there is another condition: that the organizing command was given to Moses at Sinai. Maimonides anchored this condition in his first two rules at the beginning of the *Book of Commandments*, which deal with the question: what does it mean that something was "given to Moses at Sinai"? These two rules sharpen another of the *Book of Commandments'* contributions:

articulating a theory of *halakhah* and an understanding of its hermeneutics. The original positions espoused by Maimonides in these two rules garnered scrupulous, critical, and angry criticism in Naḥmanides' glosses to the *Book of Commandments*. Naḥmanides' sharp and comprehensive objections gave rise to the most important medieval discussion of the philosophy of *halakhah* and its hermeneutics. A study of these rules will round out the portrait of the halakhic philosophy that emerged in the *Commentary on the Mishnah*.

In the first principle, Maimonides stated that he would not enumerate rabbinic commandments—rooted in rabbinic decree and not Sinai—in his count of the commandments. Maimonides would not have thought it necessary to defend this principle had not *Halakhot Gedolot*'s author enumerated rabbinic commandments like the recitation of *Hallel*, the lighting of Ḥanukkah candles, and the reading of the Scroll of *Esther*: "Know that it would not have been necessary to comment on this because it is so obvious. After all, the Talmud says: '613 commandments were spoken to Moses at Sinai.' How could we say that something of rabbinic origin would be part of this count?" (*Book of Commandments*, first principle).

This claim seems obvious, but within Maimonides' justification of his methods lurks a sharp and complex line of reasoning. He claims that one should not enumerate rabbinically enacted commandments because they were not given at Sinai, as he states later about the obligation to light Ḥanukkah candles: "I do not believe that someone would imagine or entertain the thought that it was stated at Sinai that if after many years of our kingdom such-and-such happens against the Greeks, we would be obligated to light Ḥanukkah candles" (ibid.). According to Maimonides, the distinction between commandments from the Torah and rabbinic obligations is not merely legal; rather, it delineates the content and limits of revelation. The distinction between biblical and rabbinic, "*de-Orayta*" and "*de-rabanan*," establishes that all halakhic norms not from the Torah were not given at Sinai.

Maimonides reinforced his position by arguing that nobody would claim that the Israelites were commanded at Sinai to establish a future holiday during the time of the Greeks and Hasmoneans. Yet, despite his confident tone that his claim has no objections, Maimonides is attempting to conceal a deep current in Talmudic literature and the history of *halakhah*: the claim that the entire corpus of *halakhah* was given at the Sinai revelation. Indeed, day-to-day halakhic practice comprises mainly rabbinic obligations, and thus the continuing impulse to connect these practices directly to God's word at Sinai is natural and understandable; fulfillment of *halakhah* was seen as worshipping God by realizing His will, and if this will is the product of hundreds of human rulings, with no direct connection to the revelation, what have the Rabbis accomplished with all of their enactments?

According to the alternative approach, based on the claim that even the future insights of students were stated to Moses at Sinai, the distinction between biblical and rabbinic does not set boundaries on the revelation, but merely makes internal legal differentiations. The revelation itself includes the entire corpus of *halakhah*, from the Ten Commandments to the inferences and enactments of the Rabbis. For this reason, an expression like "613 commandments were spoken to Moses at Sinai" does not require a halakhist like the author of *Halakhot Gedolot* to distinguish between biblical obligations and rabbinic decrees. One might say that the opposite is the case: his basic impulse is to blur the differences between rabbinic enactments and biblical duties so as to include the entire halakhic corpus within the revelation.

Maimonides' major move is to identify the content transmitted at Sinai with the biblical/*de-Orayta* legal category while distancing the larger layer of rabbinic law from the Sinai revelation. Maimonides knew that in order to isolate Moses' authority from the authority of the sages he must challenge the long-standing Talmudic tradition of incorporating all layers of the *halakhah*, including rabbinic enactments, in the revelation. In order to marginalize this tradition, Maimonides, further on in the first rule at the beginning of the *Book of Commandments*, makes a brilliant move. According to Maimonides, rabbinic decrees are anchored in the revelation at Sinai through the mediation of a prohibition: "you shall not deviate from what they tell you" (Deut. 17:11). This obligation, which is explicit in the Torah and mandates obedience to the rabbinical court, forms the narrow bridge that connects the mammoth Talmudic corpus to revelation:

> Every performance that the sages commanded and everything they proscribed, Moses commanded us to uphold, as he said: "According to the law that they shall instruct you and the judgment they shall tell you, you shall do." And he cautioned us against violating their pronouncements about anything they enact or infer, saying: "you shall not deviate from what they tell you." (*Book of Commandments*, first principle)

The specific contents of rabbinic decrees were not mentioned or even alluded to at Sinai. However, through the mediation of the duty to obey the sages, it can be said that even according to Maimonides, whatever the sages commanded was already given at Sinai.

Later on in the first rule, Maimonides cites a single source that can be interpreted to mean that the entire corpus of *halakhah* was given at Sinai. Maimonides reinterprets this source, by means of the mediation of the prohibition against deviating from the sages, as a second-order commandment:

> The Talmud says in Tractate *Shevu'ot*: "This implies only commandments given at Mount Sinai. What is the source for including even commandments that will be invented in the future, such as reading the Scroll [of Esther]? It is taught by the verse 'they upheld and accepted'—they upheld what they had already accepted." That is, they had accepted any commandment that the prophets and sages would enact in the future. (ibid.)

It is possible to understand the Talmudic passage cited by Maimonides as saying that the ordinance of reading the Scroll of Esther was also stated at Sinai, but only came into effect much later. Maimonides rejects the notion that revelation can prefigure a commandment relating to a future event, attaching his own interpretation to this Talmudic passage: "they shall believe in any commandment that the prophets and sages would enact in the future." The duty to read the Scroll of Esther was accepted at Sinai only in the sense that it is part of the general obligation of all Israel to obey whatever the prophets and sages would enact in the future—like signing a blank check. The principle of "you shall not deviate" as a mediating norm thus serves to anchor the authority of the sages' halakhic creativity. Similarly, Maimonides used it to reinterpret Talmudic sources, claiming that all of the principles and details of *halakhah* were given at Sinai.

Portraying the Sinai revelation as an all-embracing event—an attitude that Maimonides rejects, as we have seen—is but one expression of the trend to incorporate all halakhic life under the rubric of revelation. Another expression of this tendency, which also plays a major role in the history of *halakhah* and Jewish thought, is to view the revelation as an ongoing event, of which Sinai is just the beginning. Revelation continues from Moses to the prophets to the sages, who, if they do not prophesy, they at least possess an echo of prophecy through which *halakhah* receives divine inspiration. This approach is also implicit in *Halakhot Gedolot*, which enumerates clothing the naked as a separate commandment based on the verse in Isaiah (58:7), "when you see the naked, you will clothe him." Maimonides attacks *Halakhot Gedolot* for this as well, as he limits the revelatory authority not only of the sages, but also of the prophets. According to him, only Moses was given the authority to legislate by means of prophecy. The role of subsequent prophets is to preserve Moses' Torah, not to create an alternative or add to the present Torah.

The determination that rabbinic enactments have nothing to do with revelation or with the giving of the Torah is much easier to substantiate than claims about the status of prophecy after Moses. After all, regarding these questions about the status of rabbinic enactments, Maimonides relies on a discussion in the Talmudic Tractate *Shabbat*. There, the Talmud maintains that when reciting the benediction over Ḥanukkah candles, one still uses the standard formula of "Who has sanctified us with His commandments **and commanded us** (*ve-tzivanu*) . . ." because this duty is rooted in the commandment of "you shall not deviate."

In contrast, the duty to read the Scroll of Esther, about which Maimonides conflicts with *Halakhot Gedolot*, is considered a rabbinic law even though the scroll itself was written with Divine inspiration, and thus the holiday of Purim was apparently instituted by virtue of revelation. This holiday is an interesting case, because it breaks the otherwise complete overlap between biblical commandments and the revelation. Maimonides himself addresses this problem in the first rule:

> I have already explained that anything enacted by the post-Mosaic prophets is also rabbinic. Indeed, the [sages] explicitly stated: "when Solomon enacted *eruvin* and ablutions, a Divine echo issued forth and said: 'Be wise, My son, and make My heart glad . . . .'" And elsewhere it is explained that *eruvin* are called rabbinic laws, and ablutions are "the words of the scribes." Thus, it has been demonstrated: anything enacted after Moses is called "rabbinic." I have explained this to you so you do not think that reading the Scroll of Esther, since it was a prophetic enactment, is considered biblical law; after all, *eruvin*, though enacted by King Solomon and his court, are considered rabbinic law. (*Book of Commandments*, first principle)

Maimonides uses a Talmudic statement attributing the enactments of *eruvin* and hand-washing—rabbinic enactments—to King Solomon to exemplify his sweeping determination that anything from the prophets is considered rabbinic law. By doing so, he precludes a possible distinction between what are traditionally known as enactments by the prophets, which would be considered rabbinic law, and matters explicitly spelled out in prophetic books written under the Divine spirit. Maimonides wants his readers to conclude from these obvious cases that **whenever** the prophets legislate or enact, they function as sages. Therefore, any new halakhic content appearing in prophetic books, including the duty to observe Purim, was enacted not by virtue of revelation, but by virtue of the prophets' status as sages. Purim was thus the enactment of Mordecai and his court, just as *eruvin* and hand-washing were the enactments of King Solomon and his court.

Thus, in the first principle in the introduction to the *Book of Commandments*, Maimonides isolates the revelation to Moses from the rest of the halakhic system by means of two moves: the first, by taking a narrow view of what is considered "given at Sinai," which pushes rabbinic enactments outside the rubric of the Sinai revelation. The second, by giving the revelations to Moses exclusive status as revelations with legislative power, thereby rejecting the possibility of continuous revelation of *halakhah* and differentiating absolutely between Moses and all other prophets. These two centers of authority—the sages and the prophets—both draw their authority, according to Maimonides, from a second-order biblical obligation; rabbinic authority is derived from the prohibition "you shall not deviate," and the duty to obey the prophets from the verse "a prophet from your midst, of your brothers . . . you shall listen to him" (Deut. 18:15). Halakhic obligations that appear in prophetic books or are the result of rabbinic enactments were not included in the Sinai revelation, but their binding force derives from it directly. These two maneuvers entail, as noted, rejecting and reinterpreting the Talmudic traditions that view the revelation as an all-embracing normative event.

Revelation and Interpretation

The second principle in Maimonides' introduction to the *Book of Commandments* defines what was given at Sinai. In it, Maimonides states: "Not everything derived using the thirteen hermeneutic principles for interpreting the Torah, or by extension, is worthy of being enumerated." This continues the goals of the first rule, namely, isolating the status of Moses' revelation vis-à-vis the rest of the halakhic corpus as its exclusive, stable, and immutable core. However, the claims he makes in the second rule go much further both in terms of its intellectual boldness and in terms of its relationship with Talmudic literature.

By means of this principle, Maimonides attempts to distance not only prophecies and rabbinic enactments from the revelation to Moses, but also the Torah as it is from the rabbinic interpretation thereof. Maimonides stated that what is derived using the thirteen hermeneutic principles of the Oral Torah is not worthy of being enumerated. In his opinion, laws that the sages derived using these methods of interpretation do not have the status of a commandment stated to Moses at Sinai, and are not included in his count of the commandments. Such laws are considered rabbinic commandments even though they are derived through interpretation of biblical verses. The status of *"de-Orayta"* is accorded only to interpretations transmitted by Moses, not to laws produced by the sages.

According to Maimonides, the distinction between interpretations given to Moses at Sinai and those that the sages created through their intellectual endeavors rests upon the testimony of the sages themselves. Where the sages state explicitly that their interpretation is of "the corpus of Torah" or *de-Orayta*, it indicates that they received it as a tradition from Moses, and where they did not explicitly attest to this, the resulting law has rabbinical status:

> Since this is the case, it cannot be said of everything that the sages derived using one of the thirteen hermeneutical principles that it was said to Moses at Sinai; yet it also cannot be said that everything found in the Talmud that is based on one of the thirteen principles is rabbinic, for it is possible that it represents a received interpretation. The way to distinguish is thus: anything that is not made explicit in the Torah but which is derived in the Talmud from one of the thirteen principles—if the [sages] explicitly stated that this is part of the corpus of Torah or that it is *de-Orayta*, then it is worthy of being enumerated, for the bearers of the tradition have said it is *de-Orayta*; if they have not explained or stated thus explicitly, then it is rabbinic. (*Book of Commandments*, second principle)

Aside from the difference between these two types of *halakhah*—those received by tradition and those created via interpretation—in terms of legal status, Maimonides reintroduces another distinction between them, the distinction we discussed earlier that he raised in his introduction to the *Commentary on the Mishnah*. Legal interpretations received from Sinai are not subject to controversy. Controversies can arise about laws derived from the thirteen hermeneutical principles. The fact that a particular interpretation is not subject to dispute does not give it the status of biblical law unless it is accompanied by testimony that it was transmitted; however, lack of controversy is a necessary condition for anything received from Moses. It thus emerges from Maimonides' second rule that in order for a commandment to be enumerated and be considered a biblical obligation, it must have been received from Sinai and undisputed. Interpretations that are not attested by tradition are rabbinic.

On closer scrutiny, this structuring of *halakhah* indicates that from among the veritable sea of interpretations and controversies in the Talmud, Maimonides attempted to isolate a layer of received, indisputable laws. He claims that only this layer has *de-Orayta* status and only it was given to Moses at Sinai. Maimonides' attempt to formulate this nucleus of the halakhic corpus imposes another distinction on the content of the Talmud: the distinction between received interpretations and interpretations that were not received. The Talmud distinguishes between genuine interpretation and a loose proof-text— "*asmakhta*." In specific contexts, an interpretation is introduced only to provide textual support for a rabbinic enactment or decree; in such cases, called *asmakhta*, the presence of biblical interpretation does not attest to the biblical origin of a law. Yet the distinction between received interpretations and interpretations that were not received, and the claim that this distinction determines whether a *halakhah* is *de-Orayta* or not, is not found in the Talmud. In the Talmud, a norm that is derived via interpretation based on one of the thirteen hermeneutical principles is assumed to have the status of *de-Orayta*, even if it was not transmitted from Sinai. If, as it occasionally happens in the Talmud, such an interpretation does not grant *de-Orayta* status to the *halakhah*, it must mean that this interpretation is an *asmakhta* and not a genuine interpretation.

Maimonides' determination that laws based on the thirteen hermeneutical principles have rabbinic status registered shock among the halakhists of his day. Maimonides was asked about this matter by Pinḥas the Judge (*Responsa Rambam*, No. 355), and he reiterated the principle that a law derived by methods of interpretation and analogy is not *de-Orayta* unless explicitly stated. In the responsum, he referred Pinḥas to the rules at the beginning of the *Book of Commandments* to gain a better understanding of his position.

Maimonides' approach to rabbinic interpretation instigated one of the harshest criticisms leveled by Naḥmanides in his glosses to the *Book of Commandments*. At the end of a prolonged objection to this rule, Naḥmanides wrote:

> I am aware that many other Talmudic passages contradict the master's [Maimonides's] words. For the content of the master's work is enjoyable and entirely delightful—with the exception of this rule, which uproots large mountains of Talmud and demolishes fortified walls of Gemara; for students of the Talmud, this matter is evil and bitter. Let it drown and not be spoken.
> (*Book of Commandments with the Glosses of Naḥmanides*, second principle)

According to Naḥmanides, laws derived using the thirteen hermeneutical principles have *de-Orayta* status in Talmudic literature. He reiterates this tenet time and again: "We have not found such an opinion among the sages, for whom the hermeneutical principles were like matters stated explicitly in the Torah, though they may independently derive these matters" (ibid.); and later: "for these hermeneutical principles are like matters stated explicitly in the Torah."

Naḥmanides reinforced his claim with vast amounts of evidence from the Talmud and pointed out Maimonides' self-contradictions resulting from the discrepancy between the principle he laid out in the second rule and his halakhic rulings based on Talmudic sources. His string of proofs led *Naḥmanides* to reverse Maimonides' rule: "Therefore we should say on the contrary, that everything derived in the Talmud by any of the thirteen hermeneutical principles is *de-Orayta* unless they say is it an *asmakhta*" (ibid., p. 34). Anywhere the Talmud derives a *halakhah* exegetically, the presumption is that it is *de-Orayta*, unless explicitly stated that it is an *asmakhta*.

In addition to the incompatibility of Maimonides' position with Talmudic sources, Naḥmanides raises an internal conceptual problem with Maimonides' understanding of interpretation:

> "Such knowledge is beyond me. It is lofty; I cannot attain it" (Ps. 139:6). For if we say that the hermeneutical principles were not received from Sinai, we were not commanded to interpret and explain the Torah with them. If so, they are not true, and truth lies in the straightforward meaning of the verse, not the interpreted meaning, as mentioned in the [sages'] dictum, that a verse does not deviate from its straightforward meaning. We will thus have cut off the root of our traditional acceptance of the thirteen hermeneu-

tical principles as well as most of the Talmud, which is founded upon them. Yet [Maimonides] reiterates that this does not mean that they are not true. But if they are indeed true, why distinguish between where the [sages] mention this explicitly and where they say nothing? For if we believe that once something is not written [straightforwardly] in the Torah it is not included in the commandments, even those matters mentioned in the Talmud as being *de-Orayta* which were derived by extension or analogy were not written. (ibid.)

Nahmanides formulated the conceptual problem as a willy-nilly argument: if Maimonides believes that rabbinic interpretation is not real interpretation, and is therefore not considered actual words of Torah, he risks undermining the authority of *halakhah* as a whole. And if rabbinic interpretations are true and proper, why would they not have the status of biblically derived interpretations? Nahmanides noted that Maimonides himself claimed that he did not base his position on the unreliability of rabbinic interpretation or maintain that they are all merely *asmakhtas*: "Lest you think that we are precluded from enumerating them because they are uncertain, and the law derived using that principle is perhaps correct and perhaps not—this is not the reason" (*Book of Commandments*, p. 13).

If this is Maimonides' understanding, the following conceptual question can then be asked: how can one simultaneously consider an interpretation to be correct and yet claim that it does not have the legal status of the text it interprets? Moreover, Nahmanides' glosses demonstrate the tremendous gap between Maimonides' position and the Talmud's discussion. Maimonides was well aware of these problems and the internal contradictions stemming from the constraints imposed by his second rule. Why, then, did he see this as fundamental to his method? Alternatively: why did he construct his approach to *halakhah* in such a way that large portions of it might stand in opposition to the categories he imposed on the material? And finally, what exegetical model does Maimonides suggest in order to get out of the conceptual problem raised by Nahmanides?

Interpretation in *halakhah*: Between Explanatory Principles and Deductive Principles

Maimonides' metaphor for interpretation, the key to understanding his exegetical model, appears in the second rule at the beginning of the *Book of Commandments.* Interpretations are: "branches from the roots given to Moses explicitly, namely, the 613 commandments." Using the "branches" metaphor, Maimonides addresses the conceptual problem at the base of his exegetical model. To clarify this analogy of interpretation and text to branch and root, it is worthwhile to first distinguish between two types of interpretation: the first type, interpretation that seeks to clarify or disclose the meaning of the text's terms, and the principles that guide it are principles of discovery and definition. The second type does not explain the text, but draws additional conclusions from it.

The interpretive principles of the second type are more akin to deductive principles. For example, let us assume there is a law that says "vehicles shall not enter a public park." One who interprets this may face a problem of definition: what is the scope of the term "vehicle"? Does it include motorcycles, motorbikes, and bicycles? Similar questions abound. If an interpreter claims that the law forbids the entry of motorbikes, he is attempting to clarify one of the law's terms—"vehicle." A different type of legal interpretation is generated if an interpreter wants to deduce from this law a different prohibition: "no vehicles allowed in a schoolyard." In such a case, unlike in the first case, it is clear to the interpreter that the expression "public park" does not include schoolyards. The interpreter is not asking about the scope of the term "public park" in the manner in which he was asking the first case. Rather, he is trying to deduce a new prohibition from this law, by means of analogy or *a fortiori* argument. That is, if the legislator forbade entry of vehicles into public parks out of concern for children's security, *a fortiori* their entry into schoolyards should be prohibited. This interpreter has certain principles by means of which he attempts to derive prohibitions in addition to the existing ones; he is not trying to clarify the terms of the law and what they include, but whether a new prohibition can be deduced from it. Like this distinction between two types of interpretation, interpretive principles can also fulfill two different roles: the first—principles of discovery or definition, and the other—deductive principles.

Maimonides maintained that the "thirteen principles by which the Torah is interpreted" are deductive principles, through which it is possible to derive additional laws to those given to Moses at Sinai. The laws given to Moses at Sinai are clear, whether by virtue of their straightforward meaning or explanations transmitted through the generations. The process of interpreting by means of the thirteen principles does not explain these laws or interpret their terms, but derives new laws from the existing ones.

The thirteen hermeneutic principles are deductive principles, which generate new claims from the laws given to Moses at Sinai. In these interpretations, we do not explain the prior laws—the roots—from which the conclusion flows, for these laws are well known, clear, and not subject to controversy. Interpretation derives the branches that emerge from these roots, by means of accepted deductive principles—the thirteen principles by which the Torah is interpreted.

This equation of interpretation with deduction recurs everywhere Maimonides speaks about interpretation by means of the thirteen principles. In those cases he uses the verb "to derive/ take out" in describing what was derived by means of the thirteen principles, instead of the expressions "to interpret," "to explain," or "to clarify." He writes thus in his introduction to the *Commentary on the Mishnah*: "The laws derived by inference"; "the matters that we can derive through 'general and particular' (*'prat u-klal'*) and the other thirteen principles"; and many others. In addition, the analogy of commandments given to Moses with roots from which branches can be derived by interpretation recurs again and again in the introduction to the *Commentary on the Mishnah*. Maimonides calls the nucleus that appears in the Torah and about which there is no controversy "the roots/ principles" (*uṣūl*). The comparison to roots recurs in several places in the *Commentary on the Mishnah*: "The people of each generation make the statements of their predecessors into roots, from which they derive offshoots. There is no controversy about accepted roots" (Introduction to the *Mishnah*). Maimonides describes the error of those who believe there can be controversy about received laws as follows: "They have not differentiated received roots from derived offshoots" (ibid.); "for two people, if they are equal in wisdom, analysis, and knowledge of the roots from which one may derive offshoots, whatever they derive by deduction will not be subject to controversy" (ibid.). The phrasing of roots and branches with the verb "derive" represents interpretation using the thirteen principles as a process of deducing new laws from old ones using deductive principles, namely, the thirteen principles.

This characterization of the thirteen hermeneutical principles as principles guiding deduction finds expression in *Mishneh Torah* as well, in the Laws of Torah Study (1:11):

and one third to understanding and conceptualizing the end of a matter from its beginning, inferring one thing from another and comparing one thing to another; he will understand the hermeneutic principles of the Torah until he knows what the roots of those principles are and how he can derive what is forbidden and permitted and the like from the things he learned from the oral tradition. This matter is called "Talmud."

In his introduction to the *Commentary on the Mishnah*, Maimonides uses clearly technical terminology to characterize the thirteen principles:

> Matters about which he never heard anything from the prophet, from the branches—they would derive the law on these matters by inference . . . among those laws that they derived—there were matters about which there was no controversy, rather there was consensus; and others—there was controversy between two rationales, one following one inference and the other preferring another inference. For it is the nature of this sort of rhetorical principles that while using them as guiding an inference such a thing might occur. (ibid.)

In this brief description of the use of the thirteen principles, Maimonides' main metaphors to the act of interpretation recur. He uses the branches metaphor and keeps repeating the verb "to derive." But the true novelty of this paragraph lies in the technical terminology that Maimonides uses for the thirteen principles—"rhetorical principles" (*qiyas*)." Maimonides does not merely describe similarities that correspond to analogy when explaining the thirteen principles; he defines them with technical terminology—principles of deduction.

Moreover, it is important to emphasize that the term Maimonides uses, "*hekesh*" in Hebrew and "*qiyas*" in Arabic, has a long tradition within Islamic law. In this tradition, *qiyas* is the technique by which the given tradition is expanded and applied to problems not explicitly addressed; *qiyas* is the means of dealing with new questions that would not have answers if not for syllogistic expansion. As such, it does not reveal the meaning of the given tradition; rather, it serves as a vehicle for its expansion. Maimonides refers to the thirteen principles with the expression "the principles of deduction" the clearly technical concept of deduction and expansion within the Muslim legal tradition. By integrating this concept with its special meaning, Maimonides reinforces the sense that the thirteen principles are deductive principles, not principles of discovery.

This understanding, that interpretation is based on principles of deduction and not on principles of discovery, allows us to overcome our conceptual problem: how can the correct interpretation of a text, attained through the proper process, be considered a correct interpretation without being considered part of the text itself? The image of branches and roots is very effective for creating distance between the interpretation and the text. If interpretation would define the "roots," and exegetical principles would determine how to discover their meaning, it would be difficult to say about an explanation or determination that they constitute an interpretation of the text and at the same time continue claiming that they are not the text itself. If interpretation clarifies the terminology of the text, what would the text be by itself, without interpretation?

Returning to the example of the law, it would be problematic to claim that "motorbike" is an accurate interpretation of the term "vehicle" and yet still claim that this interpretation is not part of the text. In contrast, regarding the additional prohibition, "no vehicles allowed in a schoolyard" (a prohibition about which we claimed that it is not a clarification of "public park" but the deduction of a new rule from the existing one), there is room to argue that it is true but not part of the text. Maimonides' view that interpretation is by principles of deduction, its goal is to preserve the distance between the interpretation and the text without undermining the credibility of the interpretation.

Maimonides believed that there is no error regarding anything pertaining to the commandments that are from the Torah. According to him, there is complete consensus and lack of controversy regarding the *de-Orayta* core, and consequently it cannot be claimed that anyone has erred about it. When Maimonides addresses the phenomenon of controversy, he again emphasizes that the root principles are indisputable; controversy begins at the stage where additional laws are deduced from consensual roots. In this model of deduction, two opposing conclusions can be derived from the same premises, without claiming that one of the disputants does not understand the precedents as the other does, or that one of them erred regarding the premises themselves. However, it is possible that one of them errs in his deduction (indeed, I believe that Maimonides thought there are correct deductions and incorrect deductions), yet the debate is not about the premises, but what can be derived from them. In the case of a strict logical deduction, debate about the conclusion signifies a lack of understanding or lack of agreement about premises. In contrast, with regard to the exegetical deductions that Maimonides deals with, it is possible to be in a situation where the premises are understood and the controversy is about what can be derived from them. Such a controversy stems from the fact that the semantics of the principles of differentiation is not naturally precise.

Here is the place to address the nature of the exegetical deduction that Maimonides describes, and its relationship to logical deduction. Let us return to the example of the law. Let us further presume that someone has indeed inferred that if bringing a vehicle into a public park is forbidden, *a fortiori* it is forbidden to bring one into a schoolyard. Additionally, let us presume that we find someone who disagrees, maintaining that this *a fortiori* reasoning is invalid, because there is a difference between a school and a public park. According to this disputant, in the school case, unlike the case of a public park, we have an interest in parents entering the schoolyard with their vehicles. In this controversy, neither party disagrees as to the precedent, or the prohibition from which the additional prohibition is derived; they all agree that vehicles may not enter public parks. The controversy is whether the two cases are analogous, that is, whether a schoolyard is similar to a public park vis-à-vis the prohibition of bringing in a vehicle.

The semantics of deductive principles like *a fortiori* (*kal va-ḥomer*) and lexical analogy (*gezeira shava*) cannot be formulated in absolute terms. There is always liable to be some further question: in the case of lexical analogy, what similarity of content does the similarity of language signify? In the case of *kal va-homer*, is what we deem the weaker or stronger premise indeed so? In these and similar types of deduction, one can assume that the conclusions are disputed without establishing that each party actually uses a different premise. Maimonides can thus say that in the deductive interpretation, there is no controversy about the premises, only about the laws derived from them. This is why Maimonides called these analogies "rhetorical principles," emphasizing that these principles of deduction are not of a purely logical character.

This portrayal of interpretation, which emerges from the *Commentary on the Mishnah* and the *Book of Commandments*, reveals the conception of *halakhah* that Maimonides was aiming for. According to him, there is a core of content about which there is no controversy, which bears a special status, and from which the *halakhah* branches out. Its status stems from its direct connection to Moses. Interpretation built upon this core is not a part thereof, because it does not define it; the exegete does not alter or change the concepts and premises, rather he derives new laws from them.

There are disputes that might emerge at these deductions, and this is the stage at which controversy enters into the realm of *halakhah*. The core itself is impervious to controversy and is not defined by exegetes.

According to this claim, the core needs no interpretation; it is clear, whether by virtue of a plain reading or by means of tradition. Since these interpretations do not define the premises, they are not part of the text, but stem from them like branches that snake out of the roots. The exclusive status of Moses is thus preserved within this model, whether because only his words have the legal status of *de-Orayta* or because his words are the foundation from which everything else branches out, though his words are not themselves disputable.

Maimonides' conception of interpretation is particularly interesting. At first glance, interpretation refers to the exegete's attempt to participate in the text's authority, as he sees his words as an interpretation that strives to speak with the force of the authoritative text and not with his own force. According to Maimonides, no man can share Moses' authority, even by way of interpreting his text. The comparison of interpretation to branches creates distance and sets up an authority structure between the deductions of the exegete and the roots themselves: the words of Moses have the status of *de-Orayta*; the laws deduced from them have the status of rabbinic law.

Halakhah and Prophecy

The special status of Moses in Maimonides' conception of *halakhah* is apparent in another component of his philosophy of *halakhah*: the relationship between *halakhah* and prophecy. Several Talmudic discussions establish that "it is not in heaven," that once the Torah was given to Moses, no prophet has license to add to or interpret the commandments through prophetic means. The Torah was transmitted by sages, who interpret it by virtue of received traditions or their faculties of reason. This principle had exceptions in the Talmud itself, and various halakhists drew support from divine disclosures in determining the *halakhah*. Thus, for example, there is a collection of responsa from R. Jacob of Marvege entitled *Responsa from Heaven* (*She'elot u-Teshuvot min ha-Shamayim*). Among all of the medieval halakhists, Maimonides differentiates most unequivocally between *halakhah* and prophecy. Moreover, he grants this differentiation new conceptual meaning, which pertains to his conception of prophetic authority.

In his introduction to the *Commentary on the Mishnah*, Maimonides states that prophecy is completely ineffective for interpreting the Torah: "Know that prophecy is not effective in the study and interpretation of the Torah and in deriving branches via the thirteen hermeneutical principles; rather, what [prophets] Joshua and Phineas did in the realms of analysis and analogy is the same as what [Talmudic sages] Ravina and R. Ashi did" (Introduction to the *Commentary of the Mishnah*). A prophet who pretentiously makes laws or even decides controversies among the sages by means of prophecy attests that he is a false prophet and worthy of death by strangulation: "But if a prophet claims that God dictated to him a ruling regarding a certain commandment, or that so-and-so's analogy is correct—that prophet shall be put to death because he is a false prophet, as we have established; there is no Torah subsequent to the first agent [namely, Moses]— no addition or subtraction—for 'it is not in heaven'" (ibid.). The principle of "it is not in heaven" does not only set limits on prophetic intervention in the halakhic process; it also determines whether his prophecy is true or false. Thus, a prophet who prophesies about halakhic matters has no standing, and beyond that he is a false prophet deserving of the death penalty.

This understanding is deepened in *Mishneh Torah*, the Laws of the Foundations of the Torah. According to Maimonides, prophetic authority is not based on miracle-working, which is easily subjected to fraud. The prophet's personality and standing as a human being are what give him his credibility:

> Not everyone who performs signs or wonders is believed to be a prophet. Rather, if a person who was previously known to be fit for prophecy beforehand by his wisdom and actions, which surpass those of all his contemporaries, then observes the methods, sanctity, and asceticism of prophecy, and afterwards performs a sign or wonder and states that he was sent by God— there is a commandment to listen to him, as it states (Deut. 18:15): "Listen to him." (Laws of the Foundations of the Torah, 7:7)

Since miracles are a particularly unstable basis for demonstrating the credibility of revelation, even the prophecy of Moses itself does not draw its support from the miracles he performed, as great as the splitting of the sea and the giving of manna from heaven were:

> The Israelites did not believe in Moses because of the wonders that he performed. Whenever anyone's belief is based on wonders, his heart has short-

comings, for it is possible to perform a wonder through magic or sorcery. Rather, all the wonders performed by Moses in the desert were performed by necessity, not to demonstrate prophecy. It was necessary to drown the Egyptians, so he split the sea and sank them in it. We needed food, so he provided us with manna. (ibid. 8:1)

In this law, Maimonides rejects a basic attitude about the source of the religious worldview. He rejects the approach that man stands before God whenever the causal order of the world is broken. For example, many believers might often say: "according to natural causality, a particular event should have occurred. But instead a miracle happened, attesting to the intervention of a higher power." Maimonides thought that the basis of religious experience is not expressed in deviation from the natural order, but in the wisdom implicit in the natural order itself. He therefore challenges the view that miracles and exceptions are the primary foundation of the religious attitude. The great miracles performed by Moses stemmed exclusively from the immediate needs of the Israelites; they served no real role in the lives of believers. Thus, Maimonides emptied great historical events like the spectacular Exodus from Egypt of their significance as the basis of religious faith.

As for the metaphysical possibility of miracles as such, Maimonides presents a complex position which might have changed through time, as Zvi Langernman and Charles Manekin suggested. In his *Commentary to the Mishnah* he stated that miraculous events were implanted in nature itself to occur at specific times, and as such the extraordinary event doesn't represent a volitional intervention of God in the causal inertia of nature:

This occasioned the sages to say that all miracles which deviate from the natural course of events, whether they already occurred or, according to promise, are to take place in the future, were foreordained by the divine will during the six days of creation, nature being then so constituted that those miracles which were to happen really did afterward take place. Then, when such an occurrence happens at its proper time, it may have been regarded as an absolute innovation, whereas in reality it was not. (*Eight Chapters*, p. 383)

In later formulations in the *Guide* and his *Letter on Resurrection*, which we will discuss later in the book, Maimonides seems to allow for a direct volitional interference of God in the causal chain of nature. Yet, what is common to all the formulations on the nature and possibility of miracles, as it is apparent from his stance concerning prophecy, that miracles do not play any important role in shaping and forming genuine religious conviction and stance.

The prophecy of Moses was not based on the Exodus, but on the public nature of the giving of the Torah at the Sinai theophany:

> What is the source of their belief in him? The theophany at Mount Sinai, where our eyes saw, and not a stranger's; our ears heard, and not another's . . . Thus, those to whom he was sent bear witness to the truth of his prophecy; it was not necessary to perform a wonder for them, for he and they were like two witnesses who observed the same event together. (ibid. 8:1–2)

The people's participation in Moses' prophecy itself freed him from reliance on the wonders and miracles that ostensibly would reinforce his prophecy. Since a prophet cannot be believed by virtue of his miracle-working, the duty to obey the words of the prophets stems from the Torah's commandment to listen to them. When a prophet appears before us, he does not claim anything by virtue of the revelation itself, for we have no way of knowing whether God indeed appeared to him like He appeared at Mount Sinai. The duty to obey the prophet is based on the Torah. Therefore, a prophet who seeks to alter or undermine the Torah of Moses essentially undermines the duty to obey him, for this duty is itself derived from the Torah of Moses:

> Thus, we do not believe any prophet who arises after Moses because of the wonder [he performs] alone . . . rather, because of the commandment that we were instructed by Moses when he said: "If he performs a wonder, listen to him." Therefore, if a prophet arises and performs great signs and wonders, and wishes to deny the prophecy of Moses, we do not listen to him . . . since we only believe the wonders because of the commandments issued by Moses, how can we accept this wonder, which comes to deny Moses's prophecy that we saw and heard? (ibid. 8:2–3)

In the Laws of the Foundations of the Torah, a novel explanation emerges for the idea that prophecy was pushed out of the field of *halakhah* after the giving of the Torah. A prophet may not alter or add to the *halakhah*, not only because of some secondary rules that limit his power, but because of a limitation that derives from the very conception of his authority. The authority of post-Mosaic prophets stems from Moses' Torah itself, and therefore any attempt on their part to undermine its status eradicates the very basis of their authority. It is like a judge who determines in court that the law is mistaken, and therefore his ruling is against the law. Such a determination would automatically undermine the authority of the judge, since the court derives its authority from the fact that the law determined it. Moses is thus the exclusive legislator through prophecy because the revelation to Moses was public and not based on miracles, which can always be doubted. A post-Mosaic prophet does not draw his authority from the revelation upon which Moses' authority is based; the duty to obey him stems from the Torah of Moses, from whence his authority derives.

In this innovative construction Maimonides was trying to constrain the potential antinomian power of prophetic authority. A prophet appeals to direct revelation the same source of authority that the law itself rests upon. If he can establish through miracles an independent access to revelation, he might use it in order to undermine the law which bases itself on revelation. Maimonides, by establishing the uniqueness of the revelation at Sinai, claims that a prophet has no direct access to revelation as an independent source of his authoritative voice. His power is always mediated through the commandment given at Sinai, which is the only legal moment that can be based directly on revelation.

The principle that the prophet plays no role in innovating or interpreting *halakhah* also defines the role of the prophet: to encourage observance of the Torah received by Moses. Post-Mosaic prophets ostensibly turned to the same source of authority that the Torah itself is based on—revelation. Indeed, prophets are liable to use the Torah's very source of authority in order to undermine it. Turning to revelation to undermine a religion that is itself based on revelation is not merely a theoretical possibility—Islam based its authority on a claim of revelation similar to that of the Torah itself.

Maimonides derives the authority of every post-Mosaic prophet from the Torah itself, and thereby tried to protect the status of the Torah. It is therefore no wonder that formulations similar to those we have seen from the introduction to the *Commentary on the Mishnah* and the Laws of the Foundations of the Torah also appear in the *Epistle to Yemen*, in which Maimonides dealt with the challenge posed by Islam. The role of post-Mosaic prophets was not to add or derogate from the Torah, but to encourage its observance:

If so, why does the Torah state: "I will appoint a prophet from among their brethren like you, and I will place My word in his mouth and he will say to you whatever I command him" (Deut. 18:18)? He is not coming to establish a religion, but to command regarding the words of the Torah and warn the people against its transgression. (Laws of the Foundations of the Torah, 9:2)

Let us return to the structure of the *halakhah* according to Maimonides. *Halakhah* has a central core, connected to Moses, about which there is no controversy. Only this core has *de-Orayta* status, because it was stated to Moses explicitly. Post-Mosaic prophets had no authority or power to add to or derogate from this core, because their authority was entirely derived by power of an instruction found in the Torah of Moses. This is true not only of prophets, but of sages as well. The thirteen principles for interpreting the Torah are rules for deducing new laws that are subject to controversy. These laws are said to be rabbinic even if they are not derived by *asmakhta*.

The existence of this core is the major innovation of Maimonides' structuring of *halakhah*, and the shape he gives it leads to the view that the thirteen principles are principles of deduction, not principles of definition. By means of this view of the thirteen principles, Maimonides distinguishes, in the second rule in the introduction to the *Book of Commandments*, between the text and its interpretation. Maimonides is attempting to block the pretensions of the exegetical endeavor by claiming that interpretation is merely an addition to the text and does not obtain the status of the text itself. Yet, it is no wonder that of all the components of Maimonides' view of *halakhah*, this one met with the most difficulty from Talmudic discussions. Ultimately, interpretation is, *inter alia*, an attempt to share in the text's authority. The exegete attempts to infuse his own words with the text's authority by means of interpretation.

The motives that dictated Maimonides' theory of *halakhah* are apparent from what he wrote in the *Guide of the Perplexed*, many years after formulating it in the *Commentary on the Mishnah* and the *Book of Commandments*. In the *Guide of the Perplexed*, the vital conditions for the authority of a divine Torah are mentioned. A divine Torah must be unchanging and uniform; otherwise, all its credibility will be undermined. This is how Maimonides explains the prohibition "you shall not add to it or derogate from it" (Deut. 13:1) and the punishment of the rebellious elder:

> Inasmuch as God, may He be exalted, knew that the commandments of this
> Law will need in every time and place—as far as some of them are con-
> cerned—to be added to or subtracted from according to the diversity of
> places, happenings, and conjunctures of circumstances, He forbade adding
> to them or subtracting from them saying: Though shalt not add thereto, nor
> diminish from it (Deut. 13, 1). For this might have lead to the corruption of
> the rules of the Law and to the belief that the latter did not come from God.
> (*Guide of the Perplexed*, III:41, Pines transl., p. 563)

Attributing controversy to the transmitted core of the Torah is considered
by Maimonides to be not merely an erroneous description of the tradition,
but a challenge to one of its foundations. He expresses it thus in his introduction to the *Commentary on the Mishnah*:

> But the notions of those who think that disputed laws were also received
> from Moses, and that controversy appeared by means of mishearing or for-
> getting . . . This—Lord knows—is a very ugly and despicable statement.
> (Introduction to the *Commentary on the Mishnah*)

His sharp formulation indicates that Maimonides viewed this not only as
an error, but as a dangerous form of heresy.

Attributing the status of the Torah itself to rabbinic interpretations not
received from Sinai entangles the core of the Torah in controversy and lack
of clarity, an intolerable approach to a legal system based on revelation:
"for this would upset the Torah's system and lead people to believe that the
Torah is not from God (*Guide of the Perplexed*, III:41, p. 585). According
to Maimonides' authority-based conception, the basic, unchanging, divine
core of the Torah, to which no law can be added but from which law is
derived, must be isolated. Moreover, this isolated core emphasizes Moses'
exclusive status—a status so central to Maimonides' conception of prophecy and law. He relates to the prophets as he relates to the sages: the former
are not equal partners in prophecy with Moses, and the latter do not become equal partners with him through their interpretations.

The *Commentary on the Mishnah* and the *Book of Commandments*, works
that Maimonides composed while in his twenties, did not achieve the same
heights as *Mishneh Torah* and the *Guide of the Perplexed*. Yet these early
works are no mere ponderings and experiments of a brilliant author starting to search for the breakthrough that would come later. Each of these
two works, original and unique, lays the foundation for what would follow

later: the *Commentary on the Mishnah* turned the *Mishnah* into a work that allows for the organization and summarization of *halakhah* and its rulings. The *Book of Commandments* construed the commandments as the organizing categories of *Mishneh Torah*, from which the *halakhah* branches out and is catalogued. In both of these works, Maimonides also developed his theory of *halakhah* vis-à-vis concepts like truth, revelation, interpretation, and controversy. This theory forged the framework into which he assimilated the vast particulars of all elements of *halakhah* in *Mishneh Torah*.

CHAPTER THREE

Ethics and Belief in the
Commentary on the Mishnah

Principles of Faith

In his *Essay on Resurrection*, Maimonides described an encounter with an illustrious scholar who had doubts about whether or not God was corporeal: "I have met some who think they are among the sages of Israel—by God, they indeed know the way of the Law ever since childhood, and they battle in legal discussions—but they are not certain if God is corporeal, with eyes hands, and feet . . . or if He has a body." Other scholars that Maimonides knew were certain about the matter: "Others, whom I have met in some lands, assert positively that He is corporeal and call anyone who thinks differently a non-believer. . . . I have received similar reports of some whom I have not met" (*Essay on Resurrection*, p. 212).

Encounters such as these bolstered Maimonides' position that knowledge of *halakhah* was in no way tied to knowledge of God and provided no guarantee of extirpating erroneous beliefs—beliefs that Maimonides considered inferior even to idolatry. Because Talmudic training does not provide the tools needed to understand the principles of the faith, a sage may be ignorant of the principles of faith even if he is learned in all the details of *halakhah*. As a result, he may worship a physical, and therefore foreign, god, even while showing great punctiliousness in observing the *halakhah*. Maimonides therefore decided that he would work the principles of faith into every halakhic treatise he wrote:

> I concluded that it was necessary that I clearly elucidate religious fundamentals in my works on law. I determined not to teach these basic truths in the idiom of inquiry . . . I therefore published principles that need to be acknowledged in the introduction to the *Commentary on the Mishnah* regarding prophecy and the roots of tradition and what every Rabbanite had

to believe concerning the Oral Law. In chapter 10 of Sanhedrin I expounded fundamentals connected with the beginning and the end, i.e., what pertains to God's unity and the world to come and the other tenets of the Torah. (*Essay on Resurrection*, pp. 212–213)

From the outset, then, Maimonides determined to introduce philosophical elements into his halakhic writings. He notes that the *Commentary on the Mishnah* was meant not only to set forth, in a comprehensive and orderly way, the underpinnings of the *halakhah* and its principles, but also to play a role in teaching opinions and beliefs.

A binding statement of the principles of faith appears in the introduction to the commentary on the chapter of the *Mishnah* known as *Pereq Heleq* (the tenth chapter of tractate Sanhedrin). Maimonides there formulates thirteen principles of faith, divided into three groups.

The first group, encompassing principles 1–5, deals with metaphysical-theological principles related to the nature of the divinity:

1. The existence of God—the knowledge that there exists a God who is the cause of all existence but that He Himself is beyond existence and not dependent on it.
2. The unity of God—the knowledge that God is one and indivisible.
3. The incorporeality of God—God is neither a body nor a force within a body, and the biblical verses that seem to refer to Him as such must therefore be read allegorically.
4. The preexistence of God—God preexisted everything and created the universe.
5. God as the exclusive object of worship—only God, and not any creature, is worthy of being worshipped.

The second group, containing principles 6–9, grounds belief in the Torah and its authoritativeness:

6. Prophecy—the knowledge that prophecy exists.
7. Supremacy of Moses' prophecy—the belief that Moses our teacher attained the pinnacle of prophecy and that no other prophet of his stature preceded or succeeded him. This principle expands in some detail on the ways in which Moses' prophecy is unique.
8. Torah from heaven—the belief that the Torah given to Moses is entirely from the mouth of God.

9. Immutability of the Torah—the Torah will never be annulled, supplemented, or subtracted from.

The third group, principles 10–13, pertains to belief in reward and punishment:

10. Divine omniscience—God knows all of man's deeds.
11. Reward and punishment—God rewards those who observe the Torah
and punishes those who transgress it.
12. The belief in the coming of the Messiah.
13. The belief in the resurrection of the dead.

These principles of faith are not merely ideas to be aspired to; they are,
for Maimonides, binding dogmas that define the boundaries of the Jewish
community. He puts it this way following his listing of the principles:

> When a man accepts all of these principles, fully believing in them, he en-
> ters into the community of Israel and we are bound to love him, to show
> mercy to him, and to fulfill with respect to him all of the duties God im-
> posed regarding love and brotherhood . . . But if he rejects one of these
> principles, he leaves the community and denies [the Torah], and he is called
> a heretic and an apostate, and we are obligated to hate him and destroy him.
> Of him it is said, "Do not I hate them, O LORD, that hate Thee." (Ps.
> 139:21) (*Introduction to Pereq Ḥeleq*)

Acceptance of these principles invests a person with membership in the
community of Israel, entitles him to the rights enjoyed by a member of
that community, and situates him as one to be treated, in solidarity, with
the love and mercy all Jews are obligated to show to one another. As long
as a person accepts these principles, his membership in the community is
maintained even if he sins. Conversely, denial of one of these principles
ousts the apostate from membership in the community. He loses his standing as one entitled to certain legal rights and becomes an object of destruction and hatred: "we are obligated to hate him and destroy him."

This formulation of binding principles of faith—principles that form
the basis for membership in the community of Israel and define who has
left that community—was a truly revolutionary step in the history of Jewish thought. Maimonides associated the principles with a *Mishnah* in tractate Sanhedrin, but the sages of the Talmud never formulated principles of
faith. Membership in the community was determined primarily by refer-

ence to norms of conduct that manifest loyalty to the *halakhah*, and a fair degree of diversity was allowed with respect to matters of opinion and belief.

The foregoing is true with respect to almost all of the principles that Maimonides formulated. Some sages thought God to be corporeal; some prayed to or through intercessors such as angels; some believed the Messiah would be a greater prophet than Moses; and some held that the Torah would be annulled at the end of days. Beyond that, the Talmud raises the possibility that the Messiah would never come, because the time for his coming was allowed to pass. Rabbinic literature is rife with beliefs and positions at odds with every one of Maimonides' principles, for that literature saw faith not as a set of firm cognitive principles, commitment to which was a precondition to membership in the Jewish community, but simply as confidence in God and dedication to Him and His word. It therefore should come as no surprise that in the generations following Maimonides, such thinkers as Hasdai Crescas, Joseph Albo, and Isaac Abarbanel set out alternatives to Maimonides' thirteen principles. The traditional opposition to this approach was well stated in the nineteenth century by R. Moses Sofer (the *Hatam Sofer*), who argued that a Jew was required to believe nothing more than that the Torah was from heaven. That belief was binding because it formed the cognitive basis for diligent observance of the commandments, and it was the necessary condition to full membership in the community of Israel.

Given all that, one might well ask what moved Maimonides to take such a radically different step. The answer involves a profound turn in his understanding of man, a turn brought about by the encounter between the Jewish tradition and Aristotelian and Arab philosophy.

What is Man: Immortality of the Soul, and the Afterlife

Maimonides' association with the cultural realm of Aristotle and his interpreters led him to propose an innovative reading of Judaism's basic theological concepts, including God and his qualities, prophecy, providence, creation, and miracle. But the encounter with the Greek world in its Arab garb involved a further clash, no less dramatic, regarding the significance of human life and the realization of human potential. How Maimonides dealt with the complexities and challenges to the concept of God is a subject we will consider in the chapters on the *Guide of the Perplexed*, for the issue is not taken up in the *Commentary on the Mishnah*. The latter is a work intended for all students of rabbinic literature and not specifically for those who have internalized an Aristotelian worldview, and it pertains more to the complex, turbulent confrontation over the meaning of mankind and of human life. The deep internalization of Aristotelian thought regarding the nature of the good life, as interpreted by al-Farabi, brought about a greater emphasis on beliefs as a central component of Jewish identity.

In the Aristotelian conception, man's defining quality is his ability to distinguish between truth and falsity. Human potential is fulfilled through apprehending, to the full extent one's intelligence is able, the truth about the world and about God. According to Aristotle, after one subtracts what man shares in common with plants (nutrition and growth) and with non-human animals (sensation), what remains is the distinctly human quality, namely, the intelligence within his soul. The human actor is characterized by his ability to act on the basis of (or contrary to) intelligent deliberation. The good life entails the fulfillment of man's characteristic ability, that of attaining knowledge. Maimonides accepted this view of the meaning of human life, and the *Guide* describes the essence of man by defining the image of God within him: "For the intellect that God made overflow unto man and that is the latter's ultimate perfection . . . It was because of this that it was said of him that he was created *in the image of God and in His likeness*" (*Guide* I:2, Pines, p. 24). Accordingly, human life attains its realization through knowledge: "His ultimate perfection is to become rational in actu, I mean to have an intellect in actu; this would consist in his knowing everything concerning all the beings that it is within the capacity of man to know in accordance with his ultimate perfection" (*Guide* III:27, Pines, p. 511).

All other human activities are meant to be subservient to this highest purpose. Because man is also a material creature, he needs an orderly, well-structured society that can provide him the necessities of life. To that end, there must be a polity ordered by law, whose purpose is to deal with bodily needs. That purpose is served as well by the development of moral qualities, both because they make possible the existence of a proper society and because they allow man to control his other impulses, a precondition to a life of inquiry and contemplation. In the introduction to the *Commentary on the Mishnah*, he offers the following formulation of human life as a means for achieving the purpose of inquiry: "For they [the sages] found that [man's] purpose is but one activity, and all the other activities are to maintain his existence so he can perfect that one activity, which is to apprehend the intelligibles and know the truths as they are." In the fifth of the *Eight Chapters* (the introduction to his commentary on tractate *Avot*), that formulation appears even more forcefully: "It is proper for a person to deploy all the powers of his soul to advance knowledge . . . and to set before his eyes a single purpose, that is, apprehension of God, may He be glorified and exalted, in accord with a person's ability, that is, his knowledge. And he should apply all his actions, his movements and speech, toward that purpose" (ibid., p. 241).

Maimonides' placement of this position at the heart of Judaism had a far-reaching effect on the status of *halakhah*. The details of the commandments requiring or prohibiting various actions are not the purpose of religious existence; they are, rather, only the means that enable a man to fulfill his purpose as a knowing creature. The Torah commands not only the construction of a proper society and the development of moral attributes, which are the means for achieving human perfection. Beyond that, it commands proper beliefs and involvement in contemplation as the way toward man's higher perfection.

The Aristotelian concept, however, is not the only one imaginable, and one might take an entirely different stance regarding the meaning of human life, a stance having deep roots in the Jewish tradition. In that view, man, alone among the creatures, is granted free will, and what characterizes him is the ability to use his will to subject his desires and lusts to laws and models of proper conduct. It is *halakhah* that directs man in doing so, and fulfillment of *halakhah* in all its particulars is the essence of human distinctiveness. The will to fulfill the action-related commandments, and certainly their actual fulfillment, are the expression of human distinctiveness and its perfection, not the ability to distinguish between truth and falsehood. Maimonides, as noted, does not accept this latter conception, and believes human perfection is attained through intellectual activity. He therefore made fulfillment of the active commandments into a means rather than an end and supplemented the *halakhah* with what he took to be an additional, very important layer of effort: the binding formulation of proper and true beliefs and opinions regarding God and the world.

This changed perception of man's essence shapes the concept of the world to come presented in the introduction to *Pereq Ḥeleq*. Maimonides there attempts to topple the idea that the world to come is a physical re-

ward or some sort of after-death physical existence. The immortality of the
soul, as he sees it, is no miracle; it simply follows causally from a certain
way of life. What remains of a person after his death is the knowledge he
acquired during his life. According to the Aristotelian approach, man is
identified with his knowledge, through which his intellect moves from
potential to actual. It is this identity that ensures the immortality of a person's soul. Rather than being a reward for observing the commandments,
the world to come is the result of a life devoted to apprehension of the
intelligibles. Life in the world to come is thus a pure and refined continuation of the life of the mind:

> And they said, peace be upon them, "In the world to come there is no eat-
> ing, no drinking, no bathing, no anointing, no sexual intercourse; rather,
> the righteous sit with their crowns on their heads, taking pleasure in the
> radiance of God's presence." By "their crowns on their heads," they mean
> the existence of the soul through the existence of what it has learned, the
> soul and its learning becoming one thing, as the erudite philosophers have
> said. . . . And when they say "taking pleasure in the radiance of God's pres-
> ence," they mean that the soul enjoys what it has learned of the Creator.
> (*Introduction to Pereq Ḥeleq*)

On the face of it, this concept of immortality of the soul leaves no room
for the distinctiveness of an individual's surviving soul, for the portion of
the soul that remains is the collection of metaphysical truths acquired by a
person during his life. And, in fact, Jewish philosophy during the Middle
Ages encompasses several strained attempts to interject an individual dimension into the Aristotelian concept of the soul's immortality.

The critics of Maimonides' philosophical concept of the world to come
were troubled, however, by the conclusion that Jews who had been punctilious in their observance of all the commandments, lesser and greater,
would be denied access to the world to come simply because they had not
engaged in the study of wisdom. And what would be the fate of simple
Jews, firm in their religious commitment, who had lived lives devoted to
Torah and commandments without paying attention to the question of
whether or not God was corporeal? Ra'abad, one of the harshest critics of
Mishneh Torah, reacted sharply to Maimonides' ruling that belief in God's
corporeality constitutes apostasy. In response to Maimonides' position that
one who holds such a belief has excluded himself from the community of
Israel and has no share in the world to come, Ra'abad stormed: "And why

does he call such a one [who believes in God's corporeality] an apostate, when some who are greater and better than he held that idea on the basis of what they saw in Scripture, more than on the basis of what they saw in the [rabbinic] *aggadot* that cause mistaken ideas" (Comment on *Mishneh Torah*, "Laws Concerning Repentance," 3:7). Ra'abad objects to treating belief in God's corporeality as apostasy, even though he himself regards it as mistaken.

This concept of human perfection and immortality of the soul calls into question two other aspects of reward and punishment within the Jewish tradition—Gehenna and the resurrection of the dead. For Maimonides, the concept of Gehenna as a place where souls suffer torment for their sins is utterly meaningless. The most severe punishment for a sinner is the termination of his soul and its departure from the world. A sinner who concentrated on the life of the body to the exclusion of spiritual life disappears from the world following his death, and nothing remains of him.

In the introduction to *Pereq Ḥeleq*, following his identification of man's greatest reward as immortality of the soul and apprehension of the Creator, Maimonides speaks of the harshest punishment: "And the ultimate evil is the cutting off of the soul and its loss, its not having the privilege of continuing to exist . . . Anyone who clung to physical pleasures, despising truth and choosing falsity, is cut off from that benefit and remains nothing more than terminated material." The traditional image—that of the soul leaving the body and appearing for judgment before the celestial court—fades away in light of this account. Immortality of the soul is attained through apprehension of the intelligibles, and disappearance is the direct outcome of a life in which one failed to actualize his potential as a human being. This view of things leaves no room for Gehenna as the abode of a full array of post-mortem punishment and torment, for the sinner's soul does not survive his death and thus cannot be tormented. Maimonides, to be sure, does mention Gehenna, but only briefly and without elaboration:

> But Gehenna is a term for the sorrow that overtakes the wicked, and the Talmud does not clarify the nature of that sorrow. Some say that the sun draws near to them and burns, citing as proof the verse "For, behold, the day comes, it burns as a furnace" (Mal. 3:19), and some say that a strange fever will appear in their bodies and burn them, citing as proof the verse "your breath is a fire that shall devour you." (Isa. 33:11) (*Introduction to Pereq Ḥeleq*)

That passage suggests, on the one hand, that Maimonides felt obligated to refer to the traditional concept of Gehenna but, on the other, that he could not integrate it into his systematic outlook in any serious way.

In his *Mishneh Torah*, "Laws Concerning Repentance," Maimonides reiterated these formulations of the world to come and the immortality of the soul, and emphasized the two key ideas associated with them. One is that immortality of the soul is, in effect, the outcome of a person's bonding with the objects of his cognition during the course of his life, not a miracle based on an inquiry by a celestial court that decides, following the soul's ascent heavenward, whether it merits the rod or eternal grace. The other idea is built on the spiritualization of religious life, in that the highest achievement of man is knowledge, and that the world to come therefore provides not physical reward but the perfected—and pleasurable—realization of a life of inquiry and knowledge.

Maimonides does not mention Gehenna in *Mishneh Torah*, in step with his consistent position on the nature of man and his soul. There, too, he determines that the worst ill that befalls a sinner is that nothing remains of him following his death and that his presence in the world is ended. In 1232, following Maimonides' death, there erupted a great controversy over the *Book of Knowledge* (*Sefer ha-Madda*, the first volume of *Mishneh Torah*) and over the *Guide*. Maimonides' critics charged that he did not believe in the existence of Gehenna, regarding that as an additional reason for banning the *Book of Knowledge*. But here, as elsewhere, Maimonides opened a door to a more traditional reading of what he had written, and his defenders in the polemic, including Naḥmanides, pointed to his mentioning of Gehenna in the introduction to *Pereq Ḥeleq* or to his reference, in *Mishneh Torah*, to the judgment of a sinner.[1] This sharp dispute over his legacy was not without reason, for his consistent position regarding the soul and its immortality contradicts his clipped reference to Gehenna. It may be that on this point, Maimonides' critics understood his true position.

Resurrection of the Dead

Maimonides' understanding of the nature and purpose of human life brought about a reexamination not only of Gehenna but also of resurrection of the dead as a central element of the traditional system of reward

[1] See Maimonides' allusions in *Mishneh Torah*, Laws of Repentance, 3, 5;6. Naḥmanides, *Kitvei ha-Ramban*, Shavel Edition, II, pp. 291–292.

and punishment. This issue came to the fore during Maimonides' lifetime, following the criticism leveled by Samuel ben Eli. The chapters of *Mishneh Torah* that speak in detail of the world to come lack any mention of resurrection, and Samuel ben Eli maintained that was no coincidence. According to Samuel, Maimonides denied resurrection of the body, taking it allegorically as survival of the soul after death. A similar claim was made toward the end of Maimonides' life, in 1202, by R. Meir Halevi Abulafia of Toledo. In response to that charge, R. Aaron Hakohen of Lunel, a Provencal admirer of Maimonides, wrote a detailed defense. Maimonides himself had replied to Samuel ben Eli in his *Essay on Resurrection*, written in 1191. But did Maimonides in fact deny something that he himself had listed as one of the principles defining membership in the Jewish people? Before attempting to answer that question, we should describe the aspects of Maimonides' teachings that allow for it even to be raised.

In the passages in the *Commentary on the Mishnah* and *Mishneh Torah* that discuss the Bible's references to physical reward and punishment, Maimonides raises a key argument: the physical rewards promised by the Torah for observing the commandments, such as rainfall, lack of illness, prosperity, and independence, are not the purpose for that observance. The purpose of the physical reward is to facilitate man's pursuit of his true purpose—knowledge of the Creator. A man facing distress, hunger, illness, or exile will not be free to pursue that which leads him toward perfection. His life will be consumed by the hardships he faces and he will have neither the psychological nor the physical leisure to devote himself to the enterprise that makes one truly able to flourish. The physical reward promised by the Torah, then, is simply a means to liberate man for higher pursuits:

> For a man cannot engage in the service of God when he is ill, or hungry, or thirsty or during time of war; and He therefore declared that all of these would be removed, and they would be healthy and at peace, so their knowledge of God might be perfected and they will merit the world to come. For it is not the purpose of the Torah that the land be richly productive or that people live long or have healthy bodies; rather they will be supported by all these things in fulfilling [the true purpose]. (*Introduction to Pereq Ḥeleq*)

The same idea is reiterated in *Mishneh Torah*:

> He has further promised us in the Torah, that, if we observe its behests joyously and cheerfully, and continually meditate on its wisdom, He will

remove from us the obstacles that hinder us in its observance, such as sickness, war, famine, and other calamities; and will bestow upon us all the material benefits which will strengthen our ability to fulfill the law, such as plenty, peace, abundance of silver and gold. Thus we will not be engaged all our days, in providing for our bodily needs, but will have leisure to study wisdom and fulfill the commandment, and thus attain life in the world to come. (*Book of Knowledge*, "Laws Concerning Repentance," 9:1)

The idea that physical reward is nothing more than a state of well-being that allows one to focus on attaining higher perfection also determines Maimonides' stance regarding the messianic age. The political liberation from foreign domination that is promised for the messianic age is meant to forge conditions suitable to achieving human perfection and the world to come:

The great benefit of that time will be that we will have respite from servitude to a wicked tyranny, which impedes our attainment of virtue, and there will be an increase in wisdom, as it is said, "for the earth shall be full of the knowledge of the LORD" (Isa. 11:9), and conflicts and wars will cease, as it is said, "nation shall not lift up sword against nation" (Isa. 2:4). Those in existence at that time will attain great perfection and merit the life of the world to come . . . Messianic times are not to be longed for because produce and wealth will be abundant or because we will ride on horses and drink from fine utensils, as believed by those whose minds are confused. (*Introduction to Pereq Heleq*)

These motifs are expanded on in *Mishneh Torah*: "Hence, all Israelites, their prophets and sages, longed for the advent of Messianic times, that they might have relief from the wicked tyranny that does not permit them properly to occupy themselves with the study of the Torah and the observance of the commandment; that they might have ease, devote themselves to getting wisdom, and thus attain life in the world to come" ("Laws Concerning Repentance," 9:2). Jews eagerly await the messianic age not because it will bring them power and glory following generations of subservience; rather, its purpose is to provide a political space that will allow for the tranquility and prosperity needed for the flourishing of human perfection that will result in attaining the world to come.

In this understanding of biblical reward and punishment, Maimonides confronted a profound existential problem in human consciousness. As he saw it, the central purpose of the Torah is to elevate human life to a dimension that transcends worldly needs and fulfillment of basic material impulses. The true fulfillment of human life lies in elevation to the spiritual realm of thought and consciousness. A person who sees physical reward as the purpose for observing the commandments may transform the Torah itself into a means for satisfying his base impulses. If the world to come is a place where man's physical desires—including those for things forbidden in this world—will be satisfied, then the whole purpose of the Torah is reduced to a concern for future physical satisfaction, in the messianic age and the world to come. Indeed, when Maimonides explains the purpose of the messianic age and of the Torah's commandments, he argues that physical reward is not the reason for which the commandments should be observed; on the contrary, they are meant to liberate man from subservience to his physical impulses. The physical reward is nothing more than the means that will allow him to develop the higher aspects of his existence.

Let us return to the question of resurrection. If physical reward is merely a means for attaining the higher existence of human intellectual perfection, why should the soul be reunited with the body after a person's death? On the face of it, returning the soul to the body seems more a punishment than a reward. Moreover, we have seen that immortality of the soul is not a wondrous miracle but simply the natural result of a person's life. Resurrection of the dead, in contrast, is very much an incomprehensible and wondrous event—as well as unnecessary. Not surprisingly, Maimonides' philosophical disciples took the view that resurrection is nothing more than an allegory for immortality of the spiritual soul. Maimonides himself noted that some understood him in that way, and he was asked about it even before he wrote the *Essay on Resurrection*:

> In the course of 1185 a letter reached me from Yemen inquiring about various matters. It also related that some among them decided that the body would decompose after death, the soul would not return to the body after separation, and reward and punishment would be reserved only for the soul. They relied on what I had written about the members of the world to come. When the clear and explicit statements of the sages were brought to their attention as well as some verses from the prophets they disposed of them by maintaining they were metaphorical and required interpretation. (*Essay on Resurrection*, p. 217)

We have already seen the difficulty in finding a place for Gehenna in Maimonides' systematic and philosophical worldview, and it is no less difficult to find a place for resurrection of the dead in its plain sense.

In the *Essay on Resurrection*, Maimonides exonerated himself of that charge. He mentions resurrection of the dead as a principle of the faith, denial of which makes one an apostate who has excluded himself from the community of Israel, and he insists that nowhere in his writings did he ever suggest that the belief be understood allegorically. He applied allegorical interpretations to verses that speak of God in corporeal terms, for it is utterly implausible that God is corporeal, but a miracle such as resurrection of the dead is certainly within the range of the possible. One who denies belief in resurrection in effect denies the possibility of a miracle and therefore must treat as allegories not only resurrection but also all the miracles recounted in the Torah, such as the descent of the manna, the parting of the Red Sea, and the changing of Moses' staff into a serpent. That sort of interpretive line is inconceivable, and it is rejected in the *Epistle*. Still, Maimonides doesn't give detailed consideration to resurrection or its purpose. In his view, the wondrous and miraculous nature of the subject precludes discussion, and one must simply accept belief in this principle on the basis of prophetic and rabbinic statements regarding it.

A reading of the *Essay on Resurrection* leaves one largely unsatisfied. Maimonides forcefully rejects the charge that he takes an allegorical view of resurrection, repeatedly citing his references to the concept in its plain sense. Nowhere, however, does he give any explanation of the purpose of resurrection. Resurrection certainly may occur, for God is free to do things that transcend the bounds of nature, but why would He want to do this? What would be the purpose of resurrection? Moreover, Maimonides determined in the *Epistle* that resurrection would be something temporary. Those who were resurrected would thereafter again die, and only then would they attain the life of the world to come. But if that is so, resurrection is merely an odd pause in a process whose entire purpose is a higher sort of existence in the world to come.

The suggestion that Maimonides may not have believed in one of the principles of faith that he himself established compels us to reconsider his understanding of what is meant by "principles of faith." In the *Guide*, he refers to the distinction, which we will consider extensively below, between true beliefs and necessary beliefs. The distinction has its source in Greek and Arab political thought, which holds that the social order rests on the dissemination of necessary, useful beliefs. Plato, al-Farabi, and others believed that the legislator or ruler had to propagate a view of the world that would facilitate the existence of the state, without regard to the truth or falsity of that view. For example, belief in a God who exercises oversight, granting reward and imposing punishment, is the sort of belief that can play a highly useful role in promoting social order. A society might well unravel if its members did not believe that transgressors were destined to account for every one of their actions.

This notion that the political order could not endure in circumstances of absolute metaphysical transparency, and that the masses require necessary beliefs, was part of political thought until the eighteenth century. It was shared by prominent Enlightenment thinkers, such as Spinoza and Locke. The first who dared to suggest that a well ordered yet atheistic society might be possible were Hume and Bayle. Given this venerable tradition of seeing myth as a necessary part of the political order, one should not assume that when Maimonides promulgated principles of faith, he meant only to impart the true opinions essential to the achievement of human perfection. Promulgation of such principles also serves the purpose of establishing the necessary beliefs that facilitate a proper social order.

In the *Guide*, Maimonides formulates this dual purpose of the beliefs set forth in the Torah:

> Among the things to which your attention ought to be directed is that you should know that in regard to the correct opinions through which the ultimate perfection may be obtained, the Law has communicated only their end and made a call to believe in them in a summary way—that is, to believe in the existence of the deity, may He be exalted, His unity, His knowledge, His power, His will, and His eternity . . . In the same way, the Law also makes a call to adopt certain beliefs, belief in which is necessary for the sake of political welfare. Such, for instance, is our belief that He, may He be exalted, is violently angry with those who disobey Him and that it is therefore necessary to fear Him and to dread him and to take care not to disobey. (*Guide*, III:28; Pines, p. 512)

While the metaphysical beliefs regarding the divinity are true beliefs, the belief in God's anger against sinners is not a true belief, for God does not have a soul, and it is impossible to portray Him as angry. Still, the belief is required to deter people from sinning. The distinction between true beliefs and necessary beliefs is reiterated at the conclusion of that chapter:

> Sum up what we have said concerning beliefs as follows: In some cases a *commandment* communicates a correct belief, which is the one and only thing aimed at—as, for instance, the belief in the unity and eternity of the deity and in His not being a body. In other cases, the belief is necessary for the abolition of reciprocal wrongdoing or for the acquisition of a noble moral quality—as, for instance, the belief that He, may He be exalted, has a violent anger against those who do injustice, according to what is said: And My wrath shall wax hot, and I will kill, and so on, and as the belief that He, may He be exalted, responds instantaneously to the prayer of someone wronged or deceived: And it shall come to pass, when he crieth unto Me, that I will hear; for I am gracious. (ibid.; ibid., pp. 513–514)

And so, the principles of faith that serve a dual purpose include a layer of necessary beliefs that the masses would do well to assimilate and believe in and whose truth should be proclaimed by philosophers. Whether a belief should be classified as true or as necessary is a fundamental difficulty in Maimonides' thought. At this stage, before we examine the question in depth, we can say that several of the principles listed in the introduction to *Pereq Heleq* are formulated in a manner consistent with their being necessary beliefs. Belief in God's overseeing human behavior and in reward and punishment are in that category: God oversees human action, rewarding those who fulfill the commands of the Torah and punishing those who transgress. These beliefs are certainly essential to a proper social order, but Maimonides' view of providence and of reward and punishment, to be considered below, differs from the formulations in the thirteen principles and is much more complex. It is entirely possible that the belief in resurrection, like the other beliefs related to providence and reward and punishment that are included among the thirteen, were interpreted by Maimonides as necessary beliefs after having been identified by the sages as basic articles of faith.

The Ethics of Virtue and the Ethics of Obligation

A way of life encompasses more than a community's shared beliefs and duties. It includes as well a notion of an ideal human type, whose characteristics are recognized implicitly if not explicitly. For example, various cultures sometimes generate a normative mood, be it melancholy or joyful, and sometimes even a normative way of walking in the public square: should one walk slowly and calmly, or is it better to walk briskly, conveying a sense of urgency and busyness? Should one's head be held erect, eyes looking forward, or is it better to adopt a more modest attitude, with eyes lowered? A particular sort of choreography, of course, is not always shared by the entire community—that of men will differ from that of women, for example, and that of the wealthy will differ from that of the poor. A change in the community's basic values will sometimes bring about a significant change in the qualities that are considered admirable. An ideological change of this sort will make its way into the most basic layers of a community's life, shaping personalities and even affecting such details as verbal tone, body language, and presentation of oneself in the public square.

Avot is the Mishnahic tractate whose subject matter is the most reflective of these concerns. It does not formulate behavioral prohibitions or requirements, as do the other tractates, nor does it present creedal dogmas. It depicts a personality—more accurately, several personalities—and tries to construct a human model on the basis of their qualities and inclinations. Accordingly, it was only natural that Maimonides would use his commentary on this tractate, especially its introduction, to describe his view of the proper human character. That design, as we have seen earlier, grew out of his ties to the Greco-Arab philosophical tradition.

Aristotelian ethics is an ethics of virtues and personal characteristics rather than duties and rules. Because its basic concern is the nature of the good and proper life, it cannot rest content with defining the rules that govern interpersonal relations in situations where people are able to harm or benefit each other; it encompasses a much broader domain. It considers such questions as a person's attitude toward wealth or the degree of gravity or nonchalance that should mark his interaction with others. It details and formulates the qualities of the human soul, such as generosity, courage, magnanimity, friendship, and self-restraint.

This sort of approach assumes that emotional reactions are a profound expression of judgments and affinities. Consider, for example, the emotion of fear. A person who is afraid believes that something bad may happen to him and harm him. The feeling is not simply a physical sensation, like pain or hunger; it is, rather, an expression of belief about the surrounding state of affairs. The feeling of guilt, unlike fear, expresses the belief that the person has done something wrong, but not that something bad will happen to him. The belief expressed through an emotional reaction determines the feeling that will be sensed. How can we tell, for example, that we are feeling fear rather than guilt? We can do so not because fear and guilt entail different sensations but because the two emotions express different beliefs about the nature of the world. Moreover, the emotion expresses an attitude toward the world, an assessment of the situation. A person who feels fearful is saying something not only about the belief that loss is possible but also about his attachment to the object he does not want to lose or that is causing him concern.

This conception of emotional life bears on the role of the sage and the philosopher as a healer of souls and on the essence of philosophy as psychological therapy. Psychological illness describes a situation in which a person's emotional reactions are inappropriate to the actual state of affairs in the world. If we return to the example of fear, we may say that anxiety is irrational if it fails to recognize that the belief it expresses is a delusion. One who obsessively returns home to check that he has turned off his kitchen gas valve experiences that sort of anxiety. But a fearful reaction may accurately reflect the state of affairs in the world, while still expressing an inappropriate attitude toward what is taking place. Someone who is worried about losing skin cells when rubbing his hands together has an accurate perception of reality but is inappropriately attached to the particular cells that are being lost, for we know they will be replaced by others. To heal the psyche is to promote emotional reactions that reflect appropriate beliefs and attachments. In line with this tradition, Maimonides regards the sage as a healer of souls.

The mark of sound dispositions and qualities is that an individual possessed of them will act virtuously by reason of his personality and will have no need to use his will to suppress his inclinations. The perfected person will not feel that he is suffering when he acts virtuously, for he will have trained himself and his emotions to do so. A generous person will feel joyful when he gives to charity, for the action is consistent with his personality. A miser, in contrast, will feel distress when he uses his wealth to help a poor person. The difference between a superior person and an ordinary one will be evident in the degree of distress he perceives in performing a virtuous action. The distress or pain that may be associated with the performance of a virtuous action reflects a character flaw in the actor and his need to be strong enough to subject his inclinations to his will. Distress of that sort signals that even though a person acted properly and did what needed to be done, his psychic qualities remain far removed from those that should be aspired to. An ethical life is one in which one's emotional inclinations correspond to virtuous actions. One thereby integrates into his emotional reactions his uniqueness as a creature equipped to exercise judgment and realizes the true human ideal in his personality.

This aptitude for doing good is not the only model of morality, however; an alternative moral stance is centered on the concept of obligation, of duty. The position was stated most profoundly by Immanuel Kant, who denied that there was any moral significance to an action taken merely in accord with one's natural inclination. A person who gives charity because he feels merciful may be acting in accord with his duty, but he is not acting out of a sense of duty. The moral act must be performed independently of a person's inclinations; it must reflect the capacity to subject one's inclinations to a categorical imperative. Moral education, accordingly, is not based on training meant to make one's dispositions compatible with virtuous actions; rather, it is based on the premise that a person has the capacity, as a free agent, to act out of duty notwithstanding his inclinations. A moral person will discharge his obligations without regard to his state of mind or the leanings of his heart; and the moral life, fundamentally, is a heroic expression of human will, functioning in accord with the duty imposed on it.

Kant's philosophical position reflects in many ways a venerable approach that sees the moral life as one in which a person successfully resists his desires. A perspective centered on duty will maintain—contrary to the Aristotelian view—that the harder a person has to struggle against his urges and his instincts, the greater his stature. In battling mightily against his instincts, such a person expresses not only the force of his will but also his ability to sacrifice his desires—including the most fundamental desire of all, the desire to live—on the altar of duty. Traces of this view appear in rabbinic literature and in the Jewish tradition through the ages, for the Jewish tradition sets the concept of commandment at the center of religious and moral awareness. It should come as no surprise, therefore, that Kant's teachings proved attractive to more than a few modern Jewish thinkers, who identified the similarity between Kant's categorical imperative and Judaism's absolute commandment.

Maimonides internalized the Aristotelian ethics of good character and brought it into the very core of Judaism. Doing so required him to confront the elements of duty-based morality grounded in the tradition. Chapter 6 of his introduction to *Avot* is the arena in which he sets virtues-based morality and duty-based morality against each other. He begins with a statement of the Aristotelian position:

> Philosophers maintain that though the man of self-restraint performs moral and praiseworthy deeds, yet he does them desiring and craving all the while for immoral deeds, but, subduing his passions and actively fighting against a longing to do those things to which his faculties, his desires and his psychic disposition excite him, succeeds, though with constant vexation and irritation, in acting morally. The saintly man, however, is guided in his actions by that to which his inclination and disposition prompt him, in consequence of which he acts morally from innate longing and desire. Philosophers unanimously agree that the latter is superior to, and more perfect than, the one who has to curb his passions, although they add that it is possible for such a one to equal saintly man in many regards. (*Eight Chapters*, pp. 376–377)

A fit person does not overpower his desire to do a bad act; rather, the good act flows naturally from him and comports with his predispositions. But Maimonides is well aware of the other stream of thought, which appears in the Talmud, and he sets it against the philosophical stance:

> When, however, we consult the rabbis on this subject, it would seem that they consider him who desires iniquity and craves for it (but does not do it), more praiseworthy and perfect than the one who feels no torment at refraining from evil; and they even go so far as to maintain that the more praiseworthy and perfect a man is, the greater is his desire to commit iniquity and the more irritation he feels at having to desist from it. This they express by saying "Whosoever is greater than his neighbor has likewise greater evil inclination" (Sukkah 52a). Again, as if this were not sufficient, they even go so far as to say that the reward of him who overcomes his evil inclination is commensurate with the torture occasioned by his resistance, which thought they express by the works, "According to the labor is the reward." (*Avot*, 5:23) Furthermore, they command that man should conquer his desires but they forbid one to say, "I, by my nature, do not desire to commit such and such a transgression, even though the Law does not

forbid it." Rabbi Simeon ben Gamliel summed up this thought in the words, "Man should not say, 'I do not want to eat meat together with milk; I do not want to wear clothes made of a mixture of wool and linen; I do not want to enter into an incestuous marriage,' but he should say, 'I do indeed want to, yet my Father in heaven has forbidden it.'" (ibid.)

This collection of rabbinic dicta, which Maimonides contrasts with the Aristotelian stance, clearly reflects the traditional approach to duty, according to which the moral drama reaches its peak as a person passes the test he faces and triumphs, in however much pain, over his desires.

To resolve this tension while maintaining the Aristotelian sensibility, Maimonides proposed to distinguish between two sorts of commandments. One group, which he terms "conventional," are those that people would have to follow even if they had not been set forth in the Torah; "had they not been written, they would have deserved to be written." The second group, termed "revealed," are binding only because the Torah imposes them. With respect to the conventional commandments—such as the prohibitions on murder, theft, fraud, or harming an innocent—one who observes them by triumphing over his impulses is on a lower plane than one who has no inclination whatsoever to sin. The desire to commit wicked actions of this sort, even if successfully overcome, attests to the person's flawed character: "There is no doubt that a soul which has the desire for and lusts after the above-mentioned misdeeds is imperfect; that a noble soul has absolutely no desire for any such crimes and experiences no struggle in refraining from them" (*Eight Chapters*, p. 378). In contrast, actions prohibited by the revealed commandments would not be considered wicked had they not been proscribed by the Torah, and the obligation to avoid such actions stems entirely from the divine command. In such cases, a person need not lose the desire to perform the prohibited action, and one who overcomes that desire thereby expresses his subordination to God's will. In Maimonides' view, it is no coincidence that the examples cited by the *midrash* in declaring the superiority of a person who overcomes sinful desires pertain only to prohibitions that lack a rational moral basis, such as those against mixing meat and milk, mixing wool and linen, and having illicit sexual relations. Maimonides' preference for a morality based on character rather than duty leads him to relegate the ideal of withstanding the test and triumphing over one's inclinations to the realm of those commandments lacking any intrinsic moral meaning.

The Sage and the Pietist

The human type depicted in Aristotle's *Nicomachean Ethics* is characterized by the idea of the middle way, the idea that a good attribute is to be found between the two extremes. One extreme reflects a harmful excess; the other, a destructive deficit. Courage, for example, represents the mean between cowardice and impetuous daring. Unlike the coward, the courageous person will take genuine risks, but unlike the impetuously daring person, he will do so only for a proper goal. Generosity represents the mean between profligacy and miserliness, and satisfaction represents the mean between gluttony and apathy. This idea of the mean does not provide guidance for proper action in a particular case; rather, it offers a general account of a harmonious and balanced personality. A person of this sort will act properly because his psychic makeup will lead him to do so. The inclinations of such a level-headed and reasonable man make him into a virtuous man, and he has measured and appropriate attitudes toward such goods as security, wealth, pleasure, and honor. He is a man who can be trusted, a man who reflects in the deepest way the civic ideal of the Greek political tradition.

In contrast to this figure, which so captivated the Greco-Roman world, stands the pietist or saint. Piety, taken to excess, is religious radicalism. The pietist—in effect, a religious bohemian—is an outsider, constantly testing, in the name of religious intimacy, the boundaries of legal and bourgeois existence. He does not consider himself bound by the details of the law, and he casts his lot with God, who will fulfill his needs. He tends to go beyond the law's requirements.

One of the most fascinating cultural encounters in Maimonides' writing involves the complex relationship between the aristocrat and the saint, two types quite foreign to each other. To go beyond the law's requirements, as the saint does, would appear to be a form of excess, having no place in the Aristotelian picture. The saint, meanwhile, regards the noble citizen, for all his virtues, as a self-satisfied bourgeois. Not surprisingly, the Kotzker Rebbe—one of the most radical and independent figures in Jewish history—is reputed to have ironically said that "When I look at the roads, I see that only the horses walk in the middle. Human beings walk on the edges, on the sidewalks."

Maimonides accepted the basic notion that a fit person was characterized by his pursuit of the middle way. The fourth of the *Eight Chapters* opens with a clear formulation of the Aristotelian stance: "Good deeds are such as are equibalanced, maintaining the mean between two equally bad extremes, the too much and the too little. Virtues are psychic conditions and dispositions which are midway between two reprehensible extremes, one of which is characterized by an exaggeration the other by a deficiency" (*Eight Chapters*, pp. 367–378). A similar statement appears later, in *Mishneh Torah*, "Laws Relating to Moral Dispositions"—a text that outlines the figure of the ideal normative Jew. Consistent with his fundamental position, Maimonides describes such virtues as courage, generosity, caution, tolerance, and joviality as means between two extremes. But how can the pietistic ethos and the great virtue of doing more than the law demands—ideas with deep roots in the Jewish tradition—be integrated into the human ideal of the middle way? As the fourth of the *Eight Chapters* unfolds, we find the same turning point: the entry of a human ideal from the Greco-Arab cultural context brings with it a new interpretation of the traditional sources that otherwise lend support to an alternative human type.

People differ from one another in their natural inclinations. Cowardice, miserliness, and hedonism are not simply acquired traits. Their hereditary aspect is supplemented by the influence of the environment. The role of psychological healing is to direct a person's inclinations toward the mean. This sort of therapy calls for temporarily leaning toward the opposite extreme, so that equilibrium at the mean is ultimately achieved. For example, the miser who undertakes a course of repeated profligacy will attain equilibrium at the mean of generosity. A coward who pursues repeated acts of impetuous daring will emerge as a man of courage, and so forth.

In addition to this medical construct, tailor-made to the attributes of each person and influenced by his natural inclinations, there is a fixed component embedded in human nature through which Maimonides accounted for pietism and actions beyond the law's demands. In his view, the two extremes are unequal in the attraction and influence they exert. For example, it is easier to make a generous person out of a squanderer than out of a miser; easier to make a courageous person out of an impetuously daring person than out of a coward; and easier to make a moderate person out of one who is apathetic than out of a hedonist: "This subtle point, which is a canon and secret of the science of medicine, tells us that it is easier for a man of profuse habits to moderate them to generosity, than it is for a miser to become generous. Likewise, it is easier for one who is apathetic (and eschews sin) to be excited to moderate enjoyment, than it is for one, burning with passion, to curb his desires" (*Eight Chapters*, p. 370). The asymmetry results from the greater power generally exerted by inclinations that tend to preserve the self than by those that work contrary to its interests. Cowardice, miserliness, and hedonism are traits that preserve and sustain the self. Cowardice protects the self from danger; miserliness protects it from loss of wealth, and hedonism gathers pleasures. The opposites of these traits—profligacy, impetuous daring, and asceticism—work in the opposite direction, against the self. They provide for others at the expense of the self or deny the self pleasures. The greater power of the impulses and feelings that work to protect the self therefore must be balanced by a constant push in the other direction in order to attain the mean.

Maimonides suggests that this inequality between the extremes' attractive forces can account for the place of pietism and of doing more than the law demands:

> On his account, the saintly ones were not accustomed to cause their dispositions to maintain an exact balance between the two extremes, but deviated somewhat, by way of (caution and) restraint, now to the side of exaggeration, now to that of deficiency. Thus, for instance, abstinence would incline to some degree towards excessive denial of all pleasures; valor would approach somewhat toward temerity; generosity to lavishness; modesty to extreme humility, and so forth. This is what the rabbis hinted at, in their saying, "Do more than the strict letter of the law demands" (Bava Metzia 35a). (*Eight Chapters*, p. 370)

The pious are aware that one extreme naturally has a greater pull than the other; for that reason, they routinely depart somewhat from the mean in the direction of the less attractive extreme. Accordingly, the pietist is not the ideal human type, and his radicalism has no intrinsic value. The pietistic way is merely a fence, a mechanism to prevent falling too far in the (more enticing) direction of the self. Doing more than the law demands serves the same purpose. In this way, Maimonides integrates the pietistic ethos into the structure of the mean, though he thereby changes it into nothing more than a means for avoiding slippage in the more enticing direction. It follows that he permits only a minor departure from the mean.

Too sharp a move toward the self-denying extreme, however, would constitute asceticism that would be contrary to the spirit of the Torah.

Such a person should not be made into ideal exemplar, and it is entirely possible that his ascetic leanings are simply an exercise to help him move back to the mean. Asceticism may sometimes be desirable as a cure, but Maimonides unambiguously rejects any effort to elevate it to a proper way of life:

> When at times, some of the pious ones deviated to one extreme by fasting, keeping nightly vigils, refraining from eating meat or drinking wine, renouncing sexual intercourse, clothing themselves in woolen and hairy garments, dwelling in the mountains, and wandering about in the wilderness, they did so partly as a means of restoring the health of their souls . . . When the ignorant observed saintly man acting thus, not knowing their motives, they considered their deeds virtuous in and of themselves; and so, blindly imitating their acts, thinking thereby to become like them, they chastised their bodies with all kinds of afflictions, imagining that they had acquired perfection and moral worth, and that by this means man would approach nearer to God, as if He hated the human body and desired its destruction. (*Eight Chapters*, pp. 370–371)

The purpose of the Torah is to fulfill human potential, not to transform a person into an arena for suffering and trial in which the struggle against the body is elevated into a value in its own right. If the Torah's goal is to free man from control by his baser instincts and lead him to a higher purpose, asceticism runs contrary to that goal, for it represents continued obsession with the body, albeit in the form of systematic denial. Moreover, the existing halakhic prohibitions have already defined the scope of the small permissible departure from the mean in the direction of the less attractive extreme. By prohibiting certain foods and certain sexual relations, the Torah moves a person a bit off the mean in the direction of withdrawal from physical life. Similarly, the Torah's requirements related to giving— tithes, corners of the field, dropped or forgotten sheaves, debt nullification in the sabbatical year, restoration of fields at the jubilee, and charity in general—represent a slight departure from the mean in the direction of profligacy. The halakhic norms themselves call for doing more than the law demands, and supplementing them would be a further, and forbidden, move toward the extreme:

> Should, however, any one—who would without doubt be foolish if he did so—try to enforce these commands with additional rigor, as, for instance,

by prohibiting eating and drinking more than does the Law, or by restricting connubial intercourse to a greater degree, or by distributing all his money among the poor, or using it for sacred purposes more freely than the Law requires, or by spending it entirely upon sacred objects and upon the sanctuary, he would indeed be performing improper acts, and would be unconsciously going to either one or the other extreme, thus forsaking completely the proper mean. In that connection, I have never heard a more remarkable saying than that of the rabbis, found in the Talmud Yerushalmi in the ninth chapter of the treatise of Nedarim, where they greatly blame those who bind themselves by oaths and vows, in consequence of which they are fettered like prisoners. The exact words they use are, "Said Rabbi Iddai, in the name of Rabbi Issac, 'Do you not think that what the Law prohibits is sufficient for you that you must take upon yourself additional prohibitions?'" (*Eight Chapters*, p. 374)

Pietism, then, is simply a fence erected around the ideal of the mean. Moreover, the Torah itself has enacted prohibitions that accommodate the pietist's departure from that mean. Supplementing those prohibitions through vows and oaths that foreswear other things is a harmful and excessive departure from the mean.

Nobility and Saintliness

The most prominent trait of the ideal Aristotelian type is magnanimity, "greatness of soul," which is situated as the mean between pride and humility. The proud person suffers from exaggerated self-esteem, which leads him to claim honor of which he is unworthy. The humble person, meanwhile, suffers from low self-esteem and improperly degrades himself. A dignified person knows his worth, which stems from his sound moral qualities, and anticipates respect from those around him. His noble traits lend him charisma. He walks slowly, without hurrying, his voice is deep, and his speech is measured. He looks straight ahead and flatters no one; his appearance conveys security, tranquility, and reliability.[2]

The fundamental clash between the ideal citizen in the political tradition and the concept of the ideal person that draws on the religious tradition grows out of their differing assessments of the quality of humility. The harmonious and balanced structure that situates the virtuous person at the

---

[2] *Nichomachean Ethics*, book 4.

mean between two rejected extremes comes apart, in Maimonides' account, when humility is at issue.

First, the term magnanimity does not appear in Maimonides' dictionary of virtues. In his discussions of honor and self-esteem, he defines the median attribute in a different way: humility is the mean between pride and lowliness. Moreover, in the case of other desired traits, a slight departure from the mean is permitted as an act of extra piety. When humility is involved, however, Maimonides treats an inclination toward lowliness as characteristic of the ideal type. In *Avot* 4:4, the *Mishnah* teaches: "Strive to be lowly of spirit, for man's expectation is [to feed] worms." Maimonides comments:

> We have already explained in the preceding chapters that humility is one of the most elevated traits, the mean between pride and lowliness. . . . And we have explained in the fourth chapter that it is proper for a man to incline [somewhat] toward [the less enticing] of the extremes in the manner of a fence [around improper action]. But this trait—that is, pride—is an exception, alone among all traits, for the pious, recognizing how greatly flawed it is and the harm it can cause, distanced themselves from it all the way to the opposite extreme, to absolute lowliness. (*Commentary on the Mishnah, Avot* 4:4)

This departure from the mean toward the extreme of lowliness is reiterated in *Mishneh Torah*: "There are some dispositions in regard to which it is forbidden merely to keep to the middle path. They must be shunned to the extreme. Such a disposition is pride. The right way in this regard is to be not merely meek, but to be humble-minded and lowly of spirit to the extreme" (Book of Knowledge "Laws Concerning Moral Dispositions," 2:3).

Maimonides is here departing significantly from the Aristotelian stance and instead following the Talmudic sources that set humility as a central value. A certain degree of modesty, of feeling insignificant, is inherent in the religious posture toward the world. As a foil for the aristocrat, aware of his self-worth and social presence, there is set the pietist, one who suffers offense but does not offend, and values endless reticence over assertiveness. Because of those qualities, Maimonides associates the attitude toward anger with the departure from the mean associated with humility:

> Anger, too, is an exceedingly bad passion, and one should avoid it to the last extreme. . . . The sages, therefore, charged us that anger should be avoided

> to such a degree that one should train oneself to be unmoved even by things that naturally would provoke anger; and this is the good way. The practice of the righteous is to suffer contumely and not inflict it; to hear themselves reproached, not retort; to be impelled in what they do by love, and to rejoice in suffering. Of them Scripture says, "And they that love Him are like the going forth of the sun in his strength" (Jud. 5:31). (ibid.)

An Aristotelian man of gravitas would regard that stance, at best, as spineless passivity; at worst, it would be hypocrisy. That is how Machiavelli, and (especially) Nietzsche, regarded the image of the Christian saint—a lowly person who deployed his will against himself. In the religious traditions, however, humility and lowliness of spirit are regarded as the crowning virtues, reflecting the way in which one must stand before God.

Aristotle and many after him regarded humility as the internalization of a humble person's false belief about oneself. Were his opinion of himself to correspond to his true worth, he would not be humble, for he is a righteous person even if he has a poor opinion of himself. Humility is a seemingly paradoxical state, in which a person internalizes a false consciousness about his own assessment of his worth. This critique rests on the premise that humble people measure their worth in relation to others, thereby falsely diminishing their own standing while exaggeratingly augmenting that of others. In the tradition of humility, however, the lowly self-assessment does not reflect a comparison of the modest person to other people. Instead, it reflects his sense of awe, which leads him to assess himself in relation to the cosmos or to God.

Moreover, Maimonides' comments on the subject do not suggest that he regards humility as a negation of self-worth. It involves something different, which sets this tradition vis-à-vis the Aristotelian human ideal. In speaking of the virtue of lowliness of spirit, Maimonides illustrates lowliness with a story that appears to be drawn from the Sufi tradition:

> I have seen in one of the books on morals that a pious person was asked: What is the happiest day you have experienced? He replied: It was a day when I was journeying by ship, and my place aboard ship was the lowest of all, and I was dressed in old rags. Also on the ship were merchants and wealthy men. I was lying at my place, and one of the men on the ship got up to urinate. Noticing my lowliness and the inferiority of my situation, he exposed himself and urinated on me. I was amazed at the power of his audacity, but, by God, I was not distressed at all by his action. It did not anger

me, and I rejoiced greatly at having reached a level at which I would not be distressed by the action of this deficient person and could pay it no heed. And there is no doubt that this is the ultimate in lowliness of spirit, totally removed from pride. (*Commentary on the Mishnah*, Avot 4:4)

Lowliness of spirit is not at all tied to a low assessment of one's self-worth. This pietist, who was not angered by the wealthy merchant who urinated on him, did not believe himself so debased as to be worthy of being urinated on. Quite the contrary. The humble man, the man of lowly spirit, is one whose self-esteem does not depend on social recognition. It follows that humility is not a belief in the lowliness of one's stature; rather, it is indifference to the value of honor. A humble person is liberated, having achieved what later comes to be termed "the quality of equanimity." His tranquility is autonomous, independent of how his surroundings react to him. And so, the humble person's indifference to honor and social recognition is anchored in his recognition of his true self-worth, a recognition independent of anything extraneous.

There is a tension between humility so conceived and the civic ideal of the Greco-Roman republican tradition. The good citizen pursues recognition and wants to appear and be present in the public arena. Society effectively controls its citizens through the assignment of honor and shame. The self-effacing, stoic figure that Maimonides portrays is, in that sense, an apolitical creature, and Machiavelli and Rousseau had good reason to see that figure as a threat to the power and standing of the state. An indifferent person of this sort serving as a soldier would not be concerned about dying, but neither would he crave victory.

The gap between the ideal of lowliness of spirit and the virtue of dignity reflects an even more basic and profound issue related to the value of political life. A good citizen, claimed Aristotle, is a good man. As a private individual, a person is in the circular grip of the life cycle: birth, labor, rest, and death, and around again in the next generation. Only when he emerges into the public, political domain does a person fulfill himself as a human being in the complete sense. He adjudicates and legislates, evaluates things and deploys his powers of reason, and gives expression to his virtues as a human being. Hence Aristotle's dictum that "man is by nature a political animal."[3] Man's nature as a complete being is expressed in the polity; outside the polity are the animals and the gods. In the *Nicomachean Ethics*, to

[3] *Politics* book 1, chap. 2.

be sure, we find a tension between this noble civic ideal and the philosopher who devotes himself to a contemplative life; that latter figure appears in Book X of the treatise. But despite that tension, which has been widely discussed, the human figure that Aristotle masterfully depicted is one that achieves its peak in free and sovereign participation in public life.

In the *Commentary on the Mishnah* and *Mishneh Torah*, Maimonides treats the contemplative life as the peak of human perfection. The polity is merely a means to that end, needed because humanity cannot exist without a division of labor and cooperative efforts. Consistent with that view, he uses the dictum "man is a political animal" in a very different way: man's ability to realize his purpose and his goal depends on the existence of a stable political body, but that body is but a means for promoting knowledge of the world and of God.

Two ideas—that the capacity to know was the essence of humanity and that there existed beliefs necessary to maintaining the political order—led Maimonides to undertake a major shift in the character of the Jewish religion as he sought to identify a binding set of beliefs that would serve as the criterion for membership in the community of Israel. The process was begun in the *Commentary on the Mishnah* and continued in *Mishneh Torah*, in which Maimonides formulated normative Jewish theology. Moreover, this approach gave the relationship between philosophy and the Jewish tradition a distinctive meaning that is worthy of discussion. The fundamental premise of pre-Maimonidean Jewish philosophy was that there existed a rational process, independent of tradition or revelation, for gaining knowledge about God, the world, and morality. Accordingly, philosophical understanding had the capacity to reinforce faith, though occasional contradictions might require reinterpretation. That was the approach taken by the first systematic Jewish philosopher, Sa'adyah Ga'on, in his treatise *Beliefs and Opinions*, and it is the most basic element of every philosophical interpretation of Judaism.

Maimonides took a sizable step away from this premise in his understanding of the relationship between philosophy and religion. In his view, not only does philosophy carry critical weight, but the life of philosophical contemplation has a redemptive religious dimension. The basic concepts of religious existence—union with God, love and awe, the world to come, etc.—are understood as experiences profoundly linked to processes of cognition and speculation. Union with God, for example, is taken to be the pinnacle of a cognitive process, for Aristotelian epistemology teaches that the thinker becomes identified with the objects of his knowledge. Love is a burning desire to know God and the world, and it is aroused in light of earlier experiences of knowledge. Awe is a drawing back, a sense of insignificance and marginality that flows from an awareness of the universe and man's place within it; it is accompanied, though, by the desire to know, defined as love.

The pinnacle of religious life is the understanding of God to the extent of a person's ability, and it can be achieved only through knowledge of physics and metaphysics. That knowledge of nature and what is above nature, which is the foundation of religious perfection, is acquired through ongoing contact with sources of knowledge that lie outside the Jewish tradition—primarily Aristotle's teachings and their various interpretations in Arab philosophy. This view does not merely deny that there is any hostility between philosophy and religion; it makes a further claim and maintains that achieving the highest ideal of religious life requires resort to the philosophical tradition. Maimonides thus did not share the model of thought known today as *torah u-madda* (Torah and science), a model that strives to bridge the gaps between Torah and science and argues that they can coexist peacefully. For Maimonides, engaging in science is the pinnacle of religious existence, directed toward realizing the purpose of human existence on earth.

As early as in the *Commentary on the Mishnah*, when Maimonides was taking his first steps as a halakhist, his religious consciousness was already characterized by a philosophical ethos. Maimonidean studies have most often distinguished between his halakhic writings and his philosophical writings, between Maimonides as halakhist and Maimonides as philosopher, and between Maimonides the halakhist addressing himself to the public and Maimonides the philosopher addressing himself to an individual; but these distinctions were never really part of his life. The important elements of philosophical sensibility—especially those that appear to question the centrality of the *via activa* as a religious goal—appear in the earliest stages of his literary oeuvre. These elements became more pronounced in *Mishneh Torah*, and by integrating the philosophical ethos into a halakhic code, he sought to bring about a transformation unprecedented in Jewish history and make it a binding halakhic norm.

CHAPTER FOUR

What Is *Mishneh Torah*?

The Aims and Qualities of the Compilation

In the Introduction to his *Mishneh Torah*, Maimonides describes one of his accomplishments in that tract as having made *halakhah* (Jewish law) into a transparent, accessible system. Talmudic legal literature had developed as an uncontrollable organism, laden with disputes and fragmented give and take recorded in Aramaic, a language not used in daily life; as a result, the halakhic material had become unapproachable. Even one who had labored to attain a degree of mastery over the literature could not be assured of the ability to extract practical legal rulings from the Talmudic morass. He would always remain justifiably concerned that he had failed to understand the complex debate, that he had chosen wrongly among the wealth of opinions cited in the discussion, or, most of all, that he had missed a reference to his subject elsewhere in the Talmud, in some remote, unrelated context—a distinct possibility, given the Talmud's free-wheeling structure—and that the overlooked reference might have fundamentally changed the picture. This complexity of the Talmudic literature was described by Maimonides in his commentary of the *Mishnah*: "It is impossible to reach any conclusions from the Talmud but after a careful study of disparate texts" (Shabbat 4, 1). Maimonides therefore thought that the Jewish people lacked a genuine book of laws. As he mentioned in his letter that described the motivation for writing *Mishneh Torah*: "for, as God lives, I have been zealous on behalf of the Lord God of Israel, seeing a nation lacking a true and comprehensive book of its laws and lacking true and clear opinions; so I did what I did for the sake of God alone" (*Iggerot*, 401). The writing of *Mishneh Torah* was aimed to dramatically change this situation and to transform the chaotic halakhic discourse into a unified lasting and accessible legal system.

These difficulties flow from the Talmudic literature itself; to them, Maimonides added his gloomy historical account of the decline of Torah centers in his day, centers that, in the past, had produced halakhists qualified to extract sound, straightforward *halakhah* from the tangled Talmudic literature:

> In our days, severe vicissitudes prevail, and all feel the pressure of hard times. The wisdom of our wise men has disappeared; the understanding of our prudent men is hidden. Hence, the commentaries of the *Geonim* and their compilations of laws and responses, which they took care to make clear, have in our times become hard to understand so that only a few individuals properly comprehend them. (Introduction to *Mishneh Torah*, p. 39)

Prior to the writing of *Mishneh Torah* there were few attempts by the *Geonim* to compile halakhic tracts that would facilitate the orientation and decision in different areas of halakhah. The *She'iltot* of Rav Achai, *Halakhot Pesukot* ascribed to Yehudai Gaon, *Halakhot Gedolot* of Rabbi Shimeon Qayyara, *Sefer ha-Shetarot* of Saʿadya Gaon, and *Sefer ha-Shevuʿot* of Hai Gaon were among such compilations. To these we can add the great book by Rabbi Isaac Alfasi that follows the sequence of the Talmud. These books were a source of inspiration to Maimonides, but none of them contained all of the *halakhah* and they lacked the great organizational depth and momentum that mark *Mishneh Torah*: "I have been preceded by great sages and scholars who have compiled treatises and issued halakhic rulings in both Hebrew and Arabic on well-known matters. But to issue rulings with respect to the entire Talmud and all the laws of the Torah—in that, no one has preceded me since our holy Rabbi [that is, R. Judah the Prince, compiler of the *Mishnah*] and his holy colleagues" (*Iggerot*, pp. 440–441). *Mishneh Torah* as an extensive and conclusive text was supposed to secure the continuity of *halakhah* and to free it once and for all from the uncontrolled vicissitudes of historical and institutional difficulties.

Besides the need to stabilize the field of the *halakhah*, Maimonides mentioned another aim of the book: the creation of a normative belief system that is far beyond the narrow field of *halakhah* as obligating actual behavior. Besides the lack of comprehensive legal code, Maimonides mentioned as well the need for "true and clear opinions" as motivation for writing *Mishneh Torah*. The integration of law and theology in the work was expressed extensively in his *Essay on Resurrection*:

> I acted the same way in my major work, which I called *Mishneh Torah* . . . I also listed all the religious and legal roots, my objective being that those that are called disciples of the wise, or *Geonim*, or whatever you choose to name them, build their legal details on legal foundations, so that their learning will be organized and their knowledge systematically arranged. I wished to have all this established on religious dogmas. They will no longer cast the knowledge of God behind their backs, but will exert themselves to the limit of their power to attain what will perfect them and bring them nearer to their creator not to what the masses imagine to be perfection. (*Essay on Resurrection*, 213)

The great and genius literary creation was therefore supposed to initiate a total transformation of the structure of *halakhah* and to produce as well shared and obligatory religious beliefs to all of Israel.

The role of the book, following Isadore Twersky's analysis, is reflected well in its main characteristics:

1. The creation of a unanimous text that deletes the controversy and the give and take from the rendering of *halakhah*.
2. The organization of the *halakhah* in a text divided into concentrated and organized subjects that will ease access and control.
3. The writing of *Mishneh Torah* in the language of the *Mishnah* in clear, clean Hebrew.
4. The comprehensive and exhaustive nature of the text that includes all the realms of *halakhah*: the ones that are practiced and the ones that are not.

Through these qualities of compilation Maimonides made the whole *halakhah* transparent and accessible. As he mentioned in his introduction: "so that all the rules shall be accessible to young and old, whether these appertain to the Pentateuchal precepts or to the institutions established by the sages and prophets." As noted, the emphasis is on "accessible": what had previously been concealed and convoluted was made bright and lucid, even to novices unfamiliar with the complex literature underlying these rulings. The adjective "accessible" is preceded by the no less important term "all the rules," which characterizes the treatise as exhaustive as well as accessible. But Maimonides does not stop with this characterization of his treatise as a grand attempt at clarity and comprehensiveness; in the sentence immediately following, he adds the most daring and presumptuous statement ever written by a halakhist about himself: " . . . so that no other work should be needed for ascertaining any of the laws of Israel . . . a person who first reads the Written Law and then this compilation will know from it the whole of the Oral Law, without having occasion to consult any other book between them" (ibid.). Whatever the precise import of this passage—a matter to be considered below—one can readily understand the harsh reactions it elicited along with the powerful hopes to which it gave rise.

Beneath this transparency, however, lies an intense ambiguity bearing on the nature of *Mishneh Torah* itself as a tract and on the concept of authority that underlies it. Every line of the work is indeed a spectacular model of clarity, but the work overall is affected, from the outset, by a profound ambivalence that allows for strikingly varied understandings of its nature. The marvelous transparency of the tract's content compels the premise that any lack of clarity regarding its character is no happenstance, no mere failure of expressive skill or analytical clarity. On the contrary, the author himself has drawn a curtain of smoke, leaving his work's character an open question. As I shall try to show, this thick cloud is the intended result of Maimonides' ambiguous formulations in the introduction to *Mishneh Torah* and his contradictory statements in various letters in which he comments on the nature of the tract. At first glance, the question "what is *Mishneh Torah?*" has a clear and simple answer: it is an effort to create a comprehensive halakhic code. But the term "code" is itself vague, allowing for a wide range of meanings. The key to the various meanings of the work and to the reasons for that meaning's ambiguity is to be found in a close reading of Maimonides' introduction to his tract.

An attentive reading of the introduction to *Mishneh Torah* will give rise to two radically different understandings of the work. The first and more moderate option views *Mishneh Torah* as a representation of the *halakhah*; the second and more radical option sees it as the *halakhah* itself. The clarification of these two options and its implication for the nature of *Mishneh Torah* will be outlined below. Before turning to those possibilities, however, it is worthwhile to examine a preliminary question: why did Maimonides make the effort to describe the history of *halakhah* in such extensive detail in his introduction, and what can we learn from this description concerning the place and role of *Mishneh Torah?* The clarification of the role of the history of *halakhah* in the introduction will contribute a great deal to the comprehension of Maimonides' own self-understanding concerning his place in the history of *halakhah*, and it will serve as a back-

ground to the exposition of the different alternatives of the meaning of
Mishneh Torah.

Mishneh Torah and the History of *halakhah*

In the Introduction to *Mishneh Torah*, Maimonides sets out the history of
halakhah from Moses' time to his own. The history of *halakhah* is not a
halakhic subject in its own right, and Maimonides deals with it broadly
in order to provide context for *Mishneh Torah* and to make it an out-
growth of *halakhah*'s history to his day. But the question to be asked is
how this historical account of the *halakhah* serves *Mishneh Torah*, confirming its urgency or clarifying its meaning. What distinguishes Maimonides' construct of halakhic history from other such efforts, before and
since, such as the *Epistle of Rav Sherira Ga'on* or Rabbi Menaḥem ha-
Me'iri's introduction to his *Beit ha-Beḥirah*? And how can these distinctive
characteristics be explained in light of Maimonides' attempt to provide a
grounding for seeing his enterprise as a decisive moment within halakhic
history?

The plain, immediate purpose of this sort of historical account is to
portray a chain of *halakhah*, starting with the moment of revelation and
culminating in *Mishneh Torah*, a chain that provides an authoritative underpinning for the book itself. That sort of logic underlies, for example,
Abraham Ibn Daud's anti-Karaite *Sefer ha-Qabbalah*, a book whose purpose was to present an uninterrupted continuum of transmission that an-
chors Talmudic and medieval *halakhah* in the revelation at Sinai. Indeed,
the opening paragraph of Maimonides' introduction leaves that impression, for Maimonides there describes a magnificently constructed chain of
transmission of the Oral Torah from Moses to Rabbi Judah the Prince.
This ideal image is shattered at the time of Rabbi Judah the Prince, and
Maimonides' account of that breach at a decisive moment in the history of
halakhah provides the first link between the historical picture painted by
Maimonides and *Mishneh Torah*.

Until the time of Rabbi Judah the Prince, Torah was transmitted orally,
and the composition of the *Mishnah*—in Maimonides' view, the composition of a written book—thus constituted a substantive change in the nature of halakhic transmission. In the period predating the *Mishnah*, the
authoritative halakhic tradition passed orally from generation to generation, and any writing down of *halakhah* was intended only for the personal

use of a particular sage. Accordingly, the appearance of the *Mishnah* as an authoritative, written work constituted a breach of the prohibition against committing the *halakhah* to writing. This literary transgression could be justified, in Maimonides' view, as a response to a historical-political crisis: "Because he saw that the number of disciples was diminishing, fresh calamities were continually happening, the [Roman] government was extending its domain and increasing in power, and Israelites were wandering and emigrating to distant countries. He therefore composed a work to serve as a handbook for all, the contents of which could be rapidly studied and not be forgotten" (Introduction to *Mishneh Torah*, p. 36). The decline in students and the dispersal of Israel compromised the possibility of continuous, organic transmission of the oral tradition within a framework of central institutions, and the creation of a written code was an attempt to overcome that political and historical crisis.

The code was meant to bridge the broad geographic expanse that had been created and that precluded reliance on direct oral transmission with its need for proximity between transmitter and receiver. Similarly, an authoritative tractate of this sort can close the temporal gaps likely to be created in the chain of transmission. A skipped generation constitutes an irreparable breach in an oral chain of transmission, a mortal blow to a mighty body of knowledge that becomes irretrievable. But with the composition of the *Mishnah*, the *halakhah* was freed of its dependence on a continuous transmission of a living, continuous tradition, and the book ensured its existence even when the political situation precluded maintenance of a clear and ordered process of transmission. The writing thus responds to a crisis of time and space undergone by a community that previously had a definite, organic center. *Halakhah* operates within a historical framework, and the basic genre of halakhic transmission is not independent of historical happenstance. The writing of the *Mishnah*—a substantive change in how *halakhah* is transmitted—was the result of a dramatic shift in historical circumstances that demanded a response. In the connection that Maimonides created between political crisis and literary change in the days of Rabbi Judah the Prince, he laid the historical precedent to the writing of *Mishneh Torah* as it is apparent in what follows in the introduction.

After describing the geopolitical crisis in Rabbi Judah's time, Maimonides goes on to depict an ensuing period of continuity and calm in the history of *halakhah*, extending until the time of Ravina and Rav Ashi, the editors of the Babylonian Talmud. With the sealing of the Talmud, that period of continuity came to a premature end and the history of *halakhah* took a sharp new turn. From that point on, Maimonides no longer notes specific individuals who represent the Oral Torah's continuous chain of transmission; instead, he refers to the sages who follow Ravina and Rav Ashi by the general term "*Geonim.*" To convey the sense of a turning point in the orderly and consistent history of *halakhah*, Maimonides uses the literary device of identifying and enumerating a continuous series of forty generations—a round, complete number—from Moses to Ravina and Rav Ashi: "we find that from Rav Ashi [back to] Moses our Teacher there are forty men, as follows . . ." This reiteration of the sages of each generation back to Moses represents Maimonides' effort to indicate the end of the structured, orderly transmission process. As he says: "Ravina and Rav Ashi and their colleagues were the last great sages of Israel who transcribed the Oral Law, issued decrees, enacted ordinances, and instituted customs. Their decrees, ordinances, and customs spread throughout all Israel, wherever they resided."

The demise of that orderly, centralized and continuous transmission following the editing of the Talmud was grounded in a second geopolitical crisis that had a decisive influence on the history of *halakhah*:

> After the court of Rav Ashi, who compiled the Gemara which was finally completed in the days of his son, an extraordinarily great dispersion of Israel throughout the world took place. The people emigrated to remote parts and distant isles. The prevalence of wars and the march of armies made travel insecure. The study of the Torah declined. The Jewish people did not flock to the colleges in their thousands and tens of thousands as heretofore; but in each city and country, individuals who felt the divine call gathered together and occupied themselves with the Torah; studied all the words of the sages and from these learned the method legal interpretation. (Introduction to *Mishneh Torah*, pp. 37–38)

This description clearly recalls Maimonides' account of the crisis in the time of Rabbi Judah the Prince, and it depicts the disintegration even more sharply. Israel underwent "a great dispersion," more extreme than in Rabbi Judah's day. To make matters worse, it was substantially harder to maintain significant contact among the widely dispersed groups because "the prevalence of wars and the march of armies made travel insecure." Of the thousands and myriads who had continued to study in yeshivas even after the time of R. Judah, there now remained only an isolated remnant. This critical situation continued into Maimonides' own lifetime, and, after describing the work of the *Geonim*—shadowed by the loss of any possibility of centralized *halakhah*—he deepens the sense of historical collapse suffered by Israel in his time. That collapse provided the motivation for writing *Mishneh Torah*:

> In our days, severe vicissitudes prevail, and all feel the pressure of hard times. The wisdom of our wise men has disappeared; the understanding of our prudent men is hidden. Hence, the commentaries of the *Geonim* and their compilations of laws and responses, which they took care to make clear, have in our times become hard to understand so that only a few individuals properly comprehend them . . . .On these grounds, I, Moses the son of Maimon the Sefardi, bestirred myself. (ibid., p. 39)

Just as the *Mishnah* of Rabbi Judah the Prince was a dramatic literary reaction to *halakhah*'s first geopolitical crisis, *Mishneh Torah* was a literary and halakhic reaction to the second, even more intense, crisis. Rabbi Judah's change in the mode of halakhic transmission was the precedent for the no-less-significant change Maimonides intended to institute.

Maimonides appears to regard the rise of Islam, and the dispersion of Jewish communities to the Maghrib and Spain in its wake, as the "extraordinarily great dispersion" that has taken place since the completion of the Talmud. His remarks about the intensified historical crisis of his own time appear to relate to the destruction of Andalusian Jewry by the Almohads and to his sense of being an exile bereft of his no-longer-extant cultural home. By organizing his introduction as a continuum of transmission and organic development interrupted by two sharp historical breaks, he forges an immediate bond between Rabbi Judah's *Mishnah* and his own *Mishneh Torah*.

The *Mishnah* of Rabbi Judah the Prince and *Mishneh Torah*

The first role played by the formulation of halakhic history in Maimonides' introduction thus seems clear enough. Maimonides forges a fundamental connection between, on the one hand, changes in the *halakhah*'s modes of transmission and literary expression and, on the other, political and historical crises. He uses that narrative to set up Rabbi Judah's *Mishnah* as a precedent legitimating his *Mishneh Torah*. We shall see below that the specific formulation of the halakhic history has another, more substantive role with regard to *Mishneh Torah* and its essential nature. Before turning to that, however, we should first consider several points related to the parallels Maimonides draws between Rabbi Judah's *Mishnah* and his own *Mishneh Torah*.

Is the *Mishnah* in fact a precedent for *Mishneh Torah*? To see it as such is made possible by, among other things, a disputed understanding of the sort of composition it is. Because Maimonides takes the *Mishnah* as precedent for his own work, he is required to portray it in a manner that permits it to play that role in the history of *halakhah*. The first step in that process is to claim that the *Mishnah* was, in fact, written. That conclusion, however, was not universally accepted by the medieval sages who preceded Maimonides, some of whom thought the *Mishnah* was a treatise transmitted orally and disseminated by *tanna'im* scholars who recited the *Mishnah* who served, in effect, as living books within the study hall. According to that view—recognized in contemporary scholarship as the more reasonable one—the *Mishnah* was not a written composition, disseminated by copying; rather, the editing of the *Mishnah* entailed the crystallization of a precise, authoritative version of halakhic material that continued to be transmitted orally. If that is the case, the composition of the *Mishnah* was not a profound, substantive, or even halakhic departure from the ways in which *halakhah* had been transmitted in the past.

Similarly, the connection drawn by Maimonides between Rabbi Judah's *Mishnah* and the political crisis that supposedly intensified in his time leads him to argue that the *Mishnah* constitutes an exhaustive, accessible summary of the entire *halakhah* up to that point: "[Rabbi Judah] gathered together all the traditions, enactments, interpretations, and expositions of every portion of the Torah, that had either come down from Moses our Teacher or had been deduced by the courts in successive generations. All this material he redacted in the *Mishnah*, which was diligently taught in public, and thus became universally known among the Jewish people" (Introduction to *Mishneh Torah*, 36). But this view of the matter is called into question by an examination of the *Mishnah*'s nature as a composition. Was it written as a comprehensive summary of the *halakhah* as it had developed to that point, or was it a systematic treatment of the disputed points at issue in the study hall? Similarly, was it composed in a manner making it accessible to all, or did it contemplate a substantial degree of prior knowledge—

accounting for its clear need for extensive commentary to make it transparently understandable? Given the historical-political construct he creates, Maimonides had to describe the *Mishnah* as he did, thereby making it available as a precedent for *Mishneh Torah*, written, in Maimonides' opinion, under similar constraints and for similar purposes.

In his letter to Pinḥas the Judge of Alexandria, Maimonides emphasizes the innovative nature of his composition and observes that the sole precedent for such an effort is R. Judah's *Mishnah*: "I have been preceded by *Geonim* and great scholars who composed treatises and issued rulings in Hebrew and in Arabic on various subjects that are known. But to decide the *halakhah* regarding the entire Talmud and all the laws of the Torah is something no one has done before me except our Holy Rabbi [Judah the Prince] and his holy group [of colleagues]" (*Iggerot*, pp. 439–440). But the most substantial problem that arose by citing the *Mishnah* as precedent for *Mishneh Torah* grows out of the great difference between the two works. The *Mishnah*, like *Mishneh Torah*, mostly states the laws without the give and take of argumentation; unlike *Mishneh Torah*, however, it reports disagreements aplenty. In *Mishneh Torah*, Maimonides disregarded almost entirely the abundance of halakhic opinions, attempting thereby to establish a uniform, comprehensive halakhic system, in contrast to what came before him. The appearance in the *Mishnah* of disagreements raises the fundamental question of whether the work can be seen as a code. But even if it is a code, it is a flexible, temporary one. Alongside the majority positions evidently reported as *halakhah*, the *Mishnah*'s editor included minority opinions that might be relied on in the future and used to reverse what is now the decision of the majority. The two works are thus not comparable in the degree of uniformity they mean to introduce into the *halakhah*. Every act of canonization is accompanied by censorship. The editor of the *Mishnah*, however, though he decides the *halakhah* in accord with the majority position, also presents an array of dissenting views; as a result, the *Mishnah*'s determination of the *halakhah* does not censor the now rejected views out of the normative, collective memory. By preserving the minority opinions, this sort of redaction transforms the halakhic determination into something that might be challenged in the future. Maimonides, in contrast, resolutely deletes the views that differ from his own, and, in his drive toward almost absolute standardization of the *halakhah*, he declines even to mention them as rejected alternatives.

In his letter to Pinḥas the Judge, Maimonides confronts this divergence
between his tract and the *Mishnah*, clearly recognizing that it could jeopardize the usefulness of the *Mishnah* as precedent:

> Regarding matters as to which Rabbi [Judah the Prince] had no firm hal-
> akhic decision but only a dispute, and he himself was not inclined in one
> direction or the other—he reported each view in the name of its propo-
> nent . . . for at that time, many acted in accord with one view and many
> acted in accord with the other . . . It is improper [in principle] to mention
> anything other than decided *halakhah*, but at that time, some did this and
> others did that, and among the audience, some accepted the view of one
> and some accepted the view of the other—accordingly, there was a need to
> refer [to both views]. And since I have chosen the way of the *Mishnah*, and
> the *Gemara* has now ruled on each and every *halakhah*—either specifically
> or by one of the rules used to decide *halakhot*—and there are no longer two
> [sets of] practices, why should I mention the name of a person whose view
> of the *halakhah* is rejected? (*Iggerot*, pp. 441–442)

In order to close the gap between *Mishneh Torah* and the *Mishnah*, Maimonides had to recast the phenomenon of disagreement within the *Mishnah*. In most instances of disagreement, the *halakhah* is in accord with the
majority view, reported by Rabbi Judah without attribution to a particular
sage. Where a dispute between two *tanna'im* is reported without resolution, it is not because the *Mishnah* is a flexible document that sets out to
preserve multiple opinions. It is, rather, because the existence of the dispute has been imposed on the *Mishnah*'s redactor—either because he
lacked the ability to resolve it or because he lacked the power to impose
uniform practice and uproot communities' diverse practices. But once the
Talmud resolved disputes that had been left unresolved in the *Mishnah*,
and the rules of decision-making allowed for resolution of the disputes in
the Talmud itself, there was no longer any need to leave the halakhic question open, and an unambiguous *halakhah* could be presented.

Maimonides thus reaches two significant determinations that support
his presentation of *Mishneh Torah* as the pinnacle and conclusion of the
ongoing process of halakhic unification. First, he determined that Rabbi
Judah's purpose in composing the *Mishnah* was to unify the *halakhah* and
that the unresolved disputes that remained in the *Mishnah* were there because the editor had no choice but to include them. Second, he deter-

mined that the Talmud as a tract made it possible to resolve matters that had been left unresolved in the *Mishnah*.

One could have presented an opposing view of the dynamic: instead of Maimonides' account of progressively more fundamental unity, one might have depicted the literary continuum of *Mishnah* and Talmud as one of progressively broader dispute, in which the fertile field of *halakhah* constantly brought forth new possibilities. In that view, the *Mishnah* was a flexible code that included minority opinions that might come to prevail in the future, and the Talmud, rather than constraining the debate, broadened it by presenting a wealth of interpretive possibilities not contemplated by the *Mishnah* itself. It is possible, by using various rules of decision-making, to extract practical *halakhah* from the Talmud, but it seems clear that describing the Talmud as a composition tending to limit and resolve the disputes remaining in the *Mishnah* is well-suited to Maimonides' interest in presenting his treatise as a continuation of the tendency that began with the *halakhah*'s foundational documents.

The Authority of the Talmud and the Authority of the *Geonim*

The first task of halakhic history as Maimonides articulates it, accordingly, is to forge a link between literary changes and historical crises, thereby laying the foundation for regarding the *Mishnah* as a precedent for *Mishneh Torah*. As noted, that process led to a unique understanding of the *Mishnah*'s significance as a composition, reflecting Maimonides' effort to overcome the possible gap between his precedent and *Mishneh Torah* itself. The second, and more significant, role of the introduction to *Mishneh Torah* is enabling us to understand the work's nature as connected to the way in which Maimonides describes the history of *halakhah* from the moment the chain of transmission and organic development was cut off, that is, from the end of the era of Ravina and Rav Ashi. As noted, Maimonides characterizes Ravina and Rav Ashi as follows: "the last great sages of Israel who transcribed the Oral Law, issued decrees, enacted ordinances, and instituted customs. Their decrees, ordinances, and customs spread throughout all Israel, wherever they resided." Following that period, the Jews were overtaken by an even more acute crisis than in the days of Rabbi Judah the Prince; as noted earlier, Maimonides describes the two episodes in similar terms but uses more intense language in speaking of the later one. The seriousness of the geopolitical situation at the beginning of the geonic period created a new halakhic situation. The decisions of the *Geonim* were not accepted by all Jews, "because of the remoteness of Jewish settlements and the difficulties of travel" (Introduction to *Mishneh Torah*, p. 38). That historical fact resulted in the geonic rulings being local and temporary. A *ga'on*'s halakhic instruction bound neither other courts in other communities nor succeeding generations:

> No compulsion is exercised on those living in one country to observe the customs of another country; nor is any court directed to issue a decree that had been issued by another court in the same country. So too, if one of the *Geonim* taught that a certain way of judgment was correct, and it became clear to a court at a later date that this was not in accordance with the view of the Gemara, the earlier authority is not necessarily followed but that view is adopted which seems more reasonable, whether it be that of an earlier or later authority." (ibid.)

The *Geonim* themselves in no way shared Maimonides' view of their limited authority in comparison to that of the Talmud. They saw themselves as seated on the throne of Ravina and Rav Ashi, direct successors to the glorious Talmudic tradition, and they regarded their rulings as those of the Great Court, binding on the entire dispersion of Israel. Maimonides, on the other hand, declares absolute independence from the binding authority of the *Geonim*. He does not make an effort to attribute their lack of authority to any deficiency in their standing as halakhists; rather, he traces their loss of authority to the intensifying historical and political crisis following the Talmudic period. The process is readily apparent in the following paragraph, in which Maimonides contrasts the Talmud's binding authority with the non-binding nature of the geonic rulings:

> The foregoing observations refer to rules, decrees, ordinances, and customs that originated after the Talmud had been compiled. But whatever is already mentioned in the Babylonian Talmud is binding on all Israel. And every city and country is bound to observe all the customs observed by the sages of the Gemara, promulgate their decrees, and uphold their institutions, on the ground that all the customs, decrees, and institutions mentioned in the Talmud received the assent of all Israel, and those sages who instituted the ordinances, issued the decrees, introduced the customs, gave the decisions, and taught that a certain ruling was correct, constituted the

total body or the majority of Israel's wise men. They were the leaders who received from each other the traditions concerning the fundamentals of Judaism in unbroken succession back to Moses our Teacher, upon whom be peace. (ibid.)

It should be emphasized that Maimonides does not attribute the greater authority of the Talmud to its predating the geonic literature. If he did, he himself would be subordinate to the authority of the *Geonim*, who preceded him in time. Instead, he establishes a novel basis for the Talmud's authority: Talmudic *halakhah* is binding at all places and all times because it made its way to and was accepted by all Israel.

Maimonides' principled position concerning the limited authority of the *Geonim* is manifested in his diverse rulings in *Mishneh Torah*. Throughout the compilation the opinions of the *Geonim* are explicitly mentioned and cited in dozens of places, at times in agreement and at times in disagreement. Maimonides selected from the *Geonim*'s rulings only those that seemed to him correct without an a priori commitment to their authority. For example, he accepted the *Geonim*'s position that a court can administer an oath in any language in which the defended understand, against the opinion of his teachers the Rif and Joseph ibn Migash, who claimed that such an oath ought to be administered only in Hebrew:

> The judges administer the oath to the person taking it in any language that he understands. The *Geonim* ruled in this manner. My masters, however, ruled that an oath should be administered only in *leshon haqodesh* [holy tongue]. This ruling should not be relied upon. Although it has become customary to administer oaths in *leshon haqodesh*, the person taking the oath should be familiarized with the matter until he understands the wording of the oath. (Laws Concerning Oaths, 11:14)

In many places in which Maimonides rejected the position of the *Geonim*, he diverts from his policy of omitting the reasoning that led to his rulings, and he adds a short argument supporting his position, assuming that such a rejection needs justification. In the laws concerning borrowers and lenders, Maimonides quotes the position of the *Geonim* that a guarantor who formulated his commitment in general, unrestricted terms obligates himself to pay any debt that the person who he guaranteed took upon himself. Maimonides rejected this ruling while quoting the opposing geonic position and adding a justification for its rejection:

The following opinions were stated with regard to a person who did not limit the extent of the commitment he made to serve as a guarantor. For example, he told the lender: "Give him whatever you give him, I will guarantee it," "Sell to him, and I will guarantee it," or "Lend him, and I will guarantee it." There are *Geonim* who rule that even if the other person sells 10,000 *zuz* worth of merchandise or lends 100,000 *zuz* to the person named, the guarantor becomes responsible for the entire amount. It appears to me, by contrast, that the guarantor is not liable at all. Since he does not know for what he undertook the liability, he did not make a serious commitment and did not obligate himself. These are words of reason that a person of understanding will appreciate. (Laws Concerning Creditor and Debtor, 25:13)

A guarantee with no specification is null and void because such a generalized formulation lacks a genuine commitment on the part of the guarantor.

An interesting example of a relatively long polemics against the *Geonim*'s position relates to their ruling concerning a borrower who made an explicit condition with the lender that the paying of the debt will be done in the presence of particular witnesses. According to their position, if the debt was paid in the presence of other witnesses, their testimony is unacceptable. Maimonides reasoned against this position and added that the ruling of the *Geonim* is based upon a wrong version of the Talmud:

This is a scribal error. For this reason, the halachic authorities [*Geonim*] erred because of those texts. I have researched ancient versions of the text and I found that they state that the borrower's word is accepted. In Egypt, a portion of an ancient text of the Talmud written on parchment, as was the custom in the era approximately 500 years before the present era, came to my possession. I found two versions of this law among those parchments. Both state: "If he claims: 'I fulfilled the stipulation and repaid you in the presence of so-and-so and so-and-so, and they journeyed overseas or died,' his word is accepted." (ibid. 15, 2)

Maimonides thus relied on ancient manuscripts of the Talmud for ruling against the version of the *Geonim*.

His lack of commitment to the *Geonim*'s positions is manifested not only concerning their particular readings of the Talmud but also to their independent enactments. Maimonides rejected one of the most important of geonic enactments, which postulated that in the case of a wife who claimed that her husband is repulsive to her, the husband is forced to grant her a divorce with the full financial compensation of marriage contract—the ketubah. This enactment, which had immense importance concerning a woman's position, is rejected by Maimonides in his laws of marriage in the following way: "There are *Geonim* who say that in Babylonia different customs were followed with regard to a woman who rebels [avoiding sexual relationship with her husband]. These customs have not, however, spread throughout the majority of the Jewish community, and in most places within the Jewish community, there are many sages of stature who differ with them. [Therefore,] it is proper to follow the laws prescribed by the Talmud" (*Laws of Marriage*, 14:14).

Nevertheless, following his selective policy, Maimonides accepted two other important enactments of the *Geonim* though they differ from the Talmudic rulings. The Talmud states that the collection of debt from heirs can be done only from land of the estate that is mortgaged for such purpose and not from movable property. The *Geonim* who wished to protect the interests of the lenders enacted that debt can be collected from the movables of the heirs as well. In *Mishneh Torah* Maimonides accepted this enactment in a few places. One of them relates to the collection of a debt that resulted from damage: "The *Geonim* have already ordained that a debt owed a creditor can be expropriated from the movable property [in the estate]. This ruling has been accepted by all the [Jewish] courts of law. Therefore, damages may also be expropriated from movable property left to heirs" (Laws Concerning Damage to Property, 8:12).

Another enactment of the *Geonim* accepted by Maimonides against the Talmud's position aims as well to protect the interest of the creditor. According to the law of the Talmud, a borrower that has no capacity to pay his debt is exempted from such payment until he will have some property in his possession. The *Geonim* worsened the position of the borrower and obligated him in such a case to swear that he has no property and that when he does get hold of any property he will use it immediately to pay back his debt:

> When, however, the *Geonim* of the early generations who arose after the compilation of the Talmud saw that the number of deceitful people had increased and the possibility of obtaining loans was diminishing, they ordained that a debtor who claims bankruptcy should be required to take a

severe oath, comparable to a Scriptural oath, administered while he is holding a sacred article, that he does not possess any property aside from what
he is given in consideration, that he has not hidden his property in the
hands of others, or given the property to others as a present with the intent
that it be returned. (Laws Concerning Creditor and Debtor 2, 2)

Yet Maimonides made an explicit effort to limit the scope of the enactment in order that it will not harm the position granted by the Torah to a
lender in distress. The enacted doesn't give the right to the lender to search
the home of the borrower, and if it is known that the lender is poor, it is
prohibited to force him to swear an oath:

> An exception to the above practice is made with regard to a person who has
> established a reputation for being poor and virtuous, and conducts himself
> in a trustworthy manner, and this is known to the judges and the majority
> of the people. If a creditor comes and seeks to make this person take the
> oath mentioned above, and it can be presumed that the plaintiff has no
> doubt about the debtor's state of poverty, but instead wishes to cause him
> exasperation with this oath, to torment him and to embarrass him publicly,
> to take revenge upon him or to force him to borrow money from gentiles or
> take property belonging to his wife to pay this creditor and absolve himself
> from taking this oath, it appears to me that it is forbidden for a God-fearing
> judge to have this oath administered. If he does administer this oath, he
> violates the Scriptural prohibition: "Do not act as a creditor toward him."
> Moreover, the judge should reproach the creditor and castigate him, for he
> is bearing a grudge and acting according to the reckless whims of his heart.
> (ibid., 2, 4)

In Maimonides' position the reduction of the authority of the *Geonim*
is grounded in a broader theory of authority of *halakhah*. According to
Maimonides, as was mentioned, the authority of the Talmud stems from
the fact that it was accepted by the people of Israel, but the enactments of
the *Geonim* and their interpretation had not achieved such recognition.
One can envision other groundings for Talmudic authority, and they were
indeed suggested by Maimonides' opponents. Accusing him of basing the
Talmud's authority on the weak reed of random historical circumstance,
they sought to anchor that authority in something more substantial: either
the Talmud's proximity and faithfulness to the ancient halakhic tradition,
or a more general notion of ongoing generational decline, which enhanced

the stature of the *amora'im* [the Talmudic sages] in relation to those who followed them.

Maimonides blends his specific picture of halakhic history with a fundamental concept of the sources from which halakhic literature acquires authority. He thereby forges a strong link between history and *halakhah* and decisively limits the authority of the *Geonim* while enhancing that of the Talmud. The loss of centralization—a political condition—does not merely impede the spread of halakhic decisions throughout all Israel; it weakens their very authority, for that authority depends on their dissemination and acceptance. The *Geonim*, despite all their efforts, were caught up in a period of geopolitical breakdown, and that breakdown undermined their ability to generate binding *halakhah*. According to this view, the connection between *halakhah* and circumstance is an internal one: a certain degree of centralization is necessary not only to maintain *halakhah* as an effective system but, more fundamentally, for it to become *halakhah*. Maimonides uses the historical picture into which he casts his novel concept of authority as the mechanism for creating his desired gap between the absolute authority of the Talmud and the limited authority of the *Geonim*.

Mishneh Torah: The Moderate and Radical Alternatives

Maimonides' approach to the authority of the Talmud, and its connection to Jewish geopolitics, plays a significant role as well with respect to *Mishneh Torah* itself as a composition. There are two principal possibilities for understanding *Mishneh Torah* as a composition; I will call one "moderate" and the other "radical." The distinction will help us define more sharply the role played by Maimonides' concept of Talmudic authority in matters related to his tract.

The basic question regarding the essence of *Mishneh Torah* is as follows: Did Maimonides believe *Mishneh Torah* to be an accomplished, perhaps perfect, representation of the *halakhah*, or did he believe it to be the *halakhah* itself? Let me clarify the question by reference to jurisprudence in general. The literature of the law includes numerous treatises written by various experts on various areas of law—torts, contracts, criminal law, and so forth. These treatises have a considerable influence on judges' rulings and they are regarded as accomplished, crystallized representations of the law, but the legal system is not bound by them as it is bound by a statute. According to the moderate reading, *Mishneh Torah* is a treatise of this sort, dealing with the entire range of *halakhah*. It is a broad, comprehensive representation of the *halakhah*, to be taken into account by decision-makers in their rulings. But it is possible as well that Maimonides considered *Mishneh Torah* to be not a representation of the law but the law itself. In this radical reading, *Mishneh Torah* plays the role of a set of laws that are binding in the same sense as the Talmud.

The distinction between the moderate and radical readings can be set up as follows. On the radical alternative, Maimonides believed that a future judge ruling contrary to *Mishneh Torah* would have erred on a matter of law. His situation would be that of one who had erred with regard to something stated explicitly in the Talmud, and his ruling would be null, because *Mishneh Torah* is the *halakhah*. In the moderate alternative, in contrast, Maimonides believed that such a judge might have erred in his reasoning: his ruling does not contradict a halakhic principle itself, but it fails to follow, perhaps erroneously, a better understanding of the *halakhah*.

The distinction between the moderate and radical possibilities may be articulated as a distinction between retail and wholesale authoritativeness. In the moderate reading, the authority of each ruling within *Mishneh Torah* derives from its correct interpretation of the *halakhah*'s canonical sources. Each and every ruling is evaluated individually—on a retail basis—to determine whether it in fact successfully represents the halakhic literature. If, however, *Mishneh Torah* is *halakhah* itself, its authority must be considered on a wholesale basis. The instant the book is recognized as canonical, the authority of Maimonides' rulings stems from what H. L. Hart termed the "rule of recognition," which assigns force to all the rulings, without considering the reliability of each one individually.

If Maimonides in fact believed that his rulings in *Mishneh Torah* constituted *halakhah* itself and that his book had canonical status in the same sense as did the *Mishnah* and the Talmud, we may reasonably ask what he thought to be the source of his book's authority. The question would not concern us if Maimonides believed *Mishneh Torah* simply to be a representation and summary of the *halakhah*—i.e., on the moderate reading—for its authority would then derive from its accomplished review and presentation of earlier authoritative sources. But if *Mishneh Torah* is *halakhah* itself—the radical reading—what is the source of its authority and what transforms it from a magnificent representation of the law into a binding, canonical text?

Maimonides appears to answer this question by again constructing halakhic history and folding into his concept of Talmudic authority. The premise that the Talmud is binding because it spread to and was accepted by all Israel lays the groundwork for the possibility of *Mishneh Torah* being transformed into a binding halakhic book in the event it, too, is accepted by all Israel. Maimonides' claim, at the end of the introduction, that *Mishneh Torah* will ultimately obviate all other halakhic literature and that all Israel will learn *halakhah* from it is thus not merely an aspiration related to the awesome quality of the treatise; it is also, in effect, the basis for its future canonical status: when *Mishneh Torah* spreads to and is accepted by all Israel, it will become canonical in the same way as the Talmud itself. Maimonides' concept of the Talmud's distinctive authority and its integration into the historical narrative he spins thus serves a dual purpose in the introduction. It frees Maimonides from allegiance to geonic *halakhah*, which did not gain acceptance by all Israel, and it implants in halakhic history the conceptual framework that will allow for *Mishneh Torah*'s future authoritativeness as a canonical halakhic text.

In light of this unique view of the narrative of halakhic history and the potential place of *Mishneh Torah* as a canonical work, we can understand Maimonides' self-understanding in the following manner. He portrayed *halakhah* in a profound state of crisis resulting from harsh political conditions that had become progressively worse since the completion of the Talmud. In these circumstances, the prospect of centralized, institutional halakhic authority—which depends on political stability—was lost. The loss of any possibility of centralized authority, in turn, gave the *halakhah* a localized, interim quality, unraveling what had been a uniform, universally accepted system. Maimonides sought to reverse this situation through a dramatic literary exploit that would change the state of *halakhah* without changing the geopolitical conditions that had brought about its fragmentation. He wanted to overcome these harsh conditions by means of a mighty composition that, in effect, would create a virtual center able to serve as a stand-in for political stability. *Mishneh Torah* would allow for the creation of an imaginary realm, a realm centered on faithfulness to a book that would be accepted throughout Israel's dispersion. This effort was particularly audacious because the sought-after change would come about solely by dint of the composition's inherent power and its author's greatness and fame; the face of *halakhah* would be totally transformed without any political or institutional change.

Maimonides' account in the introduction to *Mishneh Torah* is transformed from aspiration to vision in his letter to his student Joseph. In reassuring his student, who found himself in the eye of the critical storm raging in Baghdad over *Mishneh Torah*, Maimonides envisions a time, following that initial, resentful criticism, when *Mishneh Torah* would be accepted throughout Israel: "All you have told us about those who refuse to accept it as it ought to be accepted—that is only in my time. In future times, however, when jealousy and the drive to dominate wane, all Israel will be satisfied with it alone, and all else without doubt will be set aside." Given the way Maimonides explains why the Talmud is authoritative and the *Geonim* are not, the hoped-for universal acceptance of *Mishneh Torah* will do more than signify its success; it will be what ultimately confers authoritativeness on the composition.

Mishneh Torah and Jewish Curriculum

There are, then, two entirely different ways of understanding *Mishneh Torah* as a composition: a more moderate one that sees it as an accomplished representation of the *halakhah*; and a more radical and daring one that sees it as *halakhah* itself. The distinction between those views can be taken a step further by taking account of an additional component, no less important with regard to Maimonides' perception of his work: the status of halakhic literature predating *Mishneh Torah* now that *Mishneh Torah* has been written. Is *Mishneh Torah* a summing-up of that earlier literature or a replacement for it? Central to the question is an understanding of the reason Maimonides gives for naming his book *Mishneh Torah* (literally, "Repetition of the Torah"): "a person who first reads the Written Law and then this compilation, will know from it the whole of the Oral Law, without having occasion to consult any other book between them" (Introduction to *Mishneh Torah*, p. 40). That bold sentence, too, allows for two entirely different interpretations.

A more moderate reading will take it to mean that *Mishneh Torah* is a comprehensive, accessible summary of the *halakhah* for those unable to dwell on it in depth, either because of the intricacy and complexity of the earlier halakhic literature or because of the geopolitical crisis that made the *halakhah* fragmented and inaccessible. For such people—the vast majority of Jews—study of *Mishneh Torah* makes possible a faithful, halakhic way of life and provides a picture of the entire Oral Torah. But scholars having the intelligence, leisure, and proximity to study halls and educational institutions that enable them to maintain unmediated contact with the halakhic literature should continue to apply themselves to it, toiling in the fields of Torah as before.

The much more radical reading of the statement, however, takes it to mean that *Mishneh Torah* does not merely summarize the earlier halakhic literature; it actually replaces it. In creating a canonical work of *halakhah*, Maimonides claims, as a practical matter, to have rendered the earlier halakhic literature superfluous: "without having occasion to consult any other book between them." That far-reaching claim makes the composition of *Mishneh Torah* an act of immense consequence not only for *halakhah* itself but for all of Jewish culture. With the canonization of *Mishneh Torah*, there disappears from Jewish cultural memory the vast wealth of halakhic discourse that incorporated the many rejected opinions, alternative interpretations, and hypothetical rationales, along with the dozens of books by earlier halakhists. On this radical interpretation of *Mishneh Torah* as replacement rather than summary, Maimonides meant the work not only to reshape the face of *halakhah* but also to transform the traditional Jewish curriculum.

The radical reading of *Mishneh Torah*'s nature as a composition can be conceptualized as follows. A text's canonical status has various layers. It may have binding status, establishing what the law is and how one should act. Acting in accord with a normative canon of that sort, the authorities may confiscate a person's assets, decide whether a contract is binding, impose punishments and fines, and sometimes even take a person's life. The law of every state is a normative canon of that sort. Another sort of canonization—which we shall call "formative"—has a broader cultural significance, establishing the educational structure of a given community. A formative canon contains the texts to which members of a community are exposed in their schools and recreational activities. The formative canon generates the community's collective memory and makes it possible to speak and write in a manner that presumes unmediated familiarity with a collection of texts. In effect, it establishes the terms in which people understand themselves and one another. The formative canon is interpreted and taught; and in the Jewish world, in which the study of Torah is a core value, the diligent and rigorous engagement with the formative literature bears powerful spiritual significance.

Not every canonical text performs both functions—normative and formative—simultaneously. The laws of contract, for example, are part of a community's normative canon, having far-reaching effects on people's lives, but few will see them as core cultural assets of the community. Engagement with them is a matter for a limited group of expert judges and lawyers, whom others occasionally need to consult. So, too, not every formative canon is normative. Great literature is not a collection of instructions; rather, it instills sensitivity and contributes to establishing people's self-understanding. As great literature, it sometimes forms worldviews and occasionally provides the background narrative that gives the law its meaning, but it does not determine the law itself. Within the Jewish world, the Talmud acquired a dual role, both normative and formative. It serves not only as a normative text, telling one how to behave, but also as a text worthy of constant reflection—some would say exclusive reflection—that provides its students their language and manner of thought.

In light of this conceptual distinction between two types of canonization, let us return to consider *Mishneh Torah*. If we take the radical view and see *Mishneh Torah* as a replacement for the earlier literature, its composition becomes an intricate and complex canonical act. Within this text, Maimonides confirms the normative authority of the Talmud, establishing the *halakhah* in accord with absolutely binding Talmudic directives. Moreover, by extracting transparent and accessible practical *halakhah* from the thicket of Talmudic deliberation, he makes it possible for the Talmud to serve as a normative canon. But by that very same action, he effectively decanonizes the Talmud in the formative sense. Since *Mishneh Torah* now affords us a clear, lucid version of Talmudic *halakhah*, the Talmud itself instantly becomes a text that no longer need be engaged with. In solidifying the normative force of the Talmud, *Mishneh Torah* divests it of its formative status. In this reading, the composition of *Mishneh Torah* is not simply a reorganization of the *halakhah*; it is an action pregnant with meaning for the character of Jewish culture overall.

If, in fact, the composition of *Mishneh Torah* constituted a mighty canonical act meant to replace earlier halakhic literature, the following premises must be attributed to Maimonides: (1) The Talmudic give and take has no inherent value and does not have a value in and of itself. The literary substance and spiritual value of the Talmud are limited to its halakhic conclusions. (2) Those conclusions are presented in *Mishneh Torah* in a clear and accomplished manner and, with the tract's dissemination and acceptance, those conclusions will have become *halakhah* itself. (3) Reference to *Mishneh Torah* will be all that is needed, at least in the vast majority of cases, to derive practical *halakhah* without recourse to any of the earlier halakhic literature. (4) The matters worthy in their own right of constant reflection are "the Account of Creation" (Genesis 1) and "the Account of the Chariot" (Ezekiel), that is, physics and metaphysics, respectively. Because dealing with those matters requires prior faithfulness to and comprehensive knowledge of *halakhah*, *Mishneh Torah* affords the elite the inner space they need to pursue knowledge of the universe and of God. Conjoining all these premises produces an extremely radical picture of *Mishneh Torah* and its place in Jewish culture overall, and Maimonides' radical successors in the thirteenth century—from Samuel Ibn Tibbon to Joseph Ibn Kaspi—in fact accepted all of them.

Of course, each of those premises may be challenged. It may be that engagement with the intricacies of halakhic matters is not directed exclusively toward deriving halakhic conclusions but that it, itself, constitutes the highest spiritual activity to which a scholar can aspire. The Tosafists, for example, thought their remarks were set out in the same manner as the Talmud itself, as a collection of differing interpretive possibilities, offering multiple answers to a question.

And even granting Maimonides' first premise, regarding the nature of the Talmud and the spiritual significance of engagement with it, one could still say that Maimonides did not extract the actual *halakhah* from the Talmud; at most, he offered a reasonably persuasive interpretation requiring assessment and analysis in each and every instance. That position was taken by R. Menaḥem ha-Me'iri, who held that the Talmud's significance indeed lay in its determination of *halakhah*, but that one needed to examine the *halakhah* itself independently in each instance, rather than accepting Maimonides' interpretations as a given in all cases.

Even if one took the view that the Talmud had no interpreter more accomplished and profound than Maimonides, it might still be the case that practical *halakhah* could not be derived by reference to *Mishneh Torah* alone without an understanding of the underlying Talmudic material on the basis of which Maimonides reached his correct determination. That was the position of Rabbi Asher ben Yeḥiel (Rosh), who likely disagreed with the other premises as well. In that view, *Mishneh Torah* could never replace the Talmud, for without the Talmudic deliberations, *Mishneh Torah* itself would be of limited practical applicability.[1] It is likewise possible to accept the first three premises but still establish a framework for worthwhile contemplation entirely different from the one Maimonides means to establish. One could view the accounts of creation and of the chariot not as the physics and metaphysics of the philosophers but as the mystical literature of the kabbalists. Accordingly, every one of the premises implicit in the radical reading was subject to intense scrutiny as soon as *Mishneh Torah* had spread throughout the far and diverse reaches of the Jewish world.

Thus far, we have identified two entirely different ways of understanding *Mishneh Torah* as a literary work. The moderate understanding sees it as an accessible, accomplished representation of the *halakhah* overall, constituting a comprehensive summing up of the halakhic literature that preceded it. The radical understanding sees it as *halakhah* itself—as a canonical composition replacing, rather than summarizing, what came before. Both of these views were in fact advanced by various readers during the generations that followed Maimonides. For those who ascribed superior authority to Maimonides, a decision regarding the meaning of *Mishneh Torah* would determine not only the character of the *halakhah* but also the direction and fate of Jewish culture overall. On the other hand, for those who did not ascribe superior authority to Maimonides, the question of whether to read the work moderately or radically determined their degree of tolerance for the work and the force of their criticism of it.

The halakhists who saw *Mishneh Torah* not as binding *halakhah* but as simply one possible interpretation—perhaps even quite an important interpretation—considered its rulings on a retail basis: each and every ruling had to be checked against its sources in the Talmud. In their view, as noted by Ra'abad in his annotations to the introduction, it would have been better had Maimonides identified his sources and explained his rationales. Since the work, in their view, was not *halakhah* but only a representation of it, presentation of the underlying sources and arguments would not have detracted from its authoritativeness. On the contrary; it is possible that presentation of his arguments and sources might have strengthened Maimonides' hand against those who disagreed with him without knowing exactly how he had reached his results.

---

[1] *Rosh Responsa*, principle 31, 9.

Moreover, these scholars saw in *Mishneh Torah* a wonderful opportunity for broadening halakhic discourse itself. If it was Maimonides' intention to cut off the expansion of pointless, uncontrollable halakhic deliberations, he wound up pouring oil on the fire he hoped to extinguish. Dozens of books were written on *Mishneh Torah*, and it provided a golden opportunity for scholars who saw inherent value in Talmudic argumentation and turned the work to that end, thereby glorifying and aggrandizing Torah. The treatment of *Mishneh Torah* in later interpretations and novellae confirms the sixteenth-century great rabbinic figure Maharshal's incisive and ironic comment that every effort to close the halakhic discourse by means of a recognized, transparent work becomes another opportunity to expand that very discourse.

Ambiguity and Codification

Which of these two drastically different possibilities did Maimonides himself adopt? Did he take the moderate or the radical view of his own work? Despite the dazzling clarity and transparency of each ruling in *Mishneh Torah*, its author's comments on the nature of the work fail to clarify the matter, and repeated reading of the introduction provides no unambiguous answer to the question. To make matters worse, Maimonides himself attributes different meanings to the work in his various epistles.

In his response to the criticism of *Mishneh Torah* leveled by Pinhas the Judge of Alexandria, he clearly supports the moderate reading. Pinhas was among the first to recognize the radicalism implicit in the work itself and the possibility that Maimonides might be offering it as a replacement for all earlier halakhic literature. He words one of his complaints about the work quite sharply: "It would be fitting for your Excellency to instruct the people that they should not abandon study of the *Gemara*." Reacting to this taunt, Maimonides states: "Know, first, that I never said, God forbid, 'Do not study the Gemara or the *halakhah* or Rabbi Isaac [Alfasi; "Rif"] or anyone else'" (*Iggerot*, pp. 438–439). After describing the curriculum in his study hall, which includes broad engagement with the Rif's *halakhot* as well as study of Talmudic tractates, Maimonides returns to the point and emphasizes in an aggrieved tone: "Did I command, or even think of, burning all the books that preceded my treatise? Did I not say explicitly, at the outset of my treatise, that I had composed it only because of impatience, for those who cannot probe the depths of the Talmud and understand in that manner what is forbidden and what is permitted, and I wrote at length on the matter" (ibid., p. 439). In effect, Maimonides rejects any possibility of a radical reading of his composition. He had no intention of making earlier halakhic literature irrelevant, and the entire work is intended only for one who lacks the patience to study *halakhah* more deeply.

In reaction to Pinḥas, Maimonides refers to his comments in the Introduction, interpreting them in light of the moderate understanding of *Mishneh Torah*'s character. Such a reading of the introduction is entirely possible. Nowhere in the introduction did Maimonides argue that the earlier halakhic literature should be suppressed, and he treated his compilation as a response to a complex literary environment and a state of historical crisis. One could even argue that his observation regarding the sufficiency of the Written Law and *Mishneh Torah*—"without having occasion to consult any other book between them"—refers only to a person of limited intellect and time.

And yet, despite all this, nowhere in the introduction did Maimonides explicitly adopt the contrary position. Given the significance of the possible misreading, it would have been better had Maimonides clarified the matter in his introduction, as Pinḥas wanted him to. In any case, if we had nothing to go on other than the introduction and the letter to Pinḥas the Judge, we could say that the moderate reading clearly was the one intended by Maimonides and that the radical interpretation was ruled out by his own clarification of the matter. Maimonides comments in a similar vein in his *Essay on Resurrection*: "When I concentrated on a compilation of the law of the Torah and an exposition of its statutes, my object was to find favor with God, not to look forward to honor or reward from people. I wished to the best of my ability to provide guidance, understanding, and comprehension to whomever is not qualified to grasp the teachings of the scholars of the law who lived before me" (*Essay on Resurrection*, pp. 211–212).

In addition to the letter to Pinḥas—which casts *Mishneh Torah* as summary of halakhic literature rather than as replacement—we may cite the evidence of a letter to Rabbi Jonathan Hakohen of Lunel and his academy; there, Maimonides declares *Mishneh Torah* to be a sometimes limited effort to represent the *halakhah* and certainly not the *halakhah* itself. Maimonides opens that letter by acknowledging that his involvement with philosophy and science had detracted to a degree from his knowledge of Torah.

He describes his pursuit of those disciplines as marginal, meant only to glorify the Torah; nevertheless, he states, "the time [I devote to Torah] has diminished, for my mind is divided into many segments, related to all manner of wisdom" (*Iggerot*, p. 502). That fragmentation of his thought, Maimonides says, along with the diffuse character of the halakhic sources and the universal tendency of people to forget, all increase the possibility of error in *Mishneh Torah*'s rulings. Maimonides therefore calls on his admirers, the great *halakhists* of Lunel—who accepted *Mishneh Torah* enthusiastically and contributed much to the Maimonidean culture's penetration of Provence—to verify his words well:

> For all these reasons, it is worthwhile to peruse my words and check up on me, and let not one who reads my compilation say, "Who is the person who second-guesses the king?" For I have given permission; the king says "come." And you will have done me a great favor—you sages and all who find something [amiss] and tell me; you will have done well by me, [aiming to attain] the point that there remains no stumbling block, God forbid, in it. For I intended in this compilation only to clear the paths and remove stumbling blocks from before the students, so they are not made weary by the abundant give and take, resulting in an error in ruling on the *halakhah*. (ibid. 2, p. 502)

Remarks such as these, presented to a friendly audience of recognized scholars and calling for a "retail" approach to the work's rulings, are far removed from any claim on Maimonides' part that his tract is canonical and binding. He urges his readers to check his work carefully, lest there be an error in it; and he looks forward to incorporating their corrections in a future, improved, version. He thus takes *Mishneh Torah* as a solid starting point for analysis, not as a binding end point. These letters, accordingly, lead the reader to conclude that Maimonides himself held the moderate interpretation of the composition's meaning.

But that is only part of the picture. We have various statements by Maimonides himself, sent to his close and prominent disciples, that clearly point to the radical reading of *Mishneh Torah*. In one of his letters to Joseph, he calls for his compilation to become the center of the curriculum:

> I have already attested to him that he should not rest until he has apprehended the compilation in its entirety and made it his book, teaching it

everywhere to disseminate its benefit. For the proper purpose of what is compiled in the Talmud and elsewhere has been wholly incorporated within it. But the purpose of the scholars—wasting time with Talmudic give and take, as if meaning and purpose resided in an exercise in debate—is something else. But that was not the initial purpose; rather, the give and take and the debate entered into it by happenstance: when the matter was under consideration, and one interpreted it one way and another interpreted it differently, each of them was required to present his proof and show his interpretation to be persuasive. But the primary purpose was to know what was to be done or avoided. And this is clear to one like him. Accordingly, we have returned to the primary destination . . . and left what is extraneous to one who chooses to occupy himself with it. (ibid., pp. 257–259)

The purpose of the Talmud, then, is instruction in practical *halakhah*. Talmudic give and take is a by-product of the effort to clarify the *halakhah*, and *Mishneh Torah*, as a book of *halakhah*, accomplishes this purpose in a clear, focused way. Since engagement in Talmudic give and take is not in itself a purpose to be pursued, *Mishneh Torah* replaces the Talmudic literature with a more useful instrument for attaining its purpose.

In another statement, at least as unambiguous, Maimonides provides his student Joseph with guidance in respect to the proper course of study. The *Geonim* in Baghdad had unleashed a storm of criticism of *Mishneh Torah*, and this devoted disciple of Maimonides found himself at the center of it. Maimonides wrote to his student to encourage and calm him. At the beginning of his letter, he strives to diminish the disciple's shock and surprise over the harsh criticism, noting that he himself anticipated the critical reaction, which stems from narrow horizons, jealousy, and religious zealotry. To raise his disciple's spirits, Maimonides notes that, in contrast to the bad news from Baghdad, there is good news from Provence:

I have already received a communication from the sages of France and others in their name, amazed at what has been done and requesting it in its entirety; and it has already spread to the ends of the inhabited world. And everything you have told us about those who do not accept it as it should be accepted—that is so in my time, but in the future, when jealousy and the drive for dominion depart, all Israel will be satisfied with it alone and will doubtless set aside all else, except for those who want something they can engage with all their days without achieving any purpose. (ibid., pp. 301–302)

Maimonides sees *Mishneh Torah*'s penetration of the French world as a clear sign of its spreading acceptance, for the French community is not the domestic one whose support for Maimonides could be taken for granted. There is a familiar ring to the account of the tract's spread to the ends of the settled earth and the vision of its ultimate transformation, in the eyes of all Israel, into the exclusive halakhic work: they clearly recall the concept of the Talmud's authoritativeness articulated by Maimonides in the introduction to *Mishneh Torah* and the premise that *Mishneh Torah* could gain similar authoritativeness once it spread and was accepted.

In another letter to the same disciple, Maimonides identifies the proper course of study:

> Study nothing except the *halakhot* of the Rabbi (Isaac Alfassi), of blessed memory, and compare them to the compilation [*Mishneh Torah*], and if you find a dispute, know that examination of the Talmud brought it about, and inquire into it where it is found [in the Talmud]. But if you waste your time on commentaries and interpretations of debates in the *Gemara*, and those things set aside as burdensome—you will be wasting your time and accomplishing little. (ibid., p. 312)

After the composition of *Mishneh Torah*, then, the debates of Abayye and Rava become a useless waste of time. It is possible that if Maimonides had available to him a work like *Mishneh Torah*, written by someone who had preceded him, he might have directed his attention to matters more worthy of constant contemplation, for the purpose of Talmudic study would already have been achieved by a comprehensive, decisive code.

And so, the question "what is *Mishneh Torah?*" has no clear answer at all. At the foundation of this landmark work of clarity and transparency lies a profound ambiguity. Is the compilation a representation of the *halakhah* through a clear and accessible summary of the earlier literature, or is it a work of *halakhah* itself that replaces the earlier literature? These widely divergent possibilities imply profoundly different concepts of the compilation's authoritativeness and role and of the degree to which it presumed to work a fundamental change in the character of Jewish culture overall. The divergence stems not merely from the two senses of the word

"code"; it is augmented by the differences between Maimonides' own accounts of his composition in the letters in which he speaks of his enterprise. But while each of the letters conveys a particular position on the
part of their writer, in the introduction to *Mishneh Torah* itself, Maimonides withholds any answer to the question regarding the work's nature. As
written, the introduction allows for either understanding of the book, and
each of the opposing letters in fact refers to it, directly or indirectly. Maimonides thus provides various readings of *Mishneh Torah*'s meaning as a
composition, and he formulates the introduction in a way that leaves the
question open.

Codification and Self-Esteem

The question of Maimonides' position regarding the alternative understandings of *Mishneh Torah* that he himself set up may be answered as
follows. Maimonides' true position is the radical one he conveys to his
close disciples. *Mishneh Torah* is *halakhah* itself, and the composition is a
replacement for the halakhic literature that preceded it. But Maimonides
has good reason to conceal that stance: to declare that *Mishneh Torah* is the
halakhah and that rulings contrary to it err as a matter of law would be to
claim unprecedented authority. That sort of presumptuousness would justifiably anger other scholars who would regard *Mishneh Torah* as divesting
them, for no apparent reason, of the authority to decide the *halakhah* in
accord with their own views. Moreover, setting up *Mishneh Torah* as a replacement for previous halakhic literature would effect a significant intellectual change opposed by other rabbinic authorities. It therefore is proper
to mask that viewpoint, as Maimonides does in his letter to Pinhas the
Judge. True to that stance, Maimonides—the master of concealment and
ambiguity—formulates the introduction in a way that allows him to argue
that he intended only the moderate understanding of his composition's
meaning and that it never entered his mind to think otherwise.

That understanding of Maimonides' position can be supported on general exegetical grounds. Of the two clear alternatives that Maimonides suggests, it is fair to assume that it is the radical one he supports but that he
also wants to conceal. Otherwise, why would he even have raised that
possibility? That exegetical approach has been suggested in connection
with the *Guide*, as we will see in what follows, and it lends itself to application here as well.

But in the case of *Mishneh Torah*, the matter has to be formulated in a much more complex way. As noted earlier, *Mishneh Torah*'s authority is not derived from the institutional standing of its author, for Maimonides lacked any such plenary institutional authority. Like the rule of recognition applied by Maimonides to the Talmud, the transformation of *Mishneh Torah* into actual *halakhah* depends on its spreading to, and being accepted by, the entire Jewish people, wherever dispersed. From Maimonides' location in time, he could not declare that the composition constitutes *halakhah* and replaces the earlier literature—not because of the need to conceal any such presumption, but because the nature and character of the work were yet to be determined and were subject to forces beyond Maimonides' absolute control. According to this reading, Maimonides wanted his composition to be *halakhah* per se and to serve, in the future, as a replacement for the previous halakhic literature. But because of his own concept of authority, the book's standing would be determined by circumstances external to the book. If it were to spread and be accepted, it would become *halakhah* itself and replace the earlier halakhic material; if not, the concealed meaning would be forgone, and the work would simply remain a magnificent representation of the *halakhah* that deserved to be taken into account because of the importance of its author. It would serve as an accessible, transparent summary of the earlier halakhic literature.

It can be argued that the ambiguity regarding the meaning of the composition as Maimonides formulates it is grounded in matters deeper than the dependence of its authoritativeness on future historical circumstances that will determine its fate. The gap between the two possible readings does not merely set up a significant difference regarding the character of the work. Each of the two possibilities also represents a different concept of the author, his status, and his authority; and one may therefore suggest that this ambiguity opens a window on the author's complicated position regarding himself. According to the radical understanding of the work, Maimonides intended, by a single, mighty literary act, to transform the fragmented, variegated halakhic structure without any change in the geopolitical situation that brought about the fragmentation and in the face of ongoing intensification of those geopolitical circumstances. The power of the work was its ability to bring about that change, and its acceptance throughout Israel would transform it into actual *halakhah* and alter the cultural agenda of the studious elite. Meanwhile, the more moderate reading of *Mishneh Torah* reflects a different view of himself on the part of the author. His letter to the sages of Lunel clearly suggests a more modest, restrained, and limited self-image. Maimonides engages in genuine conversation with the letter's addressees, speaking to them as first among equals and requesting corrections, comments, and annotations. On the more moderate concept of Maimonides' self-image, *Mishneh Torah* represents the effort of a mighty scholar to summarize the *halakhah* for the benefit of those who have difficulty with Talmudic give and take, but it is not *halakhah* per se and does not obviate the earlier halakhic literature.

The history of literature includes situations in which the meaning of a book remains elusive and even the fundamental positions of the author cannot be discerned. That is the case with respect to the *Guide of the Perplexed*. But the uncertain nature of *Mishneh Torah* presents an unusual case. The exegetical alternatives bear not only on the author's positions but also on his self-image and on the degree of weight and power that he assumes and attributes to himself. Maimonides was conscious of having a rare historical mission, and he never deprecated his self-worth. But it seems fair to say that the difference between the sorts of self-consciousness implied by the two readings we have discussed gives voice to internal and principled conflicts over his status and role. If that is so, then the question "what is *Mishneh Torah*?" is not merely a difficult one to resolve; it is a question that will forever defy definitive answer because the author himself was ambivalent about the matter. All we can do is formulate the question "what is *Mishneh Torah*?" and uncover its fundamental ambivalence as an enigmatic work concealed within a misleading mantle of overall clarity and transparency.

CHAPTER FIVE

Philosophy and *halakhah* in *Mishneh Torah*

Love and Awe: Philosophy and Religious Experience

The sixteenth-century *Shulḥan Arukh* is the most important halakhic code to follow *Mishneh Torah*. Its author, R. Joseph Karo, began his treatise with the laws governing the practices to be followed immediately upon awakening in the morning. That opening does more than reflect a useful organizing principle, which presents the *halakhot* in accord with the rhythm of a person's day. It also conveys in a profound way the halakhic ethos of the *Shulḥan Arukh*: a person opening his eyes is immediately summoned, without hesitancy, lethargy, or delay, to fulfill the *halakhot* that govern his entire life. A halakhic life attests to spiritual prowess and faithfulness in the ongoing and ceaseless struggle to subject human inclinations to the divine law detailed in the *halakhah*.

The opening of *Mishneh Torah*, in stark contrast, affords us an entirely different picture of the *halakhah*. The first of the treatise's fourteen major divisions is *The Book of Knowledge*; its initial subject area is "Laws Concerning the Foundations of the Torah"; and its first *halakhah* is an attempt to define, in binding terms, the Jewish concept of God. There follow four entire chapters devoted to the understanding of the divinity and of the universe, presenting, in summary form, the picture of existence that Maimonides termed "the Account of the Chariot" and "the Account of Creation." The object of the *halakhah*—that is, God—must be made clear before exposition of practical *halakhah*. Moreover, this organization of the *halakhah* implies that its purpose is to promote the understanding of God to the best of a person's abilities. The goal of the divine law is to lead a person to realize his perfection, and that perfection, as explained in the *Commentary on the Mishnah*, is the actualization of a person's potential as a creature possessed of understanding.

It is worth noting that the religious-philosophical ideal can be found in the very first line of Maimonides' halakhic work: "The basic principle of all basic principles and the pillar of all sciences is to know that there is a First Being" ("Laws Concerning the Foundation of the Torah," 1:1). The duty to know is the purpose of the *halakhah*, and it transforms physical actions pursuant to *halakhah* into a means for advancing toward the philosophic ideal that lies beyond it. As we saw in discussing the *Commentary on the Mishnah*, the understanding of human perfection in *Mishneh Torah* has far-reaching implications for the concepts of immortality of the soul and of the world to come, reward and punishment, and the messianic idea.

The final *halakhah* in *Mishneh Torah* depicts the messianic world in which the *halakhah* at its best is realized and reemphasizes the philosophic ethos with which the treatise began:

> In that era there will be neither famine nor war, neither jealousy nor strife. Blessings will be abundant, comforts within the reach of all. The one preoccupation of the whole world will be to know the Lord. Hence Israelites will be very wise, they will know the things that are now concealed and will attain an understanding of their Creator to the utmost capacity of the human mind, as it is written: For the earth shall be full of the knowledge of the Lord, as the waters cover the sea (Isa. 11:9). ("Laws Concerning Kings and Wars," 12:5)

As noted, Maimonides does not play down the philosophic ideal in his halakhic works. On the contrary, that ideal is the organizing principle of the *halakhah* overall, and that is why the treatise begins and ends with the virtue of knowledge.

The first chapters of *Mishneh Torah* are devoted to formulating the philosophic ethos as a central religious duty. To that end, Maimonides had to present a novel definition of the commandment to love and fear God. He does so as follows at the beginning of chapter 2 of "Laws Concerning the Foundations of the Torah":

> And what is the way that will lead to the love of Him and the fear of Him? When a person contemplates His great and wondrous works and creatures and from them obtains a glimpse of his wisdom which is incomparable and infinite, he will immediately love Him, praise Him, glorify Him, and long with an exceeding longing to know His great Name . . . And when he pon-

ders these matters, he will recoil affrighted, and realize that he is a small creature, lowly and obscure, endowed with slight and slender intelligence standing in the presence of Him who is perfect in knowledge. ("Laws Concerning the Foundations of the Torah," 2:2)

This *halakhah* forges an inherent link between love and awe on the one hand and knowledge on the other. Contemplation of the world causes one to perceive God's wisdom in creation; as a result, one craves to know God. Given that, it is knowledge that arouses love, and the meaning of love is the desire to know more. Awe, as Maimonides defines it in this *halakhah*, refers not to dread of punishment but to awareness of man's marginal position in the universe and insignificance in the face of God.

The pinnacle of the religious experience is the joining of love and awe. In Maimonides' system, that blend acquires a unique nuance, for it is accomplished through the medium of contemplation and knowledge. Cognition is not a neutral activity, void of desire and feeling; rather, it contains the kernel of religious experience, built on the pairing of attraction and recoiling. In the philosophical reading, love—attraction—is the infinite desire to know God; awe is the recoiling expressed in the awareness of one's marginality. But that awareness is brought about by the knowledge itself, and so the cycle goes round. A religious person who has gone through this philosophical process finds himself oscillating inwardly between the desire to know and the awareness of his insignificance—a state brought about by coming to know God and the world.

At the conclusion of this *halakhah*, after having defined the love and awe of God, Maimonides draws the connection between religious obligation and science:

In harmony with these sentiments, I shall explain some large, general aspects of the Works of the Sovereign of the Universe, that they may serve the intelligent individual as a door to the love of God, even as our sages have remarked in connection with the theme of the love of God, "Observe the Universe and hence, you will know Him who spake and the world was." ("Laws Concerning the Foundations of the Torah," 2:2)

This linkage between knowledge and the commandment to love God sheds light on an unusual feature of *Mishneh Torah*. The first chapter of the treatise deals with the normative definition of the divinity, but the ensuing three chapters present a brief account of the world as seen by Aristotelian science. Maimonides there describes the structure of the universe, the separate intelligibles, the spheres, the four elements, the soul of man, and so forth. On the face of it, these topics seem far removed from the scope of a halakhic code. Would contemporary writers, for example, see any need to preface their halakhic works with a discussion of Newtonian or Einsteinian physics? This unique component of *Mishneh Torah* is included because of science's role as the means through which one attains the pinnacle of religious experience—the joining of love and awe. Because it plays that role, science becomes an integral part of religious obligation and of *halakhah*, and Maimonides therefore opens his halakhic treatise with an outline of the scientific worldview. Physics and metaphysics, accordingly, are not seen as a body of knowledge lying outside the tradition. On the contrary, they are integrated within the tradition and promote one's ability to attain the love and fear of God.

In the final *halakhah* of "Laws Concerning Repentance," Maimonides reiterates his understanding of "love":

> It is known and certain that the love of God does not become closely knit in a man's heart till he is continuously and thoroughly possessed by it and gives up everything else in the world for it as God commanded us, "with all thy heart and with all thy soul" (Deut. 6:5). One only loves God with the knowledge with which one knows Him. According to the knowledge, will be the love. If the former be little or much, so will the latter be little or much. A person ought therefore to devote himself to the understanding and comprehension of those sciences and studies which will inform him concerting his Master, as far as it lies in human faculties to understand and comprehend—as indeed we have explained in the Laws Concerning the Foundations of the Torah. ("Laws Concerning Repentance," 10:6)

The existence of the loftiest religious ideal thus depends on intimate knowledge of the corpus of scientific and metaphysical knowledge, found in sources that are not necessarily parts of the Jewish tradition. This knowledge—"sciences and studies"—is the result of great scientific advances, and it leads a person to the knowledge of God that he is capable of achieving. Philosophy thus becomes a person's highest religious obligation. The distinction between the internal and the external, between what is within the tradition and what is outside it, is absolutely abrogated, for knowledge coming from outside the tradition becomes integral to the goal of the tradition itself.

The religious role of philosophy becomes clearer in the context of a different aspect of *Mishneh Torah*'s understanding of love of God. The final chapter of "Laws Concerning Repentance" includes a further definition of fear and love of God:

> Let not a man say, "I will observe the precepts of the Torah and occupy myself with its wisdom, in order that I may obtain all the blessings written in the Torah, or to attain life in the world to come; I will abstain from transgressions against which the Torah warn, so that I may be saved from the curses written in the Torah, or that I not be cut off from life in the world to come." It is not right to serve God in this fashion, for whoever does so, serves Him out of fear. . . . Whoever serves God out of love, occupies himself with the study of the Law and the fulfillment of commandments and walks in the paths of wisdom, impelled by no external motive whatsoever, moved neither by fear of calamity nor by the desire to obtain material benefits; such a man does what is truly right because it is truly right, and ultimately, happiness come to him as a result of his conduct. ("Laws Concerning Repentance," 10:1–2)

Here, unlike the sequence in "Laws Concerning the Foundations of the Torah," fear precedes love. Fear is the state in which a person serves God to obtain a reward or avoid punishment. Love, in contrast, is a relationship unrelated to contractual ties based on quid pro quo. In a love relationship, a person acts on behalf of the beloved not to be rewarded, but solely for the good of the beloved. In divine service out of love, a person fulfills the commandments for their intrinsic value and not to be rewarded or avoid punishment.

The transition from an attitude of fear to one of love depends on knowledge, as Maimonides emphasizes at the end of that chapter: "According to the knowledge, will be the love. If the former be little or much, so will the latter be little or much." A person acting out of fear treats the universe as a resource for the satisfaction of his desires and aspirations. He sees it as a large instrument, whose purpose is the satisfaction of his urges. Knowledge frees man from that sort of attitude, teaching him to see existence as it is, independent of his own desires. A person who comes to understand the causality and wisdom implicit in the universe will reach the conclusion that the world is not simply a response to his desires; rather, it exists on its own in all its glory, and man is only a small part of it. To reach a position of love, one must come to see the other as something standing on its own and possessed of independent value—just as in the case of interpersonal relations. Children learn to love their parents, rather than simply being dependent on them, when they discover that their parents lead independent lives and exist on their own as complete and complex persons. Philosophy and science accordingly play a decisive religious role in the most important change of consciousness a person can undergo in relation to his service of God. Knowledge moves him from seeing God and the world as an instrument to one that no longer aims to achieve practical benefits. It makes it possible for him to love God and the world, freeing his perspective on reality from its dependence on his own impulses.

The human condition is initially that of fear, which reflects an instrumental attitude toward God and the world. By acquiring knowledge, a person can move from that sort of attitude to one of love, which does not seek to attain any purpose other than further knowledge of God. It is followed by awe, the opposite of fear, its more pedestrian variety. The fear that precedes love involves a person seeing himself as the center of existence, which acts either on his behalf or against him. The awe that follows love is based on a recognition of a person's marginality vis-à-vis God and the universe—he is merely the tiniest part of existence rather than its purpose, and that existence stands before him in all its might and glory. For Maimonides, at the core of human experience of the world is the attempt to free oneself from the grip of instrumentalization of the world which is so deeply grounded in our fears and hopes. Such instrumentalization is our initial response to the world given our deep anxieties and hopes and our utter dependency on the world for our basic well-being. Philosophy and science acquire a quality of redemptive spiritual exercise, because they serve as the vehicle that ushers the transformation from instrumentality to love.

The Concept of the Divine: Eternal Universe and Creation *ex Nihilo*

Whether the world has existed for all eternity or was created at some particular time is a question posed in the *Guide* as the central and most difficult question faced by Jewish thought in the Middle Ages. It became the central question not because of interest in the history of the universe but because of its profound implications for the meaning of God and the nature of human standing before Him. The traditional idea of creation assumes that at some particular time, there arose within God a desire to create the world, and by force of His will, all existence was then created *ex nihilo*. Aristotelian philosophy, however, is troubled by the attribution of a desire to God, for it impairs His perfection. A perfect being needs nothing and therefore desires nothing; attributing a desire to God would seem to suggest that God was lacking something. Similarly, the arousal of a desire implies a change in God, a move from potential to actual, yet something perfect is fixed and unchanging, an unmoved mover.

Moreover, if the world was created by force of the divine will, it cannot be maintained that God is the first cause in the chain of causation, for something must have caused His will to develop. Aristotle accordingly took the position that the world had always existed, and God's relation to it is not that of creator to creature, on the model of a carpenter's relation to a chair he built. The world exists not because of some willful act on God's part but by reason of God's very existence, just as a person's shadow is inherent in his presence or sunlight is inherent in the existence of the sun. The world is eternal, dependent on the existence of God.

Denying that God has a will bears not only on creation but on all the basic concepts of the belief in the God of Abraham, Isaac, and Jacob. For one thing, denying God's will calls into serious question the traditional concept of revelation. On the face of it, revelation, too, is a willful action on God's part—His entry into history at some particular time by force of His will, and the assertion of his dominion over man by means of a sovereign command. Judaism can carry on without the concept of creation, but revelation is its very life breath. The Aristotelian image of the divine thus poses a threat to its very essence.

But it is more than revelation that is called into question. Providence, reward and punishment, and miracles all depend on a divine personality possessed of will, a figure that continually reacts and changes, is moved and acts. The Aristotelian divinity, in contrast, is entirely self-sufficient, unchanging in its perfection and causing the universe to be by its very existence. It should come as no surprise, then, that the question of "eternity or *ex nihilo*" became the paradigmatic problem for Jewish belief as it encountered Greco-Arab philosophy. Those who had internalized the philosophical view were decidedly perplexed in their attitude toward the Jewish tradition, to the point of difficult existential burden that cuts to the core of their identity.

The issue stands at the heart of the *Guide* and we will consider it in the chapters dealing with that work. Our present concern is Maimonides' formulation, in the first chapter of *Mishneh Torah*, of how the concept of God is reflected in the light of the vexing dilemma of eternity of the world versus creation *ex nihilo*. We should note at the outset that numerous chapters of the *Guide* are devoted to arguing that the philosophers have not been able to prove the eternity of the world. From a metaphysical perspective, these chapters suggest, the question of eternity or *ex nihilo* remains an open one, for the metaphysical issue has not been resolved. Maimonides makes it clear that, given the openhanded nature of the problem, he sided with the view that the world was created *ex nihilo*, for without that belief, the religion of Israel would be entirely undermined. He could thus remain loyal to the philosophical perspective without adopting the radical conclusion that would threaten Judaism, for philosophy did not require an eternal universe or denial of God's creative will.

As we shall see, more than a few Maimonidean interpreters, beginning with Samuel Ibn Tibbon, maintained that although a belief in creation *ex nihilo* is found at the surface level of the *Guide*, Maimonides, in truth, never took that view. The *Guide*'s hidden message is that the world is indeed eternal, and Maimonides was more of an Aristotelian than he himself expressly admitted, and he concealed the idea because of its far-reaching implications for Judaism's basic beliefs. On this premise, according to Samuel Ibn Tibbon, the *Guide*'s concealed philosophical accomplishment was the proposal of a systematic reinterpretation of Judaism's basic concepts—revelation, providence, reward and punishment—in light of the belief in an eternal universe.

With that as background, let us turn to *Mishneh Torah*. The treatise's first *halakhah* formulates the concept of God and therefore deserves close attention: "The basic principle of all basic principles and the pillar of all sciences is to know that there is a First Being who brought every existing thing into being. All existing things, whether celestial, terrestrial, or belonging to an intermediate class, exist only through His true existence" ("Laws Concerning the Foundations of the Torah," 1:1). Within this brief formulation, one can see a significant tension with respect to God's relationship to the world. The first sentence implies that God created the world and describes Him as having "brought every existing thing into being." The second sentence, however, points in a rather different direction: "All existing things, whether celestial, terrestrial, or belonging to an intermediate class, exist only through His true existence." That suggests that all existence derives from the very fact of God's existence rather than from His deliberate and willful action. Packed within this brief statement is the most basic and substantive tension within medieval Jewish philosophy: is God the Creator of the world, Who brought it into being, or does the world exist simply by reason of God's existence? The reader who believes in creation *ex nihilo* will find support for his view in the first sentence, and one who favors belief in an eternally existing world will look to the second sentence. It would have been wonderful to possess the drafts of these first sentences of *Mishneh Torah*, given the fact that in them Maimonides takes upon himself the most ominous task of articulating the normative definition of God. In such a definition, every word and nuance makes an immense difference in light of the great stakes implied in the metaphysical dilemma. Either way, it is clear that the statement does not at all shy away from raising the possibility of an eternal universe.

This formulation of the concept of God makes repeated use of the Hebrew verb stem *m-z-'* with its different permutations. Maimonides does not employ the traditional descriptors of God, such as "Creator of the World," "Master of the World," and so forth. God's essence is formulated here in terms of existence rather than of personality. The point is emphasized and developed further in the two succeeding *halakhot*:

> If it could be supposed that He did not exist, it would follow that nothing else could possibly exist.
>
> If, however, it were supposed that all other beings were non-existent, He alone would still exist. Their non-existence would not involve His non-existence. For all beings are in need of Him; but He, blessed be He, is not in need of them nor of any one of them. Hence, His real essence [or: truth] is unlike that of any of them. ("Laws Concerning the Foundations of the Torah," 1:2–3)

God's existence is necessary, but the existence of the world is contingent. Similarly, there is a basic asymmetry between the existence of God and that of the world. The existence of the world depends on the existence of God, but God's existence does not depend on that of the world. Accordingly, God's existence is truer: "His truth is unlike that of any of them." This is because truth is not simply a quality of statements about the world; rather, it denotes the force of a being's existence. The more a being's existence is anchored, necessary, and non-contingent, the more true, or real, its existence. Maimonides' statement in these *halakhot* that God is a being whose existence is necessary evidences the profound influence of the Persian Muslim philosopher Ibn Sina (Avicenna) (980–1037), who described God as possessed of necessary existence.

The tension between creation and eternal existence, posed in the first *halakhah*, is resolved, as the chapter unfolds, in favor of eternal existence. After defining the concept of God, Maimonides offers a brief proof for His existence: "This being is the God of the Universe, the Lord of all the Earth. And He it is, who controls the Sphere (of the Universe) with a power that is without end or limit with a power that is never intermitted. For the Sphere is always revolving; and it is impossible for it to revolve without someone making it revolve" ("Laws Concerning the Foundations of the Torah," 1:5). The existence of God is demonstrated by the enduring motion of the sphere. Since the sphere is perpetually rotating, there must be some first cause moving it, and that cause is God. Later, in a *halakhah* dealing with God's unity and consequent incorporeality—something corporeal can be divided—Maimonides again uses the enduring motion of the sphere as proof of God's incorporeality: "And our God, blessed be his Name, since His power is infinite and unceasing—for the Sphere (of the Universe) is continually revolving—His power is not the energy of a physical body. And since he is not a physical body, the accidents that happen to physical bodies do not apply to Him, so as to distinguish Him from another being" ("Laws Concerning the Foundations of the Torah," 1:7). In these opening *halakhot* in *Mishneh Torah*, then, Maimonides proves the existence and incorporeality of God in light of his determination that the world has always existed.

One could, of course, apply a strained reading and say that what Maimonides means is that the sphere has moved ceaselessly only since the world was created. In the *Guide*, however, Maimonides expressly states that *Mishneh Torah*'s proof for the existence of God is based on the world's eternal existence. He uses a "dilemma" argument in the following manner: If the world was created, God's existence could be proven on the basis of the very fact of creation. If, on the other hand, the world is eternal, God's existence could be proven on the basis of the sphere's perpetual movement: "For this reason you will always find that whenever, in what I have written in the books of jurisprudence, I happen to mention the foundations and start upon establishing the existence of the deity, I establish it by discourses that adopt the way of the doctrine of the eternity of the world" (*Guide* I:71; Pines, p. 182). And so, in his halakhic treatise, Maimonides adopts the stance that maintains the eternity of the world, the more philosophic of the two positions. Anyone who believes that Maimonides concealed this position from his readers can refer to its express statement in the opening *halakhot* of *Mishneh Torah*.

It is important to stress the following point. The question whether the existence of God is to be proven on the basis of the enduring movement of the sphere or of the fact that the world was created is in and of itself not that crucial. What gives it the immense religious weight is the fact that the two proofs generate different images of the divinity. One who sees the creation of the world as proof of God's existence understands God to be a sovereign personality possessed of will, while one who bases the proof on the enduring movement of the sphere and the eternity of the world understands the divinity as a being from whose very existence the entire world follows. That being does not willfully intervene in creation except insofar as it is the first cause, the ultimate reason for the order through which the universe operates. In the *Guide*, Maimonides articulated the tension between the two conceptions of God as personality or as being, as the tension between will and wisdom. Though, as Maimonides claims in the *Guide*, he adopted this proof from the eternal movement of the sphere, just as one option among the two possible proofs, the fact that he selected eternity of the world with full awareness of its implications as the option presented in *Mishneh Torah* is of great significance.

Maimonides' clear leaning toward eternity of the world is evident as well in the total absence of any reference to history in his treatment of God and the world in the first four chapters of *Mishneh Torah*. He does not base the existence of God or the direct and immediate expression of his presence on such factors as the exodus from Egypt or the miracles of the ten plagues or the crossing of the Red Sea.

The view of God as first and foremost the God of history, the God who demonstrates His existence through miracles that breach the boundaries of the natural order, is a view that is deeply rooted and widely accepted within the Jewish tradition. The biblical God is often depicted as the God of history: "I am the LORD your God who brought you out of the land of Egypt" (Ex. 20:2). Nahmanides' comment on that verse shows the centrality of the exodus from Egypt in Jewish thinking about the encounter with the divine: "He said 'who brought you out of the land of Egypt' because his having done so demonstrates His existence and His will; for we went out from there with [God's] knowledge and providence. It also demonstrates creation ex nihilo, for the eternal existence of the world would imply that nothing in nature could change; and it demonstrates [His] power" (Nah-manides Commentary on Torah, Ex. 20:2). On this view, a breach in the laws of nature accomplished through the spectacle of a miracle constitutes the most basic form of divine revelation. Nahmanides was right to link awareness of the God of history to denial of the world's eternity, for the latter concept is grounded in rejection of the idea of a divine will that changes the order of creation.

That the opening chapters of *Mishneh Torah* make no reference to history is of great importance in the annals of Jewish thought. The omission follows from those chapters being meant to forge a religious consciousness constructed solely on the causality of nature itself, not on departures from the normal course of nature through the intervention of sovereign divine will. The proof for the existence of God is based on the enduring and unchanging motion of the sphere, linked in its essence to the fixed order expressed in experience. That and more: love of God and awe of God, which stand at the pinnacle of religious experience, are connected to contemplation of the natural order of the universe and the wisdom it conveys. It should come as no surprise that when Maimonides speaks of the authentication of prophecy, he refuses to treat a miracle as an event embodying the unmediated presence of God. The God of *Mishneh Torah* inclines more to wisdom than to will. In his unprecedented effort to forge a binding system of belief for all Israel, Maimonides declined to include the most fundamental common denominator within the tradition. On the contrary; in the opening chapters of his treatise, he attempted to direct religious consciousness toward the specifically philosophical concept of the divinity.

Prophecy, Faith, and the Election of Israel

The concluding four chapters of "Laws Concerning the Foundations of the Torah" deal with prophecy. In terms tied to his concept of God, Maimonides describes prophecy as wisdom, not as an act of will. He begins the discussion as follows:

> It is one of the basic principles of religion that God causes men to prophesize. But the spirit of prophecy only rests upon the wise man who is distinguished by great wisdom and strong moral character, whose passions never overcome him in anything whatsoever, but who by his rational faculty al-

ways has his passions under control, and possesses a broad and sedate mind. When one, abundantly endowed with these qualities and physically sound, enters the "Pardes" and continuously dwells upon those great and abstruse themes—having the right mind capable of comprehending and grasping them; sanctifying himself, withdrawing from the ways of the ordinary run of men who walk in the obscurities of the times, zealously training himself not to have a single thought of the vanities of the age and its intrigues, but keeping his mind disengaged, concentrated on higher things as though bound beneath the Celestial Throne, so as to comprehend the pure and holy forms and contemplating the wisdom of God as displayed in His creatures, from the first form to the very center of the Earth, learning thence to realize His greatness—on such a man the Holy Spirit will immediately descend. And when the spirit rests upon him, his soul will mingle with the angels called *Ishim*. He will be changed into another man and will realize that he is not the same as he had been, and has been exalted above other wise men. ("Laws Concerning the Foundations of the Torah," 7:1)

The *halakhah* begins with a sentence that seems to comport with the idea of divine will: taking the initiative and exercising His will, God "causes men to prophesize." This understanding, consistent with the traditional biblical view, sees the granting of prophecy as a willful choice made by God; at times, God will even impose prophecy on a prophet who hesitates to accept his mission or tries to flee from it.

As the *halakhah* unfolds, however, it becomes clear that God has no active and volitional role in prophecy. The text describes the prophet's way of life and personal perfection. He is free of domination by his urges and his life is devoted to the ideal of contemplating nature and the divinity. His total separation from the follies of the world and devotion to knowledge of God brings about prophecy: "on such a man the Holy Spirit will immediately descend." Prophecy does not partake of a miracle entailing a revelation of God's will within a human life. It is, rather, the causal outcome of a certain way of life, as a result of which the Holy Spirit alights on the prophet "immediately." Prophecy is the prophet's ascent to the divine world, not the divinity's address to a human. Prophecy, so conceived, may be seen as the prophet successfully tuning in a frequency that broadcasts constantly.

The new direction taken by a person's life following his becoming a prophet is described here as the pinnacle of an ongoing process of ascent that concludes with the person attaining the rank of the angels: "And when the spirit rests upon him, his soul will mingle with the [rank of] angels called *Ishim*." Maimonides believed in the existence, between God and the world, of what he termed "separate intelligibles"—pure intellects devoid of any material component. In his construct, these were the angels. Prophecy is not direct speech between God and the prophet; it is, rather, the result of the prophet forming a connection with the active intellect, here termed "the [rank of] angels called *Ishim*"—the final level of the separate intelligibles. The prophet bonds himself to the active intellect and prophecy alights on him through his actualization of his potential intellect. We will examine Maimonides' concept of prophecy more broadly below, in the chapters on the *Guide of the Perplexed*. For now, we can say that this *halakhah* in *Mishneh Torah* makes it evident that Maimonides explained prophecy on the basis of divine wisdom, that is, as an event that does not depend on the divinity exercising its will to address a human being. Moreover, a comparison between the *Guide* and *Mishneh Torah* shows that the positions articulated in the latter are those that are closer to those of Aristotelian philosophy. Still, the formulations in *Mishneh Torah* lack the complexity and detail that characterize the *Guide* and present the ideas only in outline form.

The novel reading of the concept of revelation is clearly evident in another important chapter of *Mishneh Torah*, the one introducing "Laws Concerning Idolatry." Maimonides there describes the figure of Abraham and his path to God, recounting the history of religion from the beginning of mankind until Abraham and then from Abraham on to Moses. According to Maimonides, humanity initially believed in the unity of God; primeval Adam was a monotheist in all respects. After some generations, in the time of Enosh, people began to worship the stars as intermediaries deserving honor as God's servants. At that stage, however, those who worshipped the stars still believed in one God and considered the stars to be only representatives of the single and unified divinity.

The next step in the descent to idolatry took place with the transformation of the stars from representatives of the divinity into divinities in their own right. Sanctuaries were built in their honor, statues representing them were placed within those sanctuaries, revelation and the power to reward and punish were attributed to them, and they became the objects of idolatrous worship. In effect, humanity's descent into idolatry represented a process in which a representative took on the qualities of what it was supposed to represent. The stars took on the attributes of God, and then the statues, in the view of the masses, took on the qualities of the stars.

The culmination of that decline, which preceded Abraham's entry onto the historical stage, is described as follows:

> As time passed, the honored and revered Name of God was forgotten by mankind, vanished from their lips and hearts, and was no longer known to them. All the common people and the women and children knew only the figure of wood and stone and the temple edifice in which they had, from their childhood, been trained to prostrate themselves to the figure, worship it, and swear by its name. Even their wise men, such as priests and men of similar standing, also fancied that there was no other god but the stars and the spheres, for whose sake and in whose similitude these figures had been made. . . . The world moved on in this fashion till that Pillar of the World, the patriarch Abraham, was born. ("Laws Concerning Idolatry," 1:2)

The masses lost all sense of the sublime. They were immersed in a world given over to physical entities, and the realm of the divine was limited, in their eyes, to statues and temples. The elite among the idolaters, meanwhile, saw the statues as representatives of the stars. God Himself was gone and forgotten, totally replaced by his representatives.

At this point, Maimonides begins to tell the story of Abraham's life, an account that makes clear his religious-philosophical consciousness. At an early age, Abraham had already begun, by force of his mind, to challenge the beliefs of his parents and those around him: "But his mind was busily working and reflecting till he had attained the way of truth, apprehended the correct line of thought, and knew that there is One God, that He guides the celestial Sphere and created everything, and that among all that exist, there is no god besides Him . . . Abraham was forty years old when he recognized his Creator" ("Laws Concerning Idolatry," 1:3). Abraham's belief was the result of a lengthy philosophical process that reached maturity when he was forty years old; it was not produced by sudden illumination or revelation.

From that point on, Abraham becomes a subversive Socratic figure, a serious political nuisance on account of the force of his arguments: "Having attained this knowledge, he began to refute the inhabitants of Ur of the Chaldees, arguing with them and saying to them, 'The course you are following is not the way of truth.' . . . When he had prevailed over them with his arguments, the king (of the country) sought to slay him. He was miraculously saved and emigrated to Haran" ("Laws Concerning Idolatry," 1:3). Maimonides' account, of course, reworks various midrashic embellishments of the biblical story. He briefly alludes, without providing detail, to the story of Abraham being cast into a furnace and miraculously rescued from it, saying only that "he was miraculously saved." The story is centered on Abraham's philosophical path to faith and on Abraham's image as an iconoclastic philosopher who became a political threat.

R. Abraham ben David of Provance, known as Ra'abad, who wrote extensive critical notes on *Mishneh Torah*, held a different view of Abraham's life and the origin of his faith. In his brief comment on this *halakhah*, he cites a rabbinic *midrash* according to which the change in Abraham took place at a much younger age than Maimonides had said: "there is an *aggadah* according to which he was three years old." This brief reference to the midrashic version of things is an ironic attack on the entire structure Maimonides built. If Abraham was three years old when he recognized his Creator, his faith could not have been the product of probing philosophical thought; rather, it must have been the result of a sudden and miraculous illumination.

After leaving Ur, in Maimonides' account, Abraham became the founder of a school and a teacher of the public:

> He then began to proclaim to the whole world with great power and to instruct the people that the entire universe had but one Creator and that Him it was right to worship. He went from city to city and from kingdom to kingdom, calling and gathering together the inhabitants till he arrived in the land of Canaan. There, too, he proclaimed his message, as it is said, "And he called there on the name of the Lord, God of the universe" (Gen. 21:33). When the people flocked to him and questioned him regarding his assertions, he would instruct each one according to his capacity till he had brought him to the way of truth, and thus thousands and tens of thousands joined him. These are the persons referred to in the phrase, "men of the house of Abraham." He implanted in their hearts this great doctrine, composed books on it, and taught it to Isaac, his son. ("Laws Concerning Idolatry," 1:3)

Abraham disseminated monotheism through instruction and persuasion, gathering thousands and myriads of disciples as he went from city to city until he came to Canaan. What is missing from this account, however, is God's call to Abraham: "Go forth from your native land and from your father's house" (Gen. 12:1). According to Maimonides, Abraham came to the land of Canaan while fleeing political persecution; en route, he gathered an ever-growing community of monotheists. Abraham discovered God by force of his intellect, not by force of a revelation that led him to pull up stakes and leave home.

Maimonides' omission of revelation as a major factor causing Abraham to move to Canaan and his unique telling of the story reveal something even more profound. The biblical story suggests a picture of the believer's life entirely different from the one Maimonides paints. According to the plain meaning of the text, faith is the readiness to follow God's word without any doubt or hesitation. Abraham—dubbed the "Prince of Faith" by Kierkegaard—leaves the warm and secure bosom of his home and native land and sets out to follow the promise. He maintains his faith that the land of Canaan will be his even as he wanders in it as a stranger, just as he maintains his faith in the promise of progeny despite his and Sarah's advanced ages. Abraham's life embodies faith at its deepest. His greatness flows not from the force of his understanding or his prowess as a debater but from his limitless faith, grounded not on certain knowledge but on God's yet-to-be-fulfilled promise.

Maimonides, as we have seen, absolutely rejected this reading of the story and took a position far removed from the idea that the greater the absurdity, the greater the faith. For him, faith is not a blind force, operating contrary to what makes sense. Idolatry has its origin in error, in the operation of the imaginative faculty uncontrolled by reason. Monotheism, in contrast, is grounded in the ability to think and the courage to persevere in affirming truth in the face of surrounding political threats. Philosophy, rather than being the enemy of faith, is in fact its stimulus. It appeared on the stage of history with the advent of monotheism, in the figure of Abraham, after generations immersed in idolatry.

In the biblical story, Abraham appears as the founder of a family, who transmits God's blessing to his progeny. The recurring struggle over inheritance of that blessing is the axis on which the stories in Genesis revolve: Is Ishmael the heir or is it Isaac? Jacob or Esau? Maimonides, however, sees Abraham not as the founder of a family who bequeaths the divine blessing to his descendants but as the initiator of a broad movement whose members are all considered part of his household: " . . . thousands and tens of thousands joined him. These are the persons referred to in the phrase, 'men of the house of Abraham.' " His son Isaac and grandson Jacob followed him in providing instruction on monotheism: "[Abraham] implanted in their hearts this great doctrine, composed books on it, and taught it to Isaac, his son. Isaac settled down, instructing and exhorting. He imparted the doctrine to Jacob and ordained him to teach it. He, too, settled down, taught, and morally strengthened all who joined him" ("Laws Concerning Idolatry," 1:3). It is the substantive ideas and the teaching that pass from generation to generation, not the blessing and the promise.

The idea that Abraham was the founder of the monotheistic school more than a father bequeathing the blessing and the promise to his progeny is grounded in Maimonides' broader view of the election of Israel. He rejected the position taken a generation earlier by R. Judah Halevi in his *Kuzari*, who understood the election of Israel to mean the transmission of unique hereditary traits that afford Jews the capacity to be prophets—something not bestowed on the nations of the world. Maimonides attacks that view at the beginning of his discussion of prophecy: "It is one of the basic principles of religion that God inspires men with the prophetic gift" ("Laws Concerning the Foundations of the Torah," 7:1). Note carefully what he says: God grants prophecy to all men, not only Israel. The path to religious perfection is open to all human beings, Jews and non-Jews alike. And so he writes as follows at the end of "Laws Concerning the Sabbatical Year and the Year of the Jubilee," in the final *halakhah* of the *Book of Agriculture*, the volume devoted to agricultural laws:

> Not only the tribe of Levi but also each and every individual of those who come into the world, whose spirit moves him and whose knowledge gives him the understanding to set himself apart in order to stand before the Lord, to serve Him, to worship Him, and to know Him, who walks upright as God had made him to do, and releases his neck from the yoke of the many speculations that the children of men are wont to pursue—such an individual is consecrated to the Holy of Holies, and his portion and inheritance shall be in the Lord forever and evermore. ("Laws Concerning the Sabbatical Year and the Year of the Jubilee," 13:13)

The tribe of Levi did not receive an allocation of territory in the Land of Israel because it was separated and consecrated to serve God. But service of God is not a hereditary or tribal role; it is a status that all inhabitants of the world can attain.

Judah Halevi posited a hereditary aptitude that passed from primeval Adam via Terah's family to Abraham. In Maimonides' view, however, Abraham could take no pride in his ancestors, for they were idolaters. His virtue lay in the transformation he wrought by disseminating monotheism. Abraham, then, was the first convert, not the bearer of a hereditary aptitude. In terms similar to those he used in *Mishneh Torah*, Maimonides told Ovadyah the Proselyte that he could refer, in his prayers, to Abraham as his father:

> The reason for this is, that Abraham our Father taught the people, opened their minds, and revealed to them the true faith and the unity of God; he rejected the idols and abolished their adoration; he brought many children under the wings of the Divine Presence; he gave them counsel and advice . . . Ever since then whoever adopts Judaism and whoever confesses the unity of the Divine Name, as is prescribed in the Torah, is counted among the disciples of Abraham our Father, peace be with him. These men are Abraham's household. . . . Thus Abraham our Father, peace be with him, is the father of his pious posterity who keep his ways, and the father of his disciples and of all proselytes who adopt Judaism. (Letter to Ovadyah, pp. 475–476)

The distinctiveness of the Jewish people lies in their monotheism, and anyone who properly affirms monotheism is a son of Abraham. As he says later in the chapter in "Laws Concerning Idolatry," "And so it went on with ever increasing vigor among Jacob's children and their adherents till they became a people that knew God" (1:3).

The chapter concludes its history of religion with the figure of Moses. After Jacob's children went down to Egypt, the Israelites themselves sank into idolatry:

> When the Israelites had stayed a long while in Egypt, they relapsed, learned the practices of their neighbors, and, like them, worshipped idols, with the exception of the tribe of Levi, which steadfastly kept the charge of the Patriarch. This tribe of Levi never practiced idolatry. The doctrine implanted by Abraham would, in a very short time, have been uprooted, and Jacob's descendants would have lapsed into the error and perversities universally prevalent. But because of God's love for us and because He kept the oath made to our ancestor Abraham, He appointed Moses to be our teacher and the teacher of all the prophets and charged him with his mission. After Moses had begun to exercise his prophetic functions and Israel had been chosen by the Almighty as His heritage, He crowned them with precepts, and showed

them the way to worship Him and how to deal with idolatry and with those who go astray after it. (ibid.)

Unlike Abraham, Moses is a legislator, not only a teacher. A school has limited power, and a tradition built on argument is of uncertain durability. The Israelites, except for the tribe of Levi, succumbed to the influence of their surroundings and sank into idolatry.

Divine law appears on the stage of history in order to introduce stability and ensure continuity once it became clear that argument alone could not carry on the tradition. Moses, accordingly, was the founder of the nation of Israel as a political unit possessed of a legal system, and Israel's election gains expression through the giving of the Torah. It follows that when a proselyte accepts the Torah, he becomes part of the nation of Israel, which likewise became a nation by virtue of having accepted the Torah. The proselyte is equal to the rest of Israel because the Torah was given to Israel and to all others who want to accept it. Maimonides makes the point to Ovadyah in these terms: "You shall certainly say the blessing, 'Who has chosen us,' 'Who has given us,' 'Who have taken us for Your own' and 'Who has separated us': for the Creator, may He be extolled, has indeed chosen you and separated you from the nations and given you the Torah. For the Torah has been given to us and to the proselytes" (Letter to Ovadyah, p. 476). To reverse the descent into idolatry, which began in the time of Enosh with the worship of intermediaries, Moses used not only philosophical argumentation but also the absolute prohibition imposed by the Torah on worshipping anything but God.

Halakhah, Magic, and Idolatry

In *Mishneh Torah*, Maimonides, with philosophical perceptiveness, formulates the basic concepts of the Jewish world: the meaning of human perfection, the purpose of the Torah, the concept of divinity, the pinnacle of religious experience through love and awe, the doctrine of prophecy, the concept of faith, and the election of Israel. But his philosophical perspective bears not only on his broad view of the world and the meaning of *halakhah* within it; it also influences his treatment of specific halakhic norms. The clearest and most profound illustration is his formulation of the range of prohibitions related to magic, sorcery, and spells, all of which are treated in chapter 11 of "Laws Concerning Idolatry."

Maimonides waged his struggle against magic through a series of expansions of the prohibitions on magic that appear in the Torah: the forbidding of sorcery, "you shall not practice divination or soothsaying" (Lev. 19:26), the legislation against "one who casts spells" (Dt. 18:11; translated below as "a charmer"), and "nor shall you follow their laws" (Lev. 18:3). Maimonides elaborates as follows on the prohibition against "divination":

> Israelites may not resort to divination like the gentiles, as it is said, "neither shall ye practice divination" (Lev. 19:26). What is divination? The following are examples. To say: "Since my piece of bread dropped out of my mouth, or my staff fell from my hand, I shall not go today to such a place, for if I go, my business will not be successfully accomplished" . . . or if one sets for himself a sign and says, "If a certain thing happens to me, I will follow this course of action; if it does not happen, I will not do so"—as Eleazar, Abraham's servant did—these and all things similar are forbidden. Whoever does any thing as a result of any of these happenings is punished with stripes." ("Laws Concerning Idolatry," 11:4)

One may not mark out for himself signs to indicate the success or failure of a future action and then proceed on the basis of whether or not the sign appears. The prohibition would be violated, for example, by someone who avoided taking a trip because a black cat crossed his path or because he had led with his left foot while climbing onto a bus. The prohibition against "soothsaying" would be violated by skipping "thirteen" when numbering the floors of a building. Maimonides' broad interpretation of the ban on soothsaying is part of his effort to eliminate non-rational elements from human life. Through expansion of this prohibition, Maimonides forbade reliance on an astrological forecast even if a person simply happened upon it, without having requested it:

> What is an "observer of times" [*me'onen*, an astrologer]? The term applies to these who assign seasons declaring that astrologically a particular day is favorable, while another day is unfavorable; that a certain day is propitious for the execution of a specific work and a certain year or month is unfavorable for a specific thing.
>
> It is forbidden to be an "observer of times" even if he committed no overt act but only uttered the lies which fools imagine are words of truth, words of the wise. And whoever is influenced in his actions by astrology and arranges his work or journey to take place at the times fixed by the astrologers,

is punished with stripes, as it is said, "Ye shall not observe times" (Lev. 19:26). ("Laws Concerning Idolatry," 11:8–9)

According to Maimonides, then, one violates a biblical-law prohibition by reading a newspaper horoscope and acting on the basis of what it forecasts to be an auspicious day for a particular activity.

The prohibition on "casting spells" is understood by Maimonides to refer to incantations. On that basis, he forbids magical use of language for purposes of healing:

> What is a charmer? One who utters words that are not part of any spoken language and are meaningless, foolishly fancying that these words are helpful. These charmers go so far as to say that if one utters certain words over a snake or scorpion, it will become harmless, and if one utters certain words over a man, he will not be harmed by the reptiles. . . . All these strange and uncouth sounds and names do no harm, nor have they power to do good. ("Laws Concerning Idolatry," 11:10)

The distinctiveness of divine names lies in their conveying understanding of the divinity and not in their capacity to bring about actions in the world. The polemical tone associated with these *halakhot* is continued in the *Guide*:

> Do not think anything other than this and do not let occur to your mind the vain imaginings of the writers of charms or what names you may hear from them or may find in their stupid books, names that they have invented, which are not indicative of any notion whatsoever, but which they call the *names* and of which they think that they necessitate *holiness and purity* and work miracles. All these are stories that it is not seemly for a perfect man to listen to, much less to believe. (*Guide* I:61; Pines, p. 149)

He reserves his harshest criticism for those who make magic use of Jewish sancta:

> One who whispers a spell over a wound, at the same time reciting a verse from the Torah, one who recites a verse over a child to save it from terrors, and one who places a scroll or phylacteries on an infant to induce it to sleep are not only in the category of sorcerers and soothsayers, but they are included among those who repudiate the Torah; for they use its words to cure the body whereas these are only medicine for the soul, as it is said, "They shall be life to your soul" (Prov. 3:22). ("Laws Concerning Idolatry," 11:12)

Reciting biblical verse as a healing incantation, or treating holy scrolls as if they themselves provide protection and possess unique capabilities, are practices that Maimonides considers to be apostasy, appropriating sancta for human needs.

In the same spirit and with an equally harsh tone, he disparages those who write holy names on the parchment in a mezuzah or regard it as a protective amulet:

> It is customary to write the *Shaddai* on the outside of the mezuzah, opposite the space between the paragraphs. Since it is on the outside, it is not objectionable. But those who write the names of angels, holy names, verses, or special shapes on the mezuzah are included in the category of those who have no share in the world to come, since these fools not only cancel the commandment but make of a great commandment, the unification of the Holy One, blessed be he, His love, and His worship, a charm for their own benefit since they, in their stupidity, think that this is a matter which benefits them concerning worldly vanities. ("Laws Concerning Tefillin, the Mezuzah and the Scroll of the Law," 5:4)

Given this *halakhah*, one can imagine what Maimonides would say about those who check the fitness of their mezuzahs in the wake of some misfortune. He objects to the view that a flaw in a mezuzah can affect a person's fate or situation and to the idea that the purpose of the mezuzah is to protect a person against material harms. Such an idea is apostasy, and one who believes it loses his place in the world to come, for the purpose of the sancta is to raise a person beyond the realm of fears and dread, yet such a person subordinates the sancta themselves to those impulses. At the end of the laws of the mezuzah, he describes its true protective power in the following terms:

> One must take great care to fulfill the commandment of the mezuzah, since it obliges everyone always. Every time one enters or leaves [his home] he will encounter the unity of God's name, remember His love, awaken from his sleep and from his concentration on temporal vanities, and realize that nothing exists forever and ever but knowledge of the Rock of the Universe; one is immediately restored to one's senses and follows the paths of the upright. The Sages said: one who has Teffilin on his head and his arm, and fringes on his clothing, and a mezuzah on his doorway is assured of not sinning, since he has many reminders; these are the angels which save him

from sinning, as it is says, *The angel of the Lord camps around those who fear Him and rescue them* (Ps. 34:8). ("Laws Concerning Tefillin, Mezuzah, Torah Scroll," 6:13)

The mezuzah reminds a person of his devotion to God and draws him out of temporal vanities. It protects him not against external hazards but against his own impulses—the same impulses that might lead him to make the mezuzah into an amulet for his own benefit.

This expanded list of prohibitions offers the best illustration of how philosophical considerations are interwoven into the *halakhah* in *Mishneh Torah*. Maimonides in effect transforms rational activity into halakhic obligation: a person is required to examine whether his motives for taking or avoiding some action are guided by natural, causal considerations that rest on sound theory. Chapter 11 of "Laws Concerning Idolatry" thus goes beyond audacious theological innovation; it effects a revolution in the most fundamental aspects of a Jew's daily life. A community that accepts these broadened prohibitions will have to uproot much of the folk religion that makes magical use of ritual objects and amulets—such practices as treating texts of the Book of Psalms as possessing protective power.

Not surprisingly, these *halakhot* in *Mishneh Torah* elicited widespread criticism from various halakhists whose view of the world was far removed from that of Maimonides and whose understanding of these prohibitions was correspondingly different. R. Solomon ben Aderet (Rashba) was among Maimonides' prominent opponents with regard to the scope of these prohibitions; like his teacher Naḥmanides, he interpreted them narrowly. In a responsum on the use of magic in medical procedures, Rashba applied his extensive erudition to cite Talmudic passages at odds with Maimonides' view.[1] It cannot be denied that Maimonides' broad construction of the prohibitions on magic impose a scientific and philosophical construction on the Talmudic material. As we know, the Talmud is replete with medical nostrums that cannot withstand Aristotelian scientific scrutiny. The sages themselves not infrequently acted in accord with astrological considerations and often made use of a range of magical techniques, from incantations and amulets to the creation of magical creatures. Maimonides was well aware of contradictory Talmudic statements that reveal belief in an astrological worldview. In his *Letter on Astrology* that was dedicated to clarify his position on the matter, he denounced the astrological

[1] *Teshuvot ha-Rahsba*, ed. H. Dimitrovsky vol. 1, *Minchat Kenaot* [Jerusalem 1990], chap. 21.

traditions as grounded in the pseudo-science of the Chasdeans, Chaldeans, Egyptians, and the Cannaites. The rational traditions of the Greeks, Indians, and Persians rejected such a worldview. As for the appearance of astrological views in the Talmud itself, Maimonides made the following preemptive claims:

> I know that you may search and find sayings of some individual sages in the Talmud and Midrashim whose words appear to maintain that at the moment of a man's birth the stars will cause such and such to happen to him. Do not regard this as a difficulty, for it is not fitting for a man to abandon the prevailing law and raise once again counterarguments and replies (that precede its enactment). Similarly it is not proper to abandon matters of reason that have already been verified by proofs, shake loose of them, and depend on the works of a single one of the sages from whom possibly the matter was hidden. Or there may be an allusion in those worlds . . . A man should never cast his reason behind him, for the eyes are set in front not in the back. (*Letter on Astrology*, p. 472)

The great transformation wrought by Maimonides' rulings on magic, which went so far as to make rationality into a religious obligation, is ultimately rooted in Maimonides' understanding of idolatry. Consistent with his overall perspective, he regarded the prohibitions on sorcery not only as banning negative forms of conduct but as striving to alter a flawed understanding of the world. He believed sorcery, astrology, and incantations to be forbidden because they are erroneous and vain, as he says in the *halakhah* that sums up Chapter 11:

> These practices are all false and deceptive, and were means employed by the ancient idolaters to deceive the peoples of various countries and induce them to become their followers. It is not proper for Israelites who are highly intelligent to suffer themselves to be deluded by such inanities or imagine that there is anything in them. . . . Whoever believes in these and similar things and, in his heart, holds them to be true and scientific and only forbidden by the Torah, is nothing but a fool, deficient in understanding, who belongs to the same class with women and children whose intellects are immature. Sensible people, however, who possess sound mental faculties, know by clear proofs that all these practices which the Torah prohibited have no scientific basis but are chimerical and inane; and that only those deficient in knowledge are attracted to these follies and, for their sake, leave

the ways of truth. The Torah, therefore, in forbidding all these follies, exhorts us, "Thou shalt be whole-hearted with the Lord thy God" (Deut. 18:13). ("Laws Concerning Idolatry," 11:16)

These comments are directed toward a long interpretive tradition, going back to the Talmud itself and continuing to Maimonides' time and beyond and including such thinkers as Naḥmanides and Ibn Ezra, which saw astrology that was regarded at the time as a thoroughly scientific worldview, incantations or sorcery as matters of substance with an actual impact on the world. In this counter-tradition, the prohibition of such matters that was defined in far narrower terms had to do with the fact that access to sorcery and magic is a rebellious attempt to force a course of action against the divine will. Employing a harshly polemical tone, Maimonides in this *halakhah* suggests that magic and astrology are follies invented by the idolatrous clergy to promote their control of the masses. Idolatry is based on the imagination, that is, on the inability to distinguish between the possible and the impossible. For one who lacks a rational standard for assessing reality, everything is possible—even worship of the stars themselves. The idolatrous clergy controls its faithful by deploying threats and promises related to their most basic fears and hopes. Lacking a critical capacity, the believers will do whatever is demanded of them to ensure the welfare of their children, their continued livelihood, and so forth. In its effort to extirpate idolatry, the Torah therefore battles against the non-rational view of the world, as Maimonides says in Part III of the *Guide*:

> In order to keep people away from all magical practices, it has been prohibited to observe any of their usages, even those attaching to agricultural and pastoral activities and other activities of this kind. I mean all that is said to be useful, but is not required by speculation concerning nature. . . . For they are branches of magical practices, inasmuch as they are things not required by reasoning concerning nature and lead to magical practices that of necessity seek support in astrological notions. Accordingly, the matter is turned into a glorification and a worship of the stars. (*Guide* III:37; Pines, p. 543)

Many believers, some of them important thinkers, take the view that faith is based in the mysterious and the supernatural. Accordingly, belief in magic, sorcery, and such beings as demons and spirits is something firmly tied to the religious worldview. Maimonides, however, held that such a view of the world opened the door to idolatry and to clerical manipulation of the masses, who failed to distinguish between the possible and the impossible. From his perspective, then, the battle against idolatry included the attempt to extirpate an entire worldview in a manner consistent with his own broad understanding that monotheism was built on the rationality of the natural causal order, reflecting the wisdom of the Creator.

In Chapter 11 of "Laws Concerning Idolatry," Maimonides attempts to sever magic's venerable link to faith in general, with which it seems to form a continuum. As we see to this day, there is no guarantee that this heroic effort will affect the daily life of the mass of believers. More than he substantively transformed the *halakhah* in this area, Maimonides left powerful testimony to the way in which a religious worldview could penetrate to the heart of halakhic action.

Messianism, *halakhah*, and Nature

The last two chapters of *Mishneh Torah* offer a halakhic formulation of Maimonides' concept of messianism. They come at the end of the treatise's final subdivision, "Laws Concerning Kings and Wars," in which Maimonides presents his concept of the halakhic polity and the role and standing of a political ruler.

The decision to conclude *Mishneh Torah* with a binding formulation of the messianic idea is no less significant than the decision to begin it with the concept of God and the universe. By concluding his halakhic treatise with the messianic concept, Maimonides makes the point that the messianic age will be within the *halakhah* purview, not beyond it. Moreover, the Messiah will institute full halakhic governance: "King Messiah will arise and restore the kingdom of David to its former state and original sovereignty. He will rebuild the sanctuary and gather the dispersed of Israel. All the ancient laws will be reinstituted in his days; sacrifices will again be offered; the Sabbatical and Jubilee years will again be observed in accordance with the commandments set forth in the Law" ("Laws Concerning Kings and Wars," 11:1). Later in the passage, the emphasis on full restoration of the Torah's laws in the messianic era takes on a polemical tone:

> Do not think that King Messiah will have to perform signs and wonders, bring anything new into being, revive the dead, or do similar things, as the fools say. . . . The general principle is: this Law of ours with its statutes and

ordinances is not subject to change. It is for ever and all eternity it is not to be added to or to be taken away from. ("Laws Concerning Kings and Wars," 11:3, p. 239)

The idea that the law will be nullified as part of mankind's redemption is typical of various utopian streams. Diverse utopian projects associated the law with the painful gap between real and ideal, a gap attributable to human will and the human capacity to do evil. The law seeks to grapple with that gap in the unredeemed world by subjecting human will to controls. The messianic expectation contains the seeds of challenge to the idea of law, for it yearns for a world in which the good appears on its own, without any need for punishment or compulsion. This element of utopian thought appears in Christianity and in some later secular utopianisms, such as Marxism, and it did not leave Judaism unaffected. In the conclusion to his halakhic code, however, Maimonides subjected the messianic age itself to the reins of *halakhah*; he was clearly aware of the anarchic potential of the messianic idea if not subjected to such restraint. The Messiah is not to be sought in some trans-halakhic era, and the messianic era will not entail a casting off of the Torah's yoke. On the contrary, its very essence is the complete fulfillment of the Torah.

In the next *halakhah*, Maimonides intensifies the link between messianism and *halakhah*:

If there arise a king from the House of David who meditates on the Torah, occupies himself with the commandments, as did his ancestor David, observes the precepts prescribed in the Written and the Oral Law, prevails upon Israel to walk in the way of the Torah and to repair its breaches, and fights the battles of the Lord, it may be assumed that he is the Messiah. If he does these things and succeeds, triumphing over all the nations that surround him, rebuilds the sanctuary on its site, and gathers the dispersed of Israel, he is beyond all doubt the Messiah. ("Laws Concerning Kings and Wars," 11:4)

This *halakhah* suggests that Maimonides rejected the idea of the End, that is, the notion of a set, predetermined time for the Messiah's coming. The complete fulfillment of the *halakhah* and the Messiah's political success do not *demonstrate* that he had been designated from the beginning of time and that the time of salvation has arrived. His achievements *constitute* him as the Messiah since he manages to finally bring about the complete fulfillment of Judaism's halakhic and political values. By placing messianism in the "Laws Concerning Kings," Maimonides teaches that the Messiah is the king who succeeds in fulfilling all the halakhic expectations of the institution of kingship, as Maimonides understood them.

Many messianic streams anticipate a change in the nature of mankind as part of the new causal order. In the world that is to succeed the known world, death and toil will be abolished. Good will prevail throughout, for the blind inertia of nature, which reacts in the same way to the good and to the bad, will be changed. In the messianic era, an innocent child who climbs onto a shaky roof will fall to the ground as gently as a leaf, for the force of gravity will be subject to the moral standing of the falling body. The expectation that law will be annulled and nature changed reflects the depth of man's grievances against reality.

Maimonides, in contrast, saw messianism as the highest fulfillment of existing human potential, not as its replacement in some more perfect situation. The permanence of nature, like the eternity of the Torah, is an additional factor in his messianic vision. That vision, to be sure, necessarily entails fundamental acceptance of reality as we know it:

> Let no one think that in the days of the Messiah any of the laws of nature will be set aside, or any innovation be introduced into creation. The world will follow its normal course. The words of Isaiah: *And the wolf shall dwell with the lamb, and the leopard shall lie down with the kid* (Isa. 11:6) are to be understood figuratively, meaning that Israel will live securely among the wicked of the heathens who are likened to wolves and leopards. ("Laws Concerning Kings and Wars," 12:1)

Nature remains in force because it is the embodiment of divine wisdom; it is not the outcome of a cosmic fall requiring correction. The continuation of the messianic era does not signify that history has come to its predetermined end and an eternal era beyond time will ensue. In the introduction to Chapter 10 of *Sanhedrin* (*Pereq Ḥeleq*) in his *Commentary on the Mishnah*, Maimonides writes of the natural political circumstances that make possible the continuation of the messianic accomplishments: "The Messiah will die and be succeeded by his son and his grandson . . . and his government will long endure . . . and it is not beyond reason that it will endure for thousands of years, for the sages already have said that a virtuous grouping, once formed, will not quickly come apart" (*Introduction to Pereq Ḥeleq*). That the days of the Messiah may introduce a new and lengthy period does not follow from some change in nature or the arrival of some pre-set End. For Maimonides, the reasons for the onset of the new period are entirely natural—a state founded on superior laws has the ability to endure for a long time, and that will be what happens in the messianic era. The endurance of the world and the eternity of the Torah are fundamental and mutually linked threads in Maimonides' messianic idea. These two principles maintain the acceptance of reality as it exists and foreclose the potential for anarchy that lurks within the messianic idea.

The messianic traditions that envisioned formation of a new world as part of the redemption contemplated as well the destruction of the old one. That idea added an apocalyptic element to the messianic era—a mighty world war along the lines of the war of Gog and Magog. Maimonides rejected a substantial portion of the apocalyptic literature in the following *halakhah*:

> Taking the words of the Prophets in their literal sense, it appears that the inauguration of the Messianic era will be marked by the war of Gog and Magog. . . .
>
> Some of our sages say that the coming of Elijah will precede the advent of the Messiah. But no one is in a position to know the details of this and similar things until they have come to pass. They are not explicitly stated by the Prophets. Nor have the Rabbis any tradition with regard to these matters. They are guided solely by what the Scriptural texts seem to imply. Hence there is a divergence of opinion on the subject. But be that as it may neither the exact sequence of those events nor the details thereof constitute religious dogmas. No one should ever occupy himself with the legendary themes or spend much time on midrashic statements bearing on this and like subjects. He should not deem them of prime importance, since they lead neither to the fear of God nor to the love of Him. No one should calculate the end. Said the Rabbis: *Blasted be those who reckon out the end* (BT *Sanhedrin* 97b). One should wait (for his coming) and accept in principle this article of faith, as we have stated before. ("Laws Concerning Kings and Wars," 12:2)

Intensive involvement in messianic apocalypse and the timing of the End thus lacks any religious value and adds nothing to our knowledge of the future, which is in any case unknown. It fosters neither love nor fear of God.

In Maimonides' view, the messianic transformation will be a change in the political situation of the Jewish nation, which will be liberated from subservience to the nations of the world, and the formation of an expanse in which they will be able to realize the Torah in full. Subservience and exile foreclose the development of human perfection, for they subject human life to preoccupation with the basic requirements of existence. The ingathering of the exiles is thus tied to liberation from subservience to the nations.

Maimonides rejected the view that the Land of Israel possesses some inherent and unique quality that makes it a sacred space in which prophecy dwells. The demise of prophecy in exile should not be associated with territorial distance from the sacred place, as R. Judah Halevi and others after him maintained. According to Maimonides, the reason that prophecy does not alight on people in exile is that they live in circumstances of subservience and stress, which confine one's horizons. In the *Guide*, after declaring that sadness and stress in a prophet cause a lapse in his prophecy, Maimonides goes on to describe the state of affairs in exile:

> This is indubitably the essential and proximate cause of the fact that prophecy was taken away during the time of the *Exile*. For what *languor* or *sadness* can befall a man in any state that would be stronger than that due to his being a thrall slave in bondage to the ignorant who commit great sins. . . . This also will be the cause for prophecy being restored to us in its habitual form, as has been promised *in the days of the Messiah, may he be revealed soon*. (*Guide* II:36; Pines, p. 373)

The return to the Land of Israel, then, represents a political transformation that allows for the renewal of human perfection. The Land of Israel is not holy in the sense of being endowed with some unique property that allows for the emergence of prophecy. Prophecy, Maimonides maintains, is tied to the existence of sovereignty, in contrast to the dreadful state of dependency associated with exile. Sovereignty allows for the leisure needed to develop the higher human perfection that is prophecy.

Life in a flawed society, a society not committed to the pursuit of knowledge and truth, is filled with social conflicts and confrontations. The political transformation in messianic times will create the conditions in which human beings can flourish, as Maimonides describes at the end of his great treatise:

> The Sages and Prophets did not long for the days of the Messiah that Israel might exercise dominion over the world, or rule over the heathens, or be

exalted by the nations, or that it might eat and drink and rejoice. The expectation was that Israel be free to devote itself to the Law and its wisdom, with no one to oppress or disturb it, and thus be worthy of life in the world to come.

In that era there will be neither famine nor war, neither jealousy nor strife. Blessings will be abundant, comforts within the reach of all. The one preoccupation of the whole world will be to know the Lord. Hence Israelites will be very wise, they will know the things that are now concealed and will attain an understanding of their Creator to the utmost capacity of the human mind, as it is written: *For the earth shall be full of the knowledge of the Lord, as the waters cover the sea* (Isa. 11:9). ("Laws Concerning Kings and Wars," 12:4–5)

In the final two chapters of *Mishneh Torah*, Maimonides integrated the messianic idea into his broader religious and halakhic concept. His innovative interpretation was meant to restrain two sorts of dangerous utopianism that may develop at the heart of the vision of redemption. One anticipated a change in human nature and the consequent end to any need for law and *halakhah* as we know it; the other expected a change in the causal natural order. With respect to the first, Maimonides foresaw no divine intervention in human nature and believed that law would remain essential for the existence of any human grouping; he therefore depicted the Messiah as a ruler who would fulfill the *halakhah* in its entirety. In that way, he sought to extirpate the anarchic potential within messianic yearnings.

As for a change in the causal order, Maimonides believed that the most profound expression of God's presence could be found in the causal order itself. Accordingly, the utopian aspiration for a change in that order, brought about by some new act of will, represented a challenge to Maimonides' basic understanding, tied, as it is, to wisdom. Nature, he maintained, will remain intact, and the world will continue in its normal way. Even if the world was created by an initial act of will, there will be no further such act that would put an end to the world and jeopardize its existence and endurance. The restrained messianic aspiration is channeled toward a change in the way society operates, a change that will create a society that allows for realization of the ultimate principle underlying Maimonides' concept of mankind and of *halakhah*—knowledge of God and of the world.

CHAPTER SIX

Mishneh Torah and the Conceptual Understanding of *halakhah*

Reorganizing the *halakhah*: Form and Content

In the introduction to *Sefer ha-Miẓvot*, his *Book of Commandments*, Maimonides describes his struggle to organize the halakhic material in *Mishneh Torah*. He initially thought to follow the sequence of orders and tractates in the *Mishnah*. That structure appeared to offer substantial benefits, for it was familiar and authoritative; in addition, Maimonides had said in the introduction to the *Commentary on the Mishnah* that it was conceptually logical and systematic. Moreover, Maimonides considered the *Mishnah* to be a precedent for *Mishneh Torah*, and it seemed only natural to adopt the earlier work's organization.

An alternative to relying on the *Mishnah* was to adopt the method used by the Rif and follow, page by page, the sequence of topics discussed in the Talmud. This had a certain advantage, in that it ensured that every area taken up by the Babylonian Talmud would be treated. But it was clear to Maimonides that the Talmudic discussion ambled casually from topic to topic and failed to provide the desired systematic framework. Ultimately, he declined to adopt either of those structures, rejecting both the Talmudic and the Mishnahic organizations; as he wrote to Pinḥas the *dayyan*, "For I follow neither the sequence of the Talmud nor the sequence of the Mishnah" (*Iggerot*, p. 444). He believed the *Mishnah* failed to provide the systematic and conceptual framework he needed and that following its structure would not allow him to encompass systematically all the areas of the *halakhah* and present them in an accessible and transparent sequence. In rejecting both the Mishnahic and the Talmudic organization, he gave rise to an important new form of halakhic writing: the original and independent presentation of the *halakhah* overall.

A glance at *Mishneh Torah*'s structure shows that the treatise's classifica-
tion system and organization go far beyond the administrative transfer of
a pile of material from one file to another or a technical arrangement of
material that could have been organized differently. In its novel organization of the *halakhah*, *Mishneh Torah* does not merely impose an external
structure on the halakhic material; it also interprets and shapes the material itself. In gathering separate, fragmented rulings into a single literary
unit, Maimonides forged new areas in *halakhah*. Similarly, the internal
organization of the units reflects a conceptual understanding of the halakhic principles. This innovative feature of *Mishneh Torah* is evident in
every one of its volumes, and we can analyze only a few instances here that
illustrate the phenomenon overall. To begin, though, we should consider
the broad structure of the treatise.

The first volume, the *Book of Knowledge* (*Sefer ha-Madda*), sets the foundation: the elements of Jewish faith and morals. It includes "Laws Concerning the Foundations of the Torah" (*Hilkhot Yesodei ha-Torah*), "Laws
Concerning Moral Dispositions" (*Hilkhot De'ot*), "Laws Concerning the
Study of the Torah" (*Hilkhot Talmud Torah*), "Laws Concerning Idolatry
and the Institutions of Heathen Nations" (*Hilkhot Avodah Zarah ve Ḥuqqot
ha-Goyim*), and "Laws Concerning Repentance" (*Hilkhot Teshuvah*).

Next is the *Book of Love* (*Sefer Ahavah*), encompassing man's recurring
duties to his God. Maimonides describes them as "precepts which are to be
continuously observed, and which we have been bidden to keep, in order
that we may always love God and be ever mindful of Him" (*Mishneh Torah*,
Introduction). The volume comprises "Laws Concerning Reading of the
Shema" (*Hilkhot Qeri'at Shema*), "Laws Concerning Prayer and the Priestly
Benediction" (*Hilkhot Tefillah u-Birkat Kohanim*), "Laws Concerning Phylacteries, Mezuzah, and the Scroll of the Torah" (*Hilkhot Tefillin u-Mezuzah
ve-Sefer Torah*), "Laws Concerning Fringes" (*Hilkhot Ẓiẓit*), "Laws Concerning Blessings" (*Hilkhot Berakhot*), and "Laws Concerning Circumcision"
(*Hilkhot Milah*). Including the laws of circumcision in this volume was
problematic, for it is not a recurring commandment in the same manner as
the others treated in the volume. In the introduction, Maimonides explains
his decision as follows: "because this is a sign in our flesh, serving as a constant reminder, even when phylacteries and fringes of the garment, are not
being worn" (*Mishneh Torah*, Introduction). Circumcision is not a recurring obligation, but it is a sign that continuously attests to one's love of
God, even when the other commandments are not being carried out.

In the third volume, the *Book of Seasons* (*Sefer Zemanim*), we find those commandments between man and God that do not apply at all times but only on designated occasions. Reflecting the cycle of the Jewish year, the volume includes "Laws Concerning the Sabbath" (*Hilkhot Shabbat*), "Laws Concerning *Eruvin*" (*Hilkhot Eruvin*), "Laws Concerning Rest on the Tenth of Tishri" (*Hilkhot Shevitat asor*), "Laws Concerning Rest on the Festivals" (*Hilkhot Shevitat Yom Tov*), "Laws Concerning Leavened and Unleavened Bread" (*Hilkhot Hamez u-Mazah*), "Laws Concerning the Ram's Horn, the Booth, and the Palm Branch" (*Hilkhot Shofar ve-Sukkah ve-Lulav*), "Laws Concerning the Shekel-Dues" (*Hilkhot Sheqalim*), "Laws Concerning the Sanctification of the New Moon" (*Hilkhot Hiddush ha-Hodesh*), "Laws Concerning Fast Days" (*Hilkhot Ta'aniyot*), and "Laws Concerning the Scroll of Esther and Hanukkah" (*Hilkhot Megillah ve-Hanukkah*).

The *Book of Women* (*Sefer Nashim*), the fourth volume, pertains to family law: "Laws Concerning Marriage" (*Hilkhot Ishut*), "Laws Concerning Divorce" (*Hilkhot Gerushin*), "Laws Concerning Levirate Marriage and Release From It" (*Hilkhot Yibbum ve-Halizah*), "Laws Concerning a Virgin Maiden" (*Hilkhot Na'arah Betulah*), and "Laws Concerning a Wayward Woman" (*Hilkhot Sotah*).

The fifth volume, *The Book of Holiness* (*Sefer Qedushah*), offers an interesting example of the joining of seemingly disparate halakhic topics into a single unit under the influence of an overarching meta-halakhic concept. The volume includes "Laws Concerning Forbidden Intercourse" (*Hilkhot Issurei Bi'ah*), "Laws Concerning Forbidden Foods" (*Hilkhot Ma'akhalot asurot*, and "Laws Concerning the Slaughtering of Animals for Food" (*Hilkhot Shehitah*). The first of these defines and sets forth the rules regarding forbidden sexual relations; the second and third treat kashrut and permitted and forbidden foods. One might have expected "Laws Concerning Forbidden Intercourse" to have been included in the preceding volume, the *Book of Women*, but Maimonides offers the following explanation for its inclusion here: "in these two regards, the Omnipresent sanctified us and separated us from the nations: [with regard to forbidden sexual relations and with regard to forbidden foods]" (*Mishneh Torah*, Introduction). The prohibition of certain sexual relations and the prohibition of certain foods are similar in that both restrain basic biological urges. They reflect the idea of holiness, which is linked to the ability to separate oneself from basic bodily impulses.

The *Book of Asseverations* (*Sefer Hafla'a*), the sixth volume, deals with prohibitions related to speech. It includes "Laws Concerning Oaths" (*Hilkhot Shevu'ot*), "Laws Concerning Vows" (*Hilkhot Nedarim*), "Laws Concerning the Nazarite" (*Hilkhot Nezirut*), and "Laws Concerning Evaluations and Things Votive" (*Hilkhot Arakhim ve-Ḥaramin*).

In the *Book of Agriculture* (*Sefer zera'im*), the seventh volume, Maimonides collects the laws related to various aspects of agriculture. It includes "Laws Concerning Diverse Kinds" (*Hilkhot Kil'ayim*), Laws Concerning Gifts to the Poor" (*Hilkhot Matanot Aniyyim*), "Laws Concerning Heave Offerings" (*Hilkhot Terumot*), "Laws Concerning Tithes" (*Hilkhot Ma'asrot*), "Laws Concerning Second Tithes and Fourth Year's Fruit" (*Hilkhot Ma'aser Sheni ve-Neta Reva'i*), "Laws Concerning First Fruits and Other Gifts to the Priesthood" (*Hilkhot Bikkurim u-She'ar Matanot Kehunah She-bi-Gevulin*), and "Laws Concerning the Sabbatical Year and the Year of the Jubilee" (*Hilkhot Shemittah ve-Yovel*). An interesting departure in the organization of this volume appears in the final four chapters of *Hilkhot Matanot Aniyyim*, which pertain to the laws of charity, unrelated to agricultural matters. Maimonides here followed the order in the *Mishnah*, where the laws of charity are included in tractate *Pe'ah* of the order *Zera'im*. The arrangement makes sense because many of the laws in the volume—for example, those related to corners of the field, missed or forgotten crops, the tithe to the poor, and some of the laws related to the sabbatical and jubilee years—pertain to gifts for the needy.

The eighth volume, "The Book of Temple Service" (*Sefer Avodah*), sets forth the laws related to the Temple and its fixed, public cult as well as the characteristics of the various sorts of sacrifices. It includes "Laws Concerning the Temple" (*Hilkhot Beit ha-Beḥirah*), "Laws Concerning the Vessels of the Sanctuary and Those Who Serve in It" (*Hilkhot Kelei ha-Miqdash ve-ha-Ovedim bah*), "Laws Concerning Entrance into the Sanctuary" (*Hilkhot Bi'at Miqdash*), "Laws Concerning Things Prohibited for the Altar" (*Hilkhot Issurei ha-Mizbeiaḥ*) "Laws Concerning the Manner of Offering Sacrifices" (*Hilkhot Ma'aseh ha-Qorbanot*), "Laws Concerning the Daily Offerings and Additional Offerings" (*Hilkhot Temidim u-Musafim*), "Laws Concerning Hallowed Offerings Rendered Unfit" (*Hilkhot Pesulei ha-Muqdashin*), "Laws Concerning the Service on the Day of Atonement" (*Hilkhot Avodat Yom ha-Kippurim*), and "Laws Concerning Trespass in Regard to Sacred Objects" (*Hilkhot Me'ilah*). The volume departs in an interesting way from the sequence in the *Mishnah*. There, the laws of the Day of Atonement are treated in tractate *Yoma*, encompassing both the day's sacrificial service in the Temple and the duty to fast and afflict oneself imposed on every individual Jew. In *Mishneh Torah*, the two aspects of the day's laws are divided: the sacrificial service in the Temple is included in *The Book of Temple Service*, while the obligations borne by the individual—affliction and refraining from work—are set forth in the *Book of Seasons*, "Laws Concerning Rest on the Tenth of Tishri."

The *Book of Offerings* (*Sefer Qorbanot*), the ninth volume, presents the laws related to individuals' sacrifices. It includes "Laws Concerning the Passover Offering" (*Hilkhot Qorban Pesaḥ*), "Laws Concerning the Festal Offering" (*Hilkhot Ḥagigah*), "Laws Concerning Firstlings" (*Hilkhot Bekhorot*), "Laws Concerning Offerings for Transgressions Committed through Error" (*Hilkhot Shegagot*), "Laws Concerning Those Whose Atonement Is Not Complete" (*Hilkhot Meḥusrei Kapparah*), and "Laws Concerning Substituted Offerings" (*Hilkhot Temurah*).

Like the two volumes that precede it, the *Book of Purity* (*Sefer Taharah*), the tenth volume, reflects Maimonides' commitment to encompass the *halakhah* in its entirety—those aspects that applied in his time and those aspects that did not. For the most part, the laws of purity apply only when the Temple is standing, for the states of purity and impurity pertain fundamentally to whether a person may enter the Temple precincts and whether he may partake of sacrificial food. The volume includes "Laws Concerning Defilement by a Corpse" (*Hilkhot Tum'at Met*), "Laws Concerning the Red Heifer" (*Hilkhot Parah Adumah*), "Laws Concerning Defilement by Leprosy" (*Hilkhot Tum'at Zara'at*), "Laws Concerning Defilement of a Couch or a Seat" (*Hilkhot Metame'ei Moshav u-Mishkav*), "Laws Concerning Other First-Order Sources of Defilement" (*Hilkhot She'ar Avot Tum'ah*), "Laws Concerning Defilement of Foods" (*Hilkhot tum'at okhalim*), "Laws Concerning Vessels" (*Hilkhot Keilim*), and "Laws Concerning Immersion Baths" (*Hilkhot Miqva'ot*).

The final section of *Mishneh Torah*, encompassing volumes eleven through fourteen, deals with criminal, civil, and constitutional law. The laws presented in these volumes pertain to perfecting the social order, establishing the authoritative institutions with respect to *halakhah* and society, and determining the manner in which they function.

Volume eleven, the *Book of Torts* (*Sefer Neziqin*), includes "Laws Concerning Damage to Property" (*Hilkhot Nizqei Mammon*), "Laws Concerning Theft" (*Hilkhot Geneivah*), "Laws Concerning Robbery and Lost Property" (*Hilkhot Gezeilah va-Aveidah*), "Laws Concerning Wounding and Damaging" (*Hilkhot Hovel u-Maziq*), and "Laws Concerning Murder and the Preservation of Human Life" (*Hilkhot Rozeiah u-Shemirat ha-Nefesh*). The volume evidences certain difficulties in organizing all these laws into a single comprehensive unit. Its structure leads one to wonder why Maimonides separated the laws of theft from the laws of robbery and joined the latter to the laws of lost property. Lost property would appear to be better treated in the *Book of Acquisition*, which deals with when and how a person acquires ownership property he has found. It is possible that the grouping of robbery with lost property reflects the connection between the prohibition on robbery and the obligation to return lost property. One who fails to return lost property in his possession is considered a robber, for the property remains within the ownership of the person who lost it. The grouping of laws in the *Book of Torts* shows the effort Maimonides put into organizing the inner structure of the various volumes. The volume moves from the less serious to the more serious forms of damage: from property damage, to theft and robbery, to battery, and finally to murder. But the conclusion of the entire unit—the end of "Laws Concerning Murder and Preservation of Human Life"—deals with a person's duties in relation to protecting his life, for example, by constructing a guard rail around his roof. The grouping is meant to show that the prohibition on murder is grounded in the sanctity of life, which requires not only prevention of terrible violence but also active protection of life.

The twelfth volume, the *Book of Acquisition* (*Sefer Qinyan*), takes up issues related to determining the ownership of property and the corollary rights and duties. It includes "Laws Concerning Sales" (*Hilkhot Mekhirah*), "Laws Concerning Original Acquistion and Gifts" (*Hilkhat Zekhiyyah u-Matanah*), "Laws Concerning Neighbors" (*Hilkhot Shekheinim*), "Laws Concerning Agents and Partners" (*Hilkhot Sheluhin ve-Shutafin*), and "Laws Concerning Slaves" (*Hilkhot Avadim*).

The *Book of Civil Laws* (*Sefer Mishpatim*), the thirteenth volume, likewise deals with civil law. Within it are "Laws Concerning Hiring" (*Hilkhot Sekhirut*), "Laws Concerning Borrowing and Depositing" (*Hilkhot She'eilah u-Piqqadon*), "Laws Concerning Creditor and Debtor" (*Hilkhot Malveh ve-Loveh*), "Laws Concerning Pleading" (*Hilkhot To'en ve-Nit'an*), and "Laws Concerning Inheritance" (*Hilkhot Nahalot*).

The fourteenth and final volume, the *Book of Judges* (*Sefer Shofetim*), is devoted to the institutions of the judiciary and governance, their authority, and their operating procedures. It includes "Laws Concerning the Sanhe-drin and the Penalties Within their Jurisdiction" (*Hilkhot Sanhedrin ve-ha-Onshim ha-Mesurim Lahem*), "Laws Concerning Evidence" (*Hilkhot Eidut*), "Laws Concerning Rebels" (*Hilkhot Mamrim*), "Laws Concerning Mourn-ing" (*Hilkhot Avel*), and "Laws Concerning Kings and Wars" (*Hilkhot Melakhim u-Milḥemoteihem*). The scope of this volume raises a troubling question that we will return to: why are the laws of mourning placed be-tween the laws of rebels and the laws of kings? The end of the *Book of Judges* is devoted to the messianic idea, directed to the political situation that will allow knowledge of God to flourish in the world. *Mishneh Torah* concludes by returning to its starting point, the commandment to know God, and the treatise as a whole suggests that the purpose of the *halakhah* is to promote knowledge and love of God.

This general overview of the components of the treatise shows that Mai-monides produced groups of laws on subjects that were unconnected to one another or did not exist as subjects in their own right in the previous halakhic literature. The clearest examples of that are the "Laws Concerning the Foundations of the Torah," the "Laws Concerning Repentance," the "Laws Concerning the Study of Torah," and the "Laws Concerning Kings." Although the Talmud includes tractates or chapters that correspond to the "Laws Concerning the Sabbath" or the "Laws Concerning Wounding and Damaging," it contains no parallels to the laws noted in the preceding sentence. Nowhere in the *Mishnah* are Judaism's fundamental theological ideas systematically arranged and set forth. The omission does not reflect sloppy editing; rather, it points to the editor's basic sense of Judaism's over-all character. Judaism is first and foremost a religion of *halakhah*, and those who adhere to it are not identified by principles of faith; those principles at most identify those who deny or betray Judaism. Following the struc-ture of the *Mishnah* would not have allowed Maimonides to achieve one of his great revolutions in how the *halakhah* and the Jewish tradition were to be understood: the elevation of philosophy and science to religious obliga-tions of the highest importance.

Placement of the *Book of Knowledge* as the first volume of *Mishneh Torah* and introducing it with the "Laws Concerning the Foundations of the Torah" convey in a profound way how an organizational principle can ef-fect a change in the overall understanding of the *halakhah*. Similarly, by grouping *halakhot* drawn from the four corners of the Talmud into a single tapestry, Maimonides generated, sometimes *ex nihilo*, novel halakhic areas.

For example, the "Laws Concerning Repentance" inspired the development of that subject as a rich and central subject in *halakhah* and Jewish thought. The "Laws Concerning Kings" constitute a branch of *halakhah* that did not exist as an independent body of knowledge before Maimonides took up the subject, and the *halakhah* of government and politics as presented there served as the vital underpinning for all ensuing Jewish thought on politics and its *halakhot*.

But *Mishneh Torah*'s innovative organization did more than lead to the formation of new areas of *halakhah*. In addition, it redefined the character of a halakhic area in light of the volume or group of *halakhot* into which it was integrated. These decisions regarding placement pertain not only to the setting of complete groups of *halakhot* within in a single volume but also to the integration of secondary subjects within a group. Every volume and every group of *halakhot* in *Mishneh Torah* contain powerful examples of how this conceptual craftsman worked. We will here consider only one of them, already mentioned: the integration of the "Laws Concerning Mourning" into the *Book of Judges*, placed between the "Laws Concerning Rebels" and the "Laws Concerning Kings."

"Laws Concerning Mourning" and the Organization of *Mishneh Torah*

In what follows, I will attempt to parse one of the most problematic decisions in the organization of *Mishneh Torah*: What can account for the placement in the midst of the *Book of Judges*—a tract that deals primarily with constitutional law and the structuring of society's authoritative institutions—of a set of laws associated with an individual's life-cycle events and his reaction to death? Maimonides himself recognized the problem and, in the heading for the section included in the introduction to *Mishneh Torah*, uncharacteristically explained the placement of those *halakhot*: "to mourn for (deceased) relatives; even a priest must defile himself (by contact with the bodies of) deceased relatives and mourn for them, but one does not have to mourn for those who have been put do death by order of the Court." Yet, the linkage Maimonides there suggests between the "Laws Concerning Mourning" and the *Book of Judges* seems contrived. Certainly, the *Book of Judges*, in the context of the "Laws Concerning the Sanhedrin," deals with people who have been executed by the court; but the rule that executed criminals are not to be mourned is only tangential to the main subject of the "Laws Concerning Mourning" and cannot really provide a satisfactory reason for their placement—indeed, citing it only accentuates the problem. As we shall see, however, further consideration of the placement anomaly provides an indication of how Maimonides understood mourning. It also can account for the organization of the material on mourning and for several halakhic decisions related to it. We begin, then, with the laws themselves.

Conventionally portrayed as a halakhic structure that helps a mourner overcome his loss and gradually return to normal life, the rules related to mourning have been rightly seen as one of the greatest psychological and social achievements of the *halakhah*. Maimonides' concept of mourning runs in a different direction, however, as is evident both from his placement of the laws in the *Book of Judges* and from the way in which he organizes them.

In Maimonides' opinion, mourning is first and foremost a statement about the status and honor of the deceased. The bereaved relatives' duty to mourn arises out of the fact that a person's death should be an event that makes a harsh impression on his surroundings. A death that does not leave a mark represents a diminution in the deceased's standing and honor, for the absence of a reaction to his death shows that his life did not carry much weight. Through mourning, society expresses its regard for the deceased, and the rituals should not be seen solely as a means for restoring the mourner's spirit. Mourning is a mechanism for constructing the basic social order, signifying the full membership and status of a person in the community.

That is why the prohibition on mourning an executing criminal is not a marginal detail that just happens to link these laws to the overall subject of the *Book of Judges*. If mourning is primarily a means for recognizing the standing of the deceased, sinners are not worthy of the recognition expressed through the mourning rituals. This concept of mourning has a bearing on the formulation of the first chapter of the "Laws Concerning Mourning." It begins, like many groups of *halakhot*, with a brief definition of the matter at hand—here, the duty to mourn. It then turns to the time when mourning is to begin and, in the ensuing *halakhot*, to the question of whom a person is obligated to mourn for. But instead of introducing that discussion with an affirmative listing of the relatives with respect to whom the duty applies (a listing that finally appears at the beginning of Chapter 2), Maimonides begins it with a negative listing of who is not to

be mourned, even by relatives. That listing includes, among others, executed criminals:

> For those, however, who are executed by order of the court, no mourning
> rites are observed; but the relatives grieve for them, for grief is a matter of
> the heart . . .
>
> As for those who deviated from the practices of the congregation—that
> is, men who cast off the restraint of the commandments, did not join their
> fellow Jews in the performance of the precepts, observance of festivals, at-
> tendance at Synagogue and House of Study, but felt free to do as they
> pleased in the manner of other nations, as well as for epicureans, apostates,
> and delators—for these no mourning is observed. In the event of their
> death, their brethren and other relatives don white garments, and wrap
> themselves in white garments, eat, drink, and rejoice, because the enemies
> of the Lord have perished. Concerning them, Scripture says: *Do not I hate
> them, O Lord, that hate thee?* (Ps. 139:21). ("Laws Concerning Mourning,"
> 1:9–10)

Mourning is a public statement that reflects the deceased's standing as a
full member of the community. One is not to mourn, therefore, for transgressors who have withdrawn from the ways of the community or for heretics, apostates, and those who have been banned, for they are considered
to be outside the social order. Mourning thus becomes a way to mark the
community's boundaries, identifying the line between those considered to
be within it and those regarded as outside it.

The idea that mourning is an expression of honor for the deceased is
conveyed as well by another important component of the "Laws Concerning Mourning." Chapter 2 begins with a precise and detailed definition of
the relatives one is obligated to mourn for. Thereafter, from *halakhah* 6 of
Chapter 2 to the end of Chapter 3, Maimonides considers the duty of the
priest to defile himself in order to tend to his deceased relatives. A priest,
as we know, is forbidden to incur the impurity brought about by proximity
to a corpse, but he is permitted—indeed, obligated—to do so in order to
bury his relatives. The group of relatives for whom a priest can become
impure is identical to those for whom a Jew must mourn: father, mother,
brother, sister, daughter, and son. The precise details, such as when, how,
and for whom the priest can become impure are integrated into the laws of
mourning, occupying one and one-half chapters, yet one might have expected them to be found in another section of *Mishneh Torah*, in the "Laws

Concerning Defilement by a Corpse" in the *Book of Purity*, which deals with such matters directly. Maimonides himself offered his reason for such an organizational decision by linking the matter of mourning to the priest's authorization to be defiled for the sake of a deceased relative in his transition between the topics: "How weighty is the command to observe mourning! The law forbidding a priest to contract uncleanness is set aside in the case of a near of kin, so that he may attend to the obsequies and observe mourning" ("Laws Concerning Mourning," 2:6). The authorization to become impure in order to bury a deceased relative can be understood against the background of honoring the dead. Because it is usually relatives who tend to a person's burial, even a priest, normally forbidden to become defiled by a corpse, is commanded to become defiled in order to bury his deceased relative. The same duty applies with respect to a deceased who is not a relative of a priest but who has no one else to bury him. Such a person is known as a *met mizvah*, and a priest is commanded to become defiled in order to bury him. Conversely, a priest may not become defiled in order to tend to those for whom one does not mourn even if they are close relatives—heretics, those who withdraw from the community, and executed criminals. His authorization to become defiled is meant to accentuate the status of the deceased, and people such as these may not be treated as having high standing.

The association of the general duty to mourn and the priest's duty to become defiled for a deceased—an association established by Maimonides' organization of "Laws Concerning Mourning"—flows from his perception that the two duties share a common source—the status of the deceased. As noted, the association influenced the placement of the mourning laws in the *Book of Judges* and the integration of the laws of priestly defilement for a corpse into the "Laws Concerning Mourning." The connection between the two ideas appears as well in *Sefer ha-Mizvot*, where Maimonides integrates the priests' duty to become impure for the sake of their deceased relatives into his discussion of the duty to mourn on the first day, the day of burial:

> By this injunction we are commanded that the Priests are to defile themselves for [those of their deceased] relatives who are enumerated in the Torah. . . . On this commandment is based the duty of mourning; that is to say, the obligation incumbent upon every man of Israel to mourn for [the loss of] relatives . . . It is to confirm the this obligation that He has expressly

declared in the case of the Priest, who is [ordinarily] forbidden to suffer defilement, that [in respect of the six relatives] he must defile himself at any rate like all other Israelites so that the law of mourning may not be lightly esteemed. (Book of Commandments Positive Commandment 37)

In treating this commandment, Maimonides provides an original interpretation of the idea, held by the *Geonim* and by the Rif and followed by Maimonides as well, that mourning on the first day was a *de-Orayta* (biblical-law) commandment. (The Tosafists disagreed, holding it to be rabbinic only.) R. Joseph Karo rejects Maimonides' proof on the following basis: "There is also reason to wonder about this proof, for impurity and mourning are different matters; and if he commanded that he defile himself for the sake of his relatives, that would not imply that he had to mourn for them" (*Kesef Mishneh*, "Laws Concerning Mourning," 1:1). Nevertheless, given Maimonides' opinion that the purpose of mourning is to honor the deceased and highlight his status, it follows that the two subjects are inherently and understandably connected.

This understanding of mourning casts light on another original ruling by Maimonides, related to a person who dies without anyone to mourn for him: "If the deceased has left no near of kin to be comforted, ten worthy people come and sit in his place all the seven days of mourning and others come (to comfort them). If ten steady attendants are unavailable, the requisite number is supplied daily by those who volunteer their services. They come and sit in his place" ("Laws Concerning Mourning," 13:4). This *halakhah* profoundly conveys the idea that the purpose of mourning is to highlight the status of the deceased: if one dies without relatives to mourn him, no one will publicly express the loss. Accordingly, ten people not his relatives must play the social role of the mourners. They sit in mourning seven days in honor of the deceased, and the public comes to comfort them. And so mourning is not a means for helping the bereaved recover; rather, it attests to the honor of the deceased and highlights his standing. A deceased who has no relatives is a sort of *met mizvah*, and everyone therefore is obligated to bury him and to mourn him.

Ra'abad, in his comment on this passage in *Mishneh Torah*, summarily and dismissively rejected it: "it has no basis." He seems to be saying it has no source in the Talmud, and it indeed appears to be based on an innovative and less than straightforward reading of a Talmudic passage. It is worth citing the Talmudic statement in its entirety:

Said R. Judah: If a deceased has no comforters, ten people come in and sit in his place. [A story is told:] Someone who died in R. Judah's neighborhood had no comforters. Each day, R. Judah would gather ten men and sit in the deceased's place. After seven days, the deceased appeared to R. Judah in his dream and said to him: May your mind be at ease, for you have put my mind at ease. (BT *Shabbat* 152a–b)

R. Judah refers to "a deceased [who] has no comforters," which suggests that the ten men who gather where he died play the role of comforters, not of mourners. Their comforting is directed toward the deceased himself, whose soul is mourning his own death. The deceased's need for comfort is demonstrated by the immediately preceding statement: "Said R. Ḥisda: A person's soul mourns for him all seven days, as it is said, 'His soul mourns for him' [Job 15:22]" (BT *Shabbat* 152a). The idea that the deceased himself requires comforting, and R. Judah's ruling on the matter, are in response to the troubles of the deceased's soul; hence the gratitude expressed by the deceased's soul to R. Judah in the story that follows his ruling. It appears, then, that the passage is based on the deceased being in mourning and the consequent need to comfort him.

Reading the passage in accord with its plain meaning alters not only the reason for the *halakhah* but its substance as well. The ten men do not sit in the deceased's home for all seven days, in the manner of mourners; and other people do not come to comfort them. Since they themselves are comforters, they come only once a day to the deceased's home, and the other members of the community do not gather round to comfort them. Given this plain reading of the Talmudic passage, Ra'abad had good reason to reject Maimonides' ruling. Ashkenazi halakhic tradition evidently interpreted the Talmud in the same manner as Ra'abad, and it ruled that ten men assemble in the home of a relation-less deceased to worship and say Kaddish. But they do not sit there as mourners all seven days, and others do not come to comfort them. The ten come together once a day in the deceased's house or in the synagogue to comfort the deceased's soul.

Maimonides himself likely knew of this opinion, for he knew well the geonic traditions, and they interpreted the passage in accord with its plain sense. R. Hai Ga'on was asked, with reference to the passage, where the ten men sat—was it at the deceased's place in the synagogue or in his home, in the place where he died? He replied in favor of the latter, explaining that the deceased's soul mourned for itself at the place of death:

So said the sages. Said R. Ḥisda: A person's soul, his spirit, mourns for him all seven days . . . And it mourns only at the place where it departed from him . . . So even if it has no comforters, when it comes and sits at the place where the soul departed, it is comforted. (*Oẓar ha-Ge'onim, Shabbat*, p. 467)

Maimonides' novel reading of the Talmudic source, contrary to the geonic interpretation and the plain meaning of the text, evidently follows from his rejection of the idea that a person's soul mourns the death of the body for seven days following death. That notion is alien to Maimonides and his metaphysical approach, for the souls of the deceased do not tarry at the place of death for seven painful days. It follows that gathering to comfort the deceased's soul, still regarded as inhabiting the house, is a meaningless custom. Maimonides' alternative interpretation, and the *halakhah* that follows from it, reflect the vast cultural gulf between him and those who disagreed with him, for he reinterpreted the Talmudic passage in accord with his overall concept of the purpose of mourning: recognizing the honor of the deceased. In that light, a person who dies without anyone to mourn him is considered a *met miẓvah*, and there is a duty to assemble ten men to mourn for him. The ruling does not only resolve a difficult Talmudic passage; it also corresponds well with Maimonides perspective on the significance of mourning in general.

Maimonides' wording allows us to infer how he reinterprets the Talmudic passage. The *Gemara* reads "if a deceased has no comforters," which he subtly changes to read "if a deceased has none to be comforted." In the Hebrew, the change is effected by inserting only one letter, a *tav*, changing "*met she-ein lo menaḥamin*" to "*met she-ein lo mitnaḥamin*." The slight change, which alters the entire meaning of the Talmudic passage, is evident in the clumsy wording of the passage in *Mishneh Torah*. Instead of simply saying, "If a deceased has no near of kin to mourn for him," he writes "If the deceased has no near of kin to be comforted." The formulation creates a sense that the Talmudic source is being paraphrased, without emphasizing the minor change in wording. Maimonides' successor in Provence, R. Menaḥem Ha-Me'iri, followed Maimonides' lead and offered this interpretation of the Talmudic passage: "If a deceased has no comforters—that is, has no mourners who would be in need of comforting—then ten men come all seven days and sit in the house in which he died, and others come and surround them as if they are in need of comforting. And that is to the honor of the deceased" (*Beit ha-Beḥirah, Shabbat* 152a).

This ruling provides a clear example of the great creativity Maimonides exercised in crystallizing the *halakhah*. In this instance, his ruling is tied to a broad conceptual understanding of the nature of mourning, to a rejection of metaphysical principles that he finds unacceptable, and to his exegetical technique, which does not shy away from making a minor change in wording that transforms the entire understanding of the text.

The problematic placement of the "Laws Concerning Mourning" in the *Book of Judges* is one of many examples of the linkage in *Mishneh Torah* between an original organizational structure and a new conceptual understanding of important halakhic principles. That understanding affected not only the location of this group of laws within the broad context of *Mishneh Torah* but also the internal organization of the group and the halakhic decisions themselves.

Forging Concepts, Distinctions, and Generalizations

Systematic and continual exegesis of *Mishneh Torah* goes back as far as the fourteenth century, when Shem Tov ibn Ga'on wrote his *Migdal Oz* and R. Vidal di Tolosa wrote his *Maggid Mishneh*. These commentators were relatively marginal figures in the fourteenth-century halakhic world, but the sixteenth century saw the writing of commentaries on *Mishneh Torah* by major halakhists. R. Joseph Karo wrote his *Kesef Mishneh*; R. Abraham di Boton of Salonika titled his commentary *Leḥem Mishneh*; and R. David Ibn Zimra (Radbaz), one of the leading halakhists of the generation following the expulsion from Spain, wrote a commentary on portions of *Mishneh Torah* known as *Peirush ha-Radbaz*. In addition, Ibn Zimra's large collection of responsa, *Teshuvot ha-Radbaz*, included an extensive series of entries called *Leshonot ha-Rambam* (Maimonides' statements), encompassing responsa dealing with hard-to-understand rulings in *Mishneh Torah*. These interpreters of *Mishneh Torah* came to be known as Maimonides' "armor-bearers," and their treatises, included in the widely disseminated printed editions of *Mishneh Torah*, adorn and surround the text of *Mishneh Torah* itself. The "armor-bearers" treated *Mishneh Torah* primarily as a source of halakhic rulings. They considered its sources in the Talmud and attempted to resolve the occasional divergence between the talmudic sources and Maimonides' rulings. These divergences had been noted earlier by, among others, *Mishneh Torah*'s critical annotators, the Provencal sages

R. Abraham ben David (Ra'abad) and R. Moses ha-Kohen (Ramakh), contemporaries of Maimonides.

The early twentieth century saw the onset of a new wave of writings about *Mishneh Torah* and a more in-depth approach to the treatise. Noteworthy among these innovative writers are R. Hayyim Halevi of Brisk, author of *Hiddushei Rabbi Hayyim Halevi*; R. Meir Simhah Hakohen of Dvinsk, author of *Or Sameah*; and R. Yitzhaq Ze'ev Soloveitchik, son of R. Hayyim of Brisk and author of a collection of novellae on *Mishneh Torah*.

These great works, and other contemporaneous ones like them, differ from their sixteenth-century predecessors in that they do not treat *Mishneh Torah* as a source for halakhic decision-making. Instead, they use it to gain a better grasp of the underlying Talmudic discussion and to develop a conceptual understanding of the halakhah. This new approach to *Mishneh Torah* coincided with the rise of a new method of Talmudic study, heralded—not surprisingly—by the same leading scholars. This method of study, which took hold in the great Lithuanian yeshivas, was centered on an effort to understand the *halakhah* as a conceptual system. An internal anomaly within a Talmudic passage, or a contradiction between two passages, was best resolved not by local steps, such as a proviso regarding the statement or a textual correction, but by drawing substantive distinctions that bear on halakhic categories and definitions. This process—the forging of substantive distinctions that establish conceptual categories—allows not only for differentiation between various phenomena but also for the joining of seemingly diverse halakhic phenomena within a common category.

Many examples could be cited of this new analytic approach and its association with the changed attitude toward *Mishneh Torah*. One of them involves the analysis of the concept of *kavvanah* (loosely, "intention," "deliberateness," or "concentration"; because of the varied English senses, the Hebrew term will be used in what follows) in its various halakhic contexts. In *Mishneh Torah*'s "Laws Concerning Prayer," two of Maimonides' rulings appear to contradict each other. On the one hand, he rules that because prayer without *kavvanah* is not considered real prayer, one who recites a mandatory prayer without *kavvanah* has not discharged his obligation and must repeat the prayer. Elsewhere, however, he rules that discharge of the obligation requires only that the first blessing of the *amidah*[1] be recited with *kavvanah*; if one lacks *kavvanah* during the remainder of the *amidah*, his obligation is nonetheless discharged. One could maintain, as did several interpreters of *Mishneh Torah*, that the latter statement is simply a qualification of the first, limiting the reach of the obligation to maintain *kavvanah*. On this local reading of the issue, Maimonides rules that even though *kavannah* is prayer's defining feature, a person who maintains *kavannah* only during the first blessing has nevertheless fulfilled his duty to pray.

R. Hayyim Soloveitchik, who shrank from this kind of explanation, sought to account for the difference in a more substantive way, proposing that there were, in fact, two sorts of *kavannah*. In first ruling that prayer without *kavavanah* was not prayer, Maimonides was using the term *kavvanah* to mean an awareness of standing before God. Maimonides himself put it this way, when he wrote: "How does one achieve correct intention? One must free his mind of all thoughts and see himself as standing before the divine Presence. Therefore, one should sit awhile before prayer in order to direct his mind, and then pray gently and beseechingly" ("Laws Concerning Prayer and Priestly Blessing," 4, 16). Later, however, when he writes of the minimal requirement—that one have *kavvanah* only during the first blessing—he is using the term in a different sense, to mean attentiveness to the meaning and wording of the passage being recited.

There is a practical difference between these two sorts of *kavvanah*. One can rise to pray with a sense that one is standing before God—the form of *kavvanah* required for the prayer to be considered prayer—without necessarily directing one's attention to what the words of the prayer mean. Accordingly, the demand that one attend to the meaning of the words is confined to the first blessing; throughout the remainder of the prayer, a person discharges his obligation even without attending to the words as long as he remains conscious of standing before God. Following up on this distinction, R. Hayyim's grandson, R. Joseph B. Soloveitchik, coined a new conceptual term—*qiyyum she-be-lev* (lit., fulfillment in one's heart)—to refer to those commandments in which *kavvanah* was a defining ele-

[1] The *amidah* (lit., [the prayer recited while] standing) is the central mandatory prayer of the liturgy, comprising nineteen blessings to be recited thrice daily on weekdays (originally eighteen; hence its alternative name of *shemoneh esreh*). In rabbinic literature, including *Mishneh Torah*, it is often referred to as *tefillah*, "prayer." It is the *amidah* that Maimonides is speaking of in the passages under discussion.

ment of the required action and not only a condition of properly carrying it out. One may reasonably debate, for example, whether a person who takes a *lulav* on Sukkot without *kavvanah* has nevertheless discharged his obligation. When it comes to prayer, however, it is inconceivable that the obligation would be considered discharged, for the substance of prayer is standing before God, and *kavvanah* is the essence of the commandment's fulfillment.

Whatever its place in Maimonides' own writings—the issue is much debated by Maimonides scholars—the distinction proposed by R. Ḥayyim of Brisk reflects the new scholarly sensitivity. The solution to a local problem may lie in a substantive conceptual distinction, referred to as a *ḥiluq* (distinction). This approach, though, does not merely raise distinctions; it also allows for generalizations. Once the substantive distinction between the two sorts of *kavvanah* is established, it becomes possible to show how one of them represents a general category that allows for a better understanding of other halakhic cases. For example, having established the category of *qiyyum she-be-lev* in the context of prayer, that distinctive category can be extended to encompass additional commandments, such as repentance. Like prayer, the act of repentance is rooted in the heart's intention, notwithstanding its required verbal articulation in confession.

Mishneh Torah's distinctive qualities endow it with the capacity to serve as a source of inspiration for this analytical turn. The process of conceptualizing the *halakhah* requires, first and foremost, a precise and systematic use of language. The linguistic quality of *Mishneh Torah* and its rich, precise formulations invite this sort of reading. Stylistically, *Mishneh Torah* is one of the pinnacles of Hebrew literature. In its blend of frugality and lucidity, which come at no cost to precision and fine distinction, *Mishneh Torah* is the most linguistically striking Hebrew halakhic document since the time of the *Mishnah*. Its every word is measured and carefully weighed, and clarifications of particular formulations do not entail over-interpretive readings or eisegesis. At the same time, the precise and careful wording does not interfere with the marvelous flow of the writing. The great effort invested in the choice of words goes unnoticed at first glance, and what we have is a multi-dimensional and profound work with no rough edges. No one has been able to duplicate this literary accomplishment on so grand a scale, and a reading of the *Shulḥan Arukh*, for example, immediately demonstrates the difference between them. When R. Joseph Karo, author of the *Shulḥan Arukh*, quotes *Mishneh Torah* without attribution—a not infrequent occurrence—the attentive reader can identify Maimonides' unique literary quality, several orders of magnitude above that of the halakhists before and since.

Beyond these literary qualities and their invitation to precise analysis, Maimonides hoped to produce a systematic picture of the *halakhah* in toto within the framework of a new organizational structure. This required him to formulate models of conceptual thought that both differentiate and generalize. An interpreter moving from topic to topic does not necessarily employ a form of thinking that, with respect to each *halakhah*, takes account of the halakhic system overall while simultaneously assessing the ways in which this *halakhah* resembles or differs from others. Let us briefly examine one instance in which Maimonides distinguishes between two halakhic situations by the addition of a few words.

The *halakhah* differentiates in several ways between real property and chattels. Among them is the manner in which they are acquired by a new owner. Chattels are acquired by transfer from hand to hand, referred to as *meshikhah* ("pulling"); realty is acquired by written deed. Similarly, real property may be taken by a creditor in satisfaction of debts on which the property owner has defaulted, and even after the realty is sold, it remains subordinate to the interest of a pre-sale creditor. That is not the case with respect to chattels, which are not subject to a creditor's rights.

Real property and chattels differ as well with respect to the laws of bailment. If an unpaid bailee loses the item entrusted to his care, he is not liable to pay for it as long as he swears that the item is not in his possession and that he did not act negligently in caring for it. Such an oath applies, however, only to a bailment that is considered to be chattel but not to real property. Similarly, a paid bailee is liable to pay for chattels entrusted to him if it is stolen or lost, but not for real property. Classifying a given item as real property or as chattel is thus important in several respects. The Talmud reports a disagreement over whether fruit on a tree but ready for picking is considered chattel or real property. On the one hand, the fruit remains connected to the land and may be seen as part of the field; on the other, it is ready to be picked and, in that sense, may be considered chattel.

In *Mishneh Torah*, Maimonides rules, as suggested by the discussion in the Talmud, that fruit, even unpicked, has the legal status of chattel. But Maimonides also rules, consistent with a discussion in BT *Shevu'ot*, that fruit about to be picked has the status of real property, not of chattel: "If a man delivered to his fellow for safekeeping something which is attached to the soil, even if it be grapes ready to be cut, it is deemed like landed property with respect to the law of bailment" ("Laws Concerning Hiring," 2:4). Commentators have considered the seeming contradiction regarding the status of fruit. But Maimonides included an important reservation in his ruling: "it is deemed like landed property with respect to the Law of bailment," indicating a distinction between the status of fruit under the laws of bailment and otherwise. Rabbi Vidal of Tolosa, author of the *Maggid Mishneh*, saw the qualification but noted his inability to account for it: "He appears to distinguish between laws of bailment and other laws, and I do not know a sound reason for doing so" ("Laws Concerning Pleading," 5:4).

Maimonides did not explain his rationale for the distinction, but its meaning becomes apparent in the novellae on BT *Shevu'ot* by R. Joseph Ibn Migash, whom Maimonides regarded as his teacher and held in high esteem. Ibn Migash argued that the fruit about to be harvested had the status of chattel in all respects, except under the laws of bailment, where they are considered to be real property. The reason is that the bailee is obligated to return the property entrusted to him in a condition the same as that in which he received it, and he may not change the status of the fruit entrusted to him. Accordingly, even though fruit about to be picked normally has the status of chattel, if they came into the bailee's care while still attached to the ground, he must return them as he received them, namely, as real property. The brief addition to the wording in *Mishneh Torah*—"with respect to the law of bailment," a mere two words in Hebrew—thus reflects a substantive distinction that allows us to differentiate between different manifestations of a *halakhah* that on their face appear identical.

Maimonides' conceptual precision as a halakhist does not follow solely from an effort to resolve the contradictions between Talmudic passages. At times, he draws substantive distinctions that lack any such external impetus, doing so on the basis of an internal analysis of the halakhic institution itself. A clear example appears in Maimonides' wording of the laws related to the commandment to rebuke one's fellow. A Jew is obligated to rebuke a fellow Jew who is transgressing a law of the Torah. The commandment is inferred from the verse "you shall surely rebuke your neighbor" (Lev. 19:17) and is extensively elaborated on in halakhic *midrashim* and in the Talmud.

A reading of Maimonides' treatment of the commandment reveals two different sorts of rebuke:

> 5. Whoever entertains in his heart hatred of any Israelite, transgresses a prohibition, as it is said, "You shall not hate your brother in your heart" (Lev. 19:17). . . .
>
> 6. When a man sins against another, the injured party should not hate the offender and keep silent, as it is said concerning the wicked, "And Absalom spoke to Amnon neither good nor evil, for Absalom hated Amnon" (2 Sam. 13:22). But it is his duty to inform the offender and say to him "Why did you do this to me? Why did you sin against me in this matter?" And thus it is said, "You shall surely rebuke your neighbor" (Lev. 19:17). If the offender repents and pleads for forgiveness, he should be forgiven. The forgiver should not be obdurate, as it is said, "And Abraham prayed unto God (for Abimelech)" (Gen. 20:17).
>
> 7. If one observes that a person committed a sin or walks in a way that is not good, it is a duty to bring the erring man back to the right path and point out to him that he is wronging himself by his evil courses, as it is said, "You shall surely rebuke your neighbor" (Lev. 19:17). ("Laws Concerning Moral Dispositions," 6:5–7)

In *halakhah* 6, Maimonides links the duty to rebuke to the proscription of hating. One who is harmed by his fellow has a duty to rebuke the injurer, for in the absence of that verbalized rebuke, he will come to hate his injurer. This sort of rebuke is meant not only to prevent hatred of the injurer from festering in the injured party's heart; it may also bring about actual reconciliation, for if the injurer, in the wake of the rebuke, asks for forgiveness, the injured party is duty bound to set aside his anger and grant that forgiveness. In *halakhah* 7, however, Maimonides moves to a different category of rebuke. Here, one is commanded to rebuke one's fellow if he sees him sinning, in order to return him to the proper path. The duty is entirely unrelated to any relationship between injurer and injured, and it is borne by every person who witnesses transgression. The duty is based not on the prohibition of "You shall not hate" but on the interdependence of members of a community. As Maimonides says at the end of *halakhah* 7, "Whoever is in a position to prevent wrongdoing and does not do so is responsible for the iniquity of all the wrongdoers whom he might have restrained."

Maimonides thus divides the duty to rebuke into two entirely different categories, each based on its own logic and each applicable to different people. A review of the Talmud's treatment of the commandment shows that it deals extensively with the second category of rebuke: how to rebuke, whom to rebuke, how long to go on rebuking someone who does not respond. Maimonides' innovation is in his construction of an additional category within the commandment, related to an injured party's duty to express his grievance to the injurer so that his sense of affront does not turn into blazing hatred. As far as I know, this distinction cannot be found in the pre-Maimonidean halakhic tradition. Maimonides' first category of rebuke can be found in the Dead Sea Scrolls and in the Second-Temple-period apocryphal literature, but in rabbinic literature it is unconnected to "you shall surely rebuke."

Maimonides created this additional category by direct reading of Scripture, in which the obligation to rebuke follows immediately after the prohibition on hatred: "You shall not hate your brother in your heart; you shall surely rebuke your neighbor, and not bear sin because of him" (Lev. 19:17). On this reading, the duty to rebuke is derived from the prohibition on hating; they are internally and psychologically continuous. The prohibition on hating someone in one's heart, which seems at first glance to be an inexplicable effort to insist on responsibility for one's feelings, is made feasible by the duty to externalize those feelings and rebuke the offender. Maimonides supports his reading of the flow of the verse, and of the psychological dynamic that posits a linkage between the prohibition on hating and the duty to rebuke, by citing Scripture's linkage between Absalom's silence and his hatred of Amnon. In this case, the conceptual thought process in *Mishneh Torah* is based not on a contradiction in the halakhic sources but on an internal distinction between two very different appearances of what had appeared to be a single halakhic institution. The distinction also provides a nice example of Maimonides as Bible exegete.

Conceptual thinking moves in two different yet interconnected directions. One, which we have considered and illustrated, formulates substantive distinctions within a single halakhic institution, as in the case of *kavvanah* or rebuke. The other brings seemingly diverse halakhic matters within a common conceptual rubric.

An interesting instance of such process was noted by the great Lithuanian scholar of the late nineteenth century and early twentieth century R. Meir Simḥah Hakohen of Dvinsk in his book *Or Sameaḥ*; it pertains to

Maimonides' broad political outlook. The starting point for analysis of this example is the peculiar location of the seven Noahide commandments within *Mishneh Torah*. According to *halakhah*, Noahides (the sons of Noah which include all of humanity) are bound by seven commandments: the prohibitions on idolatry, cursing God, murder, incest, eating a limb torn from a living animal, and robbery, and by the obligation to establish courts that will render judgment on matters related to those commandments.

The *halakhot* regarding the Noahide commandments are included in *Mishneh Torah* under the "Laws Concerning Kings." On the face of it, the subject should be treated elsewhere. The prohibition on murder could have been included in the "Laws Concerning Murder"; the prohibition on eating a limb torn from a living animal could have been in the "Laws Concerning Forbidden Foods," and so forth. The only element of the Noahide Laws that pertains to the *Book of Judges*—which, as noted, deals with issues of constitutional law—is the duty of Noahides to establish courts and hear cases within them. It is possible that Maimonides wanted to maintain the seven Noahide commandments as a single unit rather than disperse them throughout the books of *Mishneh Torah*, and that would make considerable organizational sense. But the "Laws Concerning Kings" deals entirely with laws applicable to the kings of Israel, and there would appear to be no reason to include the Noahide commandments among them.

As we have seen, unique organizational aspects of *Mishneh Torah* are based on conceptually deep structures. In this case, the placement of the Noahide commandments in the "Laws Concerning Kings" is linked to Maimonides' distinctive concept regarding the political role of the King of Israel. By his placement of the Noahide laws, Maimonides takes the view that the Noahide commandments fall within the purview of the Jewish community. The King and courts of Israel are responsible for ensuring that the Noahides observe their seven commandments. This idea is evident from a series of rulings on the subject, though it must be noted that medieval halakhists disagreed with those rulings. Israel's responsibility for fulfillment of the Noahide commandments is stated programmatically at the outset of the discussion: "Moreover, Moses our Teacher was commanded by God to compel all human beings to accept the commandments enjoined upon the descendants of Noah. Anyone who does not accept them is put to death" ("Laws Concerning Kings," 8:10). On that basis, Maimonides justified the acts of Jacob's sons Simeon and Levi, who killed the people of Shekhem following the rape of their sister Dinah; in his view, they were punished by Jacob's sons because they had not established courts that could try Shekhem for taking Dinah. Naḥmanides, in contrast, maintained that fulfillment of the seven Noahide commandments was not a matter within Israel's legal purview: "for Jacob's sons were not given the authority to pass judgment on them" (Commentary on Gen. 35:13).

Consistent with his idea that ensuring fulfillment of the Noahide commandments is not exclusively the responsibility of the Noahide nations and that Jewish authority extends to them as well, Maimonides includes in the "Laws Concerning Kings" two rulings with significance for the law of war. First, the Torah forbids Israel from entering into a treaty with the seven Canaanite nations and requires warring against them to the end, with no possibility of peace. Maimonides ruled that if the Canaanite nations accept the seven Noahide commandments, Israel could enter into a peace treaty with them and it would become forbidden to wage war against them. Ra'abad disagreed, seeing no basis in Talmudic sources for that ruling.

Second, with respect to wars against non-Canaanite nations—referred to as "optional wars"—the *halakhah* requires Israelite forces to invite and allow peaceful surrender before attacking. If the enemy agrees to become subject to Israelite rule and to pay tribute, it is forbidden to wage war against him. Maimonides held that the proposal for peaceful surrender had to include the enemy's obligation to submit to the seven Noahide commandments. Here, too, Ra'abad disagreed, seeing no Talmudic source for the ruling. But Maimonides maintained that one of the substantive purposes of waging war was to impose the Noahide commandments. Accordingly, in the context of both commanded war (that is, against the Canaanites) and permissive war, it would be forbidden to wage war against an enemy that undertook to fulfill these commandments: "No war is declared against any nation before peace offers are made to it. This obtains both in an optional war and a war for a religious cause, as it is said: *When you draw near unto a city to fight against it, then proclaim peace unto it* (Deut. 20:10). If the inhabitants make peace and accept the seven commandments enjoined upon the descendants of Noah, none of them is slain" ("Laws Concerning Kings," 6:4).

These two unique rulings follow from Maimonides' concept that the political responsibility of the Israelite kingdom extends to compelling fulfillment of the seven Noahide commandments. These innovations, pointed out by Gerald Blidstein in his book on Maimonides' political principles, reveal Islamic influences on Maimonides' rulings and on the universal vision of the Jewish sovereign's political responsibility. In this context of the Jewish polity's universal mission Maimonides makes a normative and theological claim concerning the religious standing for a Noachaite who fulfills his obligations that drew the attention of generations of readers:

> Whoever accepts the seven commandments and observers them scrupulously is among the *Pious of the Gentiles* and will have a portion in the world to come, provided that he accepts them and performs them because of the Holy One, blessed be He, commanded them in the Torah, and made known through Moses, our teacher, that the descendants of Noah were commanded to follow them early on. But if his observance is based upon a reasoned conclusion he is not deemed as resident alien, or one of the pious of the Gentiles, but one of their wise men. ("Laws of Kings and Wars," 8, 11)

It is therefore not only Israel's mission to enforce the universal commandments, but rather the acceptance of such commandments and the full religious standing that is implied by such acceptance has to be based on a recognition that they were commanded in the Torah and known through Moses. A fulfillment of the Noahides laws that stems from reason alone grants the Noachide a status of the wise gentiles, but not the pious of the gentiles. The point Maimonides wants to stress is that the authority of these universal laws is grounded not in universal reason or in other religious tradition, but solely in the Torah of Moses. The universal mission of the Jewish polity is grounded in the very source of authority of such universal creed.

A further deep-seated connection between the "Laws Concerning Kings" and the seven Noahide commandments was noted by R. Meir Simḥah Hakohen of Dvinsk. One of Maimonides' important halakhic innovations in the political sphere pertains to the king's role as judge and penal officer. The *halakhah* sets forth very rigorous standards governing when punishment, especially capital punishment, may be imposed by a court— standards so rigorous as to preclude, in effect, all possibility of punishment. To convict someone, there must first be two eyewitnesses who warn the transgressor about the offense before he carries it out. Among other restrictions, these witnesses must be together when they observe the transgression. The *halakhah* rejects any reliance, in reaching a conviction, on circumstantial evidence, such as a clear motive for the offense, or on the testimony of a single witness or invalid witnesses. Witnesses are interrogated so strictly as to render conviction virtually impossible, and the *halakhah* sets a high bar with respect to defining the elements of the offense. The forbidden act must be committed directly, by the hand of the defendant; if his action is indirect, he will not be convicted even if his responsibility for the offense is clear. Consistent with that principle, a person will avoid punishment by the court if he binds another, sets him before a lion, and allows the lion to devour the victim; in such a case, death is caused indirectly, not by the perpetrator's own hand. *Halakhah* recognizes the moral responsibility of such a perpetrator and holds him liable before the heavenly court, but it exempts him from punishment by a human court.

As noted, these strict standards of proof and narrowly defined offenses preclude almost any possibility of punishment by a court and create a vacuum that could result in anarchy. In Maimonides' view, one of the king's functions is to fill that vacuum. In the "Laws Concerning Murder," after citing the strict standards that must be met before a court can impose punishment, Maimonides adds: "Regarding any of these or similar murderers who are not subject to being condemned to die by verdict of the court, if a king of Israel wished to put them to death by royal decree for the benefit of society, he has a right to do so" ("Laws Concerning Murder and the Preservation of Life," 2:4). He reiterates his unique view of the king's role in "Laws Concerning Kings": "If a person kills another and there is no clear evidence, or if no warning has been given him, or there is only one witness, or if one kills accidentally a person whom he hated, the king may, if the exigency of the hour demands it, put him to death in order to insure the stability of the social order" (ibid. 3:10). The king thus operates in those areas where the *halakhah* recognizes a murderer's moral responsibility but does not allow for his punishment by a human court, either because of a lack of acceptable proof or because the criminal act was performed indirectly. The king is seen here as responsible for the social order and stability; to that end, he is given broad legal authority to fill the vacuum left by the *halakhah*.

The commentators on *Mishneh Torah* wondered about Maimonides' source for the king's broad authority to impose capital punishment where the *halakhah* itself did not allow for it. The Talmud refers to royal law but contains no reference to so broad a concept of it and certainly does not mention it as a way to fill a halakhic gap. But a reading of the Noahide laws in the "Laws Concerning Kings" reveals the source and inspiration for the broad concept of royal law, as R. Meir Sim<u>h</u>ah of Dvinsk showed in his book *Or Sameia<u>h</u>*. Noahides are forbidden to murder, and they are subject to capital punishment if they do. In discussing the laws of evidence related to Noahides, Maimonides, following the Talmud, rules that "a Noahide is slain on the evidence of one witness, on the ruling of one judge, and without previous warning. He is condemned on even (on the evidence of) a relation" ("Laws Concerning Kings," 9:14). The possibility of a Noahide being punished is increased not only by easing the rules of evidence but also by broadening the definition of the punishable offense. According to Maimonides, a Noahide is to be killed even if he murders by indirection: "So, too, if he kills one suffering from a fatal disease, or ties a man with a rope and puts him before a lion, or leaves him in a famished condition in consequence of which the man dies of starvation, he is executed, for in the last analysis he caused the death of the victim" ("Laws Concerning Kings," 9:4). In *Mishneh Torah*, then, the laws of evidence and definition of the offense applicable to a Noahide correspond to those applied in adjudication by the king. The parallel between the law applicable to Noahides and Israelite royal justice stems from the fact that both are tied to the pursuit of social stability and harmony. This is a universal aspect of justice that binds every human society, Noahide and Israelite alike. The law grants the king the authority to improve society and the world, and that responsibility is derived from the Noahide laws and corresponds to them.

This inquiry into the relationship between the law of the Israelite king and the seven Noahide commandments shows how Maimonides created structural and organizational parallels and, on that basis, brought two seemingly different halakhic principles under a shared conceptual rubric that clarifies their nature. Generalizing moves such as this, as well as the drawing of distinctions between the various appearances of similar *halakhot*, are the kernel of conceptual thought about the *halakhah*. It is no mere coincidence that this sort of halakhic thought developed during the twentieth century out of intensive exegesis of *Mishneh Torah*. Each chapter of the treatise is a repository of profound conceptual thinking, which shaped the categories of halakhic thought.

Mishneh Torah and Talmudic Sources

Maimonides' original, conceptual understanding of the *halakhah* becomes evident as well in his treatment in *Mishneh Torah* of talmudic sources. The

Babylonian Talmud comprises various layers of traditions. The first layer comprises the statements of the *amora'im* as quoted in the Talmud, including the central kernel of their debates. That stratum was supplemented by a layer known in talmudic research as *stamma* (from *stam*, meaning anonymous); it comprises the anonymous talmudic give and take, clarifying and interpreting the amoraic statements and positions. Scholars such as Jacob Levinger and Meir Simḥah Feldblum have noted that Maimonides did not see the anonymous talmudic give and take as absolutely authoritative and binding. At times he rules in accord with the amoraic statements themselves, rejecting what is implied by the ensuing anonymous debate. This approach allowed him a considerable degree of independence in understanding the *halakhah* and reaching halakhic decisions. Moreover, Maimonides is not necessarily committed to the rationales for *halakhot* that appear in the Talmud. He sometimes suggests other rationales, and his original rationales can, in rare instances, lead to substantive differences in the halakhic ruling itself.

It is no simple matter to come up with a consistent picture of Maimonides' approach to his sources. On the face of things, such a picture might be able to be derived by comparing Maimonides' rulings, as we have them, to our own understanding of the Talmudic passages on which the ruling are based. But in the absence of express rationales for the *halakhot* in Maimonides' treatise, the finding of a divergence between the Talmudic give and take and the manner in which Maimonides understood the *halakhah* will often rely on mere speculation. We do not know how Maimonides understood the passage, and we therefore cannot easily claim that he knowingly diverged from its meaning. From the many examples of such divergence, therefore, it is best to focus on those in which Maimonides declared, in reaction to questions about his ruling, that he was not absolutely committed to the Talmudic give and take. He twice took that position as a matter of principle, and those instances are worth examining.

One of his responses relates to a ruling in *Mishneh Torah* that troubled the sages of Lunel because it departed from what is clearly implied by the Talmudic discussion. In his reply, Maimonides says he struggled with the issue for several days: "When I wrote the book, I considered this matter for several days, and the original version, which I retracted and did not include, evidently reflected this *halakhah* per the view of R. Isaac" (*Teshuvot*, sec. 345). In the first draft of *Mishneh Torah*, then, which Maimonides did not include in the authoritative version, the *halakhah* was resolved in accord with the view of R. Isaac, the resolution reached by the Talmudic deliberations. But after study of the issue, Maimonides changed his mind and explained why: "we should not set aside established teaching and decide the *halakhah* in accord with the *Gemara*'s discussion . . . we certainly should not decide the *halakhah* on the basis of discussion" (ibid.).

An additional response that reveals Maimonides' complex attitude toward Talmudic debate involves the first passage in *Bava Batra*. The passage considers whether the co-owners of a shared courtyard may compel each other to divide the courtyard and construct a partition between them, providing each a degree of privacy. The Talmud resolves the issue on the basis of whether the harm caused by seeing another's private domain is considered cognizable harm that would justify the demand by one co-owner that the other share the expenses of constructing a four-cubit-high partition. At one point in the inquiry, the Talmud raises the possibility that such a partition might be built only by agreement, for the harm caused by seeing is not cognizable harm. It then challenges that view, citing the rule that building a partition may be compelled in the case of a vegetable field and asking why that should not be so in a shared courtyard as well. The Talmud responds by distinguishing the vegetable field on the grounds that construction of the partition may be compelled there because of concern about the evil eye. The plain meaning of the Talmud's resolution is that in the case of a field, construction of a partition may be compelled because one partner might harm the other's crop through the evil eye, a consideration that does not apply in the case of a courtyard, where there are no crops.

In *Mishneh Torah*, the *halakhah* is decided in accord with what follows in the Talmudic passage, namely, that harm caused by seeing is indeed cognizable harm, and the co-owners of a courtyard therefore may compel each other to construct a four-cubit-high partition. Nevertheless, Maimonides rules that the partition in a vegetable field need be only ten handbreadths high, not four cubits. A ten-handbreadth-high partition is not high enough to cut off a person's field of vision, and it merely indicates that the parcels on either side of it are under different ownership. On its face, this ruling would seem to be at odds with the Talmudic view that a four-cubit-high partition should be built in a vegetable field because of concern about the evil eye. Indeed, Ra'abad comments that Maimonides' ruling is in error; in his view, one may compel construction of a four-cubit-high partition in a vegetable field. The sages of Lunel asked Maimonides to explain his ruling. He replied:

This is a question that should not have been asked by great men such as yourselves. For do you see no difference between the [sort of] harm caused by seeing—a great and genuine harm, in that one sees his fellow as he stands and sits and goes about his business—and the [sort of] harm caused by seeing one's fellow's produce with an evil eye? For it is an act of piety that one not look at another with an evil eye [that is, jealously; see discussion below], and that response is an anonymous explanation not in accord with the *halakhah*. The essence of harm by seeing is in a courtyard, a place where people live; but in a garden, there is no need for four cubits, for it is not the way of people to live there, and a partition of ten handbreadths suffices, such that one may be caught as a thief [if he takes vegetables on the other side of the partition]. And that is a fortiori the case in a vegetable field. (*Teshuvot*, sec. 395)

Maimonides opens his response with a reasoned principle: there is a considerable difference between a courtyard and a vegetable field, for harm caused pertains to protecting privacy. Protection of privacy is relevant only to a place in which a person lives, such as a courtyard. In contrast, partitions between gardens or vegetable fields, where people do not reside, are meant not to protect privacy but only to mark ownership. Accordingly, a partition in a courtyard must be four cubits high, so that the field of vision will be cut off, but that in a field need be only ten handbreadths, sufficient to mark the extent of each person's ownership.

The Talmud's comments about the partition in a field, which must be built on account of the evil eye, in fact contradicts the foregoing distinction, but Maimonides rejects them as an anonymous, non-binding explanation. He takes that view in part because he objected to magical beliefs and did not believe in the evil eye as an agent of harm. In his view, the reference to "evil eye" in the Talmud denotes not protection against harm but protection of the viewer's soul from feelings of avarice and jealousy: "For it is an act of piety, that one not look at another with an evil eye." In his view, the discussion in the Talmud must withstand the test of reason. In this instance, that discussion is not binding, for one cannot compel construction of a partition out of considerations of piety, and the suggestion appears in the Talmud as a rejected explanation.

The response illustrates two elements of Maimonides' approach to the Talmud. First, in light of his philosophical stance, he attempts to expunge from halakhic decision-making and from the interpretation of a Talmudic passage any elements that he considers to have a magical character. Second, he is not unequivocally committed to the implications of Talmudic discussion.

A similar independence is evident in the reasons provided by Maimonides for various *halakhot*, reasons that appear to differ from those provided by the Talmud itself. A statement of principle regarding such divergences appears in his response regarding the difference between a rationale he advanced in *Mishneh Torah* and that of the Rif and the Talmud. As a matter of Torah law, the prohibition on eating leaven on Passover goes into effect at the beginning of the seventh hour[2] on 14 Nisan, Passover Eve, before the start of the festival itself. The rabbis broadened the prohibition, extending it to include the entire sixth hour and even the fifth. The stated reason in the Talmud and repeated by the Rif is that on a cloudy day, people might confuse the seventh hour with the fifth. In *Mishneh Torah*, Maimonides says that the sages extended the prohibition to the sixth hour and later decreed that it applied to fifth as well, since people might confuse the sixth hour with the fifth. Maimonides was asked about this divergence from the Talmud's rationale and he replied as follows: "What appears in the *Halakhot* [of the Rif]—that is, lest he confuse the fifth hour with the seventh—is, in fact, accurate; it is the Talmud's statement in response to the question there posed. But I referred to what commonly happens, which is to confuse an hour with the hour that follows it, for my intention throughout this treatise is to draw the laws near to reason or to what commonly happens" (*Iggerot*, p. 654). A two-hour error is unusual and Maimonides therefore specified a somewhat different rationale, in order to make the matter more reasonable, and he did so even though the Rif's version cites the reason mentioned in the Talmud. Maimonides declares this to be his method throughout his treatise.

Often, the independent rationales do not alter the *halakhah*. Moreover, a reading of the Talmudic passage will show that Maimonides' rationale is grounded in an exact understanding of the passage itself. On occasion, however, the different rationale will suggest a novel understanding of the *halakhah* at hand. An instructive example appears in one of his responsa, where he suggests an innovative formulation of a Talmudic ruling that appears to incorporate magical considerations. The Talmud (BT *Yevamot* 64b) determines that a twice-widowed woman should not marry a third time because

---

[2] A halakhic "hour" is one-twelfth of the time between sunrise and sunset; its duration thus varies with the season. The beginning of the seventh hour is, in effect, midday.

she is considered to be "a lethal woman." The discussion offers two rationales for that decision: that "the fountain is the cause," that is, sexual relations are the cause of death, or that "the stars are the cause," that is, there are
astrological reasons for the deaths of this woman's husbands.

Maimonides considered the question in response to a question about
whether a twice-widowed woman whose second husband died childless
might enter into levirate marriage with his brother (*yibbum*). He replied:
"I greatly wonder about dear scholars, constantly engaged in Torah, who
have doubts about the relative degree of admonitions and fail to distinguish between something forbidden by the Torah, something forbidden by
their [that is, the rabbis'] words, and something that is simply repugnant
but not forbidden" (*Iggerot*, p. 622). He determines at the outset that the
halakhah restricting remarriage of a twice-widowed woman invokes no actual prohibition and simply finds that sort of marriage to be offensive. He
goes on to characterize the offensiveness in the remarriage of a woman
whose first two husbands have died: "Possible risk of mortality that is
grounded in divination or imaginary concerns, which sometimes affect
weakly constituted bodies" (ibid.). The offensiveness in the remarriage
does not entail any actual influence by the widow on her third husband's
health but is grounded in psychosomatic considerations: a concern based
on superstition may nevertheless exert an actual effect on a person. The
transformation of the Talmud's express prohibition into a mere declaration
of offensiveness, grounded in the psychological influence of a superstition,
shows that Maimonides had a different approach to the practical problem
presented to him. He based his argument on Andalusian practice as well:

> The practical *halakhah* that we have always applied in all the cities of Anda-
> lusia is that if a woman is repeatedly widowed, she should not be prevented
> from remarrying, especially if she is young, for there is concern about the
> detriments that may result . . . How can we put the daughters of Israel at
> risk of going astray? What the God-fearing and pious people among us did
> was to refrain from arranging a marriage for a multiple widow but to say to
> her explicitly: if you are able to find someone to marry you, we will not re-
> quire him to divorce you. And the woman and her husband would contrive
> for her to be betrothed to him before two witnesses alone, and she would
> then come to the court, which would write a *ketubbah* (marriage contract)
> for her, and she would enter the wedding canopy and the court would recite
> the seven blessings for her, since she had already been betrothed. That was

the practice of the court of Rabbeinu Isaac of blessed memory, author of the *Halakhot* [that is, the Rif] as well as of the court of Rabbeinu Joseph Halevi [that is, Ibn Migash], his student, of blessed memory, and that was the practice of all who followed after them; and that is how we have taught and how we have acted in the land of Egypt since arriving there. (*Iggerot*, pp. 622–623)

A concern grounded in magical divination cannot have the power to leave a woman stranded in widowhood. Accordingly, the practice in Andalusia was to circumvent the prohibition by advising the woman to become betrothed on her own, and the court would then confirm the marriage as a fait accompli. This position has its source in long-standing Andalusian tradition, and Maimonides uses it in halakhic practice. His ruling on the subject in *Mishneh Torah* is based both on the changed rationale for the *halakhah* and on Andalusian practice: "If a woman had been successively married to two husbands and both died, she should not marry for a third time, but if she does so, she need not be divorced. Even if only the betrothal has taken place, the third husband may consummate the marriage" ("Laws Concerning Forbidden Intercourse," 21:31). According to this ruling, once a marriage of this sort has taken place, it should not be annulled, and that is so even if all that has occurred is betrothal, and the wedding canopy is yet to be entered.

It should not be surprising that the Andalusian tradition, which Maimonides followed in practice, was harshly criticized by halakhists having a radically different view of magical considerations. Rabbi Yom Tov Ishbili (Ritva) of the fourteenth century, a student of Naḥmanides' students, wrote as follows:

> With regard to marriage, [even if] a man wants to marry a lethal woman and cause harm to himself, we do not enable him to do so, for it is forbidden and within the rubric of bloodshed [that is, suicide]; and the court bans him until he divorces her. And so I have seen as the opinion of [Naḥmanides], of blessed memory, who so acted. (Novellae of Ritva on *Yevamot* 64b, s.v. "*nesu'in*)

Ritva, loyal to the Talmudic rationale, took the view that marriage of this sort was suicidal and subject to the prohibition on endangering oneself. Accordingly, not only was such a marriage forbidden in the first instance, but even after the fact it must not be allowed and the husband should be compelled to divorce—contrary to the ruling in *Mishneh Torah*. The dispute indicates the linkage between scientific worldviews and halakhic decision-making and the way in which a change in halakhic rationale can lead to a different halakhic understanding.

Mishneh Torah's independent organization, unrelated to the sequence of Talmudic passages, and its formulation of the *halakhah* in a novel and original context, contribute to a degree to the remoteness between Maimonides' rulings and the Talmudic debates and rationales. It is possible, however, to go far beyond that, for the approach is based on Maimonides' unique position regarding the authority of the Talmud. As he saw it, the authoritativeness of the Talmud was not based on the superior wisdom and understanding of the *amora'im* (Talmudic sages) or on the work having its source in the Holy Spirit or being divinely supported. As we saw in chapter 4, Maimonides regarded the Talmud as binding and canonical because it had spread throughout Israel. The Talmud's canonical status was tied to the acceptance of its rulings as a practical matter; but its binding authoritativeness did not extend to the debates and rationales reported in it, for the community had accepted only so much of the content as could be expressed in practice. It may well be, therefore, that Maimonides was absolutely committed to the Talmud's rulings but not to the manner in which it understood and explained those rulings. That independence, derived from a concept that the Talmud was authoritative in principle, enabled Maimonides, among other things, to crystallize his original conceptual notion in *Mishneh Torah*.

Three Functions of *Aggadah* in *Mishneh Torah*

In the *Book of Knowledge*, *Mishneh Torah*'s first volume, Maimonides incorporated sections and chapters dealing with binding beliefs and desirable character traits. Throughout the treatise, he supplemented the halakhic principles with a large number of statements that are not within the narrow definition of *halakhah* pertaining to forbidden and permitted, pure and impure, guilty and innocent. These remarks—which for purposes of discussion can be all be termed "*aggadah*"—include explanations, emphases, words of encouragement and exhortation, polemics against opposing views, and words of consolation at the conclusion of halakhic units, in the manner of the *Mishnah*. For example, in the *halakhah* related to the obligation to pray with a congregation, he writes: "Communal prayer is always heard by God. The Holy One Blessed be He never rejects the prayers of the many, even if there are sinners among them. Therefore, a person should always participate with a congregation and never pray alone whenever he can pray with a congregation" ("Law Concerning Prayer and the Priestly Blessing," 8, 1). In the *halakhah* in which he forbids writing holy names in a mezuzah, he adds a sharp polemic:

> But those who write the names of angels, holy names, verses, or special shapes on the mezuzah are included in the category of those who have no share in the world to come, since these fools not only cancel the commandment but make of a great commandment, the unification of the Holy One, blessed be he, His love, and His worship, a charm for their own benefit since they, in their stupidity, think that this is a matter which benefits them concerning worldly vanities. ("Laws Concerning Tefillin, the Mezuzah and the Scroll of the Law," 5:4)

In the *halakhah* dealing with the rejoicing on a festival with food and drink, Maimonides establishes the duty to invite the poor to share in the joy. That duty, which goes beyond the general obligation to give charity, has no express source in the Talmud. It is accompanied by an explanation and admonition:

> And while one eats and drinks himself, it is his duty to feed the stranger, the orphan, the widow, and other poor and unfortunate people, for he who locks the doors to his courtyard and eats and drinks with his wife and family without giving anything to eat and drink to the poor and bitter in soul—his meal is not a rejoicing in a divine commandment but a rejoicing in his own stomach. . . . Rejoicing of this kind is a disgrace to those who indulge in it, as Scripture says, *And I will spread dung on your faces, even the dung of your sacrifices* (Mal. 2:3). ("Laws Concerning Rest on the Festivals," 6:18)

The regular occurrence in *Mishneh Torah* of aggadic passages of this sort shows that Maimonides had a pedagogic purpose in his halakhic writing; it encompassed motivating people to carry out the *halakhot*.

But in addition to the rhetorical and pedagogic significance of the *aggadah* in *Mishneh Torah* as a sort of an appendage to the *halakhah*, one can identify three roles that the *aggadah* plays in the treatise's construction of the *halakhah*: (1) it provides context and meaning for the *halakhah* itself; (2) it complements the *halakhah*; and (3) it subversively criticizes the *halakhah*.

Let me begin with the role of *aggadah* in providing context and meaning to specific halakhic principles—a broad context that will sometimes have a bearing on the content of the *halakhah* as well. The use of *aggadah* in this way is evident at some points where Maimonides opens a major halakhic unit with an aggadic introduction; examples include the first chapter of the "Laws Concerning Idolatry" and the first few *halakhot* of the "Laws Concerning Marriage." One of the most prominent examples is the introductory passage to the "Laws Concerning Prayer," and it is that one we will examine.

The opening *halakhot* in the "Laws Concerning Prayer" presents an original historical tapestry meant to instill meaning into the act of prayer. The first *halakhah* states that prayer is a positive commandment of biblical authority, based on the verse "serving Him with all your heart and soul" (Deut. 11:13)—"What is the Service of the heart? Prayer" ("Laws Concerning Prayer and Priestly Blessing," 1, 1). At that stage, Maimonides says, the duty to pray did not extend to a fixed time or a binding text. Prayer, that is, service of the heart, was an obligation borne by every individual, and each would discharge it in accord with his abilities and needs. The only set requirement was that the prayer include petitions and supplications for the satisfaction of one's needs, and that the petitions be preceded by praise and followed by thanksgiving, as is proper in a dignified plea presented before a king:

> The number of prayers is not fixed in the Torah, nor is their format, and neither does the Torah prescribe a fixed time for prayer . . . Rather, this commandment obligates each person to pray, supplicate, and praise the Holy One, blessed be He, to the best of his ability every day; to then request and plead for what he needs; and after that praise and thank God for all that He showered on him. One who is articulate offers up many supplications and requests, while one who is inarticulate prays to the best of his ability, whenever he wishes. ("Laws Concerning Prayer and Priestly Blessing," 1:1)

Prayer retained this individualized character until after the Babylonian Exile, during which Israel's linguistic ability was disrupted, as they lost their mastery of Hebrew and began to intermingle it with other languages. This crisis led Ezra and his court to formulate a fixed prayer text and to enact a requirement that prayer be said a fixed number of times per day, at fixed hours of the day.

This account of the history of prayer has important halakhic implications. Contrary to Naḥmanides' position, Maimonides followed the *Geonim* and the Rif in believing the duty to pray was biblical. The later institution of prayer by the sages was simply the institutionalization of a preexisting duty. The establishment of fixed prayers by the sages cannot be taken to imply that the overall duty to pray was something that they instituted in the wake of the Temple's destruction as a replacement for sacrifice.

The *aggadah*-like introduction also shapes the view taken of the meaning and essence of prayer. According to this historical account, it was a crisis that brought about the fixed formulation and times, but the crisis does not reflect the core nature of prayer. The essence of prayer is internal *kavvanah*—service of the heart—and it therefore is a duty borne by each individual, who must pray in his own language and in accord with his own needs. But the concept of prayer that Maimonides presents is not self-evident, and an alternative, entirely different view exists.

It might be argued, contrary to Maimonides' view, that prayer is, in principle, the public and the community turning to God and that the set formulation and fixed times are the only way in which one can stand before God. On this view, institutionalized fixed prayer, like communal sacrifices in the time of the Temple, is the essence of prayer. This concept appears in a *midrash* that explains why it is forbidden to pray more than thrice daily. The *midrash* is at odds with the view of R. Yoḥanan, who believes a person should pray abundantly, to the point of praying the entire day. The *midrash* uses the following colloquy to explain the prohibition on praying more than three times a day:

> Antoninus asked our holy rabbi [that is, R. Judah the Prince]: Is it permitted to pray at all times? He said to him: It is forbidden. He said to him: Why? He said to him: So that one does not act flippantly before the Mighty One [God]. He [Antoninus] was not persuaded. What did he [R. Judah] do? He went to before [Antoninus] early in the morning and said: Peace be upon you. After an hour, he went to him and said: Imperator! After an hour, he said to him: Peace be upon you, King. He said to him [Antoninus to R. Judah]: Why are you ridiculing the king? He said: Let your ears hear what your mouth utters. And if you, mere flesh and blood, say that to a person who greets you repeatedly, how much more so is it improper to ridicule the King of Kings, the Holy One blessed be He in this way? (*Midrash Tanḥuma, Miqqez*, 11)

This *midrash*, constructed on the protocol for approaching Caesar, shows that repeated prayer without a set formulation entails a degree of ridicule of God. The times for prayer and the set formulation, in the view of this *midrash*, are not merely an after-the-fact institutionalization of free, personal prayer; they are, rather, the only way in which God may be addressed without flippancy. The formulation and the time serve as the framework that makes it possible for the individual to approach God. But the historical account that Maimonides prefaces to the laws of prayer presents the opposite view. The set formulation and times are simply the institutionalization of prayer, and their entire purpose is to facilitate service of the heart on the part of individuals who have lost the ability to persevere in that sort of worship on their own.

The context into which Maimonides inserts the laws of prayer attests to the centrality he assigned to *kavvanah* in the halakhic context. As he says in defining *kavvanah* (here translated as "concentration") in prayer:

> What does correct intention involve? Any prayer recited without correct intention is not prayer. One who prays without correct intention must pray again with correct intention. One who is confused or preoccupied may not pray until he becomes tranquil. . . . How does one achieve correct intention? One must free his mind of all thoughts and see himself as standing before the divine Presence. Therefore, one should sit awhile before prayer in order to direct his mind, and then pray gently and beseechingly. ("Laws Concerning Prayer and the Priestly Blessings," 4:15–16)

These statements in *Mishneh Torah* suggest two important points regarding the centrality of *kavvanah*. One is that prayer uttered without *kavvanah* is not prayer at all, according to Maimonides. *Kavvanah* is not a duty; it is, rather, the very essence of prayer, and the fulfillment of prayer as service of the heart, is based entirely on the *kavvanah* with which it is said. *Kavvanah* refers to the sense of standing before God and is expressed through pleas and supplications. The second point, with respect to which Maimonides follows the view of the Talmud, is that a person who believes he cannot maintain *kavvanah* is not permitted to pray until he recovers his mental composure. If prayer without *kavvanah* is not prayer, then it is forbidden to pray when one believes *kavvanah* will be lacking. Uttering the words without *kavvanah* is not prayer; it is nothing more than mentioning God's name in vain.

Although Maimonides' second point follows in the course set by the Talmudic discussion of the matter, it should be emphasized that in the Middle Ages, a contrary view was widespread among halakhists. According to that view, diligent selection of a time in which one could pray with *kavvanah* was not a condition to fulfilling the obligation to pray, and one certainly should not repeat a prayer said without *kavvanah*, for the capacity to maintain proper *kavvanah* has in any event been lost. R. Meir Hakohen of the thirteenth century, a student of Maharam of Rothenberg and author of *Hagahot Maimoniyot*, which supplemented *Mishneh Torah* with the contrary rulings that had been issued in Germany and France, wrote as follows of Maimonides' approach: "Tosafot wrote that in all these matters, we are not strict nowadays . . . for we do not have that much *kavvanah* in prayer." The finding cited in the name of the Tosafists represents a dramatic shift in the relationship within *halakhah* between *kavvanah* and action, for it questions the standing of *kavvanah* in prayer and moderates the demands that followed from its central position. The prohibition against praying until one's mind is composed is taken to be an ideal, not a binding requirement. The view of the author of *Hagahot Maimoniyot* appears as well in the *Arba'ah Turim* by R. Jacob, son of Rosh; and R. Joseph Karo rules in the *Shulḥan Arukh* that one need not be strict in those matters that are derived from the rigorous insistence on *kavvanah* in prayer.

Maimonides was familiar with notions of this sort. They appear in the writings of R. Natronai Ga'on and, evidently, in the rulings of the Rif, who omitted from his treatise the *halakhah*, mentioned in the Talmud, that one was forbidden to pray until his mind was composed. That Maimonides maintained the view appearing in the Talmud even while evidently recognizing the contrary one highlights his view that prayer without *kavvanah* is not prayer. The centrality of *kavvanah* in Maimonides' rulings follows from his determination, in the introduction to the laws of prayer, that the essence of prayer is the biblically ordained service of the heart and that only afterward, in the wake of a historical crisis, did prayer receive an institutionalized and fixed nature. The aggadic context into which the halakhic unit was placed influenced the shaping of the *halakhah* itself.

The second role of *aggadah* in *Mishneh Torah* is to fill the void left by the official *halakhah*. In this capacity, *aggadah* does not afford an underpinning or explanation for halakhic principles; rather, it complements them. *Aggadot* of this sort appear in *Mishneh Torah* when the *halakhah* sets forth only a formal, basic framework that is insufficiently responsive to moral and religious aspirations or that fails to highlight the seriousness of the issue at hand.

Examples of supplements of this sort can be found in situations where there is a gap between the seriousness of a transgression and the relatively modest punishment it bears. As we know, the severity of a transgression is generally considered to correspond to the severity of the punishment imposed on a transgressor. Some offenses incur no punishment, and that would seem to suggest that they are not particularly serious. There are, however, instances in which the absence of punishment should not be taken to imply that the offense is relatively mild. In such instances, Maimonides uses *aggadah* to complement the formal limitation of the transgression's severity:

> Although one who puts another to shame is not punished with stripes, still it is a great offense. And thus the sages said, "He who shames another in public has no portion in the world to come." One ought therefore to beware of publicly shaming anyone, whether he be young or old. One should not call a person by a name of which he feels ashamed, nor relate anything in his presence which humiliates him. ("Laws Concerning Moral Dispositions," 6:8)

Shaming another is not a transgression for which one is punished, but the absence of punishment should not be taken to imply that the offense is a mild one. The reason for the lack of punishment is largely formal, and the *aggadah* completes the picture, avoiding the impression that might have been given by a narrow, legal reading of the transgression and its (lack of) punishment. A similar example appears in the ensuing chapter:

> Whoever tells tales about another person violates a prohibition, as it is said "Thou shalt not go up and down as a tale-bearer among thy people" (Lev. 19:16). And although no stripes are inflicted, it is a grave offense and leads to the death of many souls in Israel. Hence, this precept is followed immediately by the sentence "Neither shalt thou stand idly by the blood of thy neighbor." (Lev. 19:16)
>
> For an example of the tragic consequence of this transgression, read what happened after Doeg's report concerning the priests of Nob (1 Sam. 22:6–19) ("Laws Concerning Moral Dispositions" 7:1).

The social consequences of tale-bearing can go all the way to bloodshed, and tale-bearing therefore is a grave offense. That the offense incurs no punishment is due to an incidental consideration: offenses involving no physical action (as distinct, say, from speech) do not incur lashes. The *aggadah* cites the harsh biblical precedent of Doeg the Edomite, who told tales to King Saul about the priests of Nob having afforded David refuge, thereby bringing about their deaths. In so doing, it fills in the gap between the moral severity of the offense and its seemingly lenient judicial treatment, free of punishment. Later in the same chapter, when Maimonides defines slander, he expands on the aggadic characterization and sharpens his tone in telling of the offense's severity and the way in which it causes trust and closeness in society to crumble.

Other *aggadot* that play this complementary role are those that support taking actions characterized as consistent with "the attribute of piety"— the morality to which one should aspire, beyond what is required by dry law. For example, *zizit* (fringes) are required on four-cornered garments. In principle, one might exempt himself from the commandment by never wearing a four-cornered garment. At the end of the "Laws Concerning Fringes on Garments," Maimonides considers that situation:

> Even though one is not obligated to purchase tallit and wrap himself in it, so that he has to affix fringes to it, it is not fitting for a person who is pious to exempt himself from this commandment . . . Let one always take care concerning the commandment of fringes, since Scripture weighed it against all the other commandments and made them all dependent on it, as it says, *That shall be your fringe; look at it and recall all the commandments of the Lord and observe them* [*So that you do not follow your heart and eyes in your lustfull urge*] (Num. 15: 39). ("Laws Concerning Fringes," 3, 11–12)

Also within this category of complementary *aggadah* are passages in *Mishneh Torah* that present the purpose and ethos of halakhic principles not lending themselves to precise definition or quantification. That sort of aggadic presentation reaches a poetic and inspiring peak in the final chapter of "Laws Concerning Gifts to the Poor." The chapter is preceded by three others in which Maimonides defines in great detail the private and public duty to give charity. Those chapters include, among other things, the definition of a poor person, the amount that must be given, the priorities assigned to various recipients of charity, and the manner in which charitable funds are to be distributed. At the conclusion of that exhaustive and detailed account, he turns to the broad ethos of the commandment:

> It is our duty to be more careful in the performance of the commandment of almsgiving than in that of any other positive commandment, for almsgiving is the mark of the righteous man who is of the seed of our father Abraham, as it is said, *For I have known him, to the end that he may command his children*, etc., *to do righteousness* (Gen. 18:19). The throne of Israel cannot be established, nor true faith made to stand up, except through charity, as it is said, *In righteousness shalt thou be established* (Isa. 54:14); nor will Israel be redeemed, except through the practice of charity, as it is said, *Zion shall be redeemed with justice, and they that return of her with righteousness* (Isa. 1:27).
> ("Laws Concerning Gifts to the Poor," 10:1)

Charity is not just another positive commandment, part of the general list of commandments. It is, rather, the commandment that constitutes Jewish identity. It sets the basis for the existence of the Jewish nation and the Jewish religion, and it opens the door to redemption.

Maimonides incorporates *aggadah* into the ensuing *halakhot* as well, noting that giving charity will never diminish a person's own wealth and emphasizing the ethos of solidarity represented by charity: "All Israelites and those that have attached themselves to them are to each other like brothers, as it is said, *Ye are the children of the Lord your God* (Deut. 14:1). If brother will show no compassion to brother, who will? And unto whom shall the poor of Israel raise their eyes? Unto the heathens, who hate them and persecute them? Their eyes are therefore hanging solely upon their brethren" ("Laws Concerning Gifts to the Poor,"10:2).

The giving of charity has significance for the establishment of Jewish identity; conversely, refraining from giving is considered a challenge to the entire Torah, equivalent to idolatry: "He who turns his eyes away from charity is called a base fellow, just as is he who worships idols. . . . He is also called a sinner, as it is said, *And he cry unto the Lord against thee, and it be sin in thee*" (Deut. 15:10) ("Laws Concerning Gifts to the Poor," 10:1). The poor have an intimate connection to God, and harming them is several times more serious than harming someone else: "The Holy One blessed be He, stands nigh unto the cry of the poor, as it is said, *Thou hearest the cry of the poor.* One should therefore be careful about their cry, for a covenant has been made with them, as it is said, *And it shall come to pass, when he crieth unto Me, that I will hear, for I am gracious*" ("Laws Concerning Gifts to the Poor," 10:1).

Determining the broad, foundational ethos of charity opens the way to a series of guidelines that, by their very nature, do not lend themselves to precise quantification:

> He who gives alms to a poor man with a hostile countenance and with his face averted to the ground, loses his merit and forfeits it, even if he gives as much as a thousand gold coins. He should rather give with a friendly countenance and joyfully. He should commiserate with the recipient in his distress, as it is said, *If I have not wept for him that was in trouble, and if my soul grieved not for the needy.* He should also speak to him prayerful and comforting words, as it is said, *And I caused the widow's heart to sing with joy* (Job 29:14). ("Laws Concerning Gifts to the Poor," 10:4)

Charity is not merely material support; it includes identification with the poor person's travail. The giver, therefore, is duty-bound to respond to the psychological state of the person requesting alms. The high degree of sensitivity to be shown by the giver follows from his recognizing that the poor person feels humiliated by the situation in which he finds himself: "If a poor man asks you for alms and you have nothing to give him, comfort him with words. It is forbidden to rebuke a poor man or to raise one's voice in a shout at him, seeing that his heart is broken and crushed . . . Woe unto him who shames the poor! Woe unto him! One should rather be unto the poor as a father, with both compassion and words, as it is said, *I was a father to the needy* (Job 29:16) ("Laws Concerning Gifts to the Poor," 10:5).

Having determined that poverty is a psychological state as well as an economic situation, and that responsiveness to that psychological state is part of the essence of charity, Maimonides goes on to one of the best known halakhic pinnacles of *Mishneh Torah*: the gradations of charity, ranked in accord with how they respond to the dependence and humiliation associated with poverty. That ranking, which does not appear in the Talmud in this detailed and polished formulation, is Maimonides' own inspiring accomplishment. It identifies eight levels of charity, listed in descending order. The most praiseworthy level is a form of giving aimed at liberating the poor person from his state of dependence: "There are eight degrees of almsgiving, each one superior to the other. The highest degree, than which there is none higher, is one who upholds the hand of an Israelite reduced to poverty by handing him a gift or a loan, or entering into a partnership with him, or finding work for him, in order to strengthen his hand, so that he would have no need to beg from other people" ("Laws Concerning Gifts to the Poor," 10:7). At the bottom of the ladder is a form of giving that perpetuates the state of dependence and manifests no awareness of the poor man's possible sense of humiliation, "Below this is he who gives alms with a frowning countenance" ("Laws Concerning Gifts to the Poor," 10:14). Between these extremes, Maimonides enumerates the intermediate levels of charity, from donating secretly, such that neither the giver nor the recipient can identify the other, down to giving pleasantly, albeit less than the proper amount and only after being asked. The broad aggadic discussion of charity thus opens up a normative discussion in which precise definition and quantification are impossible. The *halakhah* determines the number of meals and the amount of food a poor person should receive daily from the communal charity fund, but it is the *aggadah* that sets guidelines related to giving with graciousness rather than hostility and to liberating the poor person from his dependence.

In its third role, *aggadah* offers criticism of halakhic particulars. An outstanding example of that role appears in the *aggadah* concluding the "Laws Concerning Slaves":

> It is permitted to work a heathen slave with rigor. Though such is the rule, it is the quality of piety and the way of wisdom that a man be merciful and pursue justice and not make his yoke heavy upon the slave or distress him, but give him to eat and to drink of all foods and drinks.
>
> The Sages of old were wont to let the slave partake of every dish that they themselves ate of and to give the meal of the cattle and of the slaves precedence over their own. Is it not said: *As the eyes of slaves unto the hand of their master, as the eyes of a female servant unto the hand of her mistress* (Ps. 123:2)?
>
> Thus also the master should not disgrace them by hand or by word, because scriptural law has delivered them only unto slavery and not unto disgrace. Nor should he heap upon the slave oral abuse and anger, but should rather speak to him softly and listen to his claims. So it is also explained in the good paths of Job, in which he prided himself:
>
> > *If I did despise the cause of my manservant,*
> > *Or of my maidservant, when they contended with me . . .*
> > *Did not He that made me in the womb make him?*
> > *And did not the One fashion us in the womb?* (Job 31:13, 15)

Cruelty and effrontery are not frequent except with heathen who worship idols. The children of our father Abraham, however, i.e., the Israelites, upon whom the Holy One, blessed be He, bestowed the favor of the Law and laid upon them statutes and judgments, are merciful people who have mercy on all.

Thus also it is declared by the attributes of the Holy One blessed be He, which we are enjoined to imitate: *And His mercies are over all His works* (Ps. 145:9).

Furthermore, whoever has compassion will receive compassion, as it is said: And He will show thee mercy, and have compassion upon thee, and multiply thee (Deut. 13:18). ("Laws Concerning Slaves," 9:8)

To begin his critique of the possibility of working a Canaanite slave with rigor, Maimonides invokes the attribute of piety and cites the precedent of the early sages, who treated their slaves justly and mercifully. He goes on to intensify his attack on harsh treatment of slaves through the use of three motifs that take the criticism far beyond one based only on the attribute of mercy.

The first motif is that of the fundamental equality of men, as articulated by Job: "Did not He that made me in the womb make him? And did not the One fashion us in the womb?"

Second, he refers to the definition of Jewish identity as established by the Torah. A Jew who acts with cruelty toward non-Jews, working his Canaanite slave with rigor, becomes like them and loses his character as a Jew. This concept, which posits a fundamental dissimilarity between Jew and gentile, would appear at odds with the motif of equality just noted. But it must be recognized that the distinction between Jew and gentile, according to Maimonides, does not flow from some inherent, inborn difference. It results, rather, from Israel having statutes and laws based on principles of justice and mercy. The Torah's laws are treated in this *halakhah* as the undergirding of Jewish identity: "the Israelites, upon whom the Holy One, blessed be He, bestowed the favor of the Law and laid upon them statutes and judgments, are merciful people who have mercy on all." Maimonides does not set the attribute of mercy against the laws of slaves, which are, after all, part of the Torah. Rather, he sets against them the statutes and laws of the Torah itself, noting that the authorization in principle to humiliate a Canaanite slave and work him with rigor runs contrary to the laws of the Torah, which are merciful to all.

The third motif, which appears at the end, criticizes the distinction between Hebrew slave and Canaanite slave, which runs counter to the image
of God Himself, who is merciful to all His creatures and demands that
human beings act as He does. As a halakhist, committed to the authority
and force of the *halakhah*, Maimonides presents the laws of slaves in their
entirety. But the *aggadah* that he intertwined with the halakhic principles
allowed him to question, on the basis of religious or moral considerations,
the halakhic authorization to work Canaanite slaves harshly. He did so by
critically invoking the concepts of equality, of the central determinant of
Jewish identity and the character of the Torah, and of the image of God
and the duty to imitate Him.

Mishneh Torah's *Book of Agriculture* concludes with an aggadic passage
that straddles the line between the *aggadah*'s complementary role and its
critical role. The passage appears in the last chapter of the "Laws Concerning the Sabbatical Year and the Year of the Jubilee," which deals with the
status of the tribe of Levi. That tribe received no allocation of land in the
Land of Israel; instead, it received fields in the cities of refuge and relied on
donations from the other Israelites. Maimonides justified the Levites'
unique status as follows: "Why was the Tribe of Levi granted no right to a
share in the Land of Israel and in its spoils, together with his brothers?
Because they were set apart to worship the Lord, to serve Him, and to
teach His upright ways and His righteous judgments to the many" ("Laws
Concerning the Sabbatical Year and the Year of the Jubilee," 13:12). He
then goes on, in the final *halakhah* of the book, to qualify everything implied earlier in the chapter:

> Not only the Tribe of Levi, but also each and every individual of those who
> come into the world, whose spirit moves him and whose knowledge gives
> him understanding to set himself apart in order to stand before the Lord, to
> serve Him, to worship Him, and to know Him, who walks upright as God
> had made him to do, and releases his neck from the yoke of the many spec-
> ulations that the children of man are wont to pursue—such an individual is
> consecrated to the Holy of Holies, and his portion and inheritance shall be
> in the Lord forever and evermore. The Lord will grant him in this world
> whatever is sufficient for him, the same as He had granted to the priests and
> to the Levites. Thus indeed did David, upon whom be peace, say, *O Lord, the
> portion of mine inheritance and of my cup, Thou maintainest my lot* (Ps. 16:5).
> (Laws Concerning the Sabbatical Year and the Year of the Jubilee," 13:13)

These words are not simply an extension of the Levites' position to other people; they may be seen as a challenge to the entire idea of hereditary right, which had determined that one Israelite tribe would have a unique standing before God. The criticism of tribal and familial status is made more forceful by Maimonides' extension of his opposition as far as possible, to encompass "each and every individual of those who come into the world"; that is, not only Israelites. Every person, then, has the possibility of standing before God and being Holy of Holies. So profound a change in consciousness, through which a person becomes liberated from the yoke of the world and moves to a more exalted existence, is not something hereditary; it is, rather, the product of one's complete sanctification and life's work.

In moments of occasional understatement, Maimonides described *Mishneh Torah* as an attempt to capture and summarize *halakhah* in an accessible, transparent, organized, and all-inclusive manner. His efforts at exhaustive and concise summary were expressed in a polemical context in the following way: "All of you who have read my works know well that I always aim to avoid disagreements and challenge. If I could squeeze the entire Law of the Torah into one chapter, I would not write two chapters for it" (*Essay on Resurrection*, p. 225). Accomplishing such a comprehensive goal is an immense achievement, as Maimonides himself stated while addressing the sympathetic circle of scholars in Lunel: "I am sure you realize how I labored day and night for almost ten years to compose [*Mishneh Torah*]. Men of your scholarly attainments appreciate the significance of this work. I have gathered materials that were dispersed and separated between the hills and the mountains, and I called them forth "one from a city and two from a family" (Jer. 3, 14) . . ." (*Iggerot*, pp. 542–543). And yet, *Mishneh Torah* is a far more transformative and *monumental* work. As a book that might have aimed to become not only a presentation of the law but the law itself, it posited a bold attempt to transform single-handedly the very structure of authority of *halakhah*. Through the sheer power of the compilation with no institutional backing and with no reliance on direct divine authority, it aspired to constitute a kind of virtual state that would galvanize the Jewish people in a shared obligatory code. Such an accomplishment, according to Maimonides, would be achieved without ushering in a change in the Jewish geopolitical dispersed condition, a condition which he believed was the obstacle to the creation of *halakhah* as a genuine legal system. If, as Maimonides hoped, *Mishneh Torah* would have been accepted by all of Israel, it would have acquired the status of the Talmud itself, and therefore it would have served not only the modest role of a comprehensive summary but rather the more ambitious goal of an ultimate substitute. In its integration of philosophy and *halakhah*, *Mishneh Torah* aimed at a deep normative impact on religious consciousness, touching upon the basic aspects of religious beliefs and experience. At the heart of this great reform was the attempt to establish the knowledge of the world as crucial in shifting the human stance from the grip of instrumental attitude, to that of love of God and the world, and then to awe. In placing such a central role to the pursuit of knowledge, *Mishneh Torah* legislated the philosophical ethos as the summit of religious life. This religious sensibility is grounded in the view, expressed in the opening chapters of the book, that ultimately God's revelation is in the natural order itself, and that human flourishing depends on transcending the basic urges of fear and hope, toward a spiritual pursuit of truth. Such a stance implies as well a reformulation in *Mishneh Torah* of Judaism's eschatological picture—the world to come and messianism.

In its novel organization of different fields of *halakhah*, and in its independent language and voice, *Mishneh Torah* far surpassed the mere work of an elegant restatement and summary. It reshaped the *halakhah*'s categories in all of its diverse realms, and it reinterpreted them with rare depth and clarity. Thus, *Mishneh Torah* served for future generations of scholars not only as a normative guideline for practical decisions, but as an everlasting resource for the understanding of *halakhah* and its conceptual frame. Far from the more modest formulations of creating a comprehensive manual for *halakhah* easily accessible to all, these features constitute *Mishneh Torah* as a transformative monumental work. It is no wonder that of all the works Maimonides wrote, including his *Guide of the Perplexed*, he often referred to *Mishneh Torah* as "our great compilation."

CHAPTER SEVEN

The *Guide of the Perplexed* and Its Critique of Religious Language

Concealed and Revealed in the *Guide of the Perplexed*

In the introduction to the *Guide of the Perplexed*, Maimonides takes the unusual step of adjuring his readers in the following terms:

> I adjure—by God, may He be exalted!—every reader of this Treatise of mine not to comment upon a single word of it and not to explain to another anything in it save that which has been explained and commented upon in the words of the famous Sages of our Law who preceded me. But whatever he understands from this Treatise of those things that have not been said by any of our famous Sages other than myself should not be explained to another; nor should he hasten to refute me, for that which he understood me to say might be contrary to my intention. (Pines, p. 15)

The *Guide*, then, is a work whose meaning has been hidden, and the reader must always question whether he has fully understood the author's ideas. And even if he achieves a correct understanding, he is bound by oath not to disseminate that meaning, for he may not reveal anything that the author himself had not chosen to reveal. If a reader cannot attain an understanding of the work's deeper meanings on the basis of his own reading of its allusions, he is unworthy of having its secrets disclosed to him, and one therefore may not do so. The genuine addressee of the treatise will understand on his own what he needs to understand and what he properly may understand.

Mishneh Torah is a work directed to a wide audience, elite and common folk alike. The *Guide*, in contrast, is intended for a narrower group, a group Maimonides defines early on as excluding the public at large and scholars who deal only with *halakhah*: "It is not the purpose of this Treatise to make its totality understandable to the vulgar or to beginners in speculation, nor to teach those who have not engaged in any study other than the science of the Law—I mean the legalistic study of the Law" (Pines, p. 5). The work is meant for the perplexed, people who have been educated to be faithful to the traditions of Judaism but who have also internalized the philosophical view of the world. His exposure to these two sources of authority—Torah and wisdom—brings the perplexed person to the point of an existential crisis that would seem to require him to make a tragic choice between religious faith and philosophical certainty:

> Hence he would remain in a state of perplexity and confusion as to whether he should follow his intellect, renounce what he knew concerning the terms in question, and consequently consider that he has renounced the foundations of the Law. Or he should hold fast to his understanding of these terms and not let himself be drawn on together with his intellect, rather turning his back on it and moving away from it, while at the same time perceiving that he had brought loss to himself and harm to his religion. He would be left with those imaginary beliefs to which he owes his fear and difficulty and would not cease to suffer from heartache and great perplexity. (Pines, pp. 5–6)

The *Guide* is meant to deliver the perplexed person from his spiritual crisis and it therefore does not present an orderly, clear set of teachings that will be easily accessible to all. The new interpretation of Jewish tradition suggested by Maimonides is intended to resolve the spiritual and existential quandary faced by the Jewish educated elite, a group represented by the perplexed individual. It is presented through chapter headings dispersed throughout the work, and study of that new interpretation requires diligent and systematic association of those headings—in the contemporary cliché, the reader has to "connect the dots." Maimonides asserts as well that he deliberately planted contradictions within the work, meant to conceal its meaning from the unworthy. In the past, esoteric traditions were transmitted only orally and to individuals, allowing the transmitter to control the breadth of his audience, but one who commits matters to writing surrenders that degree of control. The only way to filter out unworthy members of the audience is by writing in an allusive and obscure fashion, in outline only and using deliberate contradictions. The *Guide*'s unique character allows for overcoming the limitations of time and place associated with oral transmission while still not revealing the secrets to those unworthy of receiving them.

Maimonides' various interpreters, however, were not deterred by the adjuration or the concealment; quite the opposite. The worst way to keep a secret, of course, is to announce its existence and warn against its disclosure. It should come as no surprise, therefore, that soon after the *Guide*'s publication, during the thirteenth and fourteenth centuries, commentaries began to be written that purported to explain its secrets and offered various ways to understand it. Concealment of the work's meaning did not preserve and protect it; on the contrary, it led interpreters to advance a particularly broad array of meanings. It is only natural that important books acquire diverse interpretations, and that is all the more so when the book is one whose meaning has been concealed by the author. Moreover, the meaning of the *Guide* became a fateful religious and political question, one that set the work at the center of a mighty *Kulturkampf* that broke out following Maimonides' death. At the heart of the conflict was the question of whether the *Guide* contained far-reaching positions that undermined the faith of true Jewish believers. The question became even sharper and more profound when one took account of the book having been written by the greatest halakhist since the completion of the Talmud. Maimonides' halakhic authority secured the treatise while simultaneously making it more dangerous and problematic.

And so, Maimonides left an ambiguous legacy, one that divided his interpreters and his opponents. Unraveling the secret and meaning of the *Guide* occupies students of Maimonides to this day. As I discuss the *Guide* in this chapter and the next, I do not intend to decide among the various readings of the work. Instead, I want to offer four interpretive possibilities that differ substantially in their understanding of the meaning that Maimonides assigned to the Jewish tradition. The four readings are as follows:

- the skeptical;
- the mystical;
- the conservative;
- the philosophical.

Consideration of these various readings will also allow for the presentation of a seamless interpretation of the central issues treated in the *Guide*, following the sequence in the work itself. Looking beyond the readings, I will attempt as well to uncover the basic kernel of the religious transformation effected by this work as understood by the various schools of interpretation.

◇

Before turning to the possible meanings of the *Guide*, we should take a good look at how the treatise is written. What motives drive the esotericism that conceals the treatise's meaning? And if the writing is indeed meant to obscure the meaning, why does Maimonides, in the introduction and elsewhere, declare that the book encompasses hidden meanings and describes the means of concealment he has used? An author or playwright working under the censorship of a totalitarian regime would never announce in an introduction that a work has a hidden meaning he is not free to disclose. Such an announcement would make him immediately suspect and invite readers to interpret the work in the most subversive way possible, even if that meaning was not the intended one. Before we identify possible hidden meanings in the treatise, we must consider a different question: what is the significance of concealment as a mode of expression or of writing and how is it used in the *Guide*?

One of the justifications Maimonides offers for the *Guide*'s obscure character is the need to protect the philosopher and philosophy itself from the scorn of the masses, who are unable to plumb its depths, and even more importantly, from the heavy hand of religious or political authorities, who regard philosophy as a threat to social order or religious doctrine:

> A sensible man thus should not demand of me or hope that when we mention a subject, we shall make a complete exposition of it. . . . An intelligent man would be unable to do so even by speaking directly to an interlocutor. He then could put it down in writing without becoming a butt for every ignoramus who, thinking that he has the necessary knowledge, would let fly at him the shafts of his ignorance. (Introduction; Pines, p. 6)

The policy of speaking esoterically about philosophical matters, going all the way back to Plato's time, was influenced by the trauma of Socrates' execution at the hands of the Athenians. There is a powerful, sometimes violent tension between seekers of truth and governing authorities, and esotericism therefore is a condition vital to the existence of philosophy as a free and independent field of activity. The philosopher uses concealment to protect his freedom of thought, and he develops sophisticated ways of using *double entendres* in speech and writing in order to convey his view to those who are worthy of receiving them.

Even more important, esotericism is meant not only to protect the philosopher and the philosophical enterprise; it is meant at least as much to protect the masses. Exposing the masses—or those who have not yet had the benefit of scientific and philosophical education—to philosophical thinking would lead them to a loss of faith, for in their inability to grasp the truth, they would distort it: "If, however, he begins with the divine science, it will not be a mere confusion in his beliefs that will befall him, but rather absolute negation" (I:33; Pines, p. 71). For example, the assertion that attributes of quantity and quality do not apply to the divinity can lead to a denial of God's very existence, for the masses cannot conceive of the existence of something entirely abstract. Exposing the masses to these sorts of philosophical ideas means calling into question the very existence of God.

But the truth does more than threaten the faith of the masses. As the philosopher recognizes, it also undermines the social order and the authority of the law. When it rejects the view of God as a personality with a will, philosophy jeopardizes the masses' allegiance to the law. Philosophical doctrines that portray prophecy as a process involving the prophet's cognition augmented by his imaginative powers—in contrast to the traditional picture in which a personified, sovereign God commands the law to His prophet—can undercut the authoritativeness of the law as something grounded in the command of the divine sovereign. Maimonides' understanding of divine providence—the wicked person's fate is left to chance and is not subject to providence; his punishment flows from the destructive nature of his sinful life itself—likewise endangers the masses' devotion to the law, which is motivated by fear of punishment and hope for reward. Indeed, society's very existence is jeopardized by destabilizing challenges to the anthropomorphic concept of the deity as a commanding sovereign who exercises governance, imposes punishment, and grants recompense. Challenges of that sort have the effect of weakening discipline and subverting obedience to the law, which are grounded in the belief that the sinner will ultimately be punished even if he escapes the watchful eye of the terrestrial sovereign. The philosopher therefore bears a fateful responsibility for the well-being of society. He must disclose metaphysical truths only to those who are able to maintain their obligations to society even without the necessary beliefs in divine governance, recompense, and punishment. These few individuals, whose souls crave only knowledge, are uninfluenced by the material impulses that bring about the dissolution of social structures. Society in general cannot survive under conditions of metaphysical transparency. Maimonides therefore includes among the mysteries of the Torah not only "the Acount of the Chariot" and "the Acount of Creation," in their narrow sense, but also the doctrines of prophecy, divine governance, and divine knowledge, as they pertain to God's relationship to the world:

> [A]s well as the discussion concerning His creation of that which He created, the character of His governance of the world the "how" of His providence with respect to what is other than He, the notion of His will, His apprehension, and His knowledge of all that He knows; and likewise as for the notion of prophecy and the "how" of its various degrees, and the notion of His names, though they are many, being indicative of one and the same thing—it should be considered that all these are obscure matters. In fact, they are truly the mysteries of the Torah and the secrets constantly mentioned in the books of the prophets and in the dicta of the Sages, may their memory be blessed. They are the matters that ought not to be spoken of except in chapter headings, as we have mentioned, and only with an individual such as has been described. (I:35; Pines, pp. 80–81)

The tension that appears in Greek and Arab philosophy between truth and social order has an additional feature: the social order is grounded on the dissemination of myths that Plato refers to as "noble lies" and that Maimonides terms "necessary and useful beliefs." That idea figures prominently in Plato's *Republic*, in the writings of al-Farabi, and in Maimonides' thought, and it had a decisive influence on how the relationships among philosophy, religion, and politics were understood in the political thought of the Middle Ages. According to this view of things, the legislator and the ruler were obligated to inculcate a worldview that would promote the state's existence, without regard to its truth or falsity.

In discussing the beliefs that the Torah conveys to the community, Maimonides distinguishes between true beliefs, meant to bring man to his higher perfection, and necessary beliefs, useful for the proper functioning of society:

Among the things to which your attention ought to be directed is that you should know that in regard to the correct opinions through which the ultimate perfection may be obtained, the Law has communicated only their end . . . that is, to believe in the existence of the deity, may He be exalted, His unity, His knowledge, His power, His will, and His eternity . . . In the same way, the Law also makes a call to adopt certain beliefs, belief in which is necessary for the sake of political welfare. Such, for instance, is our belief that He, may He be exalted, is violently angry with those who disobey Him and that it is therefore necessary to fear Him and to dread Him and to take care not to disobey. (III:28; Pines, p. 512)

At the end of that chapter he says:

Sum up what we have said concerning beliefs as follows: In some cases a commandment communicates a correct belief, which is the one and only thing aimed at—as, for instance, the belief in the unity and eternity of the deity and in His not being a body. In other cases the belief is necessary for the abolition of reciprocal wrongdoing or for the acquisition of a noble moral quality—as, for instance, the belief that He, may He be exalted, has a violent anger against those who do injustice, according to what is said: *And My wrath shall wax hot, and I will kill, and so on*, and as the belief that He, may He be exalted, responds instantaneously to the prayer of someone wronged or deceived: *And it shall come to pass, when he crieth unto Me, that I will hear; for I am gracious.* (III:28; Pines, pp. 513–514)

True beliefs are conveyed with great brevity, through chapter headings only, because understanding them requires a thorough scientific background as well as natural talent. The necessary beliefs, in contrast, pertaining to such matters as divine governance and recompense, are treated broadly by Scripture, for they are directed to the masses and regarded as useful mechanisms for anchoring the social order.

Myth plays a role not only in buttressing society's political structure but also in combatting opposing myths. Idolatry's sway over the masses is tied to the power of its promise and its threat directed toward primal human fears, and idolatrous practices cannot be effectively uprooted by rational arguments that prove the idolatrous myths to involve meaningless threats and vain promises. A myth can be overthrown only by instilling a contrary myth. For example, Maimonides argued, the idolatrous priests' threat to the well-being of one's children if one failed to pass one's son through fire in devotion to Moloch could be combatted only by the Torah's opposing threat to the family of one who *did* pass his son through Moloch's fire:

> Now it is known that it is the nature of men in general to be most afraid and most wary of losing their property and their children. Therefore the worshippers of fire spread abroad the opinion in those times that the children of everyone who would not *make his son or his daughter to pass through the fire* would die. . . . Thereupon the truthful one makes known in the name of God, may He be exalted, and says: Whereas you perform this action so that the children stay alive because of it, God will cause him who performs it to perish and will exterminate his descendants: he says: *Then I will set My face against that man and against his family.* (III:37; Pines, p. 546)

Myth, in the sense of fabrication, is essential to the social order.

Having justified esotericism by the distinction between true beliefs and necessary beliefs, Maimonides forced his interpreters to confront a difficult question: which traditional beliefs are merely necessary, meant only to preserve the social order and to promote obedience to the law, and which are true? Where does the line between the two groups run? The more radical and counter-traditional one's interpretation of the *Guide*'s hidden meaning, the greater the number of beliefs that are seen as merely necessary. The profound differences between conservative and radical readers of the *Guide* involve, among other things, the scope of the domain of necessary beliefs. It is a question to which we shall return when we examine the various interpretations of the *Guide* in greater detail.

Despite the vast responsibility borne by the philosopher, the *Guide* does not confine itself to concealment; it reveals as well. Maimonides recognized that in writing the *Guide*, he breached the bounds of the concealed. In the foreword to the treatise and the introduction to Part III, he writes of his misgivings over departing from the tradition of treating matters secretly and his justifications for doing so. To justify his revealing of mysteries, Maimonides used a sophisticated—and invented—reconstruction of the history of those mysteries, a history in which he occupied a unique place. In his view, the esoteric tradition was lost to Israel in part because the limits of esotericism were strictly enforced:

> And it has been made clear that even that portion of it that becomes clear to him who has been given access to the understanding of it, is subject to a legal prohibition against its being taught and explained except orally to one

man having certain stated qualities, and even that one only the chapter headings may be mentioned. This is the reason why the knowledge of this matter has ceased to exist in the entire religious community, so that nothing great or small remains of it. And it had to happen like this, for this knowledge was only transmitted from one chief to another and has and has never been set down in writing. (III: Introduction; Pines, p. 415)

Because the esoteric tradition was strictly limited to transmission by word of mouth, maintaining it required territorial contiguity and institutional continuity that were simply unavailable to Jews in Exile. Moreover, the correct version of the tradition, as known to the Sages who preceded the Exile, was distorted by the influence on Jewish thinkers of the erroneous strains of thought that they encountered in the Diaspora:

> Know that the many sciences devoted to establishing the truth regarding these matters that have existed in our religious community have perished because of the length of the time that has passed, because of our being dominated by the pagan nations, and because, as we have made clear, it is not permitted to divulge these matters to all people. For the only thing it is permitted to divulge to all people are the texts of the books. (I:71; Pines, p. 175)

According to Maimonides, the internal, deep structure of the Jewish tradition was lost, and he claimed that he himself lacked the esoteric tradition: "nor did I receive what I believe in these matters from a teacher" (III: Introduction; Pines, p. 416). That position acquires extreme importance when compared with the view of some Kabbalistic thinkers, who ascribe ancient provenance to the Torah mysteries in their possession. Maimonides reconstructed the lost and forgotten esoteric world through the use of his own intellect. In the introduction to Part III of the *Guide*, he attributes his writing of the work to the crisis faced by the Jews of his time: " . . . if I had omitted setting down something of that which has appeared to me as clear, so that that knowledge would perish when I perish, as is inevitable, I should have considered that conduct as extremely cowardly with regard to you and everyone who is perplexed. It would have been, as it were, robbing one who deserves the truth of the truth, or begrudging an heir his inheritance" (III: Introduction; Pines, pp. 415–416).

Maimonides described himself as a sudden manifestation of Jewish esoteric teachings, one discontinuous with the entire past and having no prospect of continuity after his departure from the world. His life was a moment of grace in the history of a lost esoteric tradition, a moment destined to be stored away and disappear. The survival of the inner meaning of the Jewish tradition therefore depended on his own willingness to break the constraints of silence and disseminate the secrets of Torah. The picture that Maimonides drew of the history of the Jewish mystical tradition, and the unique and isolated position he saw himself as occupying within that picture, warranted the breach in the bounds of esotericism that the *Guide* effected. As he saw it, he saved the tradition of the oral Torah by codifying it in *Mishneh Torah*; similarly, he saved the orally transmitted esoteric tradition by freeing it from the bonds of secrecy and raising it to the pinnacle of human apprehension.

Moreover, the crisis that warrants weakening the constraints of secrecy becomes even more serious when the intended audience for the revealed secret is characterized as "perplexed." The perplexed person is depicted as one who is faithful to the religion of Israel, possessed of scientific and philosophical knowledge, unaware of the esoteric meanings of Scripture, and left in a difficult situation as he contemplates only the surface layer of religion. Accordingly, revelation of the esoteric layers of Torah allusively and in writing is a necessary step in rescuing the educated Jewish class from the difficult situation in which it finds itself. Maimonides raises that point expressly in the directive at the opening of the *Guide*, following his account of his qualms about writing down the Torah's mysteries:

> God, may He be exalted, knows that I have never ceased to be exceedingly apprehensive about setting down those things that I wish to set down in this Treatise. For they are concealed things. . . . However, I have relied on two premises, the one being [the Sages'] saying in a similar case, *It is time to do something for the Lord, and so on*; the second being their saying, *Let all thy acts be for the sake of Heaven.* Upon these two premises I have I relied when setting down what I have composed in some of the chapters of this Treatise.
>
> To sum up: I am the man who when the concern pressed him and his way was straightened and he could find no other device by which to teach a demonstrated truth other than by giving satisfaction to a single virtuous man while displeasing ten thousand ignoramuses—I am he who prefers to address that single man by himself, and I do not heed the blame of those many creatures. For I claim to liberate that virtuous one from that into

which he has sunk, and I shall guide him in his perplexity until he becomes perfect and finds rest. (I: Introduction; Pines, pp. 16–17)

The breach of esotericism, which constitutes a violation of the Torah, is committed for the sake of Heaven, as a sort of mortal risk assumed by the exalted individual. In characterizing the community receiving the secret as "perplexed," and in describing the difficulty of its position, Maimonides augments the sense of crisis that justifies the commitment of the mysteries to writing. The determination that the mysteries of the Torah have been forgotten and lost and that the *Guide of the Perplexed* offers the only chance for reconstructing them is supplemented by the further argument that the loss of the esoteric tradition entails perplexity and crisis for the exalted individuals. Maimonides favors protecting these exalted individuals, even if it means incurring the social and political costs of removing philosophy from the underground. The fate of the Jewish intellectual elite depends on breaching the bounds of esotericism, and Maimonides believed his teachings afforded the sole and last chance for saving that segment of society.

Taken together, Maimonides' detailed treatment of the need for secrecy, his repeated argument about the existence of the Torah's hidden meanings, and his conscious and declared focus on his way of writing and on how it breaches the bounds of secrecy all demonstrate that he was more interested in using the idea of esotericism than in preserving its secrecy. Moreover, the presence of esoteric philosophical elements within his public halakhic writings—the *Commentary on the Mishnah* and *Mishneh Torah*—undermines any idea that there is a sharp distinction between disclosed and concealed that parallels the distinction between *halakhah* and philosophy. Had Maimonides been interested only in concealment, he would not have declared his systematic treatment of the existence of mysteries, the need to conceal them, and the importance of esoteric writing. It turns out, then, that he is not set on presenting a direct continuation of the esoteric philosophical tradition so much as on constructing a new argument on its foundation.

Maimonides' detailed explanation of the need for secrecy thus constitutes a substantive component of his exegetical strategy. He offers the perplexed person the argument that Scripture include a concealed layer of meaning that can resolve his perplexity, and that in turn requires him to explain to his reader why there is a need for that layer to be concealed. Without an adequately persuasive explanation of the need for esotericism, especially with respect to those areas that Maimonides defines as mysteries of the Torah, his exegetical approach loses its credibility. His extensive discussion of the need for secrecy prepares the reader to recognize that he is obligated to seek out the true meaning of the Jewish tradition, which lies beyond the surface meaning of the canonical scriptures. The argument runs as follows: since the philosophers determined that philosophy is an esoteric science, and since Maimonides identified physics and metaphysics with "the Account of Creation" and "the Account of the Chariot," thereby linking the esoteric philosophical tradition to the esoteric Talmudic tradition, he has a basis for persuading the educated person that there is an esoteric stratum to the Torah itself, the recognition of which will resolve his perplexity. The traditional view of Maimonides' esotericism holds that shrouding ideas in mystery is a means for preserving philosophy as an autonomous area of activity. That view, however, must be supplemented by the idea of esotericism as a means for integrating philosophy into the heart of the tradition. These opposing poles establish the exquisite tension between concealment and disclosure within the new models that Maimonides created for transmitting mystery.

Idolatry and Religious Language

The justifications that Maimonides offered for engaging in esotericism are centered on the fateful effects that revealing the truth would have on philosopher and society alike. But in addition to this idea of political esotericism, one finds in the *Guide* the view that esotericism is an essential quality of metaphysical language. Seen politically, the secret itself can be clearly formulated but must not be disseminated. From the essentialist perspective of the esotericism, however, the metaphysical content cannot in principle be expressed in language and can only be alluded to through symbols:

> Know that whenever one of the perfect wishes to mention, either orally or in writing, something that he understands of these *secrets*, according to the degree of his perfection, he is unable to explain with complete clarity and coherence even the portion that he has apprehended, as he could do with the other sciences whose teaching is generally recognized. Rather there will befall him when teaching another that which he had undergone when learning himself. I mean to say that the subject matter will appear, flash, and

then be hidden again, as though this were the nature of this subject matter, be there much or little of it. (Introduction; Pines, p. 8)

The distinction between political esotericism and substantive esotericism creates two different meanings for biblical language. Sociopolitical esotericism perceives the biblical parable as an allegory, whose hidden content lends itself to direct conceptual expression. In contrast, the essential concept of esotericism sees the biblical parable as a symbol, whose hidden content cannot be formulated directly in conceptual language. According to this understanding, the esoteric mode of writing and speaking in indirect and allusive way is not the product of a strategy that philosophy adopts vis-à-vis society; it is, rather, the essential nature of the philosophical realm.

In the introduction to the work, Maimonides argues that an understanding of the truth in the realm of the divine sciences cannot be attained at will, whenever one wishes: "But sometimes truth flashes out to us so that we think that it is day, and then matter and habit in their various forms conceal it so that we find ourselves again in an obscure night, almost as we were at first" (Pines, p. 7). Proper cognition of abstract metaphysical matters, according to Maimonides, depends on liberation from matter and habit, and the ability to maintain that liberation varies with a person's proximity to perfection. The writing or teaching of metaphysical matters is, in effect, an attempt to reconstruct one's cognition in order to transfer it to someone else. But because of the evasive nature of truth, the writer can never fully duplicate his state of cognition, and he must make use of parables that point or allude to it. That approach to essential esotericism is focused on the constraints that follow from a person's existential situation as a physical being.

But Maimonides in the *Guide* goes further, developing an additional, probing notion regarding essential esotericism, one tied to the limits of language itself as a suitable means of expression. The precise meaning of this notion is linked to his approach regarding religious language generally and to one of the substantive changes he brought about in Jewish religion. Considering the limitations of language will help clarify the first of the four approaches to reading the *Guide* noted earlier: *the skeptical approach*.

In *Mishneh Torah*, Maimonides rules that one who attributes corporeality to the divinity is a heretic and has no share in the world to come. Consistent with that position, he writes in the *Guide* that belief in divine corporeality is worse than idolatry: "Know, accordingly, you who are that man, that when you believe in the doctrine of the corporeality of God or believe that one of the states of the body belongs to Him, you *provoke His jealousy and anger, kindle the fire of His wrath*, and are *a hater, an enemy, and an adversary* of God, much more so than *an idolater*" (I:36; Pines, p. 84). An idolater can always argue that the idol he is worshipping is merely a symbol of a more exalted God, but one who internalizes, in his mind's eye, a personified image of the divinity as a great person seated on a throne does not see that figure as a mere symbol, for that image of the divinity is fixed in his mind. In effect, such a person does not worship God; he worships some being that is simply a more perfected form of man. The object worshipped by a believer in corporeality is nothing more than an imaginary being on which the worshipper projects his own characteristics, and every religious act performed by such a person, therefore, partakes of self-worship.

Defining anthropomorphism as the most severe religious transgression reopened the struggle against idolatry on an entirely new front. Since the time of the Second Temple, the threat of idolatry to Judaism seemed to have been overcome, the problem resolved. During the First Temple period, Israel strayed after Baal and Astarte, built sanctuaries in their name and worshipped their statues. By the time of the Second Temple, however, as the Talmud tells, the impulse to worship idols seemed to have disappeared.[1] Maimonides renewed the struggle against idolatry not because it once again had become attractive but because he redefined the problem in a way that made it once again a pressing concern. As he saw it, the question of idolatry is centered not only on the external, plastic representation of the deity but on the worshipper's inner mental image regarding God. It is entirely possible for a person praying in a synagogue where no statue or other image is present nevertheless to commit idolatry by having a mental image of the divinity that is corrupted by anthropomorphism. It is preferable that such a person not pray at all, for every one of his prayers constitutes service of a strange God. Moreover, this redefinition of idolatry as pertaining to the internal image transforms the effort to combat it from a struggle against an external "other"—the idolatrous and seductive nations of the world—into an internal struggle that divides the community. The biblical and midrashic opposition to the worship of idols was directed toward external, plastic representation of the divinity, but Maimonides redi-

---

[1] Bavli Yoma 69b.

rected it toward mental representation; henceforth, it would be necessary to shatter the internal idol. But that redirection toward the inner mental image also brought the struggle into the inner reaches of the Jewish community.

This profound shift in the nature of the problem of idolatry had significant implications for the understanding of religious language and the way in which the divinity was represented. Jewish tradition drew a distinction between picture and word. Visual representations of God, such as statues and pictures, were forbidden acts of idolatry, but verbal representations were permitted. It was forbidden to draw or sculpt God's hand, but the Bible refers often to God's great, outstretched hand. The liturgical poem *An'im Zemirot* ("I will chant sweet hymns"), sung in many synagogues at the end of Sabbath morning prayers, speaks of the moist ringlets that adorn God's head: "With sparkling dew His head is covered, His locks with drops of the night."[2] Despite this linguistic license, no Jewish artist within any stream of Judaism would ever dare to depict this image on the ceiling of a synagogue, as Michelangelo did in the Sistine Chapel. But if Maimonides is correct in arguing that the problem of idolatry includes one's internal, mental image of God, the distinction between permissible verbal representation and forbidden visual representation collapses. A personified image of God is created not only by painting and sculpture but also by religious language. Moreover, the personified concept of the divinity is sustained by the very wording of Scripture, which is rife with personified images of God. On the face of it, the tradition itself, together with its sacred writings, foster the cardinal sin of imputing corporeality to God. Maimonides therefore devoted most of Part I of the *Guide* to clarifying the issue of religious language. The internal logic of his argument leads him to one of the most extraordinary positions to be found in the history of Jewish thought.

Once the issue of anthropomorphism is set at the center of the religious agenda, the first issue that must be dealt with is the religious language of Scripture itself. The *Guide*, accordingly, is primarily an exegetical book that administers therapy to religious language. It is not a systematic theological or philosophical work; it is, rather, interpretive, as Maimonides declares in the opening sentence of its introduction: "The first purpose of this Treatise is to explain the meanings of certain terms occurring in books

[2] As translated in *The Authorised Daily Prayer Book of the United Hebrew Congregations of the Commonwealth, Centenary Edition* (London, 1998), p. 422.

of prophecy" (Pines, p. 5). The exegetical key to liberation from perplexity is the recognition that the revealed layer of biblical language is grounded on the understanding that in any language, a single term may have multiple, diverse meanings. The Hebrew word *ayin*, for example, can denote either "eye" (the organ of sight), or a fountain. It is an equivocal word, that is, one that connotes two entirely different objects. This is even more so when it comes to expressions used metaphorically. When a person is said to have "a big heart," it is not his cardiac dimensions that are being literally referred to; the term is a metaphorical picture of his generosity, of his capacity to give. The word "big" in this context is a figure of speech; it has a literal meaning that denotes size and a metaphorical meaning. The inability to distinguish between literal and metaphorical meaning is the first factor accounting for the failure to understand biblical language.

The confounding of literal and metaphorical meaning is a specter that especially haunts religious terminology pertaining to God. That is attributable to a phenomenon that serves as Maimonides' great exegetical key: in ordinary language, or in parts of the Bible that do not refer to God, we readily distinguish between a metaphorical term and a literal term. We know, for example, that the expression "the land shall not vomit you out" (Lev. 18, 28) is metaphorical, for there is no other way to understand the land's digestive problems. It is analogous to asking "when will the wooly clouds be shorn?" Similarly, we do not take the commandment "you shall circumcise the foreskin of your hearts" (Deut. 10, 16) as requiring open heart surgery, for we understand the phrase "foreskin of your hearts" as a figure of speech. We are able to draw these distinctions—indeed, to regard them as self-evident—because of the numerous things we know about lands and hearts other than what the Bible says about them. For the same reason, we understand that "all the trees of the field shall clap their hands" (Is. 55, 12) likewise is a metaphor.

But things become much more complicated when terms refer to God. If all we know about God is what the Bible says about Him, we have no basis for distinguishing between literal and metaphorical expressions. How can we tell whether the expression "the hand of God" is to be understood literally or as a metaphor for power? Drawing that sort of distinction requires some prior metaphysical knowledge regarding God independent of Scripture. One who claims that everything he knows about God is inferred exclusively from Scripture as he reads it will often err in how he understands the verse he is reading. Without the metaphysical understanding that God cannot be material, because all material is finite and perishable, we cannot understand the biblical language itself. Accordingly, metaphysics is no threat to faith; it is a precondition to interpreting the language of faith in the most fundamental way.

Various chapters in Part I of the *Guide* are devoted to explaining biblical terms pertaining to God. In these chapters, Maimonides shows that seemingly anthropomorphic expressions, when applied to God, are only metaphors; to do so, he relies heavily on the capacity to recognize self-evident distinctions. An outstanding example is provided by verbs that appear to describe God's movement within an expanse or His coming to rest. The Torah depicts God as ascending, descending, seated, or standing. Believing God not to be a corpus that occupies physical space or moves through it, Maimonides treats these expressions as metaphors. But before arguing that a particular expression applied to God is a metaphor, Maimonides makes it clear that though the verb is not invariably used in Scripture as a metaphor, there are places where its metaphorical nature is readily identifiable. The verb "stand," for example, denotes the positioning of a corpus within an expanse, but in biblical terminology, it also denotes abstract endurance and constancy—a figure of speech that the reader easily discerns, as in the verse "his justice stands forever" (Psalms 112, 3). It is clear to the reader that justice has no legs on which it is actually standing; "stands" is a figure of speech connoting stability and constancy. Once the reader recognizes the expression as a metaphor, he can expand its metaphorical usage to encompass every place in which it refers to God. That is true as well of all other verbs indicating movement that are used as figures of speech in biblical language.

Another example relates to verbs of seeing. The Bible attributes sight to God and uses such verbs as "looked" (*hibbit*), "envisioned," (*hazah*), and "saw" (*ra'ah*). God looks and sees men's deeds; conversely, people see God or parts of Him. To attribute to God the senses of sight and sound and the associated organs is anthropomorphism of the first order, as is the claim that God can be seen, based on the premise that He has a form and surface that can be taken in by the human eye. Maimonides interprets these terms, when used in the context of religious language, as referring to apprehension or understanding rather than to sensory perception. Even in these instances, he first shows that verbs of seeing are figures of speech, both in quotidian language and in biblical language, used to connote mental processes of understanding, and that it is easy to identify their metaphorical use (or, as one might say in English too, "to *see* that they are being used metaphorically"). The verse in Ecclesiastes (1:16) that states "my heart has seen much wisdom and learning" offers a clear example of metaphorical usage—the "seeing" connotes mental understanding.[3] Accordingly, whenever terminology of seeing is used in religious language, it should be taken to connote understanding and apprehension, not actual seeing. The same may be said of verbs associated with utterance and speech, which the Bible likewise attributes to God. God creates the world through speech, and he is said to reveal himself through linguistic acts associated with the verbs "said" (*amar*) and "spoke" (*dibber*). Attributing speech to God likewise appears to be severe personification, and Maimonides took these verbs metaphorically as well. Maimonides will not determine that a given term is metaphorical without showing that the term has a metaphorical meaning in Scripture generally. He therefore demonstrates that in biblical Hebrew, "saying" (*amirah*) and "speaking" (*dibbur*) sometimes connote determination or will, as in "Do you mean [lit., "say," *omer*] to kill me" (Ex. 2:14) and sometimes connote mental apprehension, as in "So I decided [lit., "I said to myself," *amarti ani be-libbi*]" (Eccl. 3:18). When saying and speaking are attributed to God, then, the terms should be understood in an abstract, intellectual sense.

Examination of how verbs of speech and utterance are used reveals another important aspect of the *Guide*. Maimonides devotes only a single chapter (I:65) to the use of those verbs in religious language, and does not systematically go through all of their biblical usages. Nevertheless, he provides the perplexed individual the means by which he can resolve his perplexity whenever he encounters the terms in the Bible. We should make no mistake: devoting only one chapter to the matter says nothing about the force and implications of the claim Maimonides is making. In a text that from the outset declared itself limited to chapter headings, a single aside can effect a radical change in how the Jewish tradition is understood.

In fact, this one chapter has far-reaching implications in two aspects of the history of Jewish thought, namely, creation and revelation. Once the reader learns that speech cannot be attributed to God, he has no choice but to reinterpret the meaning of prophecy. Revelation cannot be a direct linguistic event in which God issues directives to the prophet by addressing

---

[3] The English versions so translate it. The King James reads, "my heart had great experience of wisdom and knowledge"; NJPS reads, "my mind has zealously absorbed wisdom and learning."

him in human language, for God Himself is not a linguistic being. The same may be said of creation, which Scripture, taken literally, treats as a linguistic event in which God generates the world through utterance. Influenced by this linguistic concept of creation, the Jewish tradition developed an idea that emphasized the creative power to be found within language. That tradition rests primarily on the ancient work known as *Sefer Yezirah*, which describes God as having created the world through the power of the twenty-two letters of the Hebrew alphabet, the building blocks of creation. On Maimonides' reading, the verse "God said, 'Let there be light'" (Gen. 1:3) does not connote speech; the verse tells only that the light was created by the force of God's will; nothing more. This interpretive move eliminates the basis for an important and venerable tradition of Jewish linguistic theology.

If Maimonides is correct, and terms referring to sight, movement, and speech, along with other personifying terms, are to be understood as metaphorical abstractions, the question arises why the Bible does not refer more directly and immediately to the more abstract meaning. To take one example, the religious experience of the elders at Sinai is described as follows: "And they saw the God of Israel: under His feet there was the likeness of a pavement of sapphire" (Ex. 24:10). If the reference to seeing in this verse actually connotes understanding, why doesn't the verse say something like "And the elders understood" or "And the elders apprehended God"? By its use of the verb to see, the verse incurs the risk of fostering the extremely serious error of attributing form to God, and it does so even more by mentioning God's feet, further contributing to a corporeal reading of the verse. At first reading, the biblical language itself, by its use of metaphor rather than more direct and abstract wording, seems to foster the personified image. Maimonides accounts for this, and explains the Bible's choice of words, by noting that the Bible is directed at an audience comprising both the masses and the educated. The masses are unable to internalize the existence of an abstract reality. "The Torah speaks in human language," thereby using concrete, sensory images to reinforce for the masses the idea that God exists. Once the existence of God is secure in the eyes of the masses, it is possible, albeit with care, to advance to a more exalted concept of God and divest it of its anthropomorphic elements. Abstract terminology in the biblical text itself, however, could promote total apostasy. The educated person possesses metaphysical knowledge independent of the divinity, so he is equipped to identify the hidden, metaphorical meaning of the expression and to interpret the verses correctly, in a manner consistent with true metaphysical concepts.

That language is not entirely transparent, and that there is no one-to-one correspondence between signifier and signified can bring about fateful errors. If one takes a metaphor literally, he internalizes a personified image of God, something worse than idolatry. At the same time, this quality of language provides vast political benefits, for it allows two audiences—the masses and the educated elite—to be addressed simultaneously. That is so not only with respect to specific expressions in biblical language but also with respect to entire literary units that present extensive parables. The first chapter of Job, for example, which describes the conversation between God and Satan in the heavenly assembly and Satan's actions on earth, are merely a parable, and Maimonides explains its inner meaning through chapter headings only. So, too, the account of Eve's seduction by the serpent and the eating of the forbidden fruit in the Garden. Parable, like metaphor, allows for two audiences to be addressed: the masses, to whom the external meaning says something fitting and useful, and the educated, who come to understand the inner meaning of the parable.

"For You, Silence Is Praise"

The *Guide*'s first forty-nine chapters offer a reinterpretation of the manifest layer of the Bible's religious language. For the most part they are devoted, chapter by chapter, to creating a dictionary that the perplexed person can use to gain an understanding of the inner structure of biblical language. In the ensuing fifteen chapters, Maimonides presents a more profound criticism of religious language as a means for representing the divinity. These chapters offer us one of the pinnacles of Maimonides' religious thought. They anticipate much of modern philosophy's critique of language, and they have far-reaching implications for the understanding of Maimonides' positions in general. In those chapters, the criticism of anthropomorphism is redirected from sensory language to conceptual language. At the conclusion of this critical journey, the perplexed reader will come to understand that language in general is limited when it sets out to describe the divinity and that silence is the apogee of the religious attitude toward God. As the maxim states, "For You, silence is praise" (*Psalm* 65, 2).

A few examples will help us gain a full understanding of this intellectual journey. In part I of the *Guide*, the reader learned that a term such as "God saw" means "God knew." Similarly, he internalized the idea that when God is said to be seated, what is being attributed to him is stable, unchanging existence. These chapters taught him that these readings are not forced or artificial because "sitting" can connote existence in other contexts as well such as the verse "Judah shall endure [lit, "shall be seated," *teishev*] forever" (Joel 1: 20). Awareness of the dual meaning of terms helps him purge biblical language of its anthropomorphized character, moving thereby from sensory expressions to conceptual or abstract expressions. That move, however, is only the first step in overcoming the pitfalls of language. The ensuing chapters of the *Guide* will teach us that even the conceptual sense of language at which he has arrived is misleading and limited. Just as we cannot say that God "sees," neither can we say that God "knows"; and just as we cannot say that God "sits," neither can we say that God "is present" or "exists."

Two key arguments underlie the critique of applying positive attributes—knowledge, existence, unity, or eternity, for example—within religious language. One is tied to the basic structure of the sentence, comprising subject and predicate. The statement "Reuben exists" assumes some entity called "Reuben" is possessed of the attribute of existence. Within religious language, that structure impairs God's unity and the relationship between Him and His attributes. Existence is not an accident encountered by God, a quality superimposed on Him; it is, rather, analytic to His essence. Attributes such as "knowing," "one," or "eternal" suffer from the same problem, inherent in the structure of language. They attribute internal multiplicity to God, treating Him as an entity encompassing numerous attributes, thereby impairing His simple and absolute unity. The fundamental rejection of conventional sentence structure as a means suitable for characterizing God follows from the fact that God's relationship with His attributes is one of necessity. Accordingly, one who reads "The Lord our God, the Lord is One" must understand well that the deep meaning of God's unity makes it impossible, in effect, for him to say "the Lord is One." Human language, then, is limited not only because it tends to use sensory terminology for the sake of the masses but also by its very structure; in Maimonides' words: "All passages that you find in the Scriptures in which it is predicated of Him, may He be exalted, that He is *the First and the Last*

are analogous to those in which it is predicated of Him that He has an eye
or an ear. . . . All these words as applied to Him are *according to the language of the sons of man*. Similarly, when we say *one*, the meaning is that He
has no equal and not that the notion of oneness attaches to His essence"
(I:57; Pines, p. 133). The limited and misleading "language of the sons of
man" considered in this paragraph is not the language of the masses, which
is incapable of attaining conceptual understanding, but human language
in general. That language is defective in the most fundamental structure of
its sentences, made up of subject and predicate. Language in general, not
only sensory language, is a limited and misleading medium through which
to come to know the divinity.

The second, more pointed argument related to the limitations of language is tied to the way in which adjectives—that is, descriptions of attributes—function and are understood in human language. We understand
an adjective such as "wise" or "good" because it applies to a number of
people. The adjective allows us to include a group of individuals within a
common category. The attribute "exists" (or the adjective "extant") applies,
for example, to tables, to people, to insects, and to the sun. All of these
things exist. To attribute adjectives to the divinity, therefore, impairs not
only the pure concept of unity but also the sublimity of God and his absolute otherness from the world. The adjective serves, in effect, as a linguistic
bridge between God and the world, incorporating God and the world
within a shared category. For example, we understand the existence of God
because we analogize it to the existence of some other individual within
the universe, and we understand God's goodness because we identify it
with the goodness of people. But if God differs in some absolute sense
from the world, adjectives cannot be predicated to Him. His existence
differs from that of any other being because it is necessary, not merely
possible; God's precedence in time differs from anything's precedence in
time to anything else, because God is not situated on the axis of time at all.

The inclusive nature of the attribute/adjective transforms religious language into a medium that ignores God's transcendence from the world.
Maimonides therefore takes the view that one can only negate the association of certain attributes with God; one can say, for example, that He is not
absent or that He is not multiple, but no positive attributes can be associated with Him. It should be emphasized that the negative attributes are
categorical negatives, that is, one may infer no positive attributes from
them. Ordinary negation differs logically from categorical negation in that

ordinary negation allows for the corresponding positive attribute—that is, the opposite of the attribute being negated—to be inferred. If a person is said not to be absent, it may be inferred that he is present. But if the number three is said not to be yellow, it cannot be inferred that it is green or red. In that sort of categorical negation, what is negated is the category of color with respect to numbers. The expression "God is not absent" does not allow for the inference that God is present, as it would in a case of ordinary negation. Categorical negation maintains that the category of absence or presence, as we know it, does not apply to God; the same is true of unity and multiplicity. Because there is no way to apply positive attributes to God, all that we know about his essence pertains to what He is not. A person who knows God advances through the sequence of negations and comes to know more and more that he does not know: "apprehension of Him consists in the inability to attain the ultimate term in apprehending Him" (I:59; Pines, p. 139).

To see positive attributes as a category that brings God and the world under a common rubric has interesting implications for Maimonides' analysis in these chapters of the names of God. Names such as *shekhinah* (Presence), *gevurah* (Might), *ribbono shel olam* (Master of the World), *adonai* (My Lord), *elohim* (God), or *ha-raḥaman* (the Merciful) are, in effect, shared qualities, which attain their meanings through the inclusion of a group of individuals under a single category. The names connote a characteristic found among men and then ascribed to God. Like the positive attributes, the names are a misleading and limited medium for relating to God. And so, for example, the name *adonai* is derived from a concept of lordship shared by God and men, and the name *shaddai* is derived, according to Maimonides, from the compound *yesh bo dai* (there is enough within Him), indicating that God is sufficient unto Himself and is not dependent on anything external to Him.

The only divine name that is not shared between men and God is the Tetragrammaton, *Y-H-W-H*. The unique quality of that name lies in its not being an attribute or adjective; it serves, rather, as the proper name of God. That the name is a proper name is evident linguistically in the fact that it alone among the names cannot take the definite article. The ability to take the definite article is what distinguishes an adjective from a proper name, and all of the other divine names can take the definite article; Scripture refers, for example to *ha-elohim* (the God). Not so the Tetragrammaton, for it is God's proper name, alluding to Him directly rather than identifying Him by means of a description. (Consider, for example, the Hebrew proper name Yoram. In contemporary daily Hebrew, it has taken on the adjectival meaning of a conformist, a straight-laced person. If one says "the *yoram* has entered the room," the word is being used adjectivally, and it can take the definite article. But if Yoram, the person so named, entered the room, the definite article could not be used.) The greatness of the Tetragrammaton is not tied to the supposed magical powers attributed to it, for Maimonides sharply rejected any association of magical powers with names. Its uniqueness as a name flows from the utterly distinct role it plays as the proper name of the Deity. The Tetragrammaton (whose grammatical root is the verb "to be") incorporates a component of existence whose meaning is tied to the fact that God's existence is necessary, but when that attribute is transformed into a name, existence comes to be identified with God's essence rather than as an attribute of His. That sort of identification cannot take place within a normal sentence, given its basic subject-predicate structure and because the attribute "exists" is shared by God and other things in the world.

Language's two limitations—its impairment of God's unity and its violation of His transcendence—are concisely formulated in the following statement in the *Guide*: "Know that when you make an affirmation ascribing another thing to Him, you become more remote from Him in two respects: one of them is that everything you affirm is a perfection only with reference to us, and the other is that He does not possess a thing other than His essence, which, as we have made clear, is identical with His perfections" (I:59; Pines, p. 139). Because language is limited in how it is understood, and every linguistic expression attempting to describe God is fundamentally flawed, the learned person does not use symbols or allusions but simply imposes silence upon himself:

> The most apt phrase concerning this subject is the dictum occurring in the *Psalms, Silence is praise to Thee*, which interpreted signifies: silence with regard to You is praise. This is a most perfectly put phrase regarding this matter. For of whatever we say intending to magnify and exalt, on the one hand we find that it can have some application to Him, may he be exalted, and on the other we perceive in it some deficiency. Accordingly, silence and limiting oneself to the apprehensions of the intellects are more appropriate—just as the perfect ones have enjoined when they said: *Commune with your own heart upon your bed, and be still, Selah*. (I:59; Pines, pp. 139–140)

The critique of religious language thus leads to a need to liberate oneself from it as a medium for properly representing God.

Silence is the pinnacle of the religious attitude; it is the highest expression of the unity and loftiness of God on the one hand and of the limitations of human cognition on the other. Still, silence cannot be imposed on the entire community of believers, for believers require some form of religious language as a concrete anchor in their lives. The liturgy contains attributes, such as "the great, mighty, and awesome God." These adjectives were put in place by the Sages, because they understood the need for some basic description—even if erroneous—of God. But religious language such as this must be kept to the minimum that is necessary. Every addition of attributes represents an affront to God's greatness and entails a failed effort to epitomize what does not lend itself to being epitomized and described. Maimonides therefore sharply disparages liturgical poetry, seeing them as excessive linguistic expansions that diminish God's stature the more they sing His praises:

> This kind of license is frequently taken by poets and preachers or such as think that what they speak is poetry, so that the utterances of some of them constitute an absolute denial of faith, while other utterances contain such rubbish and such perverse imaginings as to make men laugh when they hear them, on account of the nature of these utterances, and to make them weep when they consider that these utterances are applied to God, may He be magnified and glorified. . . . It also behooves you to consider and say that in view of the fact that *speaking ill* and *defamation* are acts of great disobedience, how much all the more so is the loosening of the tongue with regard to God, may He be exalted, and the predicating of Him qualificative attributions above which He is exalted. But I shall not say that this is an act of disobedience, but rather that it constitutes *unintended obloquy and vituperation* on the part of the multitude who listen to these utterances and on the part of the ignoramus who pronounces them. (I:59; Pines, pp. 141–142)

The Skeptical Reading and the Mystical Reading

Ludwig Wittgenstein's *Tractatus Logico-Philosophicus*, a foundational work of modern philosophy of language, concludes with the need to be silent about matters that cannot be talked about: "Whereof one cannot speak, thereof one must be silent." That demand for silence is at the base of the following critical insight: Because language is the medium through which we shape our knowledge of the world, recognizing the limits on language is tantamount, in effect, to recognizing the limits to our cognition of the world. Maimonides' doctrine of negative attributes anticipates that insight insofar as it pertains to religious language, effectively establishing the impossibility of religious cognition given the built-in limitations of language. This understanding of the critical role of philosophy, as a sort of discourse whose goal is to define the limits of cognition, gave rise to one of the principal ways in which the esoteric meaning of the *Guide* has been understood. This understanding has been advanced by Shlomo Pines, one of the greatest modern students of Maimonides. On this approach, the work means to present a fundamentally skeptical view of the possibility of gaining metaphysical knowledge of God.

The skeptical view, of course, cuts squarely against the traditional position of the believer, who supposes he is able to formulate certain principles of faith with respect to God and the world. Moreover, it profoundly challenges the philosophical certainties on which Maimonides' own world would seem to be based. Recall that when we considered *Mishneh Torah* and the *Commentary on the Mishnah*, we found a solid expression of the Aristotelian notion that man attained his highest perfection by actualizing his intellectual potential and attaining, to the extent of his ability, awareness of the universe and of God. The immortality of the soul depends, among other things, on this sort of cognitive process, in which man proves the existence of God and recognizes the reality flowing from Him. But if the critique of religious language is taken seriously, then a proof of God's existence that concludes with the statement "God exists" lacks any meaning whatsoever. God cannot be known in any positive way, and so the immortality of the soul is likewise impossible. Accordingly, human perfection must be situated in some context other than knowledge of God, for in this critical view of things, that knowledge includes only what cannot be known.

At this stage of the critical discussion of the limits on language, a different possibility opens up: the mystical reading of the *Guide*. The difference between the skeptical reading and the mystical depends on the significance of the silence that the philosopher arrives at after internalizing the inability to make any sort of statement about God. Is there some non-linguistic cognition of God? Or, to state it differently, do the limitations on language signify limits on cognition, leading us to turn to skepticism, or do they allow for some meta-linguistic cognition that cannot be formulated? It is only natural that we have forms of cognition that do not lend themselves to linguistic expression. For example, we can identify various tastes in beverages without being able to describe them. According to the mystical reading, the limits of language do not define the limits of cognition and experience. The silence is followed by a great illumination incapable of being formulated. Any attempt at verbal formulation of that illumination, that flash, will be misleading and may even impugn God's unity and loftiness. The critique of language thus leaves the philosopher with a pure experience that cannot be expressed. He made his way to that experience through the nullification of language, which leaves the field clear for intimate, meta-linguistic cognition.

It is important to note that this mystical illumination must make its way through the refiner's fire of philosophy, which plays a dual role in this mystical journey. As we know, various mystical traditions attempt to liberate man from the clutches of earthly images and impulses and, primarily, to purge and empty his human consciousness. It is that process that ultimately allows for mystical illumination. Different mystical strains achieve that emptiness in different ways, some of them ecstatic. Among the methods that have been used to dissolve the self and its embodied consciousness have been ceaseless dancing and movement, repetition of mantras, and breathing exercises. In the mysticism of the doctrine of negative attributes, the sought-for emptiness is attained through an exhausting philosophical process whose purpose is to negate language. At the end of the process, consciousness is emptied of all content, in view of the limitations on language indicated by philosophic endeavor.

But philosophy has a further role in the mystical experience, going beyond the voiding of consciousness. The mystical experience follows the journey through the negation of positive attributes, and that ensures that the object of the experience will not be illusory or personified. Without that rigorous process preceding it, the usual mystical experience seizes on illusory objects that have no ties to reality. Accordingly, the purity of the experience depends on the precise philosophical regimen that prepares the way for it. Silence redirects consciousness from language to experience.

The mystical reading of the *Guide* has a footing in the philosophical atmosphere in which Maimonides worked, and it may well be that the treatise was so read in his immediate environs. His son Abraham was closely tied to mystical traditions of Sufi Islam, and he may have drawn those inclinations from an interpretation of his father's writings. These two readings—the skeptical and the mystical—are not to be found in Maimonides' earlier writings. The skeptical position appears only in the *Guide*, and none of Maimonides' medieval interpreters espoused that view. A similar position was attributed to al- Farabi, and Samuel Ibn Tibbon devoted his commentary on Ecclesiastes to a refutation of skepticism, which calls into question the philosophical basis for human existence. Regardless of whether there is any truth to the interpretation of the *Guide* suggested by Shlomo Pines, the work is certainly much less Aristotelian than Maimonides' halakhic works. The latter, as we have seen, interpreted the *halakhah* and its meaning in the broad context of an Aristotelian concept of man and his ability to know God. According to Pines' interpretation, Maimonides over the years became less committed to his earlier philosophical beliefs, and by the time he wrote the *Guide*, he had come to adopt a critical stance toward the philosophical ethos. As we shall see, it is precisely in his most clearly philosophical work that this turn in his thinking led him to formulate the direction of human life in terms much closer to the conventional halakhic ethos.

Let us return to the skeptical reading. According to this reading there is more to the doctrine of negative attributes than its critical perspective. It has a further key component: the redirection of man toward the world once he has come to understand that he cannot attain understanding. The key to understanding this step can be found in Chapter 54 of Part I of the *Guide*, which interprets Moses' request— mentioned in chapter 33 of the book of Exodus— to see God's face and God's reply that while His face cannot be seen, He will reveal His back to Moses. Maimonides of course rejected any literal, visual reading of the revelation. According to Maimonides' dictionary, Moses' request to see God should be taken as his yearning to know God's essence, just as a man knows the face of his friend. That desire is foreclosed to him, just as it is foreclosed to every man, as a physical and linguistic creature. All that can be known of God is His back, which Maimonides understands to mean His actions rather than His essence. On this interpretation, the term "back" connotes that which is brought about by someone: the causal order of nature is the only sign of God that we possess, and through it, one can attain limited cognition of the divine. Moses' achievement was not in knowing God's essence, which cannot be known; but in knowing the Universe in its entirety. God responds to

Moses' request by saying "I will make all My goodness pass before thee" (Ex. 33:19), which Maimonides interprets as follows:

> This dictum—*All my goodness*—alludes to the display to him of all existing things of which it is said: *And God saw every thing that He had made, and, behold, it was very good.* By their display, I mean that he will apprehend their nature and the way they are mutually connected so that he will know how He governs them in general and in detail. This notion is indicated when it says: *He is trusted in all My house*; that is, he has grasped the existence of all My world with a true and firmly established understanding. For the opinions that are not correct are not firmly established. Accordingly, the apprehension of these actions is an apprehension of His attributes, may He be exalted, with respect to which He is known. (I:54; Pines, p. 124)

Man, who cannot know God's essence, looks to the world, which he can understand and know. By understanding God's actions in the world, he comes to attribute to God the qualities that would characterize a person performing the same actions. For example, as he considers the delicate care exercised by nature in forming a mammal's fetus and the fetus's capacity to survive and grow, he comes to attribute to God the characteristic of compassion—the quality that would lead a human being to act in that way. When he sees things that cause harm to people, he attributes anger and vengeance to God, for it is those characteristics that cause human beings to act in that way. But when those qualities are attributed to God, there must be a clear recognition that God himself does not act out of internal passions. As Maimonides says, "Similarly, all [His] actions are such as resemble the actions proceeding from the Adamites on account of passions and aptitudes of the soul, but they by no means proceed from Him, may He be exalted, on account of a notion superadded to His essence" (I:54; Pines, p. 126).

When he internalizes the limitations on religious cognition and comes to see the natural order as the sole medium through which the characteristics of God's actions can be known, the philosopher is led to take a turn toward the world. Human perfection is not to be found in a life of speculation, in which man actualizes his potential essence. That sort of perfection is foreclosed to him. What is left once he realizes his limitations is the area of activity in which he imitates God through his activities in the world, as Maimonides says: "For the utmost virtue of man is to become like unto Him, may He be exalted, as far as he is able; which means that we should make our actions like unto His, as the Sages made clear when interpreting the verse, Ye shall be holy. They said: He is gracious, so be you also gracious; He is merciful, so be you also merciful" (I:54; Pines, p. 128). What began as a critique of language and of metaphysical cognition concludes as a turn toward society and the exercise of moral and political responsibility.

Maimonides grew up in a society in which the relationship between the truth-loving philosopher and the broader society was the focus of a clash between the ways in which Greek tradition was understood in different streams of Arab philosophy. In his Allegory of the Cave, set out in the *Republic*, Plato depicts the philosopher as one able to extricate himself, by force of his intellect, from the cave to which other human beings are relegated. The people in the cave are those who are trapped within their transitory and variable sense impressions, which they believe to be the sum and substance of the Universe. In Plato's allegory, they face the cave's wall and see only the shadows cast by the light outside the cave, thinking all of existence to be exhausted by them. The philosopher, who makes his way to the truth, manages to turn around, face the sun, and see reality as it truly is, beyond transitory sense impressions. But even though he extricates himself from the murkiness of the cave, he returns to it because he feels a duty to the members of his community who remain there. Plato formulates the philosopher's social and political responsibility in terms of a duty—he must return to the cave to direct society in accord with the enlightenment he was privileged to attain. That return to darkness pains him, for it entails abandoning the narcissistic delights of the pure life of the intellect, and his doing so is an act of great altruism.

The philosopher's return to society is presented differently in al-Farabi's writings, which depict the return as something more than the discharge of a burdensome moral duty. The closer a person comes to perfection, the greater the bounty within his soul and emanating from it. The philosopher's return to the community, therefore, entails not only responsibility but also an overflowing of his bounty.

However they view his return to society, both of these positions call for the philosopher to be involved in the political life of the community. A different, more fatalistic position developed during the Middle Ages, however, identified with the philosopher Ibn Bājja. According to Ibn Bājja, the philosopher must do everything he can to avoid excessive involvement with society. Leaving the cave frees him from the violent and superficial conditions of political life in all its destructiveness and corruption. His cruel awakening teaches him that there is no real way to improve society and, even worse, that he will corrupt his own soul through fruitless efforts to change his surroundings. The philosopher's life is a spiritual journey that rescues him from the bonds of society and leads him to splendid isolation.

As one who was committed to *halakhah* and involved in the leadership of Egyptian Jewry, Maimonides rejected Ibn Bājja's position. *Mishneh Torah* is an impressive statement of a leader's commitment and responsibility to his community. In Platonic terms, therefore, Maimonides can be described as a man of action. Conscious of his political and moral duty, he withdrew from the blissful seclusion of the philosopher. Nevertheless, the critical and skeptical reading of this chapter links the turn back to the community not only to a sense of duty but also to the essence of the philosophical act.

We can gain a better understanding of this internal linkage by examining a different version of the Allegory of the Cave. Here, when the philosopher turns his head toward the sun, he realizes that he cannot bear its dazzling light, which brings about blindness and, one might say, silence. He returns to the cave because all he can know about the sun itself is based on the light it spreads and the shadows it casts. He does not return, as Plato would have it, out of a sense of responsibility that summons him to give up his life of pure and redemptive contemplation. Rather, his contemplation itself leads him back to the world, for he comes to understand that he lacks the ability to consider God's essence and can deal only with His world. It is the ideal of the contemplative life itself that leads the philosopher to action.

The final chapter of the *Guide* recounts the philosopher's complex spiritual journey out of the world and back to it. At the beginning of the chapter, the Aristotelian philosophical position regarding the perfection of man is formulated in particularly sharp terms. After describing man's moral perfection, Maimonides turns to a perfection that is still higher, speculative perfection:

> [T]he true human perfection . . . consists in the acquisition of the rational
> virtues—I refer to the conception of intelligibles, which teach true opinions
> concerning the divine things. This is in true reality the ultimate end; this is

> what gives the individual true perfection, a perfection belonging to him
> alone; and it gives him permanent perdurance; through it man is man.
> (III:54; Pines, p. 635)

Assiduous fulfillment of the *halakhah* is merely preparation for attaining a
higher perfection: "all the actions prescribed by the Law—I refer to the
various species of worship and also the moral habits that are useful to all
people in their mutual dealings—that all this is not to be compared with
this ultimate end and does not equal it, being but preparations made for
this ultimate end" (III:54; Pines, p. 636). This wording recalls Maimonides' positions in his halakhic writings—the *Commentary on the Mishnah*
and *Mishneh Torah*—regarding human perfection and the role of *halakhah*
as a means for attaining it.

Had the *Guide* ended there, it would have been entirely consistent
with the Aristotelian tendencies of Maimonides' halakhic works. The
chapter continues, however, with an elaborate interpretation of two verses
in Jeremiah, through which Maimonides expresses the critical turn in his
later thought. Jeremiah declares: "Thus saith the Lord: Let not the wise
man glory in his wisdom, neither let the mighty man glory in his might,
let not the rich man glory in his riches; but let him that glorieth glory in
this, that he understandeth and knoweth me, that I am the Lord who
exercise loving-kindness, righteousness, and judgment in the earth, for in
these things I delight, saith the Lord" (Jer. 9:22–23). The verses in Jeremiah set the knowledge of God as the great human accomplishment.
Maimonides points out, however, that the verses conclude not with metaphysical knowledge—for example, "that he understandeth and knoweth
Me that I am one, eternal and omniscient"—but with the idea that God
exercises loving-kindness, righteousness, and judgment. Maimonides
links the emphasis on these aspects of the knowledge of God to the doctrine of active attributes. In the ensuing paragraph, he refers back to
Chapter 54 of Part I, which dealt with God's revelation to Moses. He
there described Moses' recognition of the limits on metaphysical apprehension, following which there were revealed to him only the attributes
of God's actions in the world:

> But he says that one should glory in the apprehension of Myself and in the
> knowledge of My attributes, by which He means His actions, as we have
> made clear with reference to its dictum: *Show me now thy ways, and so on.* In

this *verse* he makes it clear to us that those actions that ought to be known and imitated are *loving-kindness, judgment, righteousness*. . . . Thus the end that he sets forth in this *verse* may be stated as follows: It is clear that the perfection of man that may truly be gloried in is the one acquired by him who has achieved, in a measure corresponding to his capacity, apprehension of Him, may He be exalted, and who knows His providence extending over all His creatures as manifested in the act of bringing them into being and in their governance as it is. The way of life of such an individual, after he has achieved this apprehension, will always have in view *loving-kindness, righteousness, and judgment*, through assimilation to His actions, may He be exalted, just as we have explained several times in this Treatise. (III:54; Pines, pp. 637–638)

Knowledge of God, then, is knowledge of His actions on earth. The man who imitates God through acts of loving-kindness, righteousness, and judgment is the man who knows God to the extent of human ability.

By concluding the *Guide* with knowledge of God's loving-kindness, righteousness, and judgment and with the duty to imitate His ways, Maimonides teaches that at the end of the philosophical journey, a man returns to active perfection directed toward the world. This understanding of Maimonides' position undermines the distinction sometimes drawn between Maimonides, the halakhist of *Mishneh Torah*, and Maimonides, the philosopher of the *Guide*. In *Mishneh Torah*, Maimonides takes the view that practical *halakhah* is but a means to the philosophical ideal of apprehension and contemplation. But in the *Guide*—presumably the vehicle in which Maimonides the philosopher is to express himself—he raises the idea of the limitations on man's capacity for metaphysical apprehension and shows how speculation leads man to the practical halakhic ideal of loving-kindness, righteousness, and judgment.

This transition from *Mishneh Torah* to the *Guide* entails a far-reaching alteration in how one is to view the destiny of man and his relationship to the world. One could well attribute the change in emphasis to the development of Maimonides' thinking as his critique of religious language led him to adopt a skeptical attitude toward philosophy's speculative ideal. It could be as well that such a view of religious language is accompanied by growing skepticism that he had about the capacity of reason to resolve crucial metaphysical questions. In one moving statement in his medical writings written after he completed the *Guide*, Maimonides describes the limits and problems of medical knowledge and gives a personal expression of his growing doubts in all fields of inquiry:

> However, do not dear reader, think that this [observation] applies only to medicine, for if you delve into natural and religious sciences you will find the same. For the more proficient and erudite a person is in a given discipline and the more he delves into it, the more doubts he has; and [many] questions are difficult for him and he delves more into the subject but he cannot provide answers. On the other hand, a person lacking in knowledge finds every difficulty easy to explain. (Rosner, ed., *Treatise on Asthma*, pp. 113–114)

Even given that progression, however, we need not see *Mishneh Torah* and the *Guide* as posing an unresolved conflict. Maimonides's oeuvre overall presents the various stages that are necessary and appropriate in a person's spiritual biography—a spiritual biography that Maimonides himself experienced. At the first stage, the life of action is preparation for realizing human perfection as a creature endowed with the ability to know, and the desire to know is expressed as a burning love for God. At the second stage, after a person has attained the level of cognition that would appear to allow him to escape the narrow confines of material human existence, it is that cognition itself that returns him to the world, for he comes to understand that knowledge, when all is said and done, is simply an understanding of the limits of knowledge. Philosophy has taught him that humans lack the ability to know God's essence and are able to know only His actions and His world. He therefore returns to the world as one who acts in imitation of God's actions in the world.

This intellectual journey out of and back to the world never ends, and a person oscillates along its path all his life. That is the meaning of Jacob's dream, which symbolizes that movement. At Beth-El, Jacob dreams of a ladder planted on the ground with its top reaching the heavens; angels of God ascend and descend on it. Maimonides took "angel" to be an equivocal word that also connoted a prophet (for a prophet, like an angel, is a messenger), and he took the dream to symbolize the spiritual life of a prophet, who moves beyond the world and then back into it. Ascending the ladder symbolizes the prophet's ever-higher degrees of apprehension; "Everyone who ascends does so climbing up this ladder, so that he necessarily apprehends Him who is upon it" (I:15; Pines, p. 41). Descending the ladder is described as follows: "How well put is the phrase *ascending and descending*, in which *ascent* comes before *descent*. For after the *ascent* and the attaining of certain rungs of the ladder that may be known comes the descent with whatever decree the prophet has been informed of—with a view to governing and teaching the people of the earth. . . . it is on this account that this is called *descent*" (ibid.). The return to engagement in the affairs of the world follows the ascent through the rungs of knowledge. The skeptical reading of the *Guide* teaches us that this return does not obligate one to give up the rewarding delights of cognition, nor does it come from any overflowing excess of bounty that the philosopher dispatches down-ward, as Maimonides himself suggests at some points. It follows, rather, from the nature of knowledge itself and its critical role. At the top of the heavenward ladder, a person realizes that the only thing he is able to appre-hend is God's movement within reality, and in the wake of that realization, he returns to reality as an active participant.

CHAPTER EIGHT

The *Guide of the Perplexed*: Will or Wisdom?

The Creation of the World: The Conservative Reading and the Philosophical Reading

After the first seventy chapters of the *Guide*, which deal for the most part with biblical language and religious language in general, Maimonides turns to the work's great and central metaphysical issue: was the world created *ex nihilo* or has it existed for all eternity, like God? This portion of the work encompasses thirty-seven chapters, running from Chapter 71 of Part I to Chapter 31 of Part II. It is the most technical and philosophical part of the treatise, but it is important to note that the discussion is not meant to provide a systematic presentation of the philosophical positions in their own right. Like the first part of the treatise, this section was written to provide a response to the existential crisis of a perplexed person.

The question to which these chapters are devoted was the most fundamental one confronting Judaism in the Middle Ages. The position one took on whether the world was created *ex nihilo* or had existed for all eternity had implications for the basic concepts of Judaism overall, and the tension raised by this metaphysical problem is a presence throughout the remainder of the *Guide*. The various approaches to the problem of creation radiate into the four subjects dealt with in the second half of the *Guide*, and the present chapter will deal with them in the following order: (1) the concept of prophecy; (2) the problem of evil and the purpose of existence; (3) the idea of divine providence and knowledge; and (4) the reasons for the commandments. Beyond that, the various interpretations of Maimonides' position on the question of creation, a matter on which his interpreters have been divided from the Middle Ages to the present day, present us with the two remaining overall approaches to the *Guide* (in addition to the *skeptical* and *mystical* readings already discussed)—the *conservative* reading and the *philosophical* reading.

Why did the question of the cosmos's eternity or creation *ex nihilo* become the ultimate question for the perplexed of the time? Numerous other issues, going far beyond simple curiosity about the world's origins, were dependent on this one. The choice between alternative views of the world's beginning reflected, in effect, two opposing positions regarding the concept of the divinity. The traditional idea of creation assumes that at some specific time, the will to create the world arose within God, and by force of that will, the Universe was created *ex nihilo*. From the perspective of Aristotelian philosophy, however, attributing will to God impairs His perfection. That which is perfect lacks nothing and desires nothing, but the arousal of God's will assumes that God was lacking something—that is, imperfect. Similarly, the arousal of God's will implies a change in the divinity, the actualizing of a potential. A perfect entity does not change; it is stable and fixed, the unmoved mover. Moreover, if the world was created by force of God's will, it cannot be argued that God was the first cause in the chain of causation, for there would appear to have been some other factor that moved his will and thus acted as the Prime Mover. Aristotle therefore held the view that the world had existed from eternity and that God's relation to the world was not that of a creator to his creature—of, say, a carpenter to a chair he had fabricated. The world exists by reason of the very fact of God's existence and not in consequence of a volition on his part, just as a man's shadow follows from the very fact of his existence or the light radiated by the sun follows from the very existence of the sun. Accordingly, the world is eternal and it is dependent, in an ongoing way, on the existence of God.

The alternative position, which affirmed the creation of the world *ex nihilo*, is likewise driven by a notion of God's perfection, albeit an opposite one. If will cannot be attributed to God, He is denied the basic component of sovereignty and power. The omnipotent God has no limitations. He can create *ex nihilo* by force of His will, and His perfection is characterized by the free exercise of His will.

The struggle between creation and preexistence thus entails a clash between two different notions of perfection. In the Aristotelian version, God's perfection means that the existence of the world is causally derived from God's very presence, without any willful move. The situation may be compared to that of a leader who has no need to raise his voice, to issue commands, to punish, or to threaten in order to motivate his followers. He exercises his influence by the simple fact of his existence, through the inspiration provided by his presence. The view that affirms creation, in contrast, sees the expression of God's perfection in His total freedom to exercise His will to change existence however He wishes. Beyond the detailed technical efforts to prove or disprove one or the other position, one can see reflected within them fundamentally different approaches to power. One sees power as unchanging stability; the other sees it as free and constant movement. In the *Guide*, Maimonides formulated these alternative approaches to the concept of God in terms of wisdom and will: causal necessity reflects structured order and wisdom; freedom of will reflects the breach of order and structure and the creation of something *ex nihilo*.

Rejecting divine will bears not only on creation but also on all the basic concepts of the belief in the God of Abraham, Isaac, and Jacob. First and foremost, denial of divine will undermines the traditional concept of prophecy. Revelation, on the face of it, would also seem to be an act of divine will. God reveals Himself at a particular time by force of his will, exercising His authority over man by means of a sovereign command. Judaism can carry on without the concept of creation, but its very essence is revelation, and the Aristotelian notion of divinity would therefore seem to threaten its very existence. But it is not only revelation that is at stake in the clash between wisdom and will. Fundamental notions of biblical religion and Jewish tradition—providence, reward and punishment, and miracles, among others—depend on God having a personality possessed of will, motivated and active, continually responding and changing. The Aristotelian divinity, in contrast, is entirely self-absorbed, unalterable in its perfection, moving the Universe by its very existence. It comes as no surprise, therefore, that the question of preexistence or creation became the ultimate problem for Jewish belief in its encounter with Greco-Arab philosophy. Those who internalized the philosophical notion of preexistence faced a harsh existential decision with respect to their Jewish religious identity.

Maimonides analyzed three possibilities with respect to creation. The first, that of Aristotle, denied that there had been any event of creation *ex nihilo*. The world as we know it has existed forever; the universe is eternal. The second position, the traditional one of the Torah of Moses, holds that God created the world *ex nihilo* and that the world represents something novel. The third position, attributed to Plato, maintains that before the creation of the world there existed some primeval raw material, which God formed into the world. With regard to the concept of the divine, it is clear that a profound tension exists between Aristotle's view and that of the Torah; that is, between an eternal, preexisting world and a newly created one. The Platonic idea of creation, however, does not deny the willful act of God in imposing form on the primeval material. A faithful Jew would have no difficulty digesting that position, which might even embody the plain meaning of the biblical text. The serious challenge is posed by the Aristotelian position, and it therefore receives the most attention in the chapters of the *Guide* that deal with creation. And it is in those chapters that the tension between the conservative reading of the *Guide* and the radical reading becomes evident.

The conservative reading rests on Maimonides' express words in the chapters in which he considers creation, extending from Part I, Chapter 71 to Part II, Chapter 31. He there defends the idea of creation as a reasonable possibility, rejecting Aristotle's proof for a preexisting world. In his view, reason is limited in its ability to resolve this metaphysical question; neither creation nor preexistence can be proven or disproven. The limitations grow out of the fact that consideration of the world's origins requires analyzing matters as they now exist and attempting to project the results of that analysis into the distant past. That sort of thought experiment, however, can produce only conjecture. Assume, Maimonides suggests, that a child became orphaned of his mother while he was still an infant and was raised by a group of men on an isolated island, never seeing a woman, pregnancy, or birth. Were he to be told that man was born of a woman's womb, where the fetus was enclosed in a liquid container unable to breathe or discharge its secretions, he would reject the idea as absurd and assert with certainty that a human being could not survive in that sort of situation for nine months. The flaw in projecting from the present to the past lies in the premise, often simply incorrect, that things remain the same. This fundamental argument raised by Maimonides resembles, albeit in the opposite direction, the objection to induction raised by David Hume hundreds of years later. Our knowledge about the world originates in our direct experience with the present state of affairs. Hume questions our ability to draw inferences from the present about the future, a situation with which we have no experience. Why can we assume, for example, that because the sun rose this morning it will do so tomorrow morning as well? We believe it will because throughout our lives we have experienced the daily appearance of the sun. But there is a problem in this sort of induction, for the future itself is not something we have experienced. Our inferences about it might place us in the situation of the animal that has been fattened for slaughter: the good life it has enjoyed leads it to expect that life to continue as it lives into a ripe old age. Maimonides cites analogous limitations on our ability to draw inferences from our present experiences about the distant past.

Moreover, Maimonides believed that even though neither creation nor preexistence could be proven, creation was nevertheless the more reasonable of the two positions. Medieval astronomy could offer no reasonable explanation of stellar and planetary motion. If the world followed causally from divine wisdom alone, one would expect the planets and stars to move in regular, circular paths. Observation, however, shows that they move at different speeds and in different directions and are distributed around the heavens in rather arbitrary clusters. To account for these observations, medieval astronomy posited all manner of epicycles, but the picture that emerged was complex, messy, and inelegant. It suggested the existence within the Universe of an element of free choice and will that was responsible for all this disorder. Accordingly, the world does not follow by necessity from the very fact of God's existence, and the departures from an orderly structure reflect an exercise of will and deliberate intention. Had Maimonides known of the achievements of Copernicus and Kepler and of Newtonian physics, he likely would not have raised that argument. Modern astronomy obviated the complexity of cycles and epicycles and offered an elegant structure of celestial motion that the proponents of wisdom rather than will would have been delighted with. Maimonides, in any event, believed that the idea of innovation and creation *ex nihilo*, though not necessary, was more reasonable than the alternative.

Attributing will to God, as we have seen, stands at odds with the Aristotelian notion of divine perfection, and the tension between those ideas generates serious metaphysical problems. To resolve those problems, Maimonides argues that one cannot compare "will" as we know it in a human context with divine will; they share only the term that designates them. Divine will is not caused by some lack or by some external driver, and does not imply any change in the divinity itself. The substantive difference between the human and the divine allows for will to be attributed to God without implying the attribution of some shortcoming. According to the conservative reading of the *Guide*, this treatment of the problem of divine will explains the connection between Part I, which deals with the limitations of language, and the ensuing chapters, which consider the creation of the world. The discussion of language teaches that one cannot draw any analogies between a human phenomenon and the divinity.

The skeptical reading of the *Guide*, however, maintains a need for a further, consistent step in the criticism of language. If it is indeed true that it is meaningless to associate positive attributes with God, that is true of the attributes "will" and "wisdom" as well. We do not know what it means to ascribe will to God, and we do not know the meaning of divine wisdom. Silence therefore is the recommended posture with respect to this great metaphysical problem, for the limitations on language make it a question that simply cannot be formulated. There is, accordingly, an important and interesting difference between the conservative reading's limited and specific skepticism regarding the metaphysical question of creation versus preexistence, and the overarching, generalized skepticism of the skeptical reading. The conservative position maintains that the limitations on our knowledge regarding the origins of the world rule out the possibility of proving either creation or preexistence; and it calls for accepting creation for the reasons described earlier. The skeptical reading, in contrast, maintains that no position at all can be taken regarding the issue, for the limitations on apprehension do more than preclude proving either creation or preexistence; they prevent a coherent formulation of the very question itself. Because the question pertains to the nature of the divinity and the attributes of God, it becomes meaningless and unanswerable.

Maimonides' great achievement, according to those who uphold the conservative reading, lies in his proving that preexistence is not a logical necessity, thereby enabling the perplexed Jew to remain devoted to Torah and commandments without sacrificing his commitment to philosophy. As a philosophical matter, preexistence versus creation remains an open issue; the perplexed believer is therefore free to take the side of creation in view of his affinity to the Torah; and he is similarly free to believe in revelation as an act of God's will, the basis of the entire Torah. Because of his philosophical inclinations, however, he will adopt the principle of creation only to the limited extent necessary. Maimonides took pains to reiterate the point often: the possibility of creation does not negate the idea that nature, with the wisdom implicit in it, is the central, most substantive revelation of God in the world. God's willful interventions, whether in creating the world or giving the Torah, are extraordinary departures from the norm, atypical of the broader picture of the world. The possibility of willful creation exists only at the starting point, the moment when the system is set in place; thereafter, the stage is left clear for wisdom.

For the very same reason, Maimonides rejected the apocalyptic notion of the end of the world. That the world has its origins in an act of will does not entail the premise that it also will have an end. Nature, formed by God's will, will endure forever without change:

> The matter has now become clear to you and the doctrine epitomized. Namely, we agree with Aristotle with regard to one half of his opinion and we believe that what exists is eternal a parte post and will last forever with that nature which He, may He be exalted, has willed; that nothing in it will be changed in any respect unless it be in some particular of it miracu-lously—although He, may He be exalted, has the power to change the whole of it, or to annihilate it, or to annihilate any nature in it that He wills. (II:29; Pines, p. 346)

At a later stage of the *Guide*, he adds:

> If you consider this opinion [that is, the Torah's] and the philosophic opin-ion, reflecting upon all the preceding chapters in this Treatise that are con-nected with this notion, you will not find any difference between them re-garding any of the particulars of everything that exists. You will find no difference other than that which we have explained: namely, that they re-gard the world as eternal and we regard it as produced in time. Understand this. (III:25; Pines, p. 506)

Maimonides emphasized the narrow bounds of his support for creation in time by taking pains to distance himself from the streams of Islamic thought whose picture of the world was influenced in its entirety by the idea of creation. These streams—the Mu'tazilite and the Ash'arite, part of the Kalam movement—arose during the eighth century and again during the tenth, and based their proof for the existence of God on their argu-ment that the world had been created in time. If the world was created, there must have been a creator. Moreover, they maintained, God's willful actions did not end with the event of creation, for no causal nature exists independent of God's will. For example, if heat turns water to vapor, God must be involved by force of his will to cause the water's vaporization. That heat vaporizes water provides no evidence of an independent causal rela-tionship between the events. The linkage between the events is, rather, the

result of God's choice to activate his will in a fixed way, so that people will
be able to anticipate results. Occasionally, God will choose to act in a way
that differs from His usual choice, in which case we will perceive a miracle
taking place, but God's willful intervention is involved in every event that
takes place in the world. Behind this picture of reality is a religious position that aims to establish God's absolute sovereignty. The premise that
there exists an independent causal order impairs God's absolute dominion
within the world.

In Maimonides' view, the Kalam's outlook, which denied what appeared
to be the existence of an independent causal order so as to prove thereby
the existence of God, represented religious apologetics rather than genuine
philosophy:

> To sum up: All the first Mutakallimūn from among the Greeks who had
> adopted Christianity and from among the Moslems did not conform in
> their premises to the appearance of that which exists, but considered how
> being ought to be in order that it should furnish a proof for the correctness
> of a particular opinion, or at least should not refute it. (I:71; Pines, p. 178)

The creation of the world is not subject to proof, and it follows that proof
for the existence of God cannot be based on the idea of creation. Similarly,
a rational effort cannot be harnessed in service of faith, even to defend
what is regarded as the fundamental premise of religious existence: "To
sum up: I shall say to you that the matter is as Themistius puts it: that
which exists does not conform to the various opinions, but rather the correct opinions conform to that which exists" (I:71; Pines, p. 179). Moreover,
even if we assume that the world was created in time, we would not on that
account have a reason to deny the reality of the causal order. God created
the world though an act of will, but He instilled within it an independently
operating causal order, just as a watchmaker creates a watch with an internal mechanism that causes it to operate continuously.

Maimonides believed he had revealed fundamental errors in the thinking of the Kalam, but he did not stop there; he regarded as invalid the
overall religious attitude of that stream, with its emphasis on absolute divine will. In Maimonides' view, the creation of the world in time does not
conflict with the existence of a stable causal order, which is the wondrous
expression of God's revelation in the world. The principle of creation allows for willful intervention on God's part, such as revelation or providence, but it does not dominate the overall picture of the world or the

concept of the divine. The conservative reading of the *Guide* makes it possible to accept creation without rejecting nature and science.

The various comments by the *Guide*'s first translator and interpreter, Samuel Ibn Tibbon, suggest that he rejected the conservative reading even though it is the one implied by a plain reading of the manifest layer of the treatise. Instead of the conservative reading, Ibn Tibbon adopted a *philosophical* one, according to which the secret of the *Guide* is rooted in the idea of the eternal preexistence of the world and creation in time is a necessary belief rather than a true one. The necessity of belief in creation arises out of the fact that the authority of law and the social order would be undermined without widespread acceptance of acts of divine will, manifest in revelation and providence. Maimonides therefore took pains, and properly so, to conceal his philosophical stance, fraught as it was with dangerous political consequences, and the many chapters he devoted to refuting the Aristotelian position are meant to mask his true position. A close, informed reading of the actual chapters on preexistence, as well as others, will show that Maimonides affirmed the view that the world was eternal and preexistent.

From Ibn Tibbon's time to our own, there have been those who read the work this way, particularly given Maimonides' own claim to have concealed his position from the reader; that suggests, it is argued, that Maimonides' true view is the more radical one, for otherwise there would be no need for concealment. Further support is drawn from Maimonides' reliance, when called upon to explain certain phenomena, on principles derived from preexistence notwithstanding his declared affirmance of creation in time. An example appears in the Work of Creation itself: in explaining the various days of creation, the process by which the various species are created, or the appearance of the continents and the formation of the oceans, he looks to natural causal processes drawn from Aristotelian science. He suggests, for instance, that God did not create man through a direct act of will. The creation of man involved both the movement of the sphere, which blended the various elements making up man's body, and the active intellect, which instilled in him his human essence.

From the perspective of philosophical interpretation, the achievement of the *Guide* is grounded in its affording the fundamental concepts of Judaism—creation, prophecy, providence, and commandment, among others—an interpretation consistent with the concept of an eternal world. The perplexed Jew can maintain his Aristotelian stance without abandoning his affinity to Judaism, for Maimonides reveals to him how the Torah's hidden meaning is consistent with preexistence. The conservative and the philosophical readings thus differ profoundly and broadly in how they understand the *Guide* and the way in which it resolves the existential crisis of the perplexed Jew.

The origin of the world is a fascinating metaphysical question, but it is not itself a matter of decisive importance. The Bible presents no insurmountable obstacle to affirming any of the various positions, and Maimonides states that if he had proof of preexistence, he would interpret the pertinent biblical passages accordingly. Interpretation is an open door, and that interpretive move would certainly be easier than the one he undertakes in systematically reinterpreting every anthropomorphic biblical expression:

> Know that our shunning the affirmation of the eternity of the world is not due to a text figuring in the Torah according to which the world has been produced in time. For the texts indicating that the world has been produced in time are not more numerous than those indicating that the deity is a body. . . . Perhaps this would even be much easier to do: we should be very well able to give a figurative interpretation of those texts and to affirm as true the eternity of the world, just as we have given a figurative interpretation of those other texts and have denied that He, may He be exalted, is a body. (II:25; Pines, pp. 327–328)

The significance of the question lies in its implications for the concept of God, and the manner in which one is to deal with the ideas of revelation and providence. It is the interpretation of these concepts, as the *Guide* goes on to discuss them, that form the focus of the clash between the conservative and the philosophical readings.

The Doctrine of Prophecy

The *Guide* treats the concept of prophecy in the chapters following those that dealt with creation, running from Chapter 32 of Part II to the end of the part, in Chapter 48. Maimonides begins the discussion by establishing a connection between one's understanding of prophecy and one's view of creation. He sets out three alternatives that would appear to correspond to the various views regarding creation in time and preexistence. The first sees prophecy as a miraculous event, an expression of God's sovereign will. God appears to a person, imposing on him a mission or a command. The prophet is God's instrument, selected by God as He wills, and the selection is not necessarily tied to the prophet's merits or qualities. In contrast to this position, Maimonides sets the philosophical alternative, which regards prophecy as a natural event. This view, adopted by al-Farabi, considered prophecy to be a form of human perfection. A person who, over the course of his life, has achieved perfection of character and intellect would necessarily attain prophecy, for it does not at all depend on God's willful intervention. The third approach to prophecy, presented as Maimonides' own position and that of the Torah, reconciles the first two. To merit prophecy, a person during his life must achieve perfection of character and intellect. Not everyone, therefore, can attain prophecy, for when it occurs, it is a natural, causal event. Maimonides thus utterly rejected the first position, which saw prophecy as something dependent entirely on God's will, imparted to whomever God chose. But Maimonides also maintained, in contrast to the philosophical approach that saw prophecy as entirely natural, that God had the power to deny prophecy to a person otherwise worthy of it. A man might attain a stature warranting prophecy but still not achieve it because God, by act of will, withheld it from him. And so prophecy is a natural achievement that requires God's approval as well. Maimonides thereby rejected the second opinion, which saw prophecy as a natural event that would necessarily ensue once the preconditions were met.

Maimonides' interpreters pondered the nature of the correspondence between these views of prophecy and the various views of creation. Some believed that the first understanding of prophecy, which took it as something miraculous, corresponds to the affirmation of creation *ex nihilo*; the second, philosophical, position corresponds to the position of Aristotle with respect to creation; and the third, middle-of-the-road, position corresponds to Plato's view that creation involved God's willful formation of the world out of preexisting material. That array of correspondences suggests that Maimonides accepted the Platonic position on creation, which corresponds to the view he took of prophecy. But the chapters of the *Guide* dealing with creation suggest that is not the case and that Maimonides accepted the view that the world was created *ex nihilo*. That being so, the alignment between views on prophecy and views on creation appears to differ from the one just suggested. The first position with respect to prophecy corresponds to the Kalam's unconstrained view of creation in time. God acts in an entirely volitional manner and nature has no independent existence; in corresponding manner, prophecy is utterly unconstrained by any natural context. God can cause Balaam's ass to speak and can do the same for any person He may choose as His messenger. The second position on prophecy corresponds to the Aristotelian affirmation of preexistence. It sees prophecy as a necessary, causal event, just as the existence of the world follows causally from the existence of God. The third position on prophecy corresponds to Maimonides' understanding of creation in time, which stands in opposition to that of the Kalam. Maimonidean creation does not deny science and nature, but it maintains the principle of will in the limited context of the initial creative event; and so it is in prophecy. The middle-of-the-road position, then, is not that of Plato but the position of the Torah with respect to creation. It occupies the ground between the position of the Kalam, which affirms only creation in time, and the Aristotelian position, which asserts only preexistence.

Whatever the appropriate set of correspondences between creation and prophecy, Maimonides' actual view of prophecy is much closer to the philosophical-natural stance than to the willful-miraculous. When prophecy takes place, it is a natural event, as the philosophers held. We must understand it as an event tied to the natural structure of the world. God's willful intervention appears only when prophecy fails to take place even though the natural conditions for it are ripe. In that light, we must examine the implications of Maimonides' position for the concept of revelation, for the nature and character of prophecy, and for the prophet's distinctiveness as a person.

The prophet, according to Maimonides, must be distinguished from two other sorts of singular personality: the political leader and the philosopher. The leader is endowed with the capacity to enthrall people, to forge images and symbols, to legislate, and to envision the ways in which events are likely to unfold. His perfection, Maimonides says, is that of the imagination—the power by which one is able to call up, in his mind's eye, sensory impressions that are not currently present, such as the image of a friend not seen for some time. Imagination also enables one to combine familiar sense impressions into a new image that does not in fact exist; for example, one can call up an image of man with the head of a horse. And, by the same token, imagination makes it possible to depict, in one's mind's eye, as if actually under way, an event that has not yet taken place. The object of imagination will always be concrete to some extent, for imagination does not operate in the realm of abstraction; and Maimonides held it to be a physical power. The ability to summon up images differs from person to person, as does the ability to depict new images formed by combining sense perceptions. Great political leaders are graced with perfection in their imaginative faculty. They create captivating symbols and images; spin foundational and organizing tales; and enact laws. Some enjoy the capacity to envision events and see the future as if it were before their eyes.

The philosopher, in contrast to the leader, is endowed with perfection of the intellect. He is equipped to deal with abstractions and can think critically in a way that allows him to distinguish between truth and falsehood, to make balanced judgments, and to judge between good and bad. But because he lacks the imaginative force, he differs from the leader in that he is unable to translate his insights into popular language. He lacks the ability to forge symbols and images that will convey his intellectual achievements in ways that will move people to action. The political leader, on the other hand, can motivate people and shape a community, but he lacks the capacity to think critically. He resembles an efficient advertising agency, which operates without any concern about the purposes and goals it is advancing.

The prophet is the complete man, possessed of both perfections: the perfected intellectual power of the philosopher and the perfected imaginative power of the leader. He is equipped to form images and lead the community, though his perfected character and intellect mean that the goals of the community will be subjected to his careful examination of truth and falseness, good and evil. He is likewise able to translate the great truths into a form understood by the masses; his language is that of story, symbol, and allegory. He does not simply mold the social order and generate common effort, as does an ordinary political leader; he also draws the community as a whole closer to a true and appropriate view of the world. Maimonides understood the imagination to be a physical quality derivative of our sensual experience and therefore dependent on the natural makeup of each individual. Some people could never become prophets, just as some could never become marathon runners. The imaginative capacity is a natural given, and attaining the perfected character that affords a man discipline and allows him to devote himself to intellectual achievement is an entire way of life. Prophecy does not strike suddenly, like lightning; it is the outcome of natural talents and diligent moral and intellectual preparation over the course of a lifetime.

The imagination operates primarily in the absence of immediate sense impressions. The dream, therefore, is the arena in which the most creative exercise of the imagination takes place, and it is also the central arena for prophecy. Every prophecy takes place in a dream or a vision; the latter is a state in which a person, though awake, withdraws from his surroundings and is overcome by internal images and pictures. A dream is a prophetic one not because its content is derived from external intervention, even though that may appear to be the case; in fact, the content consists of images arising out of the depths of the prophet's own consciousness. The dreams of a prophet, unlike those of ordinary people, are prophecies; but the reason is not that the former were bestowed by God while the latter were not. The contents of a prophet's dream, like those of all dreams, are influenced by his waking life. But because the prophet is engaged closely with the intelligibles, the images he creates in his dreams are, in effect, a symbolic translation of profound insights regarding the true and the false, the good and the bad. It may be compared to a mathematician who awakens in the morning with a solution to a complex mathematical problem that appeared to him. The solution did not appear in the wake of conscious logical analysis; it simply appeared while he slept. Importantly, however, this sort of thing happens only to a mathematician, partly because he worked on the problem with great intensity while he was awake.

In this account of the prophetic process, there is no volitional, intentional turn by God to a person; the prophecy is an internal mental event of the prophet. The external component of the prophecy results from the fact that it reaches the imagination through the inspiration of the intellect, and Maimonides' theory of cognition holds that a person's intellect identifies with the objects of cognition and with the intellect that conceives of these objects, called the active intellect. This external component—which does not address the prophet but is activated by him—is not God Himself but the final separate intellect, the active intellect, which Maimonides terms "an angel at the level of *Ishim.*" Maimonides therefore argues that every prophecy represents contact with an angel and indirectly with God. This concept of prophecy is far removed from the traditional understanding, in which the sovereign God exercises His will to address and issue a command to His messenger. According to Maimonides, when the prophet tells of hearing God speaking to him or seeing an angel calling him, he is not reporting on an external event taking place outside his own consciousness.

God does not reveal Himself to the prophet in a dream; rather, the prophet dreams that God revealed Himself to him. The difference between these two concepts is vast, as vast as the difference between going out for a pleasant walk and dreaming about that walk. Any account of seeing or hearing God or an angel is an account of a dream or a wakeful dream, for God does not appear or speak and neither does an angel. The prophet dreams that the event is occurring: "Know again that in the case of everyone about whom exists a scriptural text that an *angel* talked to him or that speech came to him from God, this did not occur in any other way than *in a dream* or *in a vision of prophecy*" (II:41; Pines, p. 386).

It is not hard to identify the daringly novel aspect of this idea that the link between the prophecy and the dream reflects the inner consciousness of the prophet. And Maimonides makes no effort to conceal his concept of the matter, for since it is impossible to see an angel, any appearance of an angel must be a dream of the prophet. One example offered in the *Guide* is that of Jacob's struggle with the angel recounted in Genesis 32. An angel has no physical body, so Jacob could not have wrestled with an angel; he only dreamt that he was wrestling with an angel. The dream has profound symbolic significance, partly because it is the dream of a man like Jacob, but it is only a dream. Maimonides even argues that when Abraham saw the three angels at the entrance to his tent he was either in a dream state or one of wakeful vision, and that the angel who called out to him to him not to slaughter Isaac was similarly Abraham's wakeful vision. In Maimonides' view, all divine revelations in the form of appearance, statement, or speech are to be understood in this way.

More than a few of Maimonides' readers saw this concept as subversive, a challenge to the force of prophecy. In his commentary on the Torah, Naḥmanides, who usually treated Maimonides with respect and moderation, sharply attacked his approach to prophecy. Among other things, he asked how Jacob, if his encounter with the angel was only a dream, suffered the injury that left him limping in the morning, as Scripture recounts. Maimonides might have answered that the limp was a continuation of the dream, or that people sometimes awaken from a dream with physiological conditions associated with the dream. Naḥmanides was no doubt troubled by the adverse effect on prophetic authoritativeness of treating prophecy as simply a manifestation of the workings of the prophet's consciousness or the events transpiring in his inner life.

Maimonides' understanding of the prophet and the prophetic process redefines the distinction between true prophecy and false prophecy. No longer can a true prophecy be identified as one in which God in fact spoke the words to the prophet, in contrast to a prophecy originating in the prophet's own mind. According to Maimonides, every prophecy arises in the prophet's mind, for God does not address him. True prophecy is to be identified on the basis of the prophet's virtues and in light of the prophecy's purpose. The picture of prophecy painted by Maimonides, then, is close to philosophical stance, as consistently presented by al-Farabi. Maimonides differed with the philosophical view in that he believed God could withhold prophecy from one otherwise qualified to attain it, but that qualification does not really matter when prophecy in fact occurs. In such a case, the prophecy as conceived of by Maimonides cannot rely on the conventional authoritativeness of a willful revelation from God's own mouth, directed to the prophet.

Advocates of the philosophical reading of the *Guide* see Maimonides' account of prophecy as proof that he believed in the eternal preexistence of the world. They argue that in the chapters dealing with creation, he states that he affirms creation in time partly because eternal preexistence undermines the concept of revelation. He had the following to say in support of creation in time:

> Know that with a belief in the creation of the world in time, all the miracles become possible and the Law becomes possible, and all questions that may be asked on this subject, vanish. Thus it might be said: Why did God give prophetic revelation to this one and not to that? Why did God give this Law to this particular nation, and why did He not legislate to the others? Why did He legislate at this particular time, and why did He not legislate before or after? . . . The answer to all these questions would be that it would be said: He wanted it this way; or His wisdom required it this way. And just as He brought the world into existence, having the form it has, when He wanted to, without our knowing His will with regard to this. (II:25; Pines, p. 329)

According to this argument, belief in creation in time allows for revelation to be interpreted as a willful address by God to man. But, say advocates of preexistence, when Maimonides sets out to interpret prophecy itself and its nature, he systematically omits any reference at all to divine will as a factor in prophecy. Notwithstanding this persuasive argument, the dispute over whether the *Guide* should be understood to affirm preexistence or creation in time extended into the chapters on prophecy. The force of the dispute is tied to an important and recurring element of Maimonides' discussion of prophecy, namely, his emphatic exclusion of Moses' prophecy from everything he says in the *Guide* about prophecy in general. Unlike other prophets, Moses encounters not an angel but God Himself. And while other prophets prophesy in a wakeful vision or a dream, Moses prophesies directly, not in a vision or a dream. For that same reason, Moses' prophecy is not tied to the imaginative faculty, as is that of the other prophets, but is derived directly from the intellect itself. In effect, Maimonides determines that the natural explanation that underlies his view of prophecy in general simply does not apply in the case of Moses. Moses' prophecy is comparable to that of other prophets only in that they share the term "prophecy." There is a certain element that they have in common, but it is peripheral, and they differ entirely in essence: "I will let you know that everything I say on prophecy in the chapters of this Treatise refers only to the form of prophecy of all the prophets who were before Moses and who will come after him . . . For to my mind the term prophet used with reference to Moses and to the others is amphibolous" (*Guide* II:35; Pines, p. 367). Conservative readers of the *Guide* will argue that by distinguishing Moses from the other prophets not only in rank but also in substance, Maimonides was defending the authoritativeness of the Torah and of revelation. Just as the world was created through a miraculous act of divine will, so was the Torah given to Moses. As in all matters related to belief in creation in time, the action of God's will does not negate nature in its entirety. The prophecy of all the other prophets, those who preceded Moses and those who followed him, can be explained naturally. According to the belief in creation in time, the divine will is active only at the original, foundational minute; and so, too, with respect to revelation: the divine will appears in the giving of the Torah, in which the absolute standing of the divine law is established as the basis for Judaism overall.

The philosophical reading of the *Guide* will argue, however, that singling out Moses' prophecy is in the nature of a necessary belief, another instance of concealing a position that has the potential to undermine the foundations of religion. In truth, Maimonides believed that the authority of Moses' Torah, like that of the prophecy of other prophets, was not derived from God being the One who, in all His glory, revealed it to Moses.

The Torah is divine not because of its source but because of Moses' perfect merit, its content, and its purposes. Indeed, when Maimonides, in the second part of the *Guide*, chapter 40, defines divine law, he characterizes it in terms related to purpose: a divine law is one that is concerned not only about a proper society, a matter of concern to all political legislation, but also about the higher perfection of people—their true beliefs and opinions. Examination of Moses' Torah shows that it deals with these matters in a balanced, perfect manner. Something imperfect appears many times, but something perfect appears but once. If at some point a prophet of Moses' stature should appear and enact a divine law, that law would be identical to the Torah of Moses. There is, accordingly, a vast gulf between the conservative and the philosophical readings, pertaining to the source of the Torah's authority.

Despite the arguments in support of the philosophical reading, Maimonides left the door open to a conservative reading of his words, as he did in the case of creation in time. This ambiguity, which allows for multiple readings, appears as well in the context of the next issue on which the conservative and philosophical readings clash, that of providence. Before considering the nature of providence, however, we must consider the question of evil, the discussion of which is one of the most impressive pinnacles of Maimonides' religious thought.

The Problem of Evil and the Purpose of Existence

The problem of evil presents one of the most difficult problems faced by monotheistic religious thought. Conceptually, the problem can be stated as follows: How is it possible to affirm, simultaneously, the following three propositions: (1) God is omnipotent; (2) God is good; (3) evil exists. If God is not omnipotent, we can understand the phenomenon of evil; God, though good, lacks the power to prevent it. Similarly, we can understand the phenomenon if God is all-powerful but not good—God has the power to prevent evil, but because He is not essentially good, He is indifferent to the evil that occurs in the world. On the face of it, however, monotheistic religious thought seems committed both to God's omnipotence and to His goodness, so how can it account for the existence of evil?

In light of the intense religious commitments to these beliefs regarding God, evil moves from being a tragic fact that has to be dealt with to being a religious problem of the first order. It threatens, with good reason, to undermine the basic structure of faith. But beyond the conceptual challenge to the fundamentals of faith, the problem of evil creates a profound existential crisis with respect to life in general. A person facing evil becomes aware of the huge gap between his moral judgments and the causal structure of the universe. That structure seems to him utterly arbitrary, unresponsive to his basic values. The blind laws of nature harm everyone, even newborn infants who have never sinned and righteous men who have done only acts of goodness all their lives. Once a person knows good and evil, he is no longer at home in the world. He feels a tragic rending, a sense of alienation from the universe. The world appears to be meaningless, an alien place into which he is cast and left to grapple with the blind cruelty of existence and its many torments. Maimonides' treatment of the problem of evil shows him to be troubled by the existential distress no less than by the theological conundrum, and he deals with the two of them together.

Many efforts to contend with the problem of evil try to maintain both God's goodness and His omnipotence by denying that evil really exists. The history of theology is replete with such efforts, which tend to be questionable and problematic. Maimonides is part of that tradition, and in dealing with the problem, he denies the existence of evil. He thereby takes upon himself a very difficult task, which he works to discharge in a unique way, informed by his overall view of the world.

Before considering Maimonides' own way of denying the existence of evil, we should note two conventional positions on the problem of evil that he rejected. The first was to blame the sufferer. According to this view, it is divine justice that decrees suffering in the world, but we cannot perceive that justice until the end. This is the view of Job's friends, who argue that his suffering was evidence that he had sinned. He may not yet realize that he has sinned, but if he examines his actions, they say, he will find that the suffering was, in fact, imposed on him justly. Although the Book of Job goes on to reject that position, it has resonated in religious history to our own day. The death of helpless, innocent babies is seen as a punishment, sometimes for the sins of their parents and sometimes for those of other souls said to be reincarnated within them. Arguments of this sort simply make things worse: not only do they fail to resolve the problem of evil; they add to it by blaming the victim. In response to Job's horrible anguish over the death of his sons, his friends take the dreadful step of blaming him for their deaths. Job protests their allegation and God vindicates him, affirming that he is not at fault. Maimonides interpreted Job in accord with the premise that he is not to be blamed for his sufferings. He rejected the position that would resolve the problem of evil by casting all suffering as the outcome of sin.

Maimonides likewise rejected a second conventional argument, which sought to use the world to come as a device for resolving the problem of evil in this world. On this argument, the torments endured by the righteous in this world will increase their reward in the world to come, and the pleasures enjoyed by the wicked in this world will augment their punishment in the world to come. To justify God in the world that is known to us, it is necessary to posit another world, in which accounts are settled and all the problems resolved. The world as we experience it in its narrow sense cannot be just unless there is a second world in which injustices are remedied. Maimonides believed this argument, like the first, compounds the problem rather than resolving it. In discussing trials, he rejects "what is generally accepted among people regarding the subject of trial . . . : God sends down calamities upon an individual, without their having been preceded by sin, in order that his reward be increased" (III:24; Pines, p. 497). Why not augment the reward of the righteous without making him suffer? The argument seems no less vile than blaming the victim and claiming that he must have sinned. According to Maimonides, the world to come is a natural result of life in this world. It is not meant as a solution to the problem of evil, for, among other things, it fails to solve it. In the *Guide*, Maimonides suggests another way to deny the existence of evil, one based on a threefold division of the evils that may afflict a person. The first are those that arise simply because a person is a material being. Death, illness, infirmity, and wounds all result from the flawed nature of the material from which a man is formed. Evils of the second sort are caused by other people; obvious examples include wars, crimes, and injustices. Finally, there are self-imposed evils, incurred as a result of a person's own behavior. Excessive risks incurred to gain excess wealth or honor, unhelpful and warped patterns of diet and consumption, desires that cannot be fulfilled—all of these bring about physical illness and great psychic suffering. Maimonides maintains that an analysis of each type of evil can unravel the problem and lead to the conclusion that there is no evil in the world that should be attributed either to limitations on God's power or to divine indifference to suffering.

The evils suffered by a person because he is a material being, Maimonides argues, are "privations," that is, situations that have no actual existence and that appear to us as the absence of a desired situation. Illness is the absence of health, death is the absence of life, infirmity is the absence of completeness, and so forth. In these cases, God does not create the evil because the evil does not really exist, and all that exists is good. Evil is the absence of certain reality; existence as such is good.

Of all the philosophical arguments made in the *Guide*, this seems the weakest. First, the evil caused by the absence of the good can sometimes cause great pain and unbearable suffering. The pain itself can hardly be described as an absence, for it is real, extant, and scorching. Beyond that, the argument seems to be a casuistic logic game that contributes little to an understanding of the question. What is gained by calling something the absence of something else? There is, to be sure, something else in play behind the flimsy argument from absence, a more profound and significant argument: the impairments and evils that result from our material nature are necessary conditions. To ask why death, illness, or difficult old age exist in the world is to ask a meaningless question as long as we are interested in being what we are, namely, material creatures. To complain about those evils necessarily entails an expectation of being something other than what we are. By its very nature, matter is limited and finite, and hoping for it to be perfect and eternal is like hoping for a square to be circular. Destruction and impairment are part of the essence of something material, and matter is given to accident and will never be perfect. And so, in those relatively few instances when children are born with defects, the situation is tied of necessity to our being creatures possessed of bodies. That God does not create durable or perfect material does not mean that his power is limited, because God does not do the logically impossible: He is unable to create a number "two" such that multiplying it by itself will yield "five." This approach to the first category of evil is marked by a profound acceptance of limits and a recognition of our finitude. The consciousness of evil is, among other things, a consequence of expectation which confronts the limitation of what is possible. If death is necessary, we do not experience it as evil; it is part of being what we are. Recognition that something is inevitable blunts the force of the complaint.

But affirmation of reality cannot entail solely the inevitability of its deficiencies. Reality, as it is, must afford us the possibility of a good and rewarding existence. And here we turn to the two remaining sorts of evil, those wrought by other people and those that are self-imposed. The evils that men do to one another, such as wars and crimes, result, in Maimonides' view, from competition for limited resources. Nevertheless, examination of the nature of the world shows that the more basic and necessary a resource, the more abundant it is. Air, water, and basic food exist almost without limitation. The struggle for resources begins when people internalize unnatural goals, such as pursuit of wealth, honor, and pleasure. There are not enough diamonds and gold bars to go around, nor is there power and might for all. People internalize inappropriate goals and then complain that the world does not provide adequately for their desires. And this affects not only interpersonal relationships but also the life of the individual. Were a person to be satisfied with meeting his basic needs, he would not have to spend his life in risk-taking, worry, frustration, jealousy, and bitterness. Similarly, given that Maimonides believed that most illness originated in improper consumption of food, a man in control of his desires would have less exposure to illness and decline.

The goal of a human being is to develop the intellectual elements of his life and to pursue knowledge and truth. Knowledge, unlike power, wealth, and honor, is an inexhaustible resource. That one person has knowledge does not diminish the supply available to others. Other, imagined, goods entail a zero-sum game, in which one person's gain is another's loss, and a society that pursues those goods will experience conflict as a result. But a society that internalizes knowledge as its highest goal will be spared such conflict. It will possess all the material resources it needs to exist, because the world provides them in sufficient quantity, and its highest goal, knowledge, is not limited or subject to competition. And what is true of society is true of the individual as well. By internalizing the proper goal, he will free himself from the physical and spiritual torments associated with a life given over to pursuing desires. This attitude toward the problem of evil is profoundly accepting of the world as it exists. The world is a domain fit for a human being as long as the human being adopts the proper goal for his life. But if he does ill to himself or his fellow, it is ridiculous to see that as a tragic flaw in the world or the basis for a complaint against God.

The affirmation of the world involves a further attitudinal adjustment related to how one understands the purpose of existence. The tragic view of the world draws support from the idea that the purpose of existence is man and yet his needs are not responded to when he encounters the world. Maimonides attributes this idea to the writings of Razi, the tenth-century Muslim philosopher and physician:

Razi has written a famous book, which he has entitled "Divine Things." He
filled it with the enormity of his ravings and ignorant notions. Among them
there is a notion that he has thought up, namely, that there is more evil than
good in what exists; if you compare man's well-being and his pleasures in
the time span of his well-being with the pains, the heavy sufferings, the in-
firmities, the paralytic afflictions, the wretchedness, the sorrows and the
calamities that befall him, you find that his existence—he means the existence of man—is a punishment and a great evil inflicted upon him. . . . The
reason for this whole mistake lies in the fact that this ignoramus and those
like him among the multitude consider that which exists only with reference to a human individual. Every ignoramus imagines that all that exists
exists with a view to his individual sake; it is as if there were nothing that
exists except him. And if something happens to him that is contrary to what
he wishes, he makes the trenchant judgment that all that exists is an evil.
(III:12; Pines, pp. 441–442)

A proper understanding of existence teaches that man is not its purpose.
The spheres and heavenly bodies were not created to serve man, and he is
but a minuscule part of the overall universe. This attitudinal adjustment,
this turning away from the placement of man at the center of the universe,
plays an important part in changing one's view of the world. The Book of
Job tells the story of this sort of adjustment, as undergone by its protago-
nist. At the start, Job contends that everything in the world happens against
him or for him. When a tragedy befalls his household, he complains that
it happened to him even though he did nothing wrong. The psychological
process he undergoes brings him to the recognition that many things in the
world happen without regard to him; they are neither for him nor against
him and have nothing whatsoever to do with him or his actions.

The key to confronting the problem of evil, then, is to be found in a
change in human consciousness. One must internalize a proper sense of his
place in the universe and recognize the inevitability of transience, given that
one is a material body. If a person sets goals for himself that are well suited
to the nature of existence, he will enjoy bounty and blessing. Contemporary society, marked by growing consumption and ever greater dependence
on energy sources that foul the environment, show, sadly, what Maimonides means. Nature is not designed to accommodate this sort of global
purpose, and people will quickly pay a high price for this sort of attitude
toward themselves and toward existence. The universe is man's home as

long as man fulfills his lofty spiritual goal as a being capable of knowing and judging. Maimonides' approach to evil flows from a key motif in his thinking, namely, that nature and causal reality, as the embodiment of kindness and good, are the highest expression of God's revelation.

Providence

The deep-seated basis for Maimonides' position on the question of evil, then, is affirmation of reality, an idea corresponding to Maimonides' position regarding God's revelation in the world as it exists. But does existence itself react to the righteous and the wicked in the same manner? Does a man's religious and moral standing have any impact on his fate? To what extent, if any, is God involved in what goes on in the world that He created or that causally arose from Him? Given these questions, the discussion of providence is a natural extension of the inquiry into the question of evil; in the *Guide*, it follows right on its heels. Moreover, the two questions that arise with respect to God's providence—its nature and its reach—are linked to the alternative view on creation in time or eternal preexistence. It comes as no surprise, therefore, that Maimonides' comments on providence have been variously interpreted in accord with each of the views on creation, the issue that forms the basis for the *Guide*'s broad perspective.

Maimonides begins his inquiry into providence by presenting five different approaches to the subject.

The first position, which Maimonides attributes to Epicurus, denies that providence exists in the world. The happenings in the universe are a series of random events, reflecting neither purpose nor direction. Maimonides rejects this position, for existence itself reflects organization and planning, not merely happenstance. He attributes the view not to an objective assessment of the world on the part of its proponents but to their deliberate, obdurate rejection of what is evident to the eye. The second position, that of Aristotle, holds that the world has structure and order but that structure does not bear on the existence of each and every individual; rather, it is expressed in the maintenance of each species overall. Accordingly the continuation of the animal species and of humankind as a whole is ensured, but each individual is subject to random chance within the processes of destruction and formation that govern their material natures.

In Aristotle's view, then, the concept of providence acquires a new and original meaning. It does not connote God's willful involvement in a person's life or in the history of a species or a nation. It refers, rather, to the formation of natural conditions in which permanence and stability are possible and ensured. Individual men and beasts are afforded limited providence, in that they are given the means for self-preservation within the lifetime that is possible for them. Man is given the instruments of thought and movement that allow him to survive; in that sense, his life is providential. Providence, then, is not God's willful intervention from without; it is the wisdom that inheres in the natural causal order and makes existence and permanence possible.

Maimonides accepts the Aristotelian position—that is, providence pertains to species but not to individuals—with respect to beasts but rejects it with regard to man. In his view, providence bears on a certain group of individual humans, not only on humanity overall. He objects to the conclusion that nature disregards the differences among the various creatures: "Similarly he [Aristotle] does not differentiate between an ox that defecates upon a host of ants so that they die, or a building whose foundations are shaken upon all the people at their prayers who are found in it so that they die. And there is no difference, according to him, between a cat coming across a mouse and devouring it or a spider devouring a fly, on the one hand, or a ravenous lion meeting a prophet and devouring him, on the other" (III:17; Pines, p. 466). Maimonides refuses to accept the moral absurdity of Aristotle's position, which assigns the mouse and the prophet, the ant and the worshipper, to the same regime, acknowledging no differences among them. According to the Aristotelian view, the same natural causality brought about the death of the ants on which the ox defecated and the worshippers on which the building collapsed. This natural causality, moreover, follows form the very existence of God, and it is inconceivable that it might change because of the religious or moral standing of any particular person. Maimonides rejected this view of providence and associated it with the idea of an eternally preexisting world.

The third and fourth positions on providence are attributed to the Ash'arites and the Mu'tazilites, the two movements associated with the Kalam. These views, despite their differences, both reflect, with full force, the idea of creation in time and exercise of divine will. According to the Ash'arites, the reach of providence is much greater than Aristotle thought, extending to every individual being, human or otherwise. Nothing in the world takes place on its own, independent of divine will. Every leaf that falls from a tree does so as the result of a deliberate exercise of divine will.

The absolute sovereignty of divine will includes even human actions taken in conformance to divine decree, so the Ash'arites reject the possibility of free will. The differing fates of human beings also express God's will and dominion, as do the suffering and happiness of human beings whose actions are preordained. The response to any question about people's different fates can only be "God so wills it."

The Ash'arite view differs from the Aristotelian not only with regard to the reach of providence but also with regard to its very nature. The providence that Maimonides attributed to Aristotle was the causality inherent in existence, derived inexorably from the existence of God and His wisdom and allowing for permanent and stable existence. In the Ash'arite view, however, providence is ongoing volitional action, controlling all events in the universe. If Aristotle was interested in the order, permanence, and rationality that exist in the world, the Ash'arites looked for control and sovereignty. The basic intuition underlying each position relates to the tension between wisdom and will, between preexistence and creation.

Maimonides rejects the Ash'arite view, for the denial of human free will undermines the essence of Torah and commandments. How can men be directed to observe the Torah's commandments if they are unable to choose whether to observe them or transgress? Similarly, extending divine will to each and every event seems to be an absurdity that leads, among other things, to more than a few injustices. Why should people be punished for actions that they are not responsible for?

The Mu'tazilite position, the fourth that Maimonides presents, offers a corrective to Ash'arite radicalism, maintaining that God controls, through acts of his will, all details of existence except human actions. Humans exercise free choice in their actions, which are therefore subject to reward and punishment. Divine justice applies not only to men but also to beasts, and they will be rewarded in the world to come as recompense for the torments they suffered in this world. Although this position does not undermine the power of the Torah, Maimonides nevertheless rejects it because it extends divine justice to beasts as well and ties God's will to every action that takes place in the world.

The fifth position Maimonides describes is that of the Torah, his own. As long as one is speaking of non-humans, he believes, Aristotle is correct to assert that providence applies only to species overall. God does not govern the events experienced by each and every animal, and He certainly does not directly deploy His will each time a leaf falls from a tree. All such events are within the context of general causal regularity. Most human beings, too, are relegated to natural randomness and are not governed by providence. Where Maimonides departs from Aristotle is in maintaining that perfected human beings are subject to providence as individuals. He understands providence as a privilege that distinguishes the perfected among human beings from others, and the perfected human differs from other beings in the degree of providence to which he is subject. The closer a person comes to perfection, the greater the degree of divine providence to which he is subject, for he is bonded more closely to the intellect emanating onto him.

Maimonides' position departs in no uncertain terms from the traditional view of providence, which believes that God punishes the wicked and rewards the ordinary (that is, those who are neither wicked nor virtuous). According to Maimonides, the wicked and the ordinary, constituting most of humanity, are relegated to happenstance. But despite this dramatic divide, the concept he presents has an internal religious logic: providence is not a basic given and does not apply to all people; it is, rather, something achieved only by a few. Throughout existence, God attends only to species as a whole, but perfected human beings merit individual providence. How that individual providence operates, however, is subject to widely differing interpretations.

The conservative reading of the *Guide* offers one such interpretation. The causal structure is what controls all existence and the fate of most men, but perfected men are subject to God's special attention, and He exercises His will to protect them from the harms and misfortunes that befall other creatures. On this reading, nature and wisdom are maintained with respect to reality as a whole, but when necessary, divine will bursts through and acts within it. If that is so, Maimonides rejected the Ash'arite position, according to which God's willful providence governs every individual and event to the point of negating the entire causal order. But he also rejects the Aristotelian position, which sees the causal order as the exclusive principle governing all existence, wicked and perfected alike. According to the conservative reading, Maimonides' view of providence parallels his views of creation and prophecy. With respect to creation, he preserved a necessary, fundamental element of creation in time—the creation of existence *ex nihilo*—and allows for the action of divine will when necessary. With respect to prophecy, he interpreted the phenomenon as a natural one but left room for a supernatural exercise of will in the case of Moses' prophecy. The same structure can be seen in connection with providence. The causal order applies everywhere except with regard to perfected people, who are protected by God's will. Accordingly, the principle of causal wisdom is not the exclusive explanation for what happens in the universe, and it is limited in areas related to the principles of religion—creation, prophecy, and providence.

The *Guide*'s philosophical readers, for their part—that is, those who understood it as affirming eternal preexistence—took a very different view of the idea that perfected people were subject to divine providence on an individual basis. On their reading, which seems to have better internal, textual logic, perfected individuals are not providentially overseen by means of divine intervention volitionally bestowed only on them. Providential oversight is afforded them, rather, by reason of causal reality itself, and it can be accounted for in terms of wisdom, not will. The perfection of the individuals who enjoy providence is commensurate with their apprehension of God and the world, as Maimonides emphasized, and that apprehension affords them two advantages that distinguish them from other men and beasts. Those advantages are theirs without any intervention of the divine will.

The first advantage is that of a place in the world to come; their souls do not perish and they are not eliminated from the world. Like Aristotle, Maimonides believed that providence implies the possibility of eternity and stability inherent in the causal order. That capacity for eternity is granted to those who attain knowledge and become bound to the active intellect; accordingly, providence—bestowed, in Aristotle's view, only on sorts whose eternity is ensured—pertains to perfected individuals.

Samuel Ibn Tibbon read Maimonides this way, understanding him to hold the view that individual providence did not involve willful divine intervention in an individual's life. In a letter on providence that he sent to Maimonides (and that Maimonides never answered), he afforded a philosophical interpretation to the concept of prophecy as it appeared in the *Guide*. In his view, misfortunes befell perfected people in the same way as others, and God did not intervene to free them from poverty, illness, or travail. But because they adhere to the proper goal of apprehending the intelligibles, which assures them eternal life, they do not regard these events as troubles.[1] They do not consider such things as loss of wealth, ill-

---

[1] Samuel's letter was published in Z. Diesendruck, "Samuel and Moses Ibn Tibbon on Maimoindes' Theory of Providence," *Hebrew Union College Annual* 11 (1936): 352–366.

ness, or handicap to be losses, for they are bound to what truly matters and what assures a person eternal life. Accordingly, in addition to the eternal life these individuals are assured of, they experience providence in their day-to-day lives, expressed not in the form of events that happen to them but as a profound change in consciousness.

The second advantage that apprehension affords to individuals overseen by providence was formulated by Moses Ibn Tibbon, Samuel's son. Unlike his father, Moses held that those perfected in thought were protected from troubles in a practical way, but not because God willfully directed reality to their benefit, as the conservative reading would have it. Rather, the knowledge of the world that these people acquired allowed them to live better-protected lives, and that is their second natural advantage: they know how to foresee risks and properly assess situations. Moreover, their focus on the higher goal of knowing God frees them from the mental and physical woes that ensue when a person's life is controlled by his desires. Perfected individuals are distinguished, then, by being providentially protected from the afflictions of the world to a greater extent than other people, but in the understanding associated with a preexisting universe, that distinctiveness does not entail a miraculous departure from the causal order. The protection and endurance simply reflect the fact that the causal order itself does well for the good.

Conservative and philosophical readers agree that Maimonides' great innovation here was the idea that providence was something afforded only to individuals and that other people were given over to chance. He thereby rejected the position of the Kalam, which saw divine intervention in every event that transpired in the world, and dissented from the traditional Jewish view that individual providence governed all people. According to Maimonides, God's presence and providence, for most people, are mediated via the causal order that He created, an order to which people are subject. The dispute between the conservative and philosophical readings pertains to how the providence extended to perfected individuals should be understood: is it effected through willful divine intervention, as the Kalam understood it to be, or is it built into the causal order itself, to be understood in terms of eternity and immortality, as Aristotle understood providence with respect to other species? The philosophical reading affords Maimonides' acceptance of reality, emphatically declared in the discussion of theodicy, a more profound meaning. Existence itself, structured through divine wisdom, corresponds to the varying degrees of human virtue, responding to differences among people without any need for willful divine intervention.

The Reasons for the Commandments

To begin his discussion of the meaning of the commandments, Maimonides places the issue in the broader context of will versus wisdom. He thereby links the *Guide*'s final portion, devoted to the reasons for the commandments, to its preceding sections, which dealt with various aspects of the foundations of Judaism and moved around a will-wisdom axis. According to the view that treats will as key to understanding God's perfection, there is no need to inquire about the reasons for the commandments. Their authority and significance flow exclusively from the fact that they express the will of God. Indeed, assigning reasons to them might diminish their worth, for it would appear to make them dependent on some source of authority external to God Himself and His might. The religious attitude and concept of humanity associated with the emphasis on divine will call for absolute obedience. To seek out a commandment's meaning is to express a lack of faith, to question the commandment's absolute authority. But Maimonides squarely rejected the religious perspective that emphasized divine will at the expense of the meaning of the commandments, and he believed the commandments could be explained as manifestations of wisdom. Just as God's wisdom is revealed in the order and purpose evident in nature, so, too, is it revealed in the Torah through its implicit insights and purpose.

For Maimonides, as we have seen, God is revealed not in the miraculous, the exceptional, and the inexplicable but in the natural, the orderly, and the causal. The Torah likewise does not give voice to arbitrariness, will, or wonder. There are those who find religious meaning only by attributing absurdity and inexplicability to God, but Maimonides treated that attitude as a sort of illness:

> There is a group of human beings who consider it a grievous thing that causes should be given for any law; what would please them most is that the intellect would not find a meaning for the commandments and prohibitions. What compels them to feel thus is a sickness that they find in their souls . . . For they think that if those laws were useful in this existence and had been given to us for this or that reason, it would be as if they derived

from the reflection and the understanding of some intelligent being. If, however, there is a thing for which the intellect could not find any meaning at all and that does not lead to something useful, it indubitably derives from God. (III:31; Pines, pp. 523–524)

Maimonides believed every commandment had its purpose. Understanding its usefulness does not undermine its worth; on the contrary, it extends one's awareness of wisdom so it encompasses law as well as nature.

The Torah does not set itself the goal of imposing God's arbitrary will on man and putting man to the test of obedience. That concept of religion is alien to the idea of wisdom and to Maimonides' basic religious stance. The Torah aims, rather, to lead man to the fulfillment of his human potential for perfection. That perfection, as already noted, involves the full development of his capacities as a knowing creature. The Torah in that sense is natural, complementing nature by creating the social and personal conditions that will foster one's ability to realize his natural purpose. Man requires an ordered society and a stable physical grounding in order to develop to his fullest. The Torah's first goal, then, is to improve the body, by creating a just and stable society in which a person can flourish as a complete human being. Laws related to the social order—dealing with such matters as torts, loans, bailment, theft, assault, and inheritance—are among the commandments meant to improve interpersonal relationships. In addition, there are commandments meant to foster sound character traits, thereby further ensuring a sound social order and proper relationships among people. This group includes commandments forbidding hatred, envy, and vengeance on the one hand and, on the other, those requiring sharing and charity and promoting mercy. The law forbidding the slaughter of an animal and its offspring on the same day is meant to prevent the development of cruelty, as is the obligation to send away the mother bird before taking the nestlings. Prohibitions on improper sexual relations are meant to promote the control of desire. Close relatives are forbidden to each other because they are regularly in proximity to each other. The limitations on sexuality advance the purpose of the law, which is to promote sound character. God's wisdom, accordingly, is revealed in the system of commandments, just as it is in nature. As Maimonides writes: "Marvel exceedingly at the wisdom of His commandments, may He be exalted, just as you should marvel at the wisdom manifested in the things He had made. It says: *The Rock, His work is perfect, for all His ways are judgment.* It says that just as the things made by

Him are consummately perfect, so are His commandments consummately just" (III:49; Pines, p. 605).

The other purpose of the commandments is improvement of the soul, and the means for accomplishing that is social and physical betterment. This layer of the Torah differentiates it from ordinary political legislation and transforms it into divine law, a law that leads man to his highest perfection as a creature able to distinguish true from false. The commandments in question are meant to supplant erroneous beliefs about the nature of the world and free man from the dominance of imagination. Idolatry gains strength because men lack the knowledge to distinguish between the possible and the impossible, and the Torah therefore forbids not only actions directly associated with idolatry but also all activity for which there is no rational basis. But it does more than negate incorrect beliefs; it also instills in the faithful certain necessary and useful beliefs regarding providence and repentance, doing so through the obligation to fast and cry out to God in times of trouble. The commandments to observe the Sabbath and recall the Exodus from Egypt fortify belief in creation, and the commandments to love God and affirm His unity are tied to knowledge of God and reality. It can be argued, therefore, that all of the Torah's commandments are dedicated to the purpose of improving body and soul, thereby bringing a person to his highest perfection.

Any effort to assign a rational purpose to the commandments runs into the serious problem posed by the group of commandments referred to in rabbinic literature as _huqqim_ (lit., "statutes," but usually used to denote the type of law next discussed). These commandments, such as the prohibition on interweaving linen and wool, the prohibition on eating meat and milk together, or the laws of purity and impurity, appear utterly inexplicable. Their existence would appear to bolster the position that focuses on divine will, locating the religious significance of the commandments in the required submission to God's word and making no attempt at explanation. According to this view of things, the significance of the _huqqim_ is their very lack of any understandable rationale, and they bear no relationship to the fulfillment of any human purpose. Maimonides, as we have seen, rejected any such understanding of the Torah and claimed that every commandment had a reason even if we do not now know what it is. In attempting to assign meaning and explanation to the _huqqim_, he undertook one of the most original and daring ventures in the history of Jewish thought.

Maimonides maintained that the key to understanding the meaning of the *ḥuqqim* lies in the historical context in which the Torah was given. He states his overall guiding principle as follows: "In the case of most of the *statutes* whose reason is hidden from us, everything serves to keep people away from *idolatry*" (III:49; Pines, p. 612). A commandment such as the ban on mixing meat and milk is tied to an idolatrous cult that existed in biblical times, in which a kid was ritually eaten in its mother's milk. The prohibition on wearing linen and wool together reflects the use of that fabric blend in the vestments of idolatrous priests. Even the prohibition of shaving parts of the head and face grows out of similar considerations, reflecting the tonsorial practice of pagan priests. Maimonides did not rest content with speculating on these matters; he immersed himself in the available literature on idolatry which provided him the keys to the meaning of some unexplained commitment, as he reported to the circle of scholars in Motpellier while completing the *Guide*:

> I also have read in all matters concerning all of idolatry, so that it seems to me there does not remain in the world a composition on this subject, having been translated into Arabic from other languages, but that I have read it and have understood its subject matter and have plumbed the depth of its thought. From those books it became clear to me what the reason is for all the commandments that everyone comes to think of as having no reason at all other that the decree of Scripture. I already have a great composition on this subject in the Arabic language (namely the *Guide of the Perplexed*) with lucid proofs for every single commandment. (*Letter on Astrology*, pp. 465-466)

Among these idolatrous texts were those associated with the Sabians. That group was active in the Mesopotamian region, and Maimonides had access to some of its writings, such as *The Order of Nabatean Worship* (a text seems to have been a forgery). His study of those works provided the basis for his understanding of the history of idolatry, which he took as the key to understanding the commandments meant to extirpate idolatry: "I shall now return to my purpose and say that the meaning of many of the laws became clear to me and their causes become known to me through my study of the doctrines, opinions, practices, and cult of the Sabians, as you will hear when I explain the reasons for the *commandments* that are considered to be without cause" (III:29; Pines, p. 518).

The struggle against idolatry employs two strategies. The first is to require actions that are the opposite of those performed in idolatrous ritual. Idolaters would sacrifice honey and yeast; the Torah therefore forbids bringing honey to the altar. Idolaters would avoid sacrificing goats, regarding them as sacred; the Torah therefore requires the sacrifice specifically of goats.

The second strategy is to adopt pagan practices in a way that transforms them into the worship of God. An example of this strategy is the Bible's sacrificial cult itself. Underlying the practice of worship through animal sacrifice is the belief in an anthropomorphized, corporeal deity who needs to feed on the gifts offered by men. This cult, therefore, is alien to biblical monotheism, which aims to divest the image of God of any trace of anthropomorphism. But the Torah could never have annulled this form of worship in one fell swoop, for the Israelites were thoroughly immersed in and accustomed to it. Maimonides here draws a comparison between nature and the Torah. Nature makes it possible for an infant to survive without solid food, which it is not yet able to ingest, and the Torah similarly employs a pedagogic approach that takes account of the historical and spiritual conditions of the time. It does not set out to express eternal, unconditioned truths; it attempts, rather, to set out a system of rules meant to advance human beings in the actual circumstances in which they find themselves. To have attempted to eliminate sacrifice at the time the Torah was given would have been as unrealistic as an attempt by a legislator to eliminate prayer in Maimonides' own time: "At that time, this would have been similar to the appearance of a prophet in these times who, calling upon the people to worship God, would say: 'God has given you a Law forbidding you to pray to Him, to fast, to call upon Him for help in misfortune. Your worship should consist solely in meditation, without any works at all'" (III:32; Pines, p. 526). As forms of worship, prayer, and fasting are preferable to sacrifices, though they, too, fall short of the ideal. They are not premised on God's need for nourishment, to be sure, but they still assume that God is moved in some emotional way by actions directed toward Him. Nevertheless, negating those actions and confining ritual exclusively to thought—that is, internal contemplation of God—would leave the community without any way to worship God. The Torah therefore preserves the sacrificial cult but limits it to one place, forbidding use of local altars and requiring all sacrifice to be at the central sanctuary. Moreover, the sacrificial cult itself is cast in a form that combats idolatry, for there is no image or form of God at the sanctuary, and many elements of the cult as practiced there are directed against idolatrous rituals.

Maimonides' explanations for the _huqqim_ and the sacrifices represent a rather daring historicization of the Torah. He suggests that the reasons for the _huqqim_ can be uncovered only by detailed historical study of the pagan context in which the Torah was given. One may say that Maimonides here took the first step toward the study of comparative religion, doing so in his effort to provide a rational context for all the commandments. But even more, this approach determines that the Torah, sensitive to the needs of time and place, and adaptive to humans' ritual needs, commands the use of fundamentally flawed forms of worship that it rejects in principle. It does so as a necessary compromise so that some ritual may be used in worshipping God, but the usefulness of the strategy remains based on the historical and geographic context. Rationalizing the commandments in this way risks undermining their authority by transforming them into temporally conditioned rules: if there no longer exist pagans whose cult involves eating kids in their mothers' milk, why maintain the prohibition? Moreover, if the deep-seated need for a sacrificial cult no longer exists— and Maimonides sensed that it no longer did in his time—why continue to look favorably on a flawed form of ritual? It is hardly surprising that in _Mishneh Torah_, Maimonides refrained from providing a historical explanation for the sacrifices and for the laws of purity and impurity. He explains them on other grounds, avoiding those that could potentially undermine the law's authority.

It is important to note, therefore, that the historical explanation for the commandments does not question their eternal and absolute force. Maimonides saw nothing wrong in principle with the Torah incorporating elements tied to time and place. Law, in his view, might warrant changes and supplements reflecting new circumstances, but such changes were forbidden because they could undermine the law's authority:

> Inasmuch as God, may He be exalted, knew that the commandments of this Law will need in every time and place—so far as some of them are concerned—to be added to or subtracted from according to the diversity of places, happenings, and conjunctures of circumstances, He forbade adding

to them or subtracting from them, saying: Thou shalt not add thereto, nor diminish from it. For this might have led to the corruption of the rules of the Law and to the belief that the latter did not come from God. (III:41; Pines, pp. 562–563)

A court may modify the Torah's law temporarily, to deal with changed circumstances, but permanent change is forbidden, for that would call the law's authority into question. The eternity and unity of the law do not follow, as a matter of principle, from the law's essential structure and significance. Quite the contrary: the law must be suited to the time and place, taking account of changing contexts and circumstances. The need for invariance and unity arises because of political constraints related to the subjects' perception of the law's authority. One must therefore distinguish between the reasons for the commandments and the source of their authority. The reason for any given commandment is grounded in transitory historical reality, but the authority for all the commandments is eternal, beyond time. Accordingly, even though Maimonides assigns the sacrifices a rationale based on historical circumstances that no longer pertain, he has no doubt, as a halakhist, about their continued applicability. In *Mishneh Torah*, he rules that the laws regarding the sacrifices retain their binding force for all time, and major portions of *Mishneh Torah* are devoted to the details of the sacrifices, the Temple and its implements, and purity and impurity.

But there is more here than a historical battle against idolatry, waged long ago, that affords meaning to the commandments. Beneath the surface of Maimonides' teachings we find as well evidence of his sharp disagreement with the ideas regarding the reasons for the commandments that were current in his own time. According to these views, which Maimonides knew of through the writings of Abraham Ibn Ezra and Judah Halevi, the commandments had causal power and fulfilling them affected reality. The Temple, for example, had the form of stellar cosmic structures, and it played a role referred to in the Middle Ages as "talisman." Through its proper external form, it helped draw down divine powers into the world. The kabbalists, with whom Maimonides was not familiar, developed the idea of the commandments' causal force beyond the natural world, extending it to the divine world itself. Judah Halevi believed the commandments acted to bring the divine into the world, and he analogized them to medicines administered in proper doses and having their effect even though the patient does not know why. These sorts of magical and astrological interpretations developed against the background of scientific attitudes grounded in the tradition of astral magic, according to which terrestrial structures paralleled the heavenly order of constellations and stars and drew on their spiritual powers, acting through them. Maimonides associates these positions with Sabian idolatry:

> In conformity with these opinions, the Sabians set up statues for the planets, golden statues for the sun and silver ones for the moon, and distributed the minerals and the climes between the planets, saying that one particular planet was the deity of one particular clime. And they built temples, set up the statues within them and thought that the forces of the planets overflowed toward these statues. (III:29; Pines, p. 516)

In Maimonides' own view, however, the efficacy of the commandments is limited to influencing human consciousness and the social order, and they have no magical or causal effect on the natural order. That is especially so with regard to the laws of purity and impurity. An impure object has no inherently harmful or negative power. No commandment forbids incurring a state of impurity, as by touching a corpse, a dead animal, or someone with impure bodily discharges. What is forbidden is entering the Sanctuary while in a state of impurity, and that prohibition has an eminently practical rationale grounded in limiting access to the Sanctuary. If a place may be entered at any time and in any condition, its value in the eyes of the multitude is diminished. To preclude that sort of unmediated entry, persons in a state of impurity were denied access to the Temple, and the more common the type of impurity, the longer the purification process. Purity and impurity, therefore, do not refer to some positive or negative state of affairs in the world, nor do they reflect quasi-demonic forces that must be kept at bay or that one must purify himself from. The incense burned in the sanctuary, for example, is entirely practical—it mitigates the unpleasant smell of the slaughtered animals and sprinkled blood in the Temple. Without a pleasant scent, the sanctuary would be regarded simply as a slaughterhouse and the masses would have less regard for it. The goal of this ramified system, despite the many magical interpretations it has been given, is simply to enhance the awe in which people hold the Temple and the grandeur they attribute to it.

The Commandments and the Philosopher's Spiritual Exercise

As we have seen, many of the commandments are meant to supplant idolatry, inculcate necessary beliefs, and promote the acceptance of true beliefs. The philosopher, as part of the community, fulfills all of the commandments that pertain to improving society and instilling virtues. Maintaining a sound social order is a responsibility he bears along with all other members of the community. Most of the commandments associated with improving the soul do not directly pertain to him, particularly those aimed at negating idolatry and bolstering necessary beliefs. He is required to fulfill them because he is part of the public. He will bring the appropriate sacrifices if he transgresses inadvertently, he will come to Jerusalem on the pilgrimage festivals and bring the associated offerings, and he will fast and cry out in times of trouble, even though these actions are ill-suited to the concept of the divinity he has internalized. Torah, like nature, is designed to suit the majority. It does not suit every individual and may even be harmful to a few. No one, not even a philosopher, is exempt on that account from absolute faithfulness to the *halakhah*, but the philosopher's observance of *halakhah* has an added dimension. As a member of the covenantal community, the philosopher is obligated, like every else, to observe every detail of the *halakhah*; as a philosopher, his fulfillment of the commandments has a special meaning that plays a central role in his spiritual journey. Maimonides discusses this added dimension in one of the most provocative chapters of the *Guide*, at the end of his treatment of the reasons for the commandments.

Human consciousness is dominated by anxieties and desires, the consequence of our very existence as physical beings. Even when we are not actively engaged in earning a living, raising children, or going to the doctor, we are shadowed constantly by an awareness of the need to maintain our lives, and that awareness controls man's inner world. Even a man who has come to know God and the world experiences that state of consciousness. A man of that sort has refined his image of God, cleansing it of all anthropomorphism, and has even read the writings of Avicenna and learned from them that the existence of God is necessary, in contrast to the merely contingent nature of the existence of the world. He can demonstrate conclusively, following Averroes, that God is the unmoved mover, the first cause in the chain of causation that drives the entire universe. All that knowledge, however, does not necessarily bring about an internal change in his consciousness. The aspirations and difficulties of daily life may continue to dominate his consciousness like that of any other man and to preoccupy him even when he turns to lofty matters. The role of the commandments in the philosopher's life is to move his inner life from a state of knowledge to a state of passionate attachment.

Love and desire reflect a state of constant engagement with the object of knowledge. One who loves and desires something differs from one who merely knows it in that his consciousness is filled with and preoccupied by the object of knowledge. Intense love uproots a person from the world, focusing his consciousness on the sole and exclusive object of his yearning. This erotic element, familiar to anyone who has known love, does not arise immediately with respect to knowledge as abstract and lofty as knowledge of God. The move from knowledge to desire demands inner training and spiritual work. The first stage of this training entails exercises to clear one's consciousness of the worldly matters, that is, a slow process of liberation from the subjugation of one's inner world to concerns about life's mainte-nance. Observance of the commandments plays a central role in this inter-nal work:

> Know that all the practices of the worship, such as reading the *Torah*, prayer, and the performance of the other *commandments*, have only the end of training you to occupy yourself with His commandments, may He be ex-alted, rather than with matters pertaining to this world . . . From here on I will begin to give you guidance with regard to the form of this training so that you should achieve this great end. The first thing that you should cause your soul to hold fast onto is that, while *reciting* the *shema* prayers, you should empty your mind of everything and pray thus. You should not con-tent yourself with *being intent* while *reciting the first verse of shema* and say-ing *the first benediction*. When this has been carried out correctly and has been practiced consistently for years, cause your soul, whenever you read or listen to the *Torah*, to be constantly directed—the whole of you and your thought—toward reflection on what you are listening to or reading. (III:51; Pines, p. 622)

In the spiritual work of the educated person, there is an internal medi-tative goal to prayer, reading the Torah, and fulfilling the command-ments—that of freeing one's consciousness of worldly needs and cravings. The process begins with small steps in the recitation of the *shema* and in the

amidah prayer. As it continues, the trainee frees his consciousness for longer periods, including Torah reading, the prayers overall, the blessings, and
the performance of the commandments. At that stage, the worshipper
does not yet direct his consciousness to God, the great object of his desire;
rather, through concentrating on the actions themselves, he empties his
consciousness of terrestrial matters. He learns to restrict the control exercised by worldly anxieties and aspirations and to restrict his attention to
them to ever more limited times. When he is alone at night, free of life's
commotion and demands, he engages with the objects of his knowledge
and directs his consciousness to the divinity. In that way, he gradually frees
many areas of his inner world from worldly involvement and eventually
attains the pinnacle of a transformed consciousness. At the pinnacle of
religious consciousness, the lover of God can conduct the activities involved in running one's life even while his inner consciousness is suffused
in its entirety by love of God. That level of existence is a rare achievement,
one that only a few can attain:

> And there may be a human individual who, through his apprehension of
> the true realities and his joy in what he has apprehended, achieves a state in
> which he talks with people and is occupied with his bodily necessities while
> his intellect is wholly turned toward Him, may He be exalted, so that in in
> heart he is always in His presence, may He be exalted, while outwardly he is
> with people, in the sort of way described by the poetical parables that have
> been invented for these notions: *I sleep but my heart waketh; it is the voice of
> my beloved that knocketh, and so on.* I do not say that this rank is that of all
> the prophets; but I do say that this is the rank of *Moses our Master* . . . This
> was also the rank of the Patriarchs, the result of whose nearness to Him,
> may He be exalted, was that His name became known to the world through
> them . . . Because of the union of their intellects through apprehension of
> Him, it came about that He made a lasting *covenant* with each of them.
> (III:51; Pines, 623–624)

The Patriarchs and Moses attained an absolute transformation of consciousness. At the start of the spiritual process, a man's inner world is dominated by the needs of daily life, and their presence overshadows his consciousness even when he is engaged in coming to know what lies beyond
his narrow world. At the end of the process, conversely, terrestrial activities
go forward automatically, and his inner consciousness is engaged with that
which is lofty. Externally, a man maintains contact with his surroundings,

but his consciousness as a lover is preoccupied constantly by God, to Whom he is bonded through knowledge. He is engaged with the world as if on automatic pilot mode. The practical commandments play a role in this inner transformation, concentrating a man's attention and enabling him thereby to free himself internally.

The philosopher's worship and desire reach their peak when he stands before death. The survival instinct is the ultimate umbilical cord attaching a person to the world. A man's affinity to his precious individual life, and his terror over the prospect of its coming to an end, bind him firmly to reality. But the worshipper who is bonded to God and delights in his achievement is able to cut that cord. He can free himself from fear of death because he no longer sees it as a tragedy:

> Yet in the measure in which the faculties of the body are weakened and the fire of the desires is quenched, the intellect it strengthened, and its lights achieve a wider extension, its apprehension is purified, and it rejoices in what it apprehends. The result is that when a perfect man is stricken with years and approaches death, this apprehension increases very powerfully, joy over this apprehension and a great love for the object of apprehension become stronger, until the soul is separated from the body at that moment in this state of pleasure. (III:51; Pines, p. 627)

The great test of religious consciousness, then, is the confrontation with death. The moment of death itself, which fills a man with horrific anxiety and a sense of loss, is the pinnacle of the philosopher's internal spiritual training, for it completes the separation of intellect from body. When the moment of death appears in the state of consciousness in which one's inner world is separated from worldly concerns, the terror is transformed into pleasure. The death of a philosopher is termed "death by a kiss," and it is, in effect, liberation from death—or, more, precisely, liberation through death: " . . . this kind of death, which in true reality is salvation from death . . . After having reached this condition of enduring permanence, that intellect remains in one and the same state, the impediment that sometimes screened him off having been removed. And he will remain permanently in that state of intense pleasure, which does not belong to the genus of bodily pleasures" (III:51; Pines, p. 628).

With Maimonides' exposition of the reasons for the commandments, the integration of Torah and philosophy achieves full fruition since the philosophical outlook informs the most important aspect of Judaism the life of Torah and its meaning. Like all political structures, some of the commandments aim at establishing a well ordered just society, which is necessary for human flourishing. For that purpose the Torah through a variety of ritual practices inculcates necessary beliefs such as reward and punishment, repentance and forgiveness, which are crucial for the solidifying obedience to Torah and its commandments. Other commandments are aimed beyond mere social order at training of the moral virtues which is fundamental to the good of the city and crucial for the attainment of higher forms of meaningful life that depend on self-control and discipline of the passions. As a divine law oriented beyond the perfection of the body and the well-ordered society, the Torah directs humans to their ultimate perfection by the complex attempt at uprooting idolatry and establishing the truth of God's unity and transcendence. Beyond the role played by the commandments in establishing a sound society, perfecting character, and instilling necessary beliefs and appropriate truths, they also operate as a central element in a man's spiritual journey. That journey begins with the ascendance of the imaginative faculty, which fills his consciousness with anxieties and aspirations related to worldly life, but it concludes with bonding to the intelligibles and a blissful liberation from the fear of death.

CONCLUSION

Four Readings

The four readings of the *Guide* that we have seen present different ways of dealing with the fundamental questions Maimonides grappled with in his treatise. Each reading has its own way of confronting such issues as the role of philosophy, the conception of God, the standing of man in the world and its ultimate perfection, and the way in which the perplexed person overcomes his existential crisis.

The *skeptical reading* sees philosophy as a critical tool, able to uncover the fact that language, like painting and sculpture, can provide only a limited and misleading representation of God. It follows that no positive knowledge of God can be conveyed through language, and that preserving God's pristine unity and transcendence demands silence. The perplexed man sheds the traditional and accepted language of faith, understanding that any attempt to formulate positive statements of belief about God will transform the object of worship into an alien, imaginary deity. The highest level of knowledge of God is expressed in a skeptical concept refined and cleansed of anything that might sully divine sublimity, and it returns the perplexed person to the world. He comes to realize that even the greatest metaphysical problem of creation in time versus eternal preexistence defies all formulation. All that is left is God's revelation in the world, which reflects the actions of loving-kindness, righteousness, and justice. Silence leads one to action in the world, which is the exclusive and direct path to adopting the ways of God in human life.

The *mystical reading* agrees that philosophy's role is primarily a critical one, for it sets limits to what it is possible to know. But it sees the philosophical journey as a process that clears the way to direct illumination and to a meta-linguistic, meta-rational experience of God. This mystical experience takes place after one's consciousness is emptied of all positive content, especially through the negation of language. The mystical reading, unlike the skeptical, believes in direct cognition and non-linguistic illumination of God, which one can attain only after language has reached its final limit. The mystical experience is not attained through the ecstatic mechanisms familiar in the history of mysticism, such as movement, breathing exercises, or automatic repetition of fixed syllables. To clear one's consciousness in a way that makes illumination possible, one must undergo a difficult and exhausting process of precise philosophical argument. Philosophical negation of false images ensures that the object of the experience will not be the fruit of misleading imagination, for the experience will have taken place only after one's consciousness has been cleansed, by means of philosophy, of every misleading positive image of God. The perplexed person sets out on his journey in a state of existential crisis spawned by the conflict between a philosophical belief system and a traditional one. In the mystical reading, however, he does not conclude the journey, as in the skeptical reading, in a return to the world of action; rather, he does so in direct, meta-linguistic experience of the sublime.

On the *conservative reading*, the *Guide*'s great achievement is in its demonstration that eternal preexistence of the world cannot be proven. The perplexed person can adhere to the philosophical way without challenging the foundations of Judaism, which rest on the ascription to God of will. Divine will establishes existence through creation *ex nihilo*; even more, the exercise of divine will provides the basis for viewing the revelation to Moses as an event of eternal, binding authority. The principle of wisdom also plays an important role in the conservative reading, for the dimension of will is kept to narrow, extraordinary contexts. God indeed created the world *ex nihilo*, but from that point on, it is causality, not will, through which his revelation is expressed. All prophecy other than that of Moses is understood as an event having an internal causal structure related to the prophet's perfection. The providential oversight premised on God's willful intervention in human life is limited to a perfect few, and other creatures (man and beast alike) are subject only to the natural causation that follows from God's original actions. The perplexed person can accept the philosophical ethos without compromising the sacred fundamentals of faith.

The *philosophical reading*, in contrast, maintains that the *Guide* provided a systematic interpretation of Judaism's fundamental concepts on the basis of wisdom and an eternal, preexisting world. Uncovering the Torah's hidden meaning makes it possible for the perplexed person to internalize the tradition of the Greco-Arab philosophy without weakening his tie to Israel's Torah. The treatise retranslates the concepts of prophecy, providence, and creation in a manner entirely consistent with the causal structure of the world, reflective of God's wisdom. The references to divine will that abound in the language of the Bible and the tradition are tied to necessary beliefs, without which the social order and faithfulness to *halakhah* might be undermined. And the same may be said of the *Guide* itself, which conceals its deep meaning from the reader who has not been initiated into philosophy. The philosophical process leads the perplexed person from will to wisdom. He is freed from life's hustle and bustle and worldly cravings, and his consciousness is directed totally toward the object of his desire—God. The commandments are a substantive part of this journey and of the spiritual exercise that weakens the grip of worldly existence on his inner world. At the end of the process, the philosophical worshipper of God is freed from the destructive power of death.

The various readings of the *Guide* reflect views of the world that differ substantively from one another, and any attempt to propose a single, consistent reading of the treatise strikes me as doomed to failure, however great the temptation to try. Skeptical readers, for example, will argue that the philosophical reading is nothing more than a preparatory step to the much more meaningful one of skepticism and consequent return to the world. The mystical interpretation will cite the elements of revelatory illumination within the treatise, which follow upon the voiding of knowledge achieved through the skeptical reading. Proponents of the philosophical reading will maintain that ideas about creation in time, as they appears in the surface layers of the *Guide*, are nothing more than an external layer of necessary beliefs, concealing the hidden meaning of the book. And the conservative interpreters will say that taking the work to favor eternal preexistence of the world misreads it by taking account only of the principles of wisdom to be found within it and disregarding Maimonides' efforts to defend the basic elements of the faith from the corrosive effects of belief in eternity.

Efforts such as these to interpret the *Guide* in a uniform manner have been made throughout the work's history. But a deep and thorough reading shows it to defy these efforts, however sophisticated and creative they may be. How, for example, can the spirit of Part III, Chapter 51, which describes the redemption of the philosopher's soul from the fetters of the world and from death, be reconciled with that of Chapter 54, which tells of the philosopher's return to worldly life after coming to recognize that all he can know about God are His actions in the world as it exists? How can the claim of the uniqueness and miraculousness of Moses' prophecy as it is stated in the *Guide* II, 35 be harmonized with the description in the *Guide* I, 51, in which Moses's insight into nature provides the source and content of his revelation? Or, in what way can we reconcile Maimonides' stated claim that he adopts creation *ex nihilo* in the *Guide* II, 25, while other chapters in the *Guide* establish a naturalistic explanation to the basic steps in the biblical creation story? And is there a possibility to bring together the miraculous nature of providence described in the *Guide* III, 51 protecting the virtuous person from all evils, and the naturalistic version proposed in the *Guide* III 23, where the wise man, like Job, internalizes that true happiness consists in the knowledge of God no matter what happens to him? It seems to me undeniable that the *Guide of the Perplexed* leaves multiple possibilities open to the reader, and that may well have been Maimonides' intention. The distress originally felt by the student thus opened the door to a range of possibilities. In allowing for four different lines of interpretation, Maimonides tacitly addresses the perplexed person as follows: You can maintain your loyalty to Judaism whether you affirm eternal existence or creation in time, and your philosophical inquiry may lead you to mystical experience or back to the world. Your perplexity is not a paralyzing fracture that can be resolved only in an intellectual and spiritual suicide through amputation of an important part of your spirit. Your perplexity, arising from the encounter between Torah and wisdom, opens before you various possibilities for religious existence and meaning.

The treatise therefore does not suggest one exclusive way to understand the Jewish tradition. If Maimonides had such a position—certainly a possibility—he does not present it to us as such. It is also possible that he himself struggled with the various alternatives and that his basic positions underwent changes during the course of his life. In any case, the primary goal of the treatise seems to be to prevent the perplexed person from coming to a terrible decision to deny a substantive part of his world. When the perplexed reader began the book, he thought he had to forsake either the Jewish tradition or his philosophical commitment. By the time he finished it, he came to understand that his existential situation is not leading him to an awful inner fissure. Quite the contrary—it is a mighty stimulus to deepening his religious outlook. The perplexity made it possible, among other things, to identify more profound perspectives on the Jewish tradition to which he is committed.

Three Common Elements

Despite the treatise's multiple meanings, there is a kernel shared by all the approaches. It pertains to the religious transformation that Maimonides sought to bring about through his novel interpretation of the Jewish tradition, and it incorporates three key elements.

The first element is shifting the struggle against idolatry from the realm of external plastic representation to that of internal mental representation. The war against idolatry was renewed because the believer's religious problem became one of anthropomorphizing God rather than worshipping statues and images. The opening of that new front required the formulation of a new attitude toward religious language, which was the primary source for the internally held personified image of God. Religious language must be read as symbol or allegory in order to overcome the invalid image of God that can be generated by a literal reading. Similarly, the transition to emphasis on the internal image integrated a necessary element of faith into religious service. A man might be punctilious in his performance of the commandments but still be worse than an idolater if he performed the commandments with an anthropomorphic image of the divinity in his consciousness. Such a person, in effect, is worshipping not God but a lofty image of humanity. This element of the Maimonidean religious transformation is linked as well to an awareness of man's marginal status in the universe. Anthropomorphism develops, in part, out of viewing man as situated at the center of existence. The war against it, then, is a struggle against a megalomaniacal view of man's place in the universe.

The second element of the religious transformation wrought by Maimonides is the focus on the causal order and the wisdom inherent in it as the most substantive revelation of the divinity. Many faith traditions place God's appearance under the rubric of "miracle," an event in which the causal order unravels and God's outstretched hand intervenes in what transpires in the world. Maimonides considered that belief to offer a flimsy, ad hoc expression of divine revelation. At the focus of religious consciousness, the world must remain as it is, as the highest expression of God's mercy, justice, and wisdom. Relying on the wondrous and the extraordinary as the basis for religious experience rests on an inability to distinguish the impossible from the possible. Such a concept comes from the imaginative faculty, the element of the soul that fosters idolatrous thinking. Accepting the order of the world as an expression of revelation extirpates messianic expectations of a change in the natural causal order. It also offers a profound resolution to what appears to be the problem of evil. Philosophy reconciles man and the causal world. It teaches him that this is his home as long as he adjusts his goals to be consistent with what nature can provide for him. The emphasis on the principle of wisdom as an expression of divine revelation leads Maimonides to a view of the Torah itself as a system meant to lead man to his natural perfection. This teleological order, and not obedience to God's word as an arbitrary sovereign decree, is what invests the Torah with religious significance.

The third element of the new religious sensibility forged by Maimonides is the rejection of the distinction between what is within the Jewish tradition and what is external to it. Philosophy is knowledge that is not derived from the canonical sources of the tradition itself. The philosophical school with which Maimonides engages deeply draws its concepts from Aristotle, imported via Muslim thought—primarily that of Ibn Sina (Avicenna), al-Farabi, Ibn Bajja, and Ibn Rushd (Averroes). Under none of the readings presented earlier is philosophy understood to be something external that the tradition must contend with. Similarly, the interpretation of Judaism that Maimonides offers is not something meant solely to reconcile beliefs grounded in the Torah with the findings of philosophy and science; rather, philosophy plays a central role in constructing the religious outlook itself. Knowledge independent of the tradition is necessary for an understanding of the tradition, for without that knowledge we cannot tell, for example, whether a particular term in the Torah is to be taken literally or metaphorically. Philosophy therefore is the mechanism through which the Torah of Israel realizes its mission as the religion of the monotheists in confrontation with idolatry. Moreover, the pinnacle of religious experience is realized through knowledge. The immersion in wisdom is a substantive part of the religious person's inner journey to the redemption of his soul, and especially of his moving from fear of God to love of God and of his contending with the world's limitations and with death.

This central role of philosophy and science in the spiritual journey is rooted in one of Maimonides' deepest insights that relate to the human condition. Humanity's initial response to the world is one of fear and instrumentality. We confront the world as both a potential source of harm and pleasure. Being in the grip of powerful anxieties and urges we tend therefore to instrumentalize the world; the world is there either against us or for us. In that initial state, being motivated by fear and desire, we are also prisoners of our imagination, which is marked by its incapacity to distinguish between what is possible and what is impossible. The combination of fear and imagination makes humans vulnerable to manipulation. Thus, the masses are easily mobilized by promises and threats, toward magic, superstition, and idolatry. Conditions of political instability lock us even deeper into that maintenance mode, in which all our internal horizons shrink to the need for survival. This feature of the human condition is the source as well for a powerful tendency to instrumentalize the Torah itself, to obey its laws and commandments out of fear of punishment and a desire for reward.

Knowledge of the world and God is aimed at relieving us of the burden of fear and freeing us from the grip of the imagination. The stance of knowledge entails the capacity to see the world as it is, independent of its instrumental role. It is therefore the key to love which is defined as a non-instrumental relationship. In grasping the vast beauty and power of the world we learn to perceive it for what it is— a grand manifestation of God's wisdom in which we humans are one marginal aspect of its design. In internalizing this non-instrumental attitude we reconcile ourselves with the world, a world that is suited to our potential as creatures capable of knowledge and capable of transcending the initial grip of fear and the imagination. By integrating this view of the human condition and the nature of genuine human flourishing into the understanding of Judaism, Maimonides constituted science and wisdom as an integral part of the Jewish tradition, which looks toward them and commands that they be studied. The goal of Judaism in communal, and individual life depends on the philosophical ethos being internalized into the tradition's heart of hearts.

The three elements of Maimonides' new religious sensibility can be found in his halakhic writings as well. The definition of God in *Mishneh Torah* is based on causational reality as the central medium for God's revelation in the world. In *Mishneh Torah*'s early chapters, God is described in terms of essence and existence, not of personality and history. According to "Laws of Repentance," corporeal conception of God is apostasy and one who espouses it places himself outside the community of Israel and loses his share in the world to come. *Mishneh Torah* regards philosophy and science as a substantive part of the *halakhah*, for the purpose of man and of *halakhah* overall is set in terms of human perfection as a rational creature, and the pinnacle of religious experience—fear and love—is attained and realized through knowledge of the world and of God. It is knowledge that liberates man from the instrumentalist attitude toward the world and leads him to an attitude of love for God. A philosophical consciousness makes its way even into clearly halakhic areas, such as the sweeping prohibition of magic and of the prophylactic use of Jewish ritual objects.

The presence of these three factors in Maimonides' halakhic writings rules out, of course, any distinction between Maimonides the halakhist and Maimonides the philosopher. Indeed, it is specifically in the halakhic writings that the philosophical elements are more prominent and sharply drawn, as we saw in our analysis of *Mishneh Torah*. In these works, God is defined in terms of eternal preexistence of the world, as is prophecy. Moreover, Maimonides' halakhic writings allow for no doubt about man's highest purpose as a knowing creature, and that definition transforms the day-to-day fulfillment of the *halakhah* into a means rather than an end in itself. In the *Guide*, meanwhile, the belief in eternal preexistence is subjected to systematic critique, as is the idea that human perfection lies in the cognition of God. The philosophical elements appearing in the *Commentary on the Mishnah* and *Mishneh Torah* thus clearly belie any distinction between *halakhah* and philosophy in Maimonides teachings.

That the basic kernel of the Maimonidean religious transformation can be found as well in his halakhic writings has implications beyond merely demonstrating the consistency of Maimonides' internal world. The integration of philosophical elements into a halakhic code reflects an attempt to elevate the philosophical religious sensitivity from a personal suggestion, an interpretation of the tradition meant only for the perplexed individual, to a binding *halakhah*, meant to shape the beliefs and self-perceptions of Jews for all time. In giving a binding formulation to the philosophical principles in *Mishneh Torah*, Maimonides brought his full halakhic weight to bear on his effort to transform the Jewish religion. He made philosophy into a halakhic and religious duty through, among other things, his definition of the commandments to know, love, and fear God, his concept of messianism, and his treatment of the laws prohibiting idolatry. Integrating these elements into his great halakhic code made the philosophical perspective into a substantive, binding aspect of the *halakhah*. It comes as no surprise, therefore, that his attempt in *Mishneh Torah* to establish philosophical sensitivity as an integral part of binding, normative Judaism evoked more hostility on the part of his opponents than any of the innovative and daring formulations in the *Guide*.

Maimonides' Teachings in Historical Perspective

In his letter to his student Joseph, Maimonides mentions two goals he had in writing *Mishneh Torah*. The purposes represent the two great transformations he sought to accomplish over the course of his life: "for, as God lives, I have been zealous on behalf of the Lord God of Israel, seeing a nation lacking a true and comprehensive book of its laws and lacking true and clear opinions; so I did what I did for the sake of God alone" (*Iggerot*, p. 301). The first goal is centered on the true beliefs Maimonides integrated into *Mishneh Torah*. They do not reflect an attempt to formulate the most basic common denominator of Jewish belief that can be culled from the tradition; they are meant, rather, to work a profound change in the religion of Israel.

The additional goal he mentions, "a true and comprehensive book of its laws," represents the second transformation that Maimonides aimed to achieve. As a work encompassing all of *halakhah*, free of disputatious give and take and universally accessible, *Mishneh Torah* was meant to present the halakhic system once and for all time. This mighty literary endeavor aimed to create an authoritative and unitary version of the entire halakhic field, encompassing all its branches and details. The treatise's authoritativeness was to be derived not from Maimonides' institutional standing, which he lacked, but from the universal acceptance he expected it to gain throughout the Jewish world. That acceptance would vest the treatise with the status not only of a successful, first-rate representation of the *halakhah* but of *halakhah* itself. Maimonides believed that because of the political circumstances of schism and dispersal that the Jews had endured, no text or halakhic ruling had gained that sort of approbation since the time of Ravina and R. Ashi. Those circumstances worsened with the destruction of Andalusian Jewry and, to a great extent, determined the course of Maimonides' own life. Through the power of *Mishneh Torah*, which would be accepted throughout all Israel in the same manner as the Talmud itself, Maimonides meant to alter the halakhic situation without changing the political situation and its preclusion of institutional centralization. In that way, the Jewish people, despite its political dispersion and fragility, would acquire a central treatise worthy of being reckoned with on account not of its firm political and institutional structure but solely because of its literary grandeur.

In his letter to Pinḥas the Judge, Maimonides spoke of his efforts in the following terms: "I have been preceded by great sages and scholars who have compiled treatises and issued halakhic rulings in both Hebrew and Arabic on well-known matters. But to issue rulings with respect to the entire Talmud and all the laws of the Torah—in that, no one has preceded me since our holy Rabbi [that is, R. Judah the Prince, compiler of the Mishnah] and his holy colleagues" (*Iggerot*, pp. 440–441). In truth, Maimonides' enterprise eclipses even the *Mishnah* of R. Judah the Prince. The *Mishnah*, unlike *Mishneh Torah*, incorporates disagreements and minority opinions, and its editor does not seem to have intended to deal systematically with the entire Torah. Never before had any Jew attempted to bring about two such profound transformations, one in Jewish thought and one in *halakhah*. These transformations were meant to reinterpret Judaism as a religion suited to the sensibilities of philosophical religiosity and to create a unified and accessible *halakhah* that would be accepted by all Jewish communities, wherever they might be. The great refugee from Andalusia sought to effect these transformations with no institutional support and with no organization or formal authority; he relied solely on the mighty power of his spirit and intellect.

Overall, one can say that Maimonides did not succeed in bringing about the transformations he hoped for. *Mishneh Torah*, to be sure, became a uniquely important work in the history of *halakhah* and an endless source of inspiration as generations of students sought to expound its profound insights. But the treatise was not accepted as *halakhah* itself, and it certainly did not fundamentally alter the communal, fragmented halakhic structure. Parallel developments in the field of *halakhah* precluded any such possibility. The period in which Maimonides expected *Mishneh Torah* to have its effect was one of unprecedented growth in the halakhic output of Jews living in Christian Europe. The Tosafists in northern France and scholars in Provence and, later, Catalonia broadened the scope of halakhic discourse and posed alternatives in every area that Maimonides thought he had decided. These halakhic giants saw Maimonides as but one among equals, an esteemed halakhist but not an ultimate, decisive authority.

The basic concept of *halakhah* within the Ashkenazi Jewish communities was at odds, in a substantive way, with Maimonides' efforts at halakhic unification. Halakhists within these communities directed their energies toward producing novellae in every area, thereby diversifying the *halakhah* and broadening it. The Ashkenazi scholars saw *halakhah* as, first and foremost, a living tradition of communities, based on diverse ancestral customs; the authority of the rabbi, rather than that of the treatise, was central to the decision-making process. *Mishneh Torah* was seen as one person's position—a rather important one, to be sure, but certainly not a binding a halakhic work.

Things were different in the Sefardic world. There, *Mishneh Torah* became an important, authoritative text, in part because of its powerful influence on the *Shulḥan Arukh*, the halakhic code written by R. Joseph Karo in the sixteenth century. That influence is evident not only in specific halakhic resolutions but also in formulations that Karo drew from *Mishneh Torah* and in the very model itself of a treatise that organized *halakhah* by subject area. But even the *Shulḥan Arukh* was not based exclusively on Maimonides' rulings. R. Joseph Karo stated that his decisions on disputed issues were based on the positions held by the majority among three great scholars that had preceded him: R. Isaac Alfasi (the Rif), Maimonides, and R. Asher ben Yeḥiel (Rosh). Maimonides carried more weight in the design and formulation of the *Shulḥan Arukh* than did the Rif or Rosh, but when specific halakhic determinations were needed, he was only one among three.

Moreover, from a long-term historical perspective, it appears that *Mishneh Torah* in fact hastened the emergence of a tendency that Maimonides evidently wanted to forestall. Maimonides believed his treatise would stabilize the uncontrolled growth of the halakhic organism and alter the structure of Jewish study, redirecting it from exclusive attention to the four ells of *halakhah* toward greater focus on the Account of Creation and the Account of the Chariot. Ironically enough, however, the work made a decisive contribution toward the broadening of the very discourse it was meant to stabilize. Generations of scholars labored at probing Maimonides' sources and the way in which he understood Talmudic passages and at striving to resolve *Mishneh Torah*'s internal contradictions. The process is evident in the dozens of scholarly treatises written on *Mishneh Torah* to our own day. The effort to resolve a difficult passage in *Mishneh Torah*—"a difficult Rambam" in the lingo of the yeshiva—is basic to the education of every actual or potential Talmudic prodigy. A great sixteenth-century halakhist, R. Solomon Luria (Maharshal), believed this phenomenon was no coincidence; he saw it, rather, as a substantive part of the history of the *halakhah*. In his understanding, halakhic literature is a sequence of efforts at codification and stabilization, each of which turned out to have the opposite effect. Every attempt at final halakhic codification produced additional written material, and that material then generated mounds of varied and contradictory interpretations, until the cycle recurred. In effect, the great literary codifiers added fuel to the fire they meant to extinguish. The *Mishnah* of R. Judah the Prince—the precedent Maimonides had in mind when he set out to compile *Mishneh Torah*—affords a prime example. Instead of cutting off halakhic discourse with a transparent legal compilation that could be relied on in every instance, it generated a range of literary activity that ultimately produced the two Talmuds—one in Babylonia, the other in the Land of Israel. And so it was in the case of *Mishneh Torah*, which Maharshal, following R. Moses of Coucy, characterized as "a dream without an interpretation." It was precisely the effort to summarize and conclude matters, marked by the omission of discussion and give-and-take, that caused the treatise to lose its transparency. Every revolution in history has had unintended consequences, and sometimes it is the unintended consequences that are the most interesting.

The effort to comprehensively transform the interpretation of Judaism overall—its understanding of the world, the structure of its beliefs, and its religious attitude—ran into even more difficulty. By its very nature, the Jewish tradition contains a streak of stubborn resistance to the setting of shared, binding, principles of belief. The organizing principle of Judaism in antiquity and in the Middle Ages was *halakhah*; belief was left open and flexible. The intellectual and existential crisis that Maimonides dealt with generated other responses that diverged sharply from his. His Andalusian predecessor, Abraham Ibn Ezra, formulated a theological approach quite different from the one Maimonides advanced, and Judah Halevi offered a totally different view of the relationship between philosophy and religion. While Maimonides was at work writing the *Guide*, the Kabbalah appeared in Provence, and that movement, which gained strength during the thirteenth century, embodied a radically different concept of God, history, humanity, and the commandments—a concept structured in part as a reaction to Maimonides' own formulations. During the 1270s, the Zohar—

the great kabbalistic canon—appeared, with its utterly different interpretation of the Torah's hidden meaning and internal mysteries. The multiple religious perspectives that emerged in the Jewish world during the twelfth and thirteenth centuries demonstrate the great difficulty—perhaps the impossibility—of shaping a single, binding belief system that would delimit the Jewish people.

Beyond the structural obstacles that Judaism interposed to any effort to formulate binding principles of faith, it must be recognized that the Maimonidean religious attitude itself entailed a mighty rejection of other vibrant and profound streams within the tradition. Maimonides more or less succeeded in extirpating the belief in a corporeal God, but it is a long way from that to rejection of all personification of the divinity. Biblical and midrashic language makes abundant use of imagery that personifies God, attributing to Him a range of emotions and reactions—love, pity, jealousy, and rage. These deeply held religious feelings would return and reappear despite the allegorizing steamroller that Maimonides deployed against them. These images are part of the heart and soul of religion in general and Judaism in particular. The silence that Maimonides imposed on religious language was too oppressive and harsh to bear, as evidenced by the efflorescence of the liturgical and other poetry that had been so sharply criticized in the *Guide*.

Maimonides believed Judaism's great role to be releasing man from the grip of basic needs, fears, desires, and appetites and moving him to the higher spiritual and intellectual dimension of his existence, where he can appear as a fully human creature. Above all, he despised the approach that saw Judaism itself as a tool for realizing those impulses. His harshest polemical statements are directed at two set targets—personification and corporealization of God, and making religion into a magical system meant primarily to maintain man and satisfy his needs. The grip of these attitudes—seen as necessary for the maintenance of life—has a powerful influence on society overall, and Maimonides understood that dynamic fully. He well knew, for example, that more than a few of his fellow synagogue congregants believed that in the future, in the world to come, they would enjoy material reward for their Torah study in this world. Their renunciation of basic desires was nothing more than deferred gratification, premised on the desires being fulfilled posthumously. Instead of elevating them to a higher sort of longing, the Torah became, in effect, a means for attaining total fulfillment of the human drive toward pleasure. The thundering pronouncements in the "Laws of Repentance" and the introduction to *Pereq Ḥeleq*, in which Maimonides sought to extirpate this image of the world to come, were merely a small step in a hopeless, never-ending battle. In many ways, it was a battle that ended in defeat; indeed, even Maimonides' supposed grave in Tiberias has become a cultic site. To those who come to that gravesite to recount their sorrows, it matters not in the least whether Maimonides himself endorsed their attitude toward the burial sites of the righteous or stridently objected to it. For them, as for many others, religion is meant first and foremost to ensure one's livelihood, health, and progeny; its role in elevating man toward the sublime is secondary. Religion has always played a part in providing for man's basic needs. Maimonides, too, believed that observing *halakhah* would promote prosperity, a well-ordered society, bounty, and health, but he did not think it would be a direct cause of those happy results. Rather, it would promote them because observing *halakhah* is, in effect, its own reward. But his effort to present Judaism as a religion whose primary goal is to elevate man to the level of existence that lies beyond the basic fears and drives of life ran directly into the contrary tendency, which used religion itself as a means to allay those fears and satisfy those drives.

The spiritual transformation that Maimonides hoped to effect remained one important and central voice among others in the rich array of Jewish thought through the ages. He left powerful testimony to one sort of religious attitude as a possible interpretation of Judaism: a religious attitude built on purifying and exalting the image of God; on seeing divine wisdom in causality and nature; and on the Torah's commandments as the greatest source of inspiration for religious experience and redemption of the soul. Maimonides' standing as a giant among halakhists, along with the profundity of his thought, preserved the religious worldview he created as a living, challenging possibility, even if its demanding features tended to marginalize it on the stage of Jewish life. Moreover, even for those who do not share his specific metaphysical and religious perspectives and are not influenced by his basic approach, he left a more basic testimony that resonates through the generations. The perplexed who appear after the *Guide*, in other historical circumstances and different sorts of crises, have learned from Maimonides that whatever the resolution of their existential perplexity, they should never allow it to foreclose human thought and inner integrity. That sort of self-destruction is a price that is never demanded of the believer; indeed, it would diminish his world and impair what is human about it. In eliminating the distinction between exterior and interior, between what flows from the tradition within and what is external to it, Maimonides transformed the other voice, the external one, into a powerful opportunity for renewal and for deeper religiosity.

MAIMONIDES' WRITINGS

Eight Chapters (Introduction to commentary on Mishnah Avot). In Isadore Twersky, ed., *A Maimonides Reader* (New York: Behrman House, 1972), pp. 361–386.

Epistle on Martyrdom. In Abraham Halkin and David Hartman, *Epistles of Maimonides: Crisis and Leadership* (Philadelphia: Jewish Publication Society, 1985), pp. 15–45.

Epistle to Yemen. In Abraham Halkin and David Hartman, *Epistles of Maimonides: Crisis and Leadership* (Philadelphia: Jewish Publication Society, 1985), pp. 93–149.

Essay on Resurrection. In Abraham Halkin and David Hartman, *Epistles of Maimonides: Crisis and Leadership* (Philadelphia: Jewish Publication Society, 1985), pp. 211–245.

The Guide of the Perplexed, 2 vols. Trans. Shlomo Pines. (Chicago: University of Chicago Press, 1963).

Haqdamot ha-Rambam la-Mishnah [Maimonides' Introductions to the *Mishnah*, Arabic and Hebrew], ed. and trans. Yizchak Sheilat (Maʿale Edomim: Maʿaliyot Press, 1992).

Iggerot ha-Rambam [*Letters of Maimonides*, Hebrew and Arabic], 2 vols. Ed. and trans. Yizchack Shailat (Maʿaleh Edomim: Maʿaliyot Press), 1987.

"Introduction to Ḥelek" [Sanhedrin Chapter Ten] In Isadore Twersky, ed., *A Maimonides Reader* (New York: Behrman House, 1972), pp. 424–436.

Letters of Maimonides. L. Stitskin (New York: Yeshiva University Press, 1977).

Letter on Astrology. In Isadore Twersky, ed., *A Maimonides Reader* (New York: Behrman House, 2000), pp. 464–473.

Letter to Ovadiah the Proselyte. In Isadore Twersky, ed., *A Maimonides Reader* (New York: Behrman House, 1972), pp. 475–477.

Maimonides' Medical Writings, vols. 1–7. Ed. and trans. Fred Rosner (Haifa: Maimonides Research Institute, 1984).

Mishnah ʿim Perush ha-Rambam [Maimonides' Commentary on the Mishnah], trans. and ed. Yoseph Kapach (Jerusalem: Mosad ha-Rav Kook, 1964).

Mishneh Torah

The Book of Acquisition, trans. Isaac Klein (New Haven: Yale University Press, 1951).

The Book of Agriculture, trans. Isaac Klein (New Haven: Yale University Press, 1979).

The Book of Asseverations, trans. B. D. Klien (New Haven: Yale University Press, 1962).

The Book of Civil Laws, trans. Jacob Rabinowitz (New Haven: Yale University Press, 1949).

The Book of Holiness, trans. Louis Rabinowitz and Philip Grossman (New Haven: Yale University Press, 1965).

The Book of Judges, trans. Abraham Hershman (New Haven: Yale University Press, 1977).

The Book of Knowledge, trans. Moses Hyamson (Jerusalem and New York: Boys Town Press, 1974).

The Book of Love, trans. Menachem Kelner (New Haven: Yale University Press, 2004).

The Book of Seasons, trans. Solomon Gandz and Hyman Klein (New Haven: Yale University Press, 1961).

The Book of Torts, trans. Hyman Klein (New Haven: Yale University Press, 1954).

The Book of Women, trans. Isaac Klein (New Haven: Yale University Press, 1972).

Sefer ha-Mizvot [Book of Commandments], trans. Joseph Kafiḥ (Jerusalem: Mosad ha-Rav Kook, 1971).

Sefer ha-Mizvot ʿim Hasagot ha-Ramban [Book of Commandments with Naḥmanides Critique], ed. Hayim Shavel (Jerusalem: Mosad ha-Rav Kook, 1981).

Teshuvot ha-Rambam [Maimonides' Responsa, Hebrew and Arabic], ed. and trans. Yehoshua Blau, 1–4. (Jerusalem: Reuven Mass Publication, 1986).

BIBLIOGRAPHY

Chapter One

Abraham ben ha-Rambam (son of Maimonides). *Ha-Maspiq le-Ovedei ha-Shem,* N. Dana, eds. *(Ramat Gan: Bar Ilan University Press, 1989).*

Ibn Aknin Joseph. *Commentary on Song of Songs.* S. A. Halkin, ed. (Jerusalem: Mekitzei Nirdamim, 1964).

Ben Sasson, Menachem. "Maimonides in Egypt: The First Stage." *Maimonidean Studies* 2 (1992): 3–30.

Ben Sasson, Menachem. "The Jewish Identity of Forced Converts: A Study of Conversion in the Almoad Period." *Pe'amim* 42 (1990): 16–37. (In Hebrew)

Cohen, Mark. "Maimonides' Egypt." In *Moses Maimonides and His Time,* E. Ormsby, ed. (Washington, DC: Catholic University of America Press, 1989), pp. 21–34.

Cohen, Mark. *Poverty and Charity in the Jewish Community of Medieval Egypt* (Princeton, NJ: Princeton University Press, 2005).

Davidson, Herbert Alan. *Moses Maimonides the Man and His Works* (Oxford: Oxford University Press, 2005).

Fenton, Paul. "A Meeting with Maimonides." *Bulletin of the School of Oriental and African Studies* 45, 1 (1982): 1–4.

Frankel, Carlos. *From Maimonides to Samuel Ibn Tibon* (Jerusalem: Magnes Press, 2008). (In Hebrew)

Friedman, Mordechai Akiva. *Maimonides, the Messiah in Yemen and Forced Conversion.* (Jerusalem: Ben Zvi Institute Press, 2002) (In Hebrew)

Friedman, Mordechai Akiva. "Maimonides and Zuta: A Tale of Three Bans." *Zion* 74 (2005): 473–527. (In Hebrew)

Kraemer, Joel L. *Maimonides: The Life and World of One of Civilization's Greatest Minds.* (New York: Doubleday Religious Publishing Group, 2008).

"Two Letters of Maimonides form the Cairo Genizah." *Maimonides Studies* 1 (1990): 87–98.

Goitein, Shlomo Dov. "A New Light on Maimonides' Life." *Ha'arez* 14 of Nisan 1966. (In Hebrew)

Goitein, Shlomo Dov. "Maimonides' Life in Light of New Discoveries from the Cairo Geniza." *Peraqim* (1966) pp. 29–42. (In Hebrew)

Goitein, Shlomo Dov. "An Autograph of Maimonides and a Letter from His Sister Miriam." *Tarbiz* (1963): 184–194. (In Hebrew)

Goitein, Shlomo Dov. *A Mediterranean Society: The Jewish Communities in the Arab World as Portrayed in the Documents of the Cairo Geniza* (Berkeley: University of California Press, 1967–1993).

Goitein, Shlomo Dov. "Moses Maimonides, Man of Action: A Revision of the Master's Biography in Light of Geniza Documents." *Hommage a Georges Vajda* (Louvain: Peeters Press, 1980), pp. 155–167.

Havlin, Shlomo Zalman. "The Life of Maimonides." *Da'at* 15 (1985): 67–79. (In Hebrew)

Hartman, David. *Crisis and Leadership: The Epistles of Maimonides.* (Philadelphia: Jewish Publication Society, 1985).

Hirshberg, Haim Zeev. "On the Decrees of the Almohads and the Trade with India: A Letter from 1148." *Isaac Beer Jubilee Book* (Jerusalem: Israel's Historical Society, 1961), pp. 134–153. (In Hebrew)

Ibn Abi Uṣaybiʿa, ʿUyun al-anbaʾ fi tabaqat al-atibbaʾ. Nizar Rida, ed. (Beirut: Matabaʿat al-hayat, n.d.).

Mann, Jacob. *The Jews in Egypt and in Palestine under the Fatimid Caliphs* (London: Oxford University Press, 1970).

Melamed, Abraham. "Maimonides On Women: Formless Matter or Potential Prophet?" In Alfred Ivry, Eliot Wolfson, and Alan Arkush, eds. *Perspectives on Jewish Thought and Mysticism* (Amsterdam: Harwood Academic Publishers, 1998), pp. 99–134.

Netanel ben Fayyumi *Gan ha-Sekhalim.* Yosef Kafiḥ, ed. (Jerusalem: ha-Aguda le-Hatzalat Ginzei Teiman, 1954).

Rosenthal, Franz. "Maimonides and a Discussion of Muslim Speculative Theology." *Jewish Tradition in the Diaspora* (Berkeley, CA: Judah L. Magnes Memorial Museum, 1981), pp. 109–112.

Soloveitchik, Haym. "Maimonides' "Iggeret Ha-Shemad"–Law and Rhetoric." *Rabbi Joseph H. Lookstein Memorial Volume*, Leo Landmann, ed. (New York: Ktav Publishing House, 1980), pp. 281–319.

Stroumsa, Sarah. *The Beginning of the Maimonidean Polemic in the East: The Letter of Silencing Concerning Resurrection* (Jerusalem: Ben Zvi Institute Press, 1999). (In Hebrew)

Stroumsa, Sarah. *Maimonides and His World: Portrait of a Mediterranean Thinker* (Princeton, NJ: Princeton University Press, 2009).

Yuval, Israel. "Moses Revivius: Maimonides as an Assistant to the Messiah." *Zion* 72 (2007): 161–188. (In Hebrew)

Chapter Two

Abraham Ibn Daud. *The Book of Tradition.* Gershon Cohen, ed. (Philadelphia: Jewish Publication Society, 1967).

Adler, Aharon. *The Underlying Principles for Maimonides Revisions From the Commentary of the Mishnah to the Mishneh Torah.* PhD diss., Bar Ilan University, Ramat Gan, 1987.

Adler, Aharon. "Maimonides Attitude to the Jerusalem Talmud." *R. Joseph ben David Kafiḥ Memorial Book.* (Ramat Gan, 2001), pp. 202–235. (In Hebrew)

Ben Menachem, Hanina. "Individuation of Laws and Maimonides' Book of Commandments." *Shenaton ha-Mishpat ha-Ivri* 14–15 (1988–89): 95–106. (In Hebrew)

Blidstein, Jacob. "Tradition and Institutional Authority: On the Idea of the Oral Law in Maimonides' Teaching." *Da'at* 16 (1976): 11–27. (In Hebrew)

Blidstein, Jacob. *Authority and Rebellion in Maimonides Legal Works: An Extensive Commentary on The Laws of Rebels 1–4* (Tel Aviv: Ha-Kibutz Ha-Meuchad, 2002). (In Hebrew)

Brody, Yerachmiel. "On Maimonides Ruling According to the Talmud Yerushalmi against the Babylonian Talmud." *Maimonidean Studies* 4 (2000): 1–11. (In Hebrew)

Halbertal, Moshe. "Maimonides Book of Commandments, the Architecture of *Halakhah* and Its Theory of Interpretation." *Tarbiz* 59 (1990): 457–480. (In Hebrew)

Halbertal, Moshe. *People of the Book: Canon Meaning and Authority* (Cambridge, MA: Harvard University Press, 1997).

Henshke, David. "The Foundations of Maimonides Theory of *Halakhah*." *Shenaton Ha-Mishpat ha-Ivry* 20 (1997): 103–149. (In Hebrew)

Langernmann, Zvi. "Maimonides and Miracles: The Growth of a (Dis)belief." *Jewish History* 18 (2004): 147–172.

Levinger, Jacob. *Maimonides Halakic Thinking.* (Jerusalem: Magnes Press, 1965).

Liberman, Shaul. *Maimonides' Hilkhot ha-Yerushalmi* (Jerusalem: Jewish Theological Seminary of America, 1995). (In Hebrew)

Sinai, Yuval. "Maimonides' Commentary on the *Mishnah* and Clarifications of Rulings in *Mishneh Torah*." *Shenaton ha-Mishpat ha-Ivri* 23 (2005): 225–251. (In Hebrew)

Manekin, Charles. "Divine Will in Maimonides' Latter Writings." *Maimonidean Studies* (2008): 189–222.

Stern, Shmuel. "Maimonides Autograph of the Commentary of the Mishnah." *Tarbiz* 23 (1954): 72–88. (In Hebrew)

Stern, Shmuel and David Sassun. "Maimonides Autograph of the Commentary of the Mishnah." *Tarbiz* 29 (1960): 261–267. (In Hebrew)

Ta-Shma, Israel. *Interpretations of the Talmud in Europe and North Africa, 1: 1000–1200* (Jerusalem: Magnes Press, 1999).

Zussman, Jacob. "Manuscripts and Textual Variants of the Mishnah." *Divrei ha-Qongres ha-'Olami ha-Shevi'i le-Madda'ei ha-Yahadut* 3 (Jerusalem 1981), pp. 215–250. (In Hebrew)

Chapter Three

Berman, Lawrence. "Maimonides the Disciple of al-Farabi." *Israel Oriental Studies* 4 (1974): 154–178.

Breslvey-Klein, Sarah. *Maimonides' Interpretation of Stories on Adam in Genesis: Chapters in Maimonides' Concept of Humanity.* (Jerusalem: Reuven Mass Press, 1987). (In Hebrew)

Davidson, Herbert. "Maimonides' Shemonah Perakim and Alfrabi's Fulsul al-Madani." *Proceedings of the American Academy for Jewish Research* 31 (1963): 33–51.

Davidson, Herbert. "The Middle Way in Maimonides' Ethics." *Proceedings of the American Academy for Jewish Research* 54 (1987): 31–72.

Frank, Daniel. "Anger as a Vice: A Maimonidean Critique of Aristotle's Ethics." *History of Philosophy Quarterly* 7 (1990): 269–281.

"God and the Good Life: Maimonides' Virtue Ethics and the Idea of Perfection." In George Tamer, ed., *The Trials of Maimonides: Jewish Arabic, and Ancient Culture of Knowledge* (Berlin and New York: Walter De Gruyter, 2005), pp. 123–136.

Goodman, Lenn. "Maimonides on the Soul." In Jay Harris, ed., *Maimonides after 800 Years: Essays on Maimonides and His Influence* (Cambridge, MA: Harvard University Press, 2007), pp. 65–80.

Kasher, Hanna. "'Wise' 'Pious' and 'Good' in Maimonides' Thought." *Maimonidean Studies* 4 (2000): 81–106. (In Hebrew)

Kelner, Menachem. *Dogma in Medieval Jewish Thought (From Maimonides to Abravanel)* (Oxford: Oxford University Press, 1986).

Kelner, Menachem. *Maimonides on Human Perfection* (Atlanta, GA: Scholars Press, 1989).

Kreisel, Howard Theodore. "Individual Perfection vs. Communal Welfare and the Problem of Contradistinctions in Maimonides Approach to Ethics." *PAAJR* 58 (1992): 107–141.

Kreisel, Howard Theodore. *Maimonides' Political Thought: Studies in Ethics, Law and the Human Ideal* (Albany: State University of New York Press, 1999).

Lam, Noram. "The Wise and the Pious in Maimonides Teachings." *Memorial Book of Shmuel Belkin* (New York: Erna Michael College of Hebraic Studies, 1981), pp. 11–28. (In Hebrew)

Leibowitz, Yeshayahu. *Conversations on Eight Chapters* (Jerusalem: Keter Press, 1986). (In Hebrew)

Rosenberg, Shalom. "The Concept of Faith in Maimonides and His Students." *Bar Ilan* 22–23 (1988): 351–397. (In Hebrew)

Schwartz, Dov. "Avicena and Maimonides on Immortality." In R. I. Nettler ed., *Medieval and Modern Perceptions on Jewish Muslim Relations* (Luxenbourg and Oxford: Harwood Academic Publishers, 1995), pp. 185–197.

Schweid, Eliezer. *Studies in the Eight Chapters of Maimonides* (Jerusalem: Magnes Press, 1969). (In Hebrew)

Septimus, Bernard. "Literary Structure and Ethical Theory in Sefer ha-Madda." In Jay Harris, ed., *Maimonides After 800 Years: Essays on Maimonides and His Influence* (Cambridge, MA: Harvard University Press, 2008), pp. 307–325.

Shatz, David. "Maimonides' Moral Theory." In Kenneth Seeskin, ed., *The Cambridge Companion to Maimonides* (Cambridge: Cambridge University Press, 2005), pp. 167–193.

Chapter Four

Elon, Menachem. *Jewish Law: History Sources, Principles* (New York: Jewish Publication Society, 2003).

Harvey, Zeev W. "Between Political Philosophy and *Halakhah* in Maimonides Teachings." *Iyyun* 29 (1980): 198–212. (In Hebrew)

Havlin, Shlomo Zalman. "On Literary Sealing as Basis for Periodization in Halakhah." *Studies in Talmudic Literature* (Jerusalem: Israel's National Academy, 1983), pp. 148–192. (In Hebrew)

Ta-Shma, Israel. "Did Maimonides Take a Revolutionary Position Towards the Study of Talmud?" *Maimonides, Traditionalism, Originality and Revolution*, vol. 1 (Jerusalem: Merkaz Shazar Press, 2009), pp. 111–118. (In Hebrew)

Twersky, Isadore. "The Beginnings of Mishneh Torah Criticism." *Biblical and Other Studies*, A. Altmann, ed. (Cambridge, MA: Harvard University Press, 1963), pp. 161–182.

Twersky, Isadore. *Introduction to the Code of Maimonides (Mishneh Torah)* (New Haven: Yale University Press, 1980).

Zussman, Jacob. "Oral Torah Literary Speaking." *Studies in Talmud* 3, no. 1 (2005): 209–384. (In Hebrew)

Chapter Five

Funkenstein, Amos. *Nature, History and Messianism in Maimonides* (Tel Aviv: Misrad Ha-Bitachon, 1983). (In Hebrew)

Goodman, Lenn E. "Maimonides' Philosophy of Law." *Jewish Law Annual* 1 (1978): 72–107.

Hartman, David. *Maimonides: Torah and Philosophical Quest* (Philadelphia: Jewish Publication Society, 1976).

Harvey, Zeev W. "Ibn Rushd and Maimonides on the Duty of Philosophical Contemplation." *Tarbiz* 58 (1989): 75–83. (In Hebrew)

Harvey, Zeev. "The 'Mishneh Torah' as a Key to the Secrets of the 'Guide'." *Me'ah She'arim*. (Jerusalem: Magnes Press, 2001), pp. 11–28.

Kaplan, Laurence. "Maimonides on the Singularity of the Jewish People." *Da'at* 15 (1985): v–xxvii.

Kasher, Hana. "The Study of Torah as Means for Knowledge of God in Maimonides Teaching." *Mehqarei Yerushalayim be-Mahshevet Yisra'el* 5 (1086): 71–81.

Kreisel, Haym. "Love and Fear of God in Maimonides' Teachings." *Da'at* (1996): 127–151.

Lasker, Daniel. "Love of God and Martyrdom in the Thought of R. Judah Halevi and Maimonides." Uri Erlich, Haym Kreisel, and Daniel Lasker, eds., *Al Pi ha-Be'er: Studies in Jewish Thought and Halakhah, Presented to Jacob Blidstein* (Beer Sheva: Ben Gurion University Press, 2008), pp. 293–302. (In Hebrew)

Levinger, Jacob. *Maimonides as a Rabbi and a Philosopher* (Jerusalem: Mosad Bialik, 1990).

Neorai, Michael. "The Land of Israel in the Thought of Maimonides and Nachmanides." In Moshe Chalamish and Aviezer Ravitsky, eds., *Eretz Israel in Medieval Jewish Thought* (Jerusalem: Zalman Shazar Press, 1991), pp. 123–137. (In Hebrew)

Pines, Shlomo. "The Philosophical Purport of Maimonides' Halachic Works and the Purport of the Guide of the Perplexed." *Maimonides and Philosophy Papers Presented at the Sixth Jerusalem Philosophic Encounter (May 1985)* (Dordrecht: Kluwer Academic Publishers, 1986), pp. 1–14.

Ravitsky, Aviezer. "According to Man's Capacity—The Messianic Era in Maimonides Thought." *Al Da'at ha-Maqom: Studies in Jewish Thought and Its History* (Jerusalem: Keter Press, 1991), pp. 74–104. (In Hebrew)

Ravitsky, Aviezer. "'The Madness of Those Who Write Amulets': Maimonides and His Students on Language, Nature and Magic." *Maimonidean Studies* (Jerusalem: Schoken Press, 2006), pp. 181–204.

Schwartz, Dov. *Astrology and Magic in Medieval Jewish Thought* (Ramat Gan: Bar Ilan University Press, 2004). (In Hebrew)

Schwartz, Dov. *The Messianic Idea in Medieval Jewish Thought* (Ramat Gan: Bar Ilan University Press, 2006). (In Hebrew)

Shapiro, Mark. *Studies in Maimonides and His Interpreters* (Scranton and London: University of Scranton Press, 2008).

Strauss, Leo. "Notes on Maimonides' Book of Knowledge," *Studies in Mysticism and Religion Presented to Gershom G. Scholem* (Jerusalem: Magnes Press, 1967), pp. 269–283.

Twersky, Isadore. "Some Non-Halakhic Aspects of the Mishneh Torah." *Jewish Medieval and Renaissance Studies*, A. Altmann, ed. (Cambridge, MA: Harvard University Press, 1967), pp. 95–111.

Twersky, Isadore. *Introduction to the Code of Maimonides (Mishneh Torah)* (New Haven: Yale University Press, 1980).

Chapter Six

Ben Or, Ehud. *A Concept of Prayer: A Study of Prayer in Maimonides and his Sources* (Ann Arbor: University of Michigan Press, 1992).

Benedict, Binyamin Zeev. *Maimonides with no Deviation from the Talmud* (Jerusalem: Mosad Ha-Rav Kook, 1995). (In Hebrew)

Blidstein, Jacob. *Political Principles in Maimonides' Teaching* (Ramat Gan: Bar Ilan University Press, 1983). (In Hebrew)

Blidstein, Jacob. *Prayer in Maimonides' Legal Teachings.* (Jerusalem: Bialik Press, 1994). (In Hebrew)

Feldblum, Meir. "Maimonides' Rulings in Light of his Attitude to the Anonymous Material in the Babylonian Talmud." *American Academy of Jewish Studies* (Jerusalem, 1980), pp. 111–120. (In Hebrew)

HaCohen, R. Meir Simchah. *Or Sameah̠*, 4 (Jerusalem: Masoret Israel, 2002). (In Hebrew)

Harvey, Zeev W. "Aggadah in Maimonides' *Mishneh Torah*." *Dine Israel* 24 (2007): 197–207.

Henshkeh, David. "The Reason for *Halakhah* in Maimonides' Thought." *Maimonidean Studies* 4 (2000): 45–80. (In Hebrew)

Henshkeh, David. "'A Dead Person with No Comforters': More on the Reflection of Maimonides' Thought in Halakhic Teaching." *Sidra* 18 (2003): 27–39. (In Hebrew)

Kaplan, Laurence. "The Unity of Maimonides' Religious Thought: The Law of Mourning as a Case Study." *Judaism and Modernity: The Religious Philosophy of David Hartman*, J. Malino, ed. (UK: Aldershot, 2004), pp. 393–412.

Levinger, Jacob. *Maimonides Halakhick Thinking* (Jerusalem: Magnes Press, 1965). (In Hebrew)

Lorberbaum, Menachem. "'Tiqqun 'Olam according to Maimonides: An Exploration in the Goals of *Halakhah*." *Tarbiz* 94 (1985): 65–82. (In Hebrew)

Lorberbaum, Menachem. *Politics and the Limits of the Law* (Stanford: Stanford University Press, 2001).

Rapel, Dov. "Maimonides' Didactic Policy in the *Mishneh Torah*." *Mikhtam le-David: Me-*

morial Book for Rabbi David Oaks (Ramat Gan: Bar Ilan University Press, 1978), pp. 291–298.

Soloveichiek, Haym. "Reflections on Maimonides' Organization of *Mishneh Torah*: Real and Imagined Difficulties." *Maimonidean Studies* 4 (2000): 107–115. (In Hebrew)

Soloveichiek, Haym. "Mishneh Torah: Polemic and Art." *Maimonides after 800 Years* (Cambridge, MA: Harvard University Press, 2007), pp. 327–343.

Soloviechiek, R. Haym Halevi. *Novella on the Mishneh Torah* (Jerusalem, 1991).

Twersky, Isadore. "The Arrangement of the Maimonides' *Mishneh Torah*: Philosophical and Halakhic Principles." *Divrei ha-Qongres ha-Olami ha-Shishi le-Madda'ei ha-Yahadut* 3, Jerusalem 1977, pp. 179–189. (In Hebrew)

Twersky, Isadore. *Introduction to the Code of Maimonides (Mishneh Torah)* (New Haven: Yale University Press, 1980).

Chapter Seven

Altmann, Alexander. "Maimonides on the Intellect and the Scope of Metaphysics." *Von der Mittelalterlichen zur modernen Aufklärung—Studien zur jüdischen Geistesgeschichte* (Tubingen: J.C.B. Mohr, 1987), pp. 60–129.

Blumenthal, David. "Maimonides' Intellectualist Mysticism and the Superiority of the Prophecy of Moses." *Studies in Medieval Culture* 10 (1978): 51–67.

Blumenthal, David. *Philosophical Mysticism: Studies in Rational Religion* (Ramat Gan: Bar Ilan University, 2006).

Blumenthal, David. "Maimonides Philosophic Mysticism." *Philosophic Mysticism* (2006): 128–151.

Berman, Lawrence V. "The Political Interpretation of the Maxim: The Purpose of Philosophy is the Imitation of God." *Studia Islamica* 15 (1961): 53–61.

Berman, Lawrence V. "Maimonides, the Disciple of Alfarabi." *Israel Oriental Studies* 4 (1974): 154–178.

Buijs, Joseph A. "A Maimonidean Critique of Thomistic Analogy." *Journal of the History of Philosophy* 41 (2003): 449–470.

Davidson, Herbert. "Maimonides on Metaphysical Knowledge." *Maimonidean Studies* 3 (1995): 49–103.

Diamond, James. *Maimonides and the Hermeneutics of Concealment: Deciphering Scripture and Midrash in the Guide of the Perplexed* (Albany: State University of New York Press, 2002).

Halbertal, Moshe. *Concealment and Revelation: Esotericism in Jewish Tradition and Its Philosophical Implications* (Princeton, NJ: Princeton University Press, 2007).

Hyman, Arthur. "Maimonides on Religious Language." In Joel L. Kraemer, ed. *Perspectives on Maimonides* (Oxford: Littman Library, 1991), pp. 175–191.

Ivri, Alfred. "The Problematics of the Ideal of Human Perfection for Maimonides." *The Thought of Moses Maimonides*, Ira Robinson, Lawrence Kaplan, and Julien Bauer eds. (Lewiston, NY: E. Mellen Press, 1983), pp. 16–26.

Kaplan, Laurence. "'I sleep, but my heart waketh.' Maimonides' Conception of Human

Perfection." *The Thought of Moses Maimonides*, I. Robinson, L. Kaplan, and J. Bauer, eds. (Lewiston, NY: E. Mellen Press, 1990), pp. 130–166.

Klein-Berslavy, Sarah. *King Solomon and Philosophical Esotericism in Maimonides' Teachings.* (Jerusalem: Magnes Press, 1996). (In Hebrew)

Lorberbaum, Yair. "On Contradictions, Rationality, Dialectics, and Esotericism in Maimonides's "Guide of the Perplexed."" *Review of Metaphysics* 55, 4 (2002): 711–750.

Lorberbaum, Yair. "On Allegory, Metaphor, and Symbol in 'The Guide of the Perplexed'." *Studia Judaica* 16 (2008): 95–106.

Manekin, Charles. "What Is the Difference Between the Early and Late Writings of Maimonides Concerning the Limits of Human Knowledge." *Maimonides Traditionalism Originality and Revolution 2* (Jerusalem: Merkaz Shazar Press, 2009), pp. 297–314. (In Hebrew)

Pines, Shlomo. "The Limitation of Human Knowledge, According to al-Farabi, ibn Bajja and Maimonides." *Studies in Medieval Jewish History and Literature* (Cambridge, MA: Harvard University Press, 1979), pp. 82–109.

Ravitzky, Aviezer. "Esotericism and Philosophical Education." *Maimonidean Studies* (Jerusalem 2006), pp. 59–80. (In Hebrew)

Ravitzky, Aviezer. "The Political Vocation of the Philosophers: Samuel Ibn-Tibon in Contra Maimonides" *Maimonides: Traditionalism, Originality and Revolution 2* (Jerusalem: Merkaz Shazar Press, 2009).

Septimus, Bernard. "Maimonides on Language." *The Heritage of the Jews of Spain* (Tel Aviv: Levinski College of Education Pub. House 1994), pp. 35–54.

Stern, Joseph. "Logical Syntax as the Key to the Secret in the *Guide of the Perplexed.*" *Iyyun* 38, 2 (1999): 137–166. (In Hebrew)

Stern, Joseph. "Maimonides on Language and the Science of Language." *Maimonides and the Sciences* (2000), pp. 173–226.

Stern, Joseph. "Maimonides on the Growth of Knowledge and the Limitation of the Intellect." *Maimonides* (2004), pp. 143–191.

Stern, Joseph. "Maimonides' Epistemology." *The Cambridge Companion to Maimonides*, K. Seeskin, ed. (Cambridge: Cambridge University Press, 2005), 105–133.

Strauss, Leo. *Persecution and the Art of Writing.* (Glencoe, IL: Free Press, 1952).

Chapter Eight

Altmann, Alexander. "Maimonides and Thomas Aquinas: Natural or Divine Prophecy." *AJS Review* 3 (1978): 1–19.

Davidson, Herbert. "Maimonides' Secret Position on Creation." *Studies in Medieval Jewish History and Literature* (Cambridge MA: Harvard University Press, 1979), pp. 16–40.

Goldman, Eliezer. "'The Unique Worship of Those Who Attain Truth': Interpretative Comments to The Guide of The Perplexed III 51–54." *Studies in Jewish Thought of the Present and the Past* (Jerusalem: Magnes Press, 1997), pp. 16–40. (In Hebrew)

Diesendruk Zvi."Samuel and Moses ibn Tibbon on Maimonides' Theory of Providence." *HUCA* 11 (1936): 341–366.

Freudenthal, Gad. "Maimonides on the Knowability of the Heavens and of Their Mover: (Guide 2:24)." *Aleph* 8 (2008): 151–157.

Harvey, W. Z. "Maimonides and Spinoza on the Knowledge of Good and Evil." *Iyyun* 28 (1978): 167–185. (In Hebrew)

Harvey, W. Z. "A Third Approach to Maimonides' Cosmogony-Prophetology Puzzle." *Harvard Theological Review* 74 (1981): 287–301.

Ivri, Alfred. "Islamic and Greek Influences on Maimonides' Philosophy." *Maimonides and Philosophy*, S. Pines and Y. Yovel, eds. (Dordecht: Kluwer Academic Publishers, 1986), pp. 139–156.

Kaplan, Laurence. "Maimonides on the Miraculous Element in Prophecy." *Harvard Theological Review* 70 (1977): 233–256.

Kasher, Hana. "The Image and Opinions of Job in *The Guide of the Perplexed*." *Da'at* 15 (1985): 81–87. (In Hebrew)

Klein-Brelavy, Sarah. *Maimonides' Interpretation of the Creation Story* (Jerusalem: Reuven Mass Press, 1988). (In Hebrew)

Kreisel, Howard. *Prophecy: The History of an Idea in Medieval Jewish Philosophy* (Dordrecht: Kluwer Academic Publishers, 2001).

Macy, Jeffrey. "Prophecy in al-Farabi and Maimonides," In Sholom Pines and Yirmiyahu Yovel, eds. *Maimonides and Philosophy: Papers Presented at the Sixth Jerusalem Philosophical Encounter May 1985* (Dordrecht: Matinus Nihoff, 1986), pp. 185–201.

Manekin, Charles. "Divine Will in Maimonides' Later Writings." In Arthur Hyman and Alfred Ivri, eds. *Maimonidean Studies* 5 (2008), pp. 189–221.

Nuriel, Abraham. "Divine Will in The Guide of the Perplexed," *Revealed and Hidden in Medieval Jewish Philosophy* (Jerusalem: Magnes Press, 1980), pp. 41–63. (In Hebrew)

Nuriel, Abraham. "Providence in The Guide of the Perplexed *Revealed and Hidden in Medieval Jewish Philosophy* (Jerusalem: Magnes Press, 1980), pp. 83–92.

Nuriel, Abraham. "Creation of the World or Eternity According to Maimonides." *Revealed and Hidden in Medieval Jewish Philosophy* (Jerusalem: Magnes Press, 1980), pp. 25–40.

Ravitzky, Aviezer. "Maimonides Concealed Teaching in *The Guide of the Perplexed*: The Interpretation in the Past and Present." *Al Da'at ha-Maqom: Studies in the History of Jewish Thought* (Jerusalem: Keter Press, 1991), pp. 142–181). (In Hebrew)

Ravitzky, Aviezer. "R. Shmuel ibn Tibon and the Secret of *The Guide of the Perplexed*." *Maimonidean Studies* (Jerusalem: 2006), pp. 86–101.

Rozenberg, Shalom. "Biblical Interpretation in the Guide." *Jerusalem Studies in Jewish Thought* 1, no. 1 (1981): 85–157. (In Hebrew)

Rudavsky, Tamar. *Time Matters: Time, Creation and Cosmology in Medieval Jewish Philosophy* (Albany: State University of New York Press, 2000).

Seeskin, Kenneth. *Maimonides: A Guide for Today's Perplexed* (West Orange, NJ: Behrman House, 1991).

Seeskin, Kenneth. *Searching for the Distant God: The Legacy of Maimonides* (New York: Oxford University Press, 2000).

Stern, Joseph. *Problems and Parables of Law: Maimonides and Nahmanides on Reasons for the*

Commandments (ta'amei ha-mizvot) (New York: State University of New York Press, 1988).

Stroumsa, Sarah. *Maimonides and His World: Portrait of a Mediterranean Thinker* (Princeton, NJ: Princeton University Press, 2009).

Stroumsa, Sarah. "The 'Guide' and Maimonides Philosophical Sources." *The Cambridge Companion to Maimonides,* K. Seeskin, ed. (Cambridge: Cambridge University Press, 2005), pp. 58–81.

INDEX

divination. *See* magic, divination, and
    sorcery
divine intervention, 228, 339–341
divine justice, 293, 330–331, 337, 354,
    358
divine will, 2, 203, 128, 208–209, 222,
    314, 316–322, 325–328, 336–343,
    355–356

Egypt: exodus from, 127–129, 146, 207,
    215, 343; Jewish community of, 6, 19–
    20, 25, 38, 40–46, 68, 85, 92, 261, 307;
    Maimonides in, 4–5, 16, 18, 25, 31,
    33–47, 56–74, 77, 87–90
esotericism/esoteric tradition, 7, 65, 278,
    280–289, 302
evil, the problem of, 224, 312, 324, 329–
    335, 359
explanatory principles. *See* hermeneutics

fear and awe of God, 2, 50, 90, 147, 160–
    163, 197–202, 208, 216, 220, 226, 260,
    276, 283, 359–361
free will, 139–140, 337
Fustat, 24, 33–47, 56, 59, 64, 69–73, 92

Galen, 62–63, 71–72
Gehenna, 34, 141–143, 146
Geonim/geonic tradition/authority of the
    Geonim, 1, 9, 12, 19–20, 44, 76, 77, 80,
    84–85, 93–94, 96, 97, 98, 100, 102–
    109, 165, 166, 168, 170–171, 173,
    175–181, 183–184, 192, 240–242, 265,
    267
good and evil. *See* evil, the problem of
Greek philosophy and tradition, 6, 48, 51,
    79, 137, 146, 154–155, 161, 203, 221,
    282, 306, 314, 319, 355

halakhic and religious transformation: 1–5,
    10–13, 77–79, 84, 88, 90–91, 96–98,
    136, 162–163, 164–166, 173, 183–185,
    193, 195–196, 220–221, 223, 235,
    275–276, 280, 358–361, 362–368
halakhic decision-making, 31–32, 57, 79,
    84, 93–96, 113, 174–175, 182, 244,
    255–258, 262, 364
health. *See* medicine

heresy/heretics, 27–28, 79, 101, 132, 136,
    140, 146, 219, 238–239, 289, 295, 360
hermeneutics, 106, 108–112, 116–127,
    131
humility, modesty, and lowliness of spirit,
    37, 149, 156, 158–161

Ibn al-Qifti, 25–26, 39, 74
Ibn Bajja, 2, 21–22, 306–307, 359
Ibn Rushd (Averroes), 2, 21–22, 349, 359
Ibn Sina (Avicenna), 72, 349, 359
Ibn Tibbon: family, 16; Judah, 16, 68;
    Moses, 22, 340; Samuel, 13, 16, 21, 68–
    70, 73, 187, 204, 304, 320, 339, 340
idolatry, 2, 26, 29, 47–53, 75–82, 134,
    210–223, 230, 251, 264, 270, 273, 283,
    288–296, 343–348, 349–353, 358–361
image of God, 2, 138, 274, 291, 296, 345,
    349, 355, 358, 367
immortality of the soul, 137–142, 145,
    198, 302, 340
Isaac Alfasi (the Rif), 15–18, 165, 177,
    189, 193, 229, 240, 259–261, 265–
    267, 364
Isaac ben Samuel (Ri the Elder), 11
Islam/Arabic: influences on Maimonides,
    21–23, 69, 71, 78–79, 100, 123, 137–
    142, 147,149, 160, 205–206, 282, 318,
    333, 359; and the Jewish community, 6,
    9, 20–21, 24–25, 48–49; and monothe-
    ism, 29, 48, 51–54, 81–83, 89, 210–
    215, 329; oppression, 24–25. *See also* re-
    ligious persecution

Jacob ben Netanel, 47–50, 55
Jacob ben Meir (Rabbeinu Tam), 11, 12,
    77
Japhet, the dayyan of Acre 33, 42, 58–59,
    86–87
Jewish philosophy of the middle ages, 140,
    202–208, 267, 282, 306–307, 312, 365
Job, 272–273, 296, 330–331, 334, 357
Jonathan Hakohen, 10, 14, 57, 67–68,
    190
Joseph ben Aknin, 18, 25
Joseph ben Judah, 17, 37, 60–61, 63, 65–
    66, 73, 76, 84–90, 184, 191–193, 362
Joseph Karo, 197, 240, 243, 246, 267, 364